CliffsTestPrep®

TExES®: Generalist EC–4

An American BookWorks Corporation Project

Contributing Authors/Consultants

Javier Ayala, PhD

George J. Hademenos, PhD

Perry Kay Haley-Brown, EdD

Pug Deavenport Parris, EdD

Joan Marie Rosebush, MEd

Cynthia Rutledge, EdD

Ken Springer, PhD

Mark E. Turner, DMA

WILEY

Wiley Publishing, Inc.

Publisher's Acknowledgments

Editorial

Project Editor: Tere Stouffer

Acquisitions Editor: Greg Tubach

Technical Editor: Cheryl Van Camp

Production

Proofreader: Christine Pingleton

Wiley Publishing, Inc. Composition Services

CliffsTestPrep® TExES®: Generalist EC–4

Published by:
Wiley Publishing, Inc.
111 River Street
Hoboken, NJ 07030-5774
www.wiley.com

Copyright © 2006 Wiley, Hoboken, NJ

Published by Wiley, Hoboken, NJ
Published simultaneously in Canada

Library of Congress Cataloging-in-Publication Data

CliffsTestPrep TExES : generalist EC-4 / contributors, Javier Ayala . . . [et al.].
     p. cm.
 "An American BookWorks Corporation Project."
 ISBN-13: 978-0-7645-9821-0 (pbk.)
 ISBN-10: 0-7645-9821-X
1. Teaching—Texas—Examinations—Study guides. 2.
Teachers—Certification—Texas.   I. Ayala, Javier.
 LB1763.T4C58 2006
 379.1'5709764—dc22

2005034541

Printed in the United States of America

10 9 8 7 6 5 4 3 2 1

1B/SX/RS/QV/IN

Table of Contents

PART I: TExES GENERALIST EC–4 SUBJECT REVIEW

PART II: TExES GENERALIST EC–4 SAMPLE TESTS

Introduction

Every individual interested in pursuing certification as an elementary school teacher in the state of Texas must, among other requirements, obtain a passing score on the Texas Examination of Educator Standards (TExES) Generalist EC–4 exam offered through the State Board of Educator Certification (SBEC). You must also take the TExES Pedagogy and Professional Responsibilities EC–4 test.

TExES tests can be taken only in your last semester of coursework or after all your coursework for certification has been completed. Essentially, in order to take the test you must meet any one of the following:

- You are fulfilling the program requirements of an approved Texas educator preparation program (contact the advisor, director, or certification officer of your current program).
- You are already fully certified in another state or country, and wish to receive an educator certificate (contact the State Board of Educator Certification).
- You are already certified and wish to receive an additional certificate or supplemental certificate (contact the State Board of Educator Certification).
- You are seeking to demonstrate your content mastery as a charter school teacher (contact the advisor, director, or certification officer of your current program).
- You wish to receive a temporary teacher certificate (contact the State Board of Educator Certification).

You can find additional details on the following Web sites:

- www.texes.nesinc.com, where you'll find information about both the TExES and the ExCET (an earlier exam)
- www.tea.state.tx.us/tcks, the Web site for the Texas Education Agency
- www.texes.nesinc.com/prepmanuals/prepman_opener.htm, which takes you to the preparation manuals; look for the manual called *101 Generalist EC–4*
- www.sbec.state.tx.us/SBECOnline, which is for the State Board of Educator Certification

About the Test

The Generalist EC–4 exam, consisting of approximately 100 multiple-choice questions with four possible solutions to choose from, is designed to test the competency of the prospective teacher in five domains, including the following:

- Domain I: English/Language Arts and Reading (approximately 40% of the test)
- Domain II: Mathematics (approximately 15% of the test)
- Domain III: Social Studies (approximately 15% of the test)
- Domain IV: Science (approximately 15% of the test)
- Domain V: Fine Arts, Music, Health, and Physical Education (approximately 15% of the test)

The exam is five hours long and usually includes another ten nonscorable questions. Your final score, however, is based only on the 100 scorable questions; the others are merely pilot questions—questions that are being tested for future exams. These questions will not be identified on the exam.

Although the questions on this test are all multiple-choice, there are a couple of different types of these questions with which you should be familiar. Most of the questions involve some type of stimulus material, such as teacher notes, samples of student work, or descriptions of classroom situations. Following the stimulus is a question that asks you to choose the correct answer that involves analyzing a problem or making a decision.

Some questions will be single items, and some will be clustered items. A single-item question has one stimulus and one question, while a clustered question may have one or two stimuli and/or more than one question relating to these stimuli. Be sure to read the stimuli carefully to understand what material is being presented. Then read the question to see whether you can identify the correct choice.

About This Book

This book is designed to help you prepare for the Texas Examination of Educator Standards (TExES) Generalist EC–4 (early childhood through 4th grade), and as such, there's a logical organization to this book. We've divided it into two parts—the first is a review of the topics to prepare for on the actual exam, and the second part consists of two full-length simulated tests.

In the first part of this book, the review section, we present you with each of the five domains. The framework of the test requirements are fully explained so that you understand the material you're likely to encounter on the test. Each competency is its own section and begins with the official wording of the competency standard in italics. Goals within each competency are structured as individual sections, too, and examples are given when they might help clarify the information. Use the white space on goal pages for notes, examples, or ideas.

Domain I: English Language Arts and Reading

- Competency 001: Oral Language
- Competency 002: Phonological and Phonemic Awareness
- Competency 003: Alphabetic Principle
- Competency 004: Literacy Development
- Competency 005: Word Analysis and Decoding
- Competency 006: Reading Fluency
- Competency 007: Reading Comprehension
- Competency 008: Research and Comprehension Skills in the Content Areas
- Competency 009: Writing Conventions
- Competency 010: Development of Written Communication
- Competency 011: Assessment of Developing Literacy

Domain II: Mathematics

- Competency 012: Mathematics Instruction
- Competency 013: Number Concepts, Patterns, and Algebra
- Competency 014: Geometry, Measurement, Probability, and Statistics
- Competency 015: Mathematical Process

Domain III: Social Studies

- Competency 016: Social Science Instruction
- Competency 017: History
- Competency 018: Geography and Culture
- Competency 019: Government, Citizenship, and Economics

Domain IV: Science

- Competency 020: Science Instruction
- Competency 021: Physical Science

- Competency 022: Life Science
- Competency 023: Earth and Space Science

Domain V: Fine Arts, Music, Health, and Physical Education

- Competency 024: Visual Arts
- Competency 025: Music
- Competency 026: Health
- Competency 027: Physical Education

At the end of each competency are several multiple-choice questions that are similar to the types of questions you might find on the exam, and that are also designed to help test your knowledge of what you've read. Keep in mind that whatever review material we've provided, is just that: review material. Its purpose is to help refresh your memory on subjects with which you should already be familiar.

The second part of the book includes the two full-length exams. The secret of successful test-taking is to practice taking tests and answering as many questions as possible. We've given you that opportunity here. We suggest you set aside time to take these exams: Find yourself a quiet place in which to work, and begin. Don't worry about time, because the purpose of taking these tests is to become familiar with the process of taking the test and understanding the types of questions you'll see.

When you've finished, go over the answers at your leisure. We've coded all of the answers by domain name, so that you can evaluate your strengths and weaknesses on the exam. By analyzing your weaknesses, you can go back and study further any of those areas that you found difficult or didn't understand. Ask your instructor, consult your textbooks, and of course, go back and reread the section(s) in this book that are giving you trouble.

Answering Multiple-Choice Questions

Most of the standardized tests you've taken throughout your educational career have contained multiple-choice questions. For some reason, these types of questions give a large percentage of test-takers a difficult time. If you approach these questions carefully, however, they should be easier than you think.

The questions on this test are created to test your abilities to recognize the correct answer from four choices. From the start, be happy that there are only four choices, not five, as there are on many exams. This lowers your need to make too many choices.

Questions are comprised of several parts.

- The question stem
- The correct choice
- Distracters

As test-item writers create questions, they normally approach it as follows:

- One choice is absolutely correct.
- Once or two choices are absolutely incorrect (distracters).
- Once or two choices are similar to the correct answer, but contain some information that is not quite accurate or on target, or may not answer the specific question (distracters).

How do you approach the questions? First, read the question and see whether you know the answer. If you know it automatically, you can look at the choices and select the correct one. If you don't know, however, begin the elimination process. Here's an example.

---

1. Why was the Bill of Rights created?

    A.   Members of the First Congress wanted to create a description of the relationship between federal and state governments.

    B.   Members of the First Congress were concerned that the existing Constitution did not sufficiently protect citizens from the central government.

    C.   Members of the First Congress were concerned that without a Bill of Rights, the legislative branch of government would dominate the executive and judicial branches.

    D.   The Bill of Rights represents a compromise between the political interests of the individual members of the First Congress.

Do you know the correct answer? If not, here's a good time to practice the process of elimination. Look at choice A. The Bill of Rights was written after the Constitution, and the relationship between the federal and state governments was already described in the Constitution. Therefore, you can eliminate choice A.

Look at choice B. It could be correct, so you can't yet eliminate it. Thus, move on to choice C. Choice C is just plain incorrect, and factually wrong. The three branches of government were already established in order to effect a system of checks and balances. Thus, the Bill of Rights had no impact on that balance. Having eliminated two out of the four choices, you now have a 50/50 chance (50%) of guessing the correct answer if you still don't know what it is.

Finally, look at choice D. This is one of those choices that sounds almost correct, but is somewhat vague; any significant congressional document would represent a degree of compromise between the interests of members. In almost all instances, your correct choice is a clear answer.

Therefore, that leaves choice B. Members of the First Congress were concerned that the original Constitution, in providing a much stronger central government than the Articles of Confederation, jeopardized the rights of individual citizens. Members of congress still had, in their minds, the memory of the British violation of civil rights before and during the Revolution. Thus, they demanded a "bill of rights" that would spell out the immunities of individual citizens.

The process of elimination requires some knowledge of the subject, because without it, it would be hard to eliminate choices. However, in some instances, the incorrect choices are clear and obvious, making your job of eliminating those choices much easier. Anything you can do to reduce the number of choices and increase your odds will help you immeasurably.

Here's another question that may be easier.

---

2. Which of the following tends to be the most desirable goal for a business?

    A. shortage

    B. supply

    C. equilibrium point

    D. surplus

Unless you know the answer, you should begin to eliminate the incorrect choices. For example, why would a business want to have shortages? This would put them at a great disadvantage in a competitive industry. You can quickly eliminate choice A. At the same time, you probably don't want surplus, either (choice D), because it leaves unsold inventory, which means that the company is overproducing. Thus, you can eliminate that choice.

Choice B sounds like it could be correct, but supply is simply the amount of goods and services that a business produces. But it is not their goal—it is merely their function. Thus, you can eliminate choice B. That leaves you with the correct answer, choice C. The equilibrium point is defined as the price at which consumers will purchase exactly as much of a good or service as a business is producing. This keeps a business flowing, without having to worry about unsold inventory or playing "catch up" to make up for shortages and not being able to ship orders as they're received.

If you don't know the answer as soon as you read the question, the practice of the process of elimination is a time-honored technique for any multiple-choice test. Pay special attention to words like "always," "never," or "not." Most things in the world are not always or never, so you can probably eliminate those.

Finally, be careful about questions that ask you to choose which of the choices is *not . . .* or which are true *except . . . .*

Understanding Learning Styles

In any class, the content presented by a teacher will be perceived differently by each student in his or her class. Each student comes to class with different interests, knowledge levels, abilities, life experiences, learning styles, learning abilities, and reading abilities, but all must learn and be assessed over the same content. In fact, as inclusion becomes more mainstream in Texas public schools, a teacher may also have students who are special education, English Language Learners, or diagnosed with a learning disability—all of whom must be taught the same content as the other students in the classroom.

In order to maximize learning for all of the students in a class, a teacher must recognize what the different learning styles are and address these learning styles in the classroom presentation of content. Each child learns predominately through one of three different means:

- Seeing (**visual learners**)
- Hearing (**auditory learners**)
- Doing, touching, and moving (**tactile/kinesthetic learners**)

Although each child learns to some extent through all three means, each child learns more through one mean than the others. This is his or her dominant learning style. Learning styles are described in more detail in the following table.

Learning Styles		
Learning Style	*Characteristics*	*Instructional Strategies*
Visual learner	These learners tend to: ■ Express and organize thoughts by writing them down or listing them ■ Favor sitting in the front of the class so they can see what the teacher is doing ■ Respond in short answer to questions instead of using complete sentences	Learns best by: ■ Watching the teacher's movements, particularly facial expressions, body language ■ Involving graphics in lessons such as videos, illustrated books, flip charts, overhead transparencies, and graphic organizers ■ Writing or being provided written handouts of instructions, expectations, and assignments
Auditory learner	These learners tend to: ■ Have illegible handwriting ■ Be easily sidetracked by competing noises, sounds ■ Make noises while reading such as humming or whistling	Learns best by: ■ Verbal interactions through lecture, discussion, speaking their thoughts, and listening to others ■ Involving group-based work (projects) in class assignments ■ Having assignments/test questions read aloud to them

(continued)

Learning Styles *(continued)*		
Learning Style	*Characteristics*	*Instructional Strategies*
Tactile/kinesthetic learner	These learners tend to: ■ Be uncomfortable by sitting down for long periods ■ Experience difficulties in reading for extended periods ■ Have poor listening skills	Learns best by: ■ Involving hands-on activities, demonstrations, lab experiments, and field trips ■ Using science (learning) centers in which students must move from their desks to learn ■ Constructing models to illustrate concepts rather than to read or hear about them

The variation in learning styles in the elementary classroom is why it is important for a teacher to address all three learning styles in the presentation of instructional content. In presenting a concept on insects, for example, a teacher may

- Talk about insects to the class.
- Read an illustrated book on insects.
- Show a video on insects.
- Initiate a classroom discussion on the importance of insects to nature.
- Bring different types of insects into the classroom for the students to observe.
- Have the students draw a picture and/or develop a 3-D model of an insect.
- Write a short story or a scientific report on insects.
- Take the class on a nature walk around the school or to a park to look for insects.
- Take the class on a field trip to a zoo or museum where the kids can see a wider selection of insects and/or have a guest speaker such as an entomologist to speak to the kids.

By incorporating as many of these different types of activities into the classroom for as many topics as possible, the teacher addresses all of these different learning styles and increases the chances that all of the students in the class will understand the content being taught in class.

Focusing on Bloom's Taxonomy

As a teacher tries to accommodate all student learning styles, the teacher should focus on strategies and activities that promote higher-order thinking skills. Higher-order thinking skills evolved from an idea advanced by Professor Benjamin Bloom who identified six levels of learning activities, known as **Bloom's Taxonomy.** The six levels of Bloom's Taxonomy are Knowledge, Comprehension, Application, Analysis, Synthesis, and Evaluation. The lower levels of Bloom's Taxonomy (Knowledge, Comprehension, and Application) pertain to the student's ability to recall, translate, interpret, and apply factual information, while the upper levels (Analysis, Synthesis, and Evaluation) represent the student's ability to engage in higher-order thinking and reasoning skills. The following table describes all levels of Bloom's Taxonomy.

Basics of Bloom's Taxonomy in the Classroom

Level of Bloom's Taxonomy	Purpose	Demonstrated Skills	Descriptive Verbs
Knowledge	The learner demonstrates the recognition and recall of factual information such as names, dates, places, events, terms, definitions, and basic concepts.	■ Knows specific information about names, dates, places, and events ■ Knows major steps in methods and procedures ■ Knows and define terms ■ Knows basic concepts	choose, cite, collect, define, describe, find, identify, list, memorize, name, omit, pick, point to, pronounce, read, recall, relate, select, spell, state, tabulate, what, when, where, who
Comprehension	The learner demonstrates an ability to grasp material and understand facts and ideas through organizing, translation, interpretation, and estimation.	■ Understands, organizes, and selects facts and ideas ■ Translates knowledge between media (from numbers to words) ■ Interprets, compares, and contrasts facts and ideas ■ Predicts consequences	account for, associate, classify, compare, contrast, convert, demonstrate, estimate, explain, generalize, give examples, interpret, make sense out of, outline, relate, rephrase, restate (in own words), reword, summarize, transform
Application	The learner demonstrates an ability to apply acquired knowledge toward solving problems.	■ Applies information, concepts, and theories to new situations ■ Solves problems using required knowledge or skills	apply, assess, build, calculate, chart, compute, construct, contribute, develop, give examples of, illustrate, make use of, model, predict, solve
Analysis	The learner demonstrates an ability to break down material into its parts, make inferences, and find evidence to support generalizations.	■ Finds the underlying components or parts of a whole ■ Sees and recognizes patterns	analyze, break down, categorize, correlate, diagram, differentiate, dissect, distinguish, examine, infer, point out, recognize, reduce
Synthesis	The learner demonstrates an ability to combine ideas to create or produce a whole product.	■ Creates new ideas from old ones ■ Makes generalizations from facts ■ Predicts and draws conclusions	build, collaborate, combine, compile, compose, construct, create, design, propose, validate, what if
Evaluation	The learner demonstrates an ability to make judgments or express/defend opinions based on reasoning.	■ Assesses values of theories ■ Makes choices based on reasoning ■ Verifies value of evidence	appraise, assess, critique, debate, defend, disprove, dispute, judge, justify, prove, recommend, value

Bloom BS. (ed.) (1953), *Taxonomy of Educational Objectives: The classification of educational goals: Handbook I, Cognitive Domain*. New York: David McKay and Company.

PART I

TExES GENERALIST EC–4 SUBJECT REVIEW

Domain I: English Language Arts and Reading

Competency 001 (Oral Language)

The teacher understands the importance of oral language, knows the developmental processes of oral language, and provides children with varied opportunities to develop listening and speaking skills.

Review

Understand basic linguistic concepts

The beginning teacher understands basic linguistic concepts (for example, phonemes, semantics, syntax, pragmatics).

Language can be divided into several components:

- **Phonology** refers to the sounds of a language. **Phonemes** are the basic units of sound. Each language uses only a subset of all possible phonemes, and these subsets vary across languages. R and L, for example, are two different phonemes in English, but are not distinguished in Japanese. As they grow up, babies and young children must identify the subset of phonemes used in their native language. Although babies are good at hearing important phonemic distinctions, the ability to produce those distinctions in speech emerges slowly, and early pronunciation errors are common.

- **Morphology** is the set of rules for combining sounds into meaningful units. The smallest units of meaning in a language are called **morphemes.** For example, "cat" is a single morpheme in English. When prefixes and suffixes are added, the number of morphemes in a word increases, because the prefixes and suffixes are themselves meaningful units. For example, the word "cats" consists of two morphemes, because the "-s" is a morpheme meaning "more than one." As children get older, the length of their utterances increases, and the number of morphemes per utterance gets larger, too.

- **Syntax** refers to the structure of a phrase or sentence. The sentence "John smiles at Mary" contains exactly the same words as the sentence "Mary smiles at John," but the meaning is different, because each sentence has a different syntax. Taken together, syntax and morphology constitute the **grammar** of a language, and children's understanding of grammatical rules increases gradually as they get older.

- **Semantics** refers to the meanings of words and phrases. The link between a word and its meaning is a matter of convention. In English, the word "cat" identifies a particular mammal, but some other combination of sounds could have been used. There is no inherent similarity between the word "cat" and a real cat. In order to achieve fluency, a child must learn the meanings of tens of thousands of individual words. Children's understanding of word meanings increases over time, but at any age their **comprehension** of word meanings tends to be more advanced than their **production** of words in speech and writing. In short, children tend to understand more than they can express in words.

- **Pragmatics** consists of rules for effective communication in different contexts. Pragmatics covers many aspects of language, including humor, style, turn-taking, the use of nonverbal gestures such as pointing, and the use of figurative speech such as metaphors—all of which must be used appropriately in order for a person to be truly fluent. Recognizing the importance of politeness when asking a favor, and choosing polite language as well as a polite tone of voice, would illustrate one type of pragmatic competence. As children develop, they gradually learn more about the pragmatics of communicating with others in their particular culture.

Recognize developmental stages in acquiring oral language

The beginning teacher recognizes developmental stages in acquiring oral language, including stages in phonology, semantics, syntax, and pragmatics, and recognizes that individual variations occur within and across languages.

Language develops in predictable stages:

- **Phonological development:** At 2 to 3 months of age, babies begin cooing. **Cooing** consists of simple vowel sounds such as "ahhh" and "oooh." After several months of cooing, consonant sounds are added. The resulting mix of vowels and consonants is called **babbling,** which becomes increasingly complex and speech-like in later months. In the second half of the first year, babies begin to direct sounds toward objects, sometimes while pointing at them. Between 8 and 18 months of age, most babies begin to produce their **first words.**

  Although infants can hear all the phonemic distinctions in their native language, the ability to speak fluently takes years to develop. Beginning with their first words, children's speech reflects several kinds of pronunciation errors. These "errors" are actually strategies for making words easier to say. An early talker may leave out a phoneme ("appo" instead of "apple") or an entire syllable ("bana" for 'banana"). In other cases, adding a syllable makes a word easier to say—as in the case of the child who says "Jaguwar" when pronouncing the word "Jaguar." These pronunciation errors gradually diminish throughout early childhood.

- **Semantic development:** Early talkers tend to use one word at a time. Each of the first words is a **holophrase,** meaning that it stands for an entire idea or sentence. A toddler may use the word "milk" to mean "I want more milk," or "I love milk!," or "I just spilled milk on myself."

  By age 2, most children have begun to say two words at a time, and longer combinations soon follow. The rate at which new words are learned begins to accelerate. However, children's understanding of word meanings is sometimes inaccurate. An example would be the toddler who uses the word "doggy" to refer to dogs, cats, and squirrels. This example illustrates one of many kinds of semantic errors that are common in early oral language development.

- **Grammatical development:** As the length of their utterances increases, preschoolers also begin to make grammatical mistakes, such as **overregularization.** Overregularization occurs when children treat irregular forms according to the rules for ordinary cases. Examples include "mouses," "foots," "goed," and "builded." In each example, the child applies an ordinary grammatical rule to an exceptional case. Overregularization errors tell us that young children are active language learners, spontaneously coming up with general rules rather than passively copying what they hear. These occurences diminish over time but are still heard among elementary school students.

- **Pragmatic development:** Infants understand that language is used for communication. They make sounds to attract their parents' attention, and they babble in response to parental speech. Throughout early development, children's understanding of communication gradually increases. An important source of learning about communication is conversations with adults. Adults provide conversational structure, explanations of figurative speech, and explicit guidance on how to communicate effectively. Pragmatic development occurs gradually, as children learn about turn-taking, politeness, and some of the ways that language is used in a figurative, or non-literal, sense.

  Sensitivity to phonemic distinctions in words, comprehension of word meanings, and awareness of pragmatic conventions, are examples of **receptive language,** or the ability to understand a message. The ability to express oneself in language—to pronounce words, to choose correct vocabulary and grammar, and to follow pragmatic conventions—constitutes **expressive language.** Although receptive and expressive language develop in predictable sequences, there are many variations in the development of individual children. Children differ in verbal skills, in maturational level, and in the cultural, linguistic, and family environments in which they are raised. As a result, early childhood teachers must anticipate—and be receptive to—considerable variability in the oral language experiences and abilities of their students.

Assess and address individual oral language development

The beginning teacher plans and implements systematic oral language instruction based on informal and formal assessment of children's oral language development and addresses individual children's strengths, needs, and interests.

The instructional methods that teachers plan must take into account their student's age. Younger children will tend to need more help with basic skills, such as knowing how to respond when spoken to and how to listen when others are speaking. Older children will need more help with advanced skills, such as evaluating the content of their own and others' speech.

The instructional methods that teachers plan and implement should be sensitive to individual differences among children in each age group. Some children are more verbally skilled than others; some children are more attentive than others; some children have had more experience with conversation than others; and some children need more encouragement than others to express themselves. Teachers can obtain information about individual children through discussions with parents, through conversations with children, and from both informal and formal assessments of each child's oral language abilities. Formal assessments of oral language development include standardized tests such as the Peabody Picture Vocabulary Test (PPVT) and the Test of Oral Language Development (TOLD).

Although it is important for teachers to monitor the progress of their students over time, assessment is particularly important at the beginning of the year. Assessment during the first few weeks of the year provides baseline information for planning the most effective oral language instruction for individual students.

Recognize speech or language delays

The beginning teacher recognizes when speech or language delays or differences warrant in-depth evaluations and additional help or interventions.

Children vary in the rate at which they acquire oral language skills. For example, by age 4, some children are able to articulate all of the basic sounds in English. Other children will continue to struggle for several more years with sounds such as *l*, *r*, *s*, and *th*. It can be difficult for a teacher to tell the difference between a developmental lag and an actual disorder. Some children with comparatively limited skills catch up to their peers naturally, while others need additional intervention. A number of informal and formal assessment practices are available to help teachers discern whether an oral language problem exists in a child's receptive and/or expressive language.

Design activities to build language skills

The beginning teacher designs a variety of one-on-one and group activities (for example, meaningful and purposeful conversations, dramatic play, language play, stories, song, rhymes, games, discussions, questioning, sharing information) to build on children's current oral language skills.

Scaffolding refers to the way that adults help children learn complex skills such as language. For example, when talking with a young child, a parent may help the child participate in the conversation by asking key questions such as "What happened next?" The parent may then elaborate on the child's response. If the child says "He threw hats," the parent may reply "Yes, the monkeys threw the hats out of the tree." In these examples, the parent is providing a scaffold, or structure, in which the child can develop his or her language skills. One of the goals of the early childhood teacher is to choose instructional methods that provide the best scaffold for the oral language development of each child. Asking questions and elaborating on what children say are two of the important general methods that can be used. Some other instructional methods are as follows:

- **Reading to children:** When reading a story, teachers should involve the class by discussing what happens in the story and by asking about children's reactions. **Shared reading**, in which children participate in the telling of the story, also increases children's interest and involvement. Reading to children gives teachers the opportunity to discuss the meanings of new words and to engage in a variety of literacy-related activities.

- **Involving children in songs, rhymes, and games:** Teachers should use a variety of activities to keep children interested while reinforcing their oral language skills. Activities such as singing, rhyming, choral recitation, and language play help maintain children's interest while teaching new words as well as sensitivity to the sounds and rhythms of language.

- **Encouraging children to participate in conversation:** Teachers should find opportunities to talk with children about what they think and feel. Asking questions is one way of engaging children in conversation. During conversations, the teacher can provide appropriate scaffolding for a variety of language-related skills.

- **Thinking out loud:** Teachers should provide verbal descriptions of what they are thinking as they make decisions, solve problems, and observe what is happening in the classroom. "Let's see," a teacher may say, "I need to cut this paper into four pieces. How am I going to do this? I know. I'll fold the paper like this, and . . ." In other cases, the teacher may look around and talk about what various children in the classroom are doing. Thinking out loud provides children with models for oral language usage.

- **Using props:** Teachers should promote oral language activities in which children can make use of props. Talking to a puppet, or having a puppet speak for them, can sometimes help young children who are otherwise reluctant to express themselves in class. Show-and-tell facilitates oral expression among both younger and older children, because it allows children to talk about something that is both important and familiar to them. Role-play is an engaging way of involving children of all ages in oral language expression. Each of these activities is useful not only for encouraging individual children to talk, but also for stimulating conversation among students.

Reflect cultural diversity and build on individual strengths

The beginning teacher selects and uses instructional materials and strategies that promote children's oral language development, reflect cultural diversity, and respond to the strengths, needs, and interests of individual children, including English Language Learners.

English Language Learners are children whose native language is not English, and whose oral language skills (in English) are less advanced than their classmates. To some extent, the same instructional methods used for the rest of the class are appropriate for these children. At first, however, the teacher will need to do more of the talking.

As English Language Learners progress toward effective communication in English, there is a predictable sequence. At first, these children use their native language to communicate with the teacher and other students. When they realize they are unable to communicate with others in their native language, many of these children enter a period of silence in which their main attempts at communication are nonverbal (for example, through gestures). This progression is normal. English Language Learners need time to adjust to the new language. They need time to figure out what others are saying and what they themselves should say. They need time to feel comfortable expressing themselves in English. The teacher should be sensitive to these needs, while providing English Language Learners with verbal scaffolding and other forms of support. Eventually, English Language Learners will begin to communicate with the teacher and other students in English.

The English Language Learner may participate in **bilingual education,** meaning that academic content is provided in the child's native language at the same time that English language instruction is given. In some cases, the child will be placed in an English class with other English Language Learners who speak a variety of different languages. This is an **English-as-a-Second-Language** (**ESL**) classroom, and ESL teachers must be sensitive to the different backgrounds and skill levels of their students.

Acknowledging a student's cultural background, whether or not the student is an English Language Learner, helps make the student feel important and respected. There are many ways that teachers can incorporate cultural backgrounds into instructional practice. Instructional units on different cultures or subcultures would be one type of example. Another would be the use of instructional materials such as stories, reference books, and pictures that reflect cultural differences. Show-and-tell, as well as conversations about home and family, are other activities that reflect cultural diversity in ways that facilitate oral language development and help students fit into the classroom.

Build on non-English backgrounds

The beginning teacher selects and uses instructional strategies to build on children's cultural, linguistic, and home backgrounds to enhance their oral language development, including using the home language to develop English.

Standard English is the dialect of English that is taught in school and used in many contexts outside the classroom. There are many kinds of nonstandard English. It is important for the teacher to realize that nonstandard dialects are not inferior to Standard English. Linguistically, each dialect is comparable in richness and complexity. The key difference between dialects is that Standard English is more prevalent in certain contexts, such as the classroom.

The teacher should also realize that the language that a child speaks is a reflection of his or her home environment. The child who speaks a nonstandard dialect is not speaking incorrectly. Rather, the child's speech is an accurate reflection of the vocabulary and grammar that he or she has been exposed to. The teacher must find ways to teach Standard English while maintaining respect for the child's home language. It is potentially harmful for the child to feel that the home language is inferior in some sense.

When interacting with a child who speaks a nonstandard dialect, the teacher should model and encourage Standard English without being critical of the child's usage. The teacher should focus on the idea that the child is trying to convey, and restate or paraphrase the child's remarks in Standard English. By restating or paraphrasing what the child has said, the teacher is able to model standard usage without being critical of the child. In addition, the teacher can praise the child for standard usage without being openly critical of nonstandard expressions.

Although students are exposed to Standard English in school, the teacher should provide opportunities to build on the linguistic cultural practices the child is familiar with at home. Oral reports on home life, show-and-tell, and discussions of differences in dialect are among the ways that teachers can incorporate children's background into instructional practice.

Provide instruction that interrelates oral and written language

The beginning teacher understands relationships between oral language and literacy development and provides instruction that interrelates oral and written language to promote children's reading proficiency (for example, preview-review, discussion, questioning).

Oral language and literacy do not develop independently. Speaking, reading, and writing are interrelated, and effective instructional methods rarely contribute to the development of one without contributing to the development of the others.

For example, the **language experience approach** (**LEA**) is a commonly used instructional method that integrates oral and written language skills. For younger children, the LEA often involves a dictation activity. Students dictate a story to the teacher, who writes the story down in front of the students and reads it back later. LEA stories often focus on shared experiences, such as a field trip or a special event. However, the stories can be about personal experiences, imagined events, or anything else that students are interested in relating. As students get older, they play an increasingly central role in the creation of LEA text.

The LEA allows younger students to see connections between oral expression and writing. Students observe the correspondence between what they say and what the teacher does while writing the story. They notice the sequencing of words from left to right and top to bottom, as well as the spellings of individual words, the spacing between words, and other characteristics of written text. The LEA allows each student to feel that he or she has contributed to the story and provides an opportunity for the teacher to call attention to many different aspects of oral language and print.

Other activities that link oral and written language in the promotion of reading proficiency are discussed under Competencies 003 and 004.

Help children connect spoken and printed language

The beginning teacher selects and uses instructional materials, strategies, and activities to strengthen children's oral vocabulary and narrative skills in spoken language and to help children connect spoken and printed language (for example, planned read-alouds).

Children's vocabulary and narrative skills can be strengthened through a variety of methods. For example, the teacher can make use of **textless books** (also known as **wordless books**), which consist of sequences of pictures but no print. Asking young children to "read" a textless book out loud allows them to practice vocabulary and to apply their emerging appreciation of narrative.

Encouraging children to tell or retell stories also reinforces vocabulary and strengthens narrative skills. Props such as puppets may provide helpful support for younger children as they learn how to tell and retell stories.

There are many ways for teachers to emphasize connections between the spoken and written word. For younger children, observing the teacher read a book out loud provides opportunities to see connections between what the teacher says and what is printed on each page of the book. In addition, children's narrative skills can be enhanced through discussions of story events and characters. **Dialogic reading** refers to conversations between a teacher and students about a story that has just been read.

The younger the child, the more a teacher must rely on prompts to sustain dialogic reading. For example, the teacher can use open-ended prompts. A simple but effective open-ended prompt would be to show children a picture from the story and ask what is happening. Other kinds of prompts provide more verbal scaffolding. For example, the teacher may read a sentence from the story but leave a blank at the end for children to fill in ("Johnny gave his teacher an _____"). In addition, the teacher may ask specific questions ("Do you remember what Johnny did after school?").

Dialogic reading is an effective instructional activity at any age. As children get older, their participation in the reading of the stories naturally increases, and the extent to which they need to be prompted, or guided in their responses, naturally declines.

During the elementary years, greater reliance can be placed on written materials as a means for strengthening vocabulary and narrative skills. Elementary school students learn vocabulary from books and other written materials. For example, the teacher may post **word walls**, which are lists of words that students are currently learning, in places that the entire class can see.

New vocabulary words are often learned through receptive language, but teachers should give students as many opportunities as possible to use new words and thereby incorporate them into their expressive vocabularies.

Provide opportunities to adapt spoken language to various audiences

The beginning teacher provides instruction and opportunities for children to develop skills for adapting spoken language for various audiences, purposes, and occasions.

Pragmatics includes the ability to adapt one's speech to fit the needs of a particular context. The early childhood teacher helps students appreciate a number of pragmatic conventions.

Teachers of younger children focus on basic conventions, such as the importance of a polite tone of voice, and the need for responding to a teacher's question (even if only to say, "I don't know"). Teachers also help younger children appreciate the differences between communicating with a group of people versus communicating one-on-one. When addressing the entire class for an oral report or show-and-tell, the teacher will help students understand the need to speak up, make eye contact with the group, and provide an appropriate amount of information—neither too much nor too little.

Perspective-taking is a skill that increases with age. Younger children may not appreciate that other people think differently, or have different knowledge and experiences than they do. Teachers must help students appreciate some of these differences in order to tailor their speech to their particular audience. Role-playing is one kind of activity that helps children appreciate other points of view.

Teachers of older children help refine the basic skills acquired by younger children. For example, elementary school students may understand the difference between polite and impolite speech, yet still find it difficult to express constructive criticism without being excessively negative. Elementary school students will also need help appreciating some of the differences between formal and informal speech styles.

Provide opportunities to develop listening skills

The beginning teacher understands listening skills for various purposes (for example, critical listening to evaluate a speaker's message, listening to enjoy and appreciate spoken language) and provides children with opportunities to engage in active, purposeful listening in a variety of contexts.

Different types of listening are used for different purposes. **Critical listening** is used to understand and evaluate the content of what someone is saying, while **listening for appreciation** is used to appreciate and enjoy the message. Both types of listening may be needed for the same material. An example would be the strategies a teacher uses to introduce a poem. The first time the teacher reads the poem out loud, he or she may encourage listening for appreciation by alerting students to the rhymes and rhythms of the poem, and by asking students to imagine some of the scenes and situations that the poem expresses in figurative language. In subsequent readings of the poem, the teacher may encourage critical listening by asking students to think about the ideas that the poet is trying to convey, and to consider how clearly the ideas are expressed.

Because children are active learners, they tend to learn best when their listening is active rather than passive. **Active listening** is a way of focusing attention on a speaker through participation in activities relevant to the message. The goal of active listening is to keep children attentive and actively engaged. The teacher can promote active listening in a number of ways. While telling a story, for example, the teacher may ask children to contribute a repeated phrase at appropriate times. Active listening can also be encouraged by helping children to retell simple stories, to paraphrase important instructions, and to ask appropriate questions when the teacher or another student is making a presentation. For elementary school students, taking notes is one of the most important forms of active listening that develops. (Note taking is discussed further under Competency 008.)

Encourage evaluation of spoken messages

The beginning teacher provides instruction and opportunities for children to evaluate the content and effectiveness of their own spoken messages and those of others.

Metacognition refers to the ability to reflect on and evaluate one's own thought process. Examples of metacognition include the understanding that taking notes can help one remember, that people can draw different conclusions from the same evidence, and that learning is more difficult when one is tired. **Metalinguistic knowledge** is a form of metacognition that pertains to the ability to reflect on and evaluate language.

An example of metalinguistic knowledge would be the ability to evaluate a spoken message on dimensions such as clarity, relevance, and effectiveness. Teachers can encourage children to evaluate messages by asking key questions about content. For example, if there are several different red objects in a box and a child makes reference to "the red one," the teacher can ask whether anything else needs to be said about the object in order to find it.

Teachers can also encourage students to consider the effectiveness of a message. A student who has just made a request may be asked whether he or she thinks the request was loud enough, clear enough, or framed in a way that someone else can understand. With younger students, teachers may need to provide answers to some of these questions. As students progress through elementary school, they become increasing capable of evaluating the logic, style, and persuasiveness of spoken messages and, consequently, more independent in their evaluation of content and effectiveness.

Select appropriate technologies to build oral skills

The beginning teacher selects and uses appropriate technologies to develop children's oral communication skills.

The teacher has many resources to draw from to help develop children's oral language. Books, pictures, audio and video recordings, computer software, art supplies, games, puppets, and dolls are among the many materials and technologies that teachers can use.

Some resources are explicitly designed for children of particular groups or levels. For example, a **basal reader** is a collection of stories and other materials that is appropriate for children of a particular grade level. Basal readers, worksheets, games, and software programs are often designed with a particular age group in mind. Other resources, such as picture books and puppets, must be used by the teacher in age-appropriate ways to develop oral language skills.

Oral language is often taught in conjunction with some content area, and multiple resources are used. For example, **thematic units** (or thematic organizers) are designed to teach several subjects through sustained focus on a particular topic. An example of a thematic unit would be a unit on dinosaurs in which children learn about biology (for example, differences between meat-eaters and plant-eaters), geography (for example, the habitats of different dinosaurs), and math (for example, changes in the size of dinosaur populations over time). A variety of different materials and activities would be used to help children make sense out of this information.

In a thematic unit on dinosaurs, oral language skills could be developed as children engage in discussions about dinosaurs, present oral reports to the class about dinosaurs, and learn dinosaur names. For younger students, the learning of dinosaur names could be an opportunity to practice identifying the initial sounds of words ("What letter does Tyrannosaurus start with?"). For older students, the learning of dinosaur names could be an opportunity to work on spelling relatively challenging words.

Foster collaboration with families and other professionals

The beginning teacher understands how to foster collaboration with families and with other professionals to promote all children's oral language development.

From birth, babies are spoken to and overhear speech. Children develop in a language-rich environment created by parents, siblings, teachers, peers, and the media. The home environment tends to have the most significant influence on the oral language development of individual children.

It is important for teachers to maintain contact with each child's parents or guardians. Information about the home environment can be a source of useful information about the child's functioning in the classroom. Academic and behavioral problems are sometimes a reflection of problems at home. For example, young children sometimes respond to stress by regressing to more rudimentary forms of speech.

It is also important for parents to be encouraged to participate in their children's oral language development. Reading aloud, talking about stories, engaging in conversations, and many of the other activities discussed under this competency are appropriate not only for teachers but also parents. Teachers can suggest activities to parents, and encourage parents to work with their children on oral language activities that the child is participating in at school.

Sample Questions

1. During the first week of school, a pre-kindergarten teacher asks each child to bring something blue from home to talk about in a show-and-tell format. What is the main purpose of this activity?

   A. to strengthen children's pronunciation skills
   B. to provide new vocabulary words for the class to learn
   C. to help children become comfortable about talking in front of the group
   D. to support the development of critical listening

   C Any use of oral language allows children to exercise their pronunciation skills. Asking children to discuss something they have brought from home does not help pronunciation more than other ordinary uses of oral language. Hence, option A would not be the main purpose of the activity. For the same reason, option B would not be the main purpose, because there are so many opportunities, both planned and unplanned, for teaching new vocabulary. Pre-kindergarten teachers would probably not emphasize critical-listening skills so early in the school year, so option D would not be the main purpose either. Option C is the best answer. During the early weeks of school, it is important for the pre-kindergarten teacher to help children become comfortable with expressing themselves in front of their classmates. In this example, the teacher has chosen an activity that bridges the gap between school and home and also allows children to discuss something familiar to them.

2. When asking children to tell a story using a textless book, which of the following should a kindergarten teacher expect?

   A. grammatical errors
   B. irrelevant details
   C. nonstandard English
   D. all of the above

   D Option A is correct, because grammatical errors such as overregularization are normal among kindergarten students. Option B is correct, because limitations in narrative and pragmatic skills sometimes result in children speaking off-topic. Option C is also correct, because Nonstandard English is a common occurrence in the classroom. Hence, option D is the best answer.

Competency 002 (Phonological and Phonemic Awareness)

The teacher understands phonological and phonemic awareness and employs a variety of approaches to help children develop phonological and phonemic awareness.

Review

Understand how phonological and phonemic awareness develop

The beginning teacher understands the significance of phonological and phonemic awareness for reading, is familiar with typical patterns in the development of phonological and phonemic awareness, and recognizes that individual variations occur.

There is some variation among experts in how phonological awareness and phonemic awareness are defined and distinguished from each other.

Generally, **phonological awareness** refers to the ability to notice and think about the sounds of language. These sounds include words, syllables, letters, and individual phonemes. For example, the ability to count the syllables in a word reflects phonological awareness, as does the ability to distinguish between the parts of a syllable. Specifically, the consonant(s) at the beginning of a syllable are referred to as the **onset,** and the vowel(s) and consonants that follow are called the **rime.** In the word "book," the /b/ sound is the onset, and the /ook/ sound is the rime. In the word "bring," the /br/ is the onset, and the /ing/ is the rime.

Recall that phonemes are the basic units of sound in a language. The word "bat" consists of three phonemes: /b/ /a/ /t/. The word "ball" also consists of three phonemes: /b/ /a/ /l/. The word "tax" consists of four phonemes: /t/ /a/ /k/ /s/. **Phonemic awareness** is the ability to identify the phonemes that make up words, to distinguish between phonemes, and to make use of phonemes. Thus, according to some experts, phonemic awareness is one aspect of phonological awareness.

Phonemic awareness enables specific skills such as rhyming, alliteration, blending, and segmentation.

- **Rhyming** refers to repetition of sounds at the ends of words.
- **Alliteration** refers to the repetition of sounds in stressed syllables or at the beginnings of words (as in "Tick, tock . . ." or "Peter Piper picked a peck . . .").
- **Blending** is the combination of individual sounds, as when a teacher asks what /p/, /a/, /t/ spell and a child replies "pat."
- **Segmentation** is the division of words into sounds, as when a teacher asks a child to identify the first sound in "pat" and the child says "p" or makes a /p/ sound.

Phonological and phonemic awareness can be distinguished from **auditory discrimination,** or the ability to hear differences between phonemes and other units of sound. Auditory discrimination matures in infancy. It is not difficult for infants and children with normal hearing to discriminate between all of the phonemes in their native language. A young child can respond appropriately to a request for a "bat" as opposed to a "ball," because the child can hear the difference in the final phoneme of each word. Likewise, a young child can hear that the word "banana" is longer than the word "ball."

In contrast to auditory discrimination, phonological and phonemic awareness do not automatically mature at an early age. These skills must be taught to children over a period of time.

Phonological and phonemic awareness are difficult skills to master, and some children struggle more than others. The child who can hear the difference between "bat" and "ball" may not be able to describe the difference between the two words. The child who can hear that "banana" is longer than "ball" may not be able to count the syllables, even with help from a teacher. It is normal for preschoolers to have difficulty making these phonological distinctions.

Teachers of pre-readers and early readers help children develop phonological and phonemic awareness. Phonological and phonemic awareness are prerequisites for reading. Reading depends in part on the ability to break words down into individual units of sound such as syllables, letters, and phonemes, and to understand how these units are combined. Studies show that such abilities are predictors of reading achievement—the more advanced a child's phonemic awareness, for example, the greater the child's later success at reading.

Build on individual and non-English backgrounds

The beginning teacher understands differences in children's development of phonological and phonemic awareness and adjusts instruction to meet the needs of individual children, including English Language Learners.

The development of phonological and phonemic awareness varies widely from child to child. Teachers must be sensitive to developmental differences, and must keep pace with more advanced children while providing extra support for children who are struggling.

Children who seem to be struggling can be helped by extra time and attention, a focus on familiar letters and words, the use of concrete objects as props, and the incorporation of more cues into phonological activities. For example, the teacher may help a child who is having difficulty with segmentation by using the child's name as an example. The teacher may say "Let's say your name. Robert. Rrrrrrrrrrrobert. Do you hear that Rrrrrrrrrrr sound? Isn't that like the sound a tiger makes—Grrrrrrrrrrr? Can you say Grrrrrrrrrrr? Now say Rrrrrrrrrrrobert with me."

Teachers of English Language Learners should remember that these children do have experience with a language, even if it is not the English language. English Language Learners can benefit from phonological and phonemic awareness activities that build on their native language. At the same time, some activities can sharpen phonological and phonemic awareness even when the English Language Learner is uncertain about the meanings of the words. Simple rhymes and chants, for example, focus children's attention on similarities and differences in sounds. It is important, however, to help English Language Learners gain a foundation in oral language and appreciate the meanings of the words they are working with. Emphasis on isolated phonological properties of words is not recommended for any type of student.

Along with English Language Learners, teachers will encounter students who speak dialects that are different from Standard English. In classrooms where more than one dialect is spoken, teachers can develop activities that call attention to differences in sounds across dialects. Doing so helps children feel respected and avoids giving them the impression that their way of speaking is wrong.

Incorporate assessments of phonological development

The beginning teacher plans, implements, and adjusts instruction based on the continuous use of formal and informal assessments of individual children's phonological development.

Teachers can informally assess phonological and phonemic awareness through observation, as well as by involving children in simple tasks, games, and other activities. Teachers can develop checklists and other forms for keeping track of the progress of individual students. For example, a kindergarten teacher may observe how well individual children can clap along with the syllables in a word as it is articulated. Or, the teacher may monitor how well children can generate rhymes for simple words. Informal assessments can be made in group settings or in private conferences with children. Experts recommend the use of multiple methods to identify an individual child's strengths as well as areas that need work.

Formal assessment may be called for if a child does not seem to be making progress. One formal assessment of phonological development currently used in Texas is the **Texas Primary Reading Inventory** (**TPRI**). The TPRI is used for assessing skills such as phonemic awareness, listening comprehension, and reading, among children ranging from kindergarten through 2nd grade. Several other formal assessments are available to help teachers identify students who need additional support for emerging phonological and phonemic awareness skills.

Use a variety of instructional approaches

The beginning teacher uses a variety of instructional approaches and materials (for example, language games, informal interactions, direct instruction) to promote children's phonological and phonemic awareness.

Phonological and phonemic awareness can be promoted through a variety of activities:

- **Songs, stories, chants, and rhymes:** Rhymes such as "Hickory, dickory, dock, the mouse ran up the clock . . . ," for example, help refine phonological awareness by calling children's attention to similarities in the final sounds of words. Songs such as "Old MacDonald" and chants such as "Pease porridge hot . . ." also call attention to alliteration. Shared reading provides an excellent opportunity for interactive activities that promote phonological skills.

- **Motor activities:** During a singalong, for example, children can be encouraged to raise their hands, tap their feet, or clap when they hear the rhyming words: "Ding dong, bell [clap], pussy's in the well [clap] . . ." Clapping is commonly used to help children count the syllables in familiar words such as their own names.

- **Language games:** Word play and other language games help develop specific aspects of children's phonological and phonemic awareness. Asking children to generate rhymes, even if what they produce are nonsense words, is one example of a useful language game. Asking children what you get when you say "ball" without the /b/ sound would be another example. As children begin to learn the alphabet and the sounds of individual letters, written materials can be incorporated into language games. For example, showing children a simple word such as "cat" and asking what you get when you replace the first letter with a "b," is an activity that promotes segmentation.

- **Word boxes:** A **word box** (also referred to as an **Elkonin box**) is a row of boxes that correspond to different sounds in a word. The word box for "hat," for example, would consist of three boxes in a row (or a rectangle divided into three parts). A picture of a hat would be present, and each child would have markers such as plastic counters or pennies. As the teacher pronounces each sound in "hat," children would place a counter in the appropriate box (or part of the rectangle). Older children would be asked to write the appropriate letter in each box.

- **Writing:** As discussed under Competency 009, children learn about the phonology of their language through writing, beginning with their earliest efforts to create written text. The attempt to write letters that correspond to the sounds of words helps children appreciate letter-sound correspondences and improves phonological awareness.

Foster collaboration with families and other professionals

The beginning teacher understands how to foster collaboration with families and with other professionals to promote all children's phonological and phonemic awareness both at school and at home.

Generally, parents or caregivers should be kept up-to-date about what happens in the classroom. The teacher can prepare a letter that describes key classroom activities and explains how these activities promote phonological skills. Parents can be encouraged in this letter, and during conferences with teachers, to engage in specific activities with children at home. Reading in general should be encouraged, as should other materials, games, and activities that contribute to phonological development. The goal is not to have parents "drill" children, but rather to help them appreciate that many activities children enjoy can contribute to emerging phonological skills. The messages to parents should be to have fun and to focus on what their children can do rather than on what they cannot do.

Along with descriptions of the overall classroom experience, it is important for teachers to keep parents informed about individual children's progress. Parents can be given specific suggestions for games and other activities that may help their children in areas that need work. Again, parents should be encouraged to be positive and nurturing and to keep in mind that anything they do to help their child will be most effective if the child views it as a fun activity rather than a chore.

Sample Questions

1. Which of the following would be most helpful in developing phonemic awareness among preschoolers?

   A. During circle time, the teacher reads a list of words and asks children to clap each time they hear the name of an animal, but not when they hear the name of a food.

   B. During shared reading of a story about a snake, children are told that the first letter of the word "snake" is an "s," and they are asked to make an /sssss/ sound each time they hear the word.

   C. During show-and-tell, the teacher writes the name of each object on the board and pronounces it several times for the class.

   D. On the first day of class, during circle time, children take turns saying their own names, and then saying the first letter of their names.

   B Phonological awareness activities help children notice the sounds that make up words. Option A is incorrect, because the only phonological skill required is auditory discrimination of the differences between animal names. Option C is incorrect as well. By writing the names of each object on the board, the teacher demonstrates correspondences between spoken and written language, but in itself does not contribute to phonemic awareness. Option D is inappropriate, because on the first day of preschool, at least some children will not know the first letter of their name. Option B is correct. By telling children that "snake" begins with an "s," and then asking them to make an /sssss/ sound each time they hear "snake," children can become better at segmenting that particular word by identifying its initial phoneme.

2. A teacher recites "Peter Piper" very slowly for her kindergarten class. Afterward, she asks the class which sound they heard a lot of. What aspect of language is the teacher trying to sensitize her class to?

   A. rime
   B. blending
   C. phonology
   D. alliteration

   D Option A is incorrect, because rime consists of the vowel(s) and consonant(s) that follow an onset sound. The rimes in "Peter Piper" tend to be different from word to word. Option B is incorrect, because children are not given the opportunity to hear or engage in blending. Option C is incorrect, because it is much too general. Option D is the correct answer. "Peter Piper" is extremely alliterative, owing to the numerous repetitions of the /p/ sound.

Competency 003 (Alphabetic Principle)

The teacher understands the importance of the alphabetic principle for reading English and provides instruction that helps children understand the relationship between printed words and spoken language.

Review

Understand the alphabetical principle

The beginning teacher understands the elements of the alphabetic principle, including letter names, graphophonemic knowledge, and the relationship of the letters in printed words to spoken language.

English is an **alphabetic language,** because each sound or phoneme in the language is written with a letter or set of letters. For example, the /t/ sound is represented in written English by the letter "t." In contrast, a single Chinese character stands for an entire morpheme or word. In Chinese, a word such as "talk" is represented by one or two characters, and none of the characters contains a part that corresponds to the /t/ sound or any other specific sound in the word.

In alphabetic languages, the **alphabetic principle** is the idea that there are consistent relationships between sounds and letters. Understanding the alphabetic principle means appreciating that each sound or phoneme in one's language is written with a single letter or set of letters. A **grapheme** is the letter or letters that represent a phoneme. For example, the word "bay" consists of two graphemes: a "b" for the first phoneme, and an "ay" for the second one. The word "ball consists of three graphemes: a "b" for the /b/ sound, an "a" for the /a/ sound, and an "ll" for the /l/ sound.

Graphophonemic knowledge refers to knowledge about specific relationships between graphemes and phonemes; that is, between letters and sounds. In the process of acquiring literacy, children learn the names of letters as well as correspondences between each letter or set of letters and particular sounds. Adults know many rules and many exceptions—for the ways language sounds are represented in writing.

Phonological awareness, phonemic awareness, and graphophonemic knowledge about letter-sound correspondences are examples of skills and knowledge that are acquired in the process of becoming literate. These terms should not be confused with **phonics,** which refers to a method of teaching children specific letter-sound correspondences. Phonics conveys graphophonemic skills and contributes to phonological and phonemic awareness. Although educators sometimes refer to phonics as the method that children use to sound out words, a distinction can be made between phonics as a teaching method versus the phonic strategies that children use when sounding out words. These issues are discussed further under Competency 005.

Understand alphabetic skills development

The beginning teacher understands expected patterns of children's alphabetic skills development and knows that individual variations may occur.

Oral language is acquired naturally, in the sense that even if adults did not make deliberate attempts at instruction, children would gradually learn how to comprehend and produce speech. In contrast, alphabetic skills and other knowledge about writing would probably not be acquired unless some instruction were given. Children learn the names of letters, the way letters are written, and specific letter-sound correspondences through books, songs, games, and other activities.

In the process of acquiring literacy, children learn the names of the 26 letters in our alphabet. Children may learn many or all of these names by rote, before they understand that letter names are related to writing. In other words, acquisition of letter names may or may not go along with the acquisition of graphophonemic knowledge.

In order to read, children must know not only the names of letters but also how to recognize them in print. **Alphabetic recognition** is the ability to recognize printed letters based on their distinctive shapes. Alphabetic recognition tends to develop in tandem with graphophonemic knowledge, in the sense that as children learn what letters look like, they also learn how the letters sound. Teachers should remember that just as children may learn letter names without understanding how the letters are written (or the fact that letters are written in the first place), so there will be children who have alphabetic recognition before they appreciate specific links between letters and sounds.

Distinguishing between the physical appearance of letters can be difficult at first. It is common for children to confuse letters of similar appearance (for example, "p" and "q" or "E" and "F"). Not all children are equally quick to appreciate these distinctions. Although children with learning differences such as dyslexia may continue to confuse similar-looking letters, it is not necessarily indicative of a problem when young children experience such confusions.

As alphabetic recognition improves, children show increasing appreciation of the idea that the same letter can be written in a variety of different sizes and fonts, and they learn the distinction between upper- and lowercase forms of each letter. Many educators believe that by the end of kindergarten, children should be able to recognize the upper- and lowercase forms of the entire alphabet. The ability to distinguish between block letters and cursive tends to be a later development.

Understand differences among languages

The beginning teacher understands that many alphabetic languages are more phonetically regular than English, that not all written languages are alphabetic, and that English Language Learners' use of the alphabetic principle may vary based on language background.

Not all written languages are alphabetic. In Asian languages such as Chinese and Japanese, for example, a single character stands for an entire morpheme or word. Other languages use alphabets that differ to a greater or lesser extent from our own.

Languages such as French, German, and Spanish use the same alphabet as English but make regular use of **diacritic marks** to guide pronunciation. Diacritic marks (also called **diacriticals**) that are common in Spanish are the **cedilla** beneath the letter "c" to indicate an /s/ sound (as in Curaçao), and the **tilde** above the letter "n" to indicate a /ny/ sound (as in mañana).

Other alphabetic languages, such as Russian and Greek, contain some letters that are similar to or the same as our own, as well as many letters that are different. Korean is written with characters that are composed of geometric units, with each unit standing for a particular sound. In short, there are many systems for representing sounds with letters or phonemic units.

Among alphabetic languages, English is one of the most phonetically irregular. The /s/ sound, for example, can be represented by the letters "s," "c," "sc," or "ss," as in the words "soft," "ice," "science," and "mossy." Adding to the irregularity is the fact that these letters do not only convey the /s/ sound:

- An "s" is sometimes pronounced /z/, as in the word "busy."
- A "c" is sometimes pronounced /k/, as in the word "cat," and at other times, it is pronounced /sh/, as in the word "appreciate."
- An "sc" is sometimes pronounced /sk/, as in the word "screen," and at other times it is pronounced /sh/, as in the word "fascism."
- An "ss" is sometimes pronounced /sh/, as in the word "passion."

Notice that the sound /sh/ can be represented by "sh," "c," "sc," "ss," "sch," "ch," or "ti" (as in the word "motion"). These are just a few of the many examples of phonetic irregularities in English. These irregularities occur not only across words but also within them—in the word "discussions," for example, there are three different pronunciations of the "s." From these examples, it should be understandable why learning the alphabetic principle and mastering graphophonemic applications can be difficult for children.

English Language Learners face the additional challenge of applying the alphabetic principle to a language with which they are relatively unfamiliar. The specific ways that English Language Learners apply the alphabetic principle may be influenced by their home language. For example, a child whose native language is Spanish may tend to equate the letter "j" with the /y/ or /h/ sounds, as in Spanish. Teachers must be patient as they sensitize children to the differences in graphophonemic specifics between languages.

Focus instruction on letter-sound relationships

The beginning teacher selects and uses instructional strategies and materials to provide focused instruction on the letters of the alphabet and the relationships between sounds and letters.

Many strategies and materials can be used to teach letter names, alphabetic recognition, and graphophonemic correspondences between letters and sounds. Generally, the teacher should begin by teaching high frequency consonants such as "m," "t," and "b." At some point, short vowel sounds should be introduced, so that children can quickly progress to the reading of simple **CVC (consonant-vowel-consonant)** words, such as "bat."

- **Songs, rhymes, and storytelling:** The alphabet song is probably the most common source of learning about English letter names. (Some adults have difficulty reciting the alphabet without thinking of the song or unconsciously following its phrasing.) One source of the alphabet song's effectiveness is that it incorporates rhyme by pausing after the rhyming letter names "g," "p," "v" and "z." There are many other songs and rhymes that can be used to teach letter names, alphabet recognition, and letter-song correspondences. Stories, especially when interactive, always provide a good opportunity for alphabetic and graphophonemic instruction.

- **Alphabet books:** Alphabet books support alphabetic recognition and can be used to teach letter-sound correspondences. Teachers should read these books with children and help children create their own alphabet books with letters and pictures.

- **Word boxes:** Word boxes are a good method of helping children isolate the letters that constitute familiar words and to appreciate the connections between the letters and the way they sound in each word.

- **Alphabet displays and word walls:** Word walls are lists of words posted where all students can easily see them. Word walls provide support for the acquisition of graphophonemic knowledge. Alphabet displays, whether on walls or flashcards or anywhere else in the classroom, help reinforce letter names and support letter recognition. Like alphabet books, alphabet displays are particularly helpful for learning letters, because the letters are strongly emphasized.

- **Other activities:** A variety of activities can provide opportunities for learning about letters and letter-sound correspondences. Matching games encourage children to link pictures or objects with their initial letters. Simple crossword puzzles focus attention on individual letters. Writing, show and tell, and guided play can all be modified to teach or reinforce alphabetic and graphophonemic knowledge.

Use a variety of instructional approaches

The beginning teacher uses a variety of instructional materials and strategies, including multisensory techniques, to promote children's understanding of the elements of the alphabetic principle.

It is important for teachers to work with a variety of materials and strategies when teaching children about letters and letter-sound correspondences. **Multisensory techniques** teach literacy by engaging more than just the visual sense. These techniques can help children focus on the shapes and sounds of letters. Manipulable representations such as magnetic letters allow children to literally handle letters as they work with them. Letter-shaped cookie cutters can be used to cut letters out of soft materials. Sand trays can be used for writing practice, as can **skywriting** (the method of writing letters in the air). Children are active, concrete learners who benefit from these kinds of hands-on activities.

Emphasis on variety is important for several reasons. Varying materials and strategies helps maintain interest while reinforcing the same idea from different perspectives. Variety helps ensure that children with different learning styles receive at least some information that best suits their particular style. And variety tends to reflect some of the natural variation in spoken and written language that children must contend with, such as differences in font as well as phonetic irregularities.

In choosing activities, it is important for teachers to keep in mind that the ultimate goal is successful reading. Instructional methods that focus on individual letters are helpful but should be integrated as much as possible with meaningful activities that link letters to words, and words to broader uses of language. For example, if the teacher chooses to spend a week focusing on the letter "d," alphabetic activities should be linked with other aspects of instruction. If the class is learning about animals that week, the teacher can create activities in which children identify and talk about animals whose names begin with "d." Any children whose names begin with "d" or have a "d" in them can be identified. In this way, a specific letter is linked to specific words, and the words are used in meaningful and personally relevant ways.

Use formal and informal assessments

The beginning teacher uses formal and informal assessments to analyze individual children's alphabetic skills, monitor learning, and plan instruction.

Teachers should use a variety of informal assessments to monitor children's progress. Early on, children can be asked to point to the letters in a set of letters and numbers. Children can be asked to say or sing the alphabet as a way of evaluating whether they know letter names. Simply asking children to name letters, or to make a sound associated with each letter, is a straightforward approach to assessing knowledge of letter-sound correspondences. Alternatively, the teacher can point to a letter and ask children to say what they know about it. This open-ended approach gives children the opportunity to say something if they only know the letter name, and/or its sound, and/or a word that begins with it.

As children get older, increasingly sophisticated assessments of alphabetic skills can be conducted. Children can be given sets of letters and asked to separate upper- from lowercase forms or vowels from consonants. Children can be asked to write all the letters they can think of that make a particular sound or asked to write all the sounds associated with a particular letter.

The results of both formal and informal assessments can guide instructional planning for the entire class, and can be used to identify specific areas where individual students need additional support. Some students may simply need help distinguishing between two particular letters. Other students may have more general needs.

Foster collaboration with parents and other professionals

The beginning teacher understands how to foster collaboration with parents and with other professionals to promote all children's development of alphabetic knowledge.

As with other aspects of literacy, teachers should keep each parent informed about key classroom activities that involve all children, as well as his or her particular child's progress. Teachers can suggest activities that reinforce and extend what children are learning in class and can help parents support skills that need extra work. As with other literacy-related skills, parents should be encouraged to be enthusiastic and to make sure that alphabetic activities conducted at home are fun for everyone.

Sample Questions

1. Which of the following can be expected in a preschool classroom?

   A. Children struggle with the distinction between the way "b" and "d" are written.
   B. When children are shown pictures of a cat, a bat, and a hat, they find it difficult to point to the "cat."
   C. Children who know the names of the 26 letters also know how to write them.
   D. All children acquire graphophonemic knowledge at about the same pace.

   A Option B is incorrect, because accurate performance relies on auditory discrimination skills that all preschoolers should have. Children with normal hearing will have no difficulty pointing to the "cat." A child who is unable to do so may have a hearing deficit, or some other problem that should be evaluated. Option C is incorrect, because it is unlikely that by preschool age most children know how to write all 26 letters. Likewise, Option D is incorrect, because individual differences in the acquisition of graphophonemic knowledge can be expected. Option A is correct. It is normal for preschoolers to experience some difficulty distinguishing between the way highly similar-looking letters are printed.

2. Assuming that a kindergarten class already has alphabetic recognition for six high-frequency consonants, what should the teacher do next?

   A. Teach children how to recognize low-frequency consonants, such as "q" and "z."
   B. Continue teaching high-frequency consonants and make a "letter list" of consonants already learned that can be posted at the front of the room.
   C. Teach children high-frequency vowels so that they can begin to read simple words in picture books.
   D. Have children make drawings of the consonants and vowels that they already know, and then post the drawings around the room.

   C All of the options would promote literacy development. However, it is important that literacy instruction takes place in a meaningful context. The focus should not be on isolated skills but rather on the application of these skills to meaningful, interesting activities. As children acquire letter names and alphabetic recognition skills, they should be given the opportunity to apply these skills to reading as soon as possible. Options A, B, and D all reinforce children's understanding of individual letters. In contrast, option C would allow children to apply their understanding of individual letters to the task of reading actual words. Hence, option C is the best answer.

Competency 004 (Literacy Development)

The teacher understands that literacy develops over time, progressing from emergent to proficient stages, and uses a variety of approaches to support the development of children's literacy.

Review

Understand the process of acquiring literacy

The beginning teacher understands that literacy acquisition develops in an often predictable pattern from prereading (sometimes referred to as emergent literacy) to conventional literacy and that individual variations occur in literacy acquisition.

Traditionally, it was assumed that formal instruction marks a sharp distinction between pre-readers and readers. It was believed that children require about five years of maturation and exposure to oral language before they could be ready to learn reading and writing. At that point, it was believed that children should be taught **reading readiness skills,** such as alphabetic knowledge. Once they acquired reading readiness skills, children would be prepared to enter the world of literacy through formal instruction in reading and, later, writing.

Experts increasingly reject this sharp distinction between pre-readers and readers. It is believed now that the development of literacy begins at birth, because infants and children are raised in print-rich environments, and throughout childhood have meaningful interactions with adults in the context of print. Young children notice that people respond to marks printed on signs. They see their parents look at books and tell stories that seem to be "in" the books. They hear people talk about reading, and they see people writing. At some point before children learn how to read and write, they may look at books and pretend to tell stories, and they may scribble and say they have written a story.

Emergent literacy refers to children's beliefs about and experiences with reading and writing prior to formal instruction. The knowledge, skills, behaviors, and interests that fall under the heading of emergent literacy contribute to the development of **conventional literacy,** or the kind of reading and writing that is taught in elementary school. Both emergent and conventional literacy develop in predictable ways, but specific patterns of development vary across individual children as a result of differences in both maturation as well as experience.

Emergent literacy includes children's earliest efforts to create or retell stories, to convey meaning through drawing and writing, and to notice and express interest in print. Emergent literacy thus encompasses both oral and written language. Experts assume now that emergent literacy activities are not simply childish behaviors but rather important precursors to conventional literacy. It is assumed that there is a continuum of development from emergent to conventional literacy rather than a sharp distinction between the two. For example, educators once believed that children should have a foundation in reading before they are taught how to write. Experts now believe that emergent reading and writing both contribute to conventional literacy, and that writing should be encouraged among pre-readers, because it gives children practice at expressing themselves, helps them understand the relationship between reading and writing, and increases their phonological sensitivity as they try to express the sounds of familiar words with written letters.

Recognize the emergence of print awareness

The beginning teacher understands that the developing reader has a growing awareness of print in the environment, the sounds in spoken words, and the uses of print.

Print awareness is the understanding of the nature of print, the functions it serves, and the conventions governing its use. Print awareness allows children to distinguish between words and other forms of representation, such as pictures. Print awareness includes the understanding that print conveys meaning, and that its meaningfulness is enabled by conventions of punctuation, spacing between words, left-right orientation, regular spelling, and so on.

Print awareness is fostered by many sources. For example, **environmental print** is the written text that is observable in one's surroundings, such as signs, labels, stickers, billboards, and brand names. By age 2, children recognize environmental print, although at first they attend to it in a global way. That is, young children may recognize the logo for "Coke," but they attend to the design, shape, and color of the can or bottle as well as the print. As children get older, they develop the ability to focus on the printed word. This example illustrates that experience with environmental print contributes to the emergence of print awareness.

Print awareness is also facilitated by the experience of being read to by parents and other adults. As children look on, they notice that the rows of marks in storybooks are related to the story that the parent is telling. Being read to thus conveys the idea that print consists of marks that are arranged in linear rows. Being read to also reinforces the idea that print is a source of meaning. As children look on, there are opportunities to learn the alphabetic principle and to notice connections between the way familiar words sound and how they are printed.

There are many other opportunities besides storytelling for children to learn about the uses of print. Children who observe their parents as they consult menus, select programs from the TV guide, follow recipes, read street signs, and write checks or letters are afforded many opportunities to learn about the many functions of print.

As children pass from emergent to conventional literacy, their print awareness also increases, because they receive a great deal of information about print through classroom activities.

Use instructional approaches that distinguish text from non-text

The beginning teacher selects and uses instructional strategies, materials, and activities to assist young children in distinguishing letter forms from number forms and text from pictures.

Children's earliest attention to print is global. The child who is looking on while a parent reads a story may not pay much attention to the print, or may not distinguish clearly between the print and the pictures. However, the child may be developing the sense that both the text and the pictures contribute to what the parent is saying. The preschool teacher can engage in a variety of activities to help children distinguish written text from pictures. While reading, the teacher can call attention to the text by occasionally tracing it with a finger. When a question arises, the teacher can show children how the text provides an answer (for example, "Let's look back at this page. It says here that . . .").

There are many opportunities for teachers to spontaneously reinforce children's understanding of what is text versus what is not. Calling attention to environmental print is a common occurrence in the classroom (for example, "Let's see who this belongs to. It says right here that this is Maria's . . ."). And whenever the teacher writes in the vicinity of a related picture, the difference between the text and the picture is emphasized.

Initially, children will find it difficult to distinguish between letter and number forms. In some cases, letters and numbers are similar (for example, the number "2" and the letter "Z"), and in other cases, they are virtually identical (for example, the number "0" and the letter "O," or the number "1" and the letter "l"). The teacher can help children distinguish letters from numbers by pointing out contextual cues, such as the idea that names would not contain numbers, while phone numbers would not contain letters. A variety of activities can help children make the letter-number distinction. For example, sorting tasks can be used in which children are asked to select letters from a pile of forms that include both letters and numbers.

Recognize the multiple levels of literacy development

The beginning teacher understands that literacy development occurs in multiple contexts through reading, writing, and the use of oral language.

One of the key assumptions of emergent literacy is that literacy development begins at birth and is fostered through interactions with people in a variety of contexts, including conversations, games, and other oral language activities.

Being read to provides young children with the opportunity to learn new vocabulary. At first, infants simply listen to the stories that are told to them. As children take an increasingly active role in reading interactions, they ask questions about stories, talk about new words and phrases, and practice their emerging narrative skills as they attempt to retell part or all of the stories that are familiar to them. The pre-reader who picks up a book and "reads" it by looking at the pictures and telling a story is exercising early narrative skills that have been learned through storytelling interactions.

Reading to children provides a great deal of information about the nature and conventions of print. Reading to children also helps convey a sense of what stories are. Through listening to stories, children learn about narrative conventions, including the idea that stories have a beginning, middle, and end; that stories often focus on a character or group of characters; and that stories tend to present a coherent sequence of events rather than fragmentary descriptions. Understanding conventions of narrative structure helps children when they begin to read, by providing guidance about what to expect when trying to identify specific words. (This topic is discussed further under Competency 005). Awareness of narrative structure also helps children learn about differences among the various genres of stories, including an important distinction between works of fiction and expository texts (that is, texts that convey information directly).

Just as pretend reading helps exercise early narrative skills, pretend writing allows children to practice expressing themselves by making marks on paper. Children's earliest "writing" consists of random scribbles. Over time, letter-like forms begin to replace the scribbled marks. As the capacity to write letters emerges, children produce one letter at a time, often the first letter of a word, such as "d" for "dad." Combinations of letters then appear, such as "Mk" for "Mike" or "bsbl" for "baseball." The strings of letters that children create will probably not be exclusively linear and horizontal, and pictures may be incorporated into the text. Gradually, children learn to form letters more clearly, to write entire words, and to follow some of the conventions of print such as linearity, left-to-right and top-to-bottom orientation, and the introduction of spaces between words. But even before these conventions are mastered, children's writing represents an effort to convey meaning—it is a reflection of emergent literacy, and it contributes to the development of conventional literacy skills.

Once writing has developed to the point that children can form words, much of what they write consists of **invented spelling** (also known as developmental or phonetic spelling). Teachers should encourage children rather than insisting on correct spelling at this point. If the child asks for the correct spelling of a word, the teacher can provide it. Otherwise, invented spelling need not be corrected. Invented spelling contributes to conventional literacy development, because it allows children to practice expressing themselves through writing. Children develop a positive attitude about writing if they feel they are capable of expressing themselves in this medium. Moreover, the effort to write down letters that correspond to the sounds of familiar words sensitizes children to phonemic distinctions and letter-sound correspondences.

Use instructional approaches that focus on the functions of print

The beginning teacher selects and uses instructional strategies, materials, and activities that focus on functions of print, including concepts involving book handling, parts of a book, orientation, directionality, and the relationships between written and spoken words.

There are many strategies, materials and activities that can teach children about the nature and function of print.

During storytelling and shared reading, the teacher can call attention to some of the conventions of print, identifying the title before reading, pointing out how the book is held and which direction the pages are turned, and using a finger to trace the words as they are read in order to emphasize their linearity, their horizontal alignment, and their left-to-right and top-to-bottom orientation.

Wordless books, which consist of a sequence of pictures, give children the opportunity to handle books, to be the storytellers, and to express their emerging narrative skills. Teachers can write down the stories that children are composing. A **language experience approach** (see Competency 001) allows children to observe teachers in the act of writing and to experience some of the specific letter-sound correspondences in familiar words.

Along with book-oriented activities, conversation about classroom procedures and events is a source of information about print. The teacher may say "I'm writing your name on this so everyone knows that it's yours." Or, "Let's see what's written under this picture. Oh, it says 'apple' there."

As children get older, teachers can be increasingly explicit about conventions of print, such as the spacing between words, punctuation, paragraph structure, and so on.

Incorporate children's literature into instruction

The beginning teacher demonstrates familiarity with children's literature and provides multiple opportunities for children to listen and respond to a wide variety of children's literature, both fiction and nonfiction, and to interact with others about literature.

Teachers should be familiar with a variety of fiction and nonfiction genres and specific books. The teacher will need to select books written at an appropriate level of difficulty for the entire class, as well as for individual students. The teacher will also need to choose books that are relevant to various classroom activities and thematic units.

In addition, the teacher needs to have ready access to books that fit the interests and needs of particular students. A student may request more information about a topic or find another book from a particular genre or author. If the teacher notices that a student is extremely interested in a particular author, the teacher may suggest other books by that author or try to broaden the child's interest in other authors within the same genre. Having familiarity with a variety of children's literature helps teachers achieve instructional objectives by keeping individual students engaged, thereby fostering a positive attitude about reading.

The books that teachers choose for their classroom can be used for storytelling, shared reading, and dialogic reading (see Competency 001). Repeated reading of stories is helpful, because children become familiar with the stories and thereby have more basis for engaging in retells, discussions, dramatic reenactments, and other meaningful activities.

With older students, teachers will also be selecting books that the children themselves read. **Choral reading** takes place when a group of students or the entire class reads out loud. In **guided reading,** the teacher explains the purpose for reading a particular text as well as the structure for how to respond to what is read. Students are also encouraged to engage in independent reading. Choral, guided, and independent reading do not replace storytelling, shared reading, and dialogic reading but are added to them as children's own reading skills advance.

Apart from group activities, teachers can help individual students with independent reading selections, and with the choice of books for their book bags. Teachers can provide suggestions and guidance for the selection of books that fit each child's skill level and that match, or broaden, the child's interests. A "library" of books should be available to students in the classroom, as well as lists of books that can be found in the school or community library or at a local bookstore.

The genres that can be represented in teachers' book selections include folklore, realistic fiction, historical fiction, science fiction, poetry, biographies, essays, and **expository texts** (that is, informational books). In addition, teachers may make use of **basal readers** (also called **basal reading programs**), which consist of narratives and supplemental instructional materials, including workbooks, skill sheets, and teacher manuals, that are designed to foster a sequence of skills. Extensive or inflexible reliance on basal readers, however, is not recommended.

Teach children about authorship

The beginning teacher teaches children about authors and their purposes for writing.

Literacy includes the understanding that books are created by authors who have some purpose for writing them (entertainment, instruction, edification, and so on). Naming the author of each book read to a preschool class helps children understand the connection between reading and writing. Discussions of authors' lives and their purposes in writing particular books helps children understand concepts of narrative and **story grammar** (the underlying structure of a story that links episodes), as well as the nature of differences between genres. Specific events and characters in a work of fiction, as well as specific topics of discussion in an expository text, can be understood more clearly if the child realizes what purpose the author had in mind when creating the book.

Use technology to enable access to texts

The beginning teacher selects and uses appropriate technology to help children gain access to a wide range of narrative and expository texts.

There are many sources for written texts of interest to students. Along with books and other kinds of written materials available for use in the classroom, the teacher can provide both students and parents with information about the use of the school and local libraries, bookstores and book swaps in the community, and Internet sites designed to promote early literacy through interactive use.

Electronic books, educational videos, and educational computer games are sources of narrative and expository text that can contribute to literacy development through interactive, multisensory methods. Audiotapes are another alternative to conventional books as sources of narrative and expository information.

Personal computers are increasingly prevalent at home and in the classroom. PCs provide a variety of new opportunities for literacy development. Among the many kinds of software currently available are CD-ROM **talking books,** which are interactive versions of stories that contain multimedia features such as animation, music, and narrated text. The interactive nature of talking books is helpful, in that children can use a mouse to respond to prompts, influence the type of information presented, and repeat information as needed.

As with any other kind of material, guidance from teachers and parents is needed for children to make the most out of technological alternatives to conventional books.

Use assessments to meet individual needs

The beginning teacher uses formal and informal assessments of children's literacy development to plan, implement, and adjust instruction to meet the needs of individual children, including English Language Learners.

Both informal and formal assessments should be used to track children's literacy development and to both plan and adjust instructional methods. Both emergent literacy skills as well as attitudes toward literacy should be assessed. It is critical for young children to have a positive attitude about reading and writing, given the importance of these skills as well as the extent of time and effort needed for mastery.

English Language Learners can benefit from the use of concrete objects and multimedia displays to help establish an oral language foundation during the development of emergent literacy. As appropriate, teachers can use nonverbal gestures, repeat key words, avoid slang, and anticipate unfamiliar words to help these children. English Language Learners may find play and small-group activities to be especially helpful.

Foster collaboration with parents and other professionals

The beginning teacher understands how to foster collaboration with families and with other professionals to promote all children's literacy development.

Teachers should communicate regularly with parents about classroom activities. Parents should be given information about emergent literacy to help them appreciate the importance of children's interest in storytelling, reading, writing, drawing, and other literacy-related activities. Parents should be encouraged to be positive and supportive rather than correcting children or pushing them toward conventional literacy skills.

Teachers should ask parents about their children's interests and activities in order to help plan instructional activities that are most relevant to students. In addition, teachers should convey information about individual children's progress.

Teachers should also make available to parents lists of age-appropriate books, tapes, Internet sites, and computer software, along with guidance about interacting with children in the context of storytelling, shared reading, and other literacy-related activities.

Sample Questions

1. A kindergarten teacher encourages his class to tell stories from wordless books using narrative and role-play. What skill does this activity nurture?

   A. phonological awareness
   B. print awareness
   C. graphophonemic knowledge
   D. emergent literacy

   D Option A is incorrect, because this activity provides no particular exercise for the ability to notice sounds in words. Likewise, option C is incorrect, because the activity does not call children's attention to letter-sound correspondences. Although the activity does reinforce the understanding that books contain stories, the teacher uses wordless books and, thus, option B is incorrect. The correct answer is option D. By looking at the pictures in wordless books and both describing and acting out a sequence of events, children have an opportunity to practice their narrative skills and link an unfolding narrative to a sequence of pages in a book. The understanding of narrative and how it is expressed in books is one aspect of emergent literacy.

2. Which of the following would be most effective in fostering print awareness among preschoolers?

   A. a guided reading activity in which children practice identifying the main point in a passage
   B. an invented spelling activity, in which children are encouraged to write a story (children are told they can write what they want and use any spelling they prefer)
   C. a book making activity, in which each member of the class draws a picture on a "page;" the pages are then combined and jointly "read" by teachers and students
   D. a choral reading activity based on a very simple text

   C Options A and D are incorrect, because guided and choral reading are too advanced for preschoolers. Option B is incorrect for a similar reason. Some preschoolers engage in invented spelling and in spontaneously doing so, they exercise their emerging knowledge of print. But not all children are capable of making letters by preschool age and, thus, asking them to write a story may result in confusion. Option C is correct. By combining pages in a book and reading each page in succession, the teacher reinforces some basic conventions of print, such as the idea that books contain pages, the pages of books contain information, and readers examine pages in a left-to-right sequence.

Competency 005 (Word Analysis and Decoding)

The teacher understands the importance of word analysis and decoding for reading and provides many opportunities for children to improve their word-analysis and decoding abilities.

Review

Understand the development of word analysis and decoding

The beginning teacher understands that many children develop word-analysis and decoding skills in a predictable sequence but that individual variations may occur.

Word analysis refers to the recognition of written words. There are many different methods of recognizing a word. **Sight words** are recognized instantly, without analysis of the word's components. Words that are not immediately recognized may be guessed on the basis of contextual cues, such as a nearby picture. If the child can read other words in a passage, the child may be able to use syntactic cues to recognize a particular word. Likewise, if the child understands the meaning of the passage, semantic cues can be helpful.

Decoding refers to the recognition of how written words sound. Sight words can be pronounced without analysis or other conscious effort. For words that cannot be recognized by sight, children use **phonic analysis** to identify the sounds in each word and to blend the sounds together. Phonic analysis is commonly referred to as "sounding out" a word. Many different parts of a word can be attended to during the process of phonic analysis: syllables, letters, consonants, vowels, phonemes, onsets, and rimes. Phonic analysis also includes attention to **diphthongs** (pairs of adjacent vowels that are both heard, such as the "oy" in "toy"), **consonant blends** (pairs of adjacent consonants that are both heard, such as the "br" in "break"), and **digraphs** (pairs of adjacent vowels or consonants that are heard as a single sound, such as the "ch" in "cherry" or the "ee" in "meet").

The terms "word analysis" and "decoding" are not used in a consistent way by educators and educational experts. Here, word analysis refers to any strategy by which a child recognizes a written word. One of the many methods of recognizing a word is to decode it through phonic analysis.

To some extent, the development of word analysis and decoding are predictable. Three broad, overlapping phases have been observed.

1. At first, as children notice environmental print, they begin to recognize entire words that have significance for them, such as their names, the names of favorite restaurants, or the model name of the family car. At this time, children attend to the fonts, colors, designs, and backgrounds of the words they recognize. Their attention is not restricted to the words themselves or the constituent letters.

2. In the next phase, children view words in an increasingly analytical way. They begin to understand graphophonemic patterns of association between letters and sounds, and they develop a variety of word-analysis and decoding strategies. Preschool and kindergarten instruction fosters the increasingly broad and skillful use of these strategies.

3. Finally, children begin to recognize words in a relatively automatic way, without having to take time to deliberately apply decoding strategies such as phonic analysis.

Successful readers tend to rely on the components of words rather than on pictorial and contextual cues as a basis for word recognition. Their early decoding strategies tend to be consistently focused on letters and letter groups. Over time, they recognize an increasing number of words in an automatic way. Although the progression from emergent to successful reading is somewhat predictable, there will be variations from child to child in the types of strategies used, the types of errors made, and the extent of comprehension for particular passages.

Promote the use of word-recognition skills

The beginning teacher understands the importance of word-recognition skills (for example, decoding, blending, structural analysis, sight-word vocabulary) for reading comprehension and knows a variety of strategies for helping young children develop and apply word-analysis skills.

There are many ways to foster word-analysis skills in group as well as individual interactions. Word-analysis skills can be taught through direct instruction as well as by modeling and guided practice. Typically, more than one method is appropriate. For example, a teacher may explain what blending is (see Competency 002), model several examples of blending, and then guide children as they practice blending on their own.

For early readers, sorting words is an activity that helps emphasize similarities and differences between words on key dimensions. Words can be sorted according to length, common letters, common sounds, and common onsets or rimes. The teacher can identify dimensions on which words should be sorted, or children can come up with their own categories.

Word walls, spelling pattern lists, and other written materials can be incorporated into classroom activities that foster early word-analysis development. Written materials may focus on particular components of words, such as common affixes or rimes, or they may emphasize entire words. At least some materials should be manipulable, and children should be given opportunities to write as well as read.

Reading with children provides opportunities to teach virtually every aspect of literacy, including word-analysis skills. During shared reading, for example, teachers can point to words in big books and sound them out with children.

As children's own reading skills progress, teachers can introduce strategies that guide reading behavior. Pausing to think about what has been read, rereading, and skipping difficult words until more of the text has been read and understood are some of the broad strategies that support word analysis.

Teachers can also help children master word-analysis strategies that apply to individual words. A variety of semantic, syntactic, structural, and contextual cues are available. Some of these cues help children recognize difficult words based on what they already know about the content or grammar of a passage. For example, in a story about a swim in the ocean, the child can be encouraged to realize that when a character is about to "swim in" or "jump into" something, that something is probably a word such as "ocean" or "water." Other cues help children focus on the constituents of individual words. For example, when attempting to identify a difficult word, children can be taught to look for a spelling pattern (such as a rime) or an entire word embedded in the difficult word (for example, "bookstore").

Along with word-analysis strategies, young children need to acquire sight words. Being able to recognize at least a few words by sight at the outset of reading instruction helps children appreciate that written words convey meaning. In addition, it helps children maintain a positive attitude toward reading and gives them a context for applying word-analysis strategies to unfamiliar words.

Finally, teachers can teach decoding strategies based on **phonics,** a method of instruction that emphasizes specific letter-sound relationships. Phonics helps children sound out words through phonic analysis. Although appropriate phonics instruction has a positive impact on reading, teachers should not focus on phonics to the exclusion of reading for meaning. Phonics should be part of instructional activities that focus on all aspects of literacy development, from oral language to specific decoding strategies. Neither teachers nor students should lose sight of the goal of literacy instruction: meaningful communication through reading and writing.

Use assessments to meet individual needs

The beginning teacher knows a variety of formal and informal procedures for assessing children's word-analysis and decoding skills and adjusts instruction to meet the needs of individual children, including English Language Learners.

Teachers should monitor the progress of individual students as they acquire word-analysis and decoding skills. A variety of assessments can be made during both group and one-on-one interactions, and instruction should be adjusted to fit the needs and interests of individual students.

Recall that oral language is the basis of emergent and conventional literacy skills. English Language Learners may not understand spoken English well enough to appreciate word-analysis and decoding activities. These children may be unable to recognize a particular word, because they lack oral experience with the word in either English or their native language. They may struggle with the word, because it contains a sound or letter that does not appear in their native language.

English Language Learners should not be involved in word-analysis activities that focus on parts of words in isolation from their meaning. It is critical for all children to understand what they are attempting to read. English Language Learners need a foundation in spoken English, including oral experience with specific words that are being taught, before they can benefit from word-analysis instruction.

Teach word analysis in a simple-to-complex progression

The beginning teacher teaches the analysis of phonetically regular words in simple-to-complex progression (that is, phonemes, blending onsets and rimes, short vowels, consonant blends, other common vowel and consonant patterns, syllables).

As children learn how to read, teachers should introduce phonetically regular words before gradually incorporating words of greater complexity. Experts have offered a number of recommendations:

- At first, emphasis should be on words written in lowercase, unless upper- and lowercase forms are similar (for example, "S" and "s").
- At first, the words introduced to children should be familiar to them through spoken language.
- Monosyllabic words should be introduced before multisyllabic words.
- Simple consonant-vowel-consonant combinations such as "mat" or "rug" should be introduced first.
- Words with continuous sounds (such as "m") should be introduced before words with stop sounds (such as "p"), unless the stop sounds appear at the ends of the words.
- At first, words containing highly similar letters, such as the "b" and "d" in "bed," should be avoided.
- Words with single consonants should be introduced before words with consonant clusters.
- Words with high frequency consonants such as "t" should be introduced before words with low frequency consonants.
- Finally, it has been observed that 37 rimes such as "ack," "ell," and "ump" make up nearly 500 simple words that are common in elementary-level written materials. Children's earliest word lists should include at least some words created from these rimes.

Use decodable texts

The beginning teacher teaches children to read passages using decodable texts as appropriate and provides opportunities for children to progress from sounding out words orally to decoding words silently.

Decodable texts are written materials that reflect the letter-sound relationships a particular child already knows. Exclusive reliance on decodable texts is considered too restrictive, but the choice of books and other written materials provided to beginning readers should be linked as closely as possible to each child's graphophonemic skill level.

Decodable texts help children progress toward silent reading. Repeated exposure to particular words allows children to become more familiar with them and to progress from sounding them out to reading them silently. Practice with reading generally fosters silent decoding.

Although children may be capable of silent reading, there are times when reading out loud is appropriate. Oral reading is a major source of information for assessment. In addition, reading out loud as a group (**choral reading**) is appropriate for activities that involve modeling. For early readers, teachers should model strategies such as blending. Teachers should also model the reading of passages to help children appreciate phrasing and its relationship to punctuation, grammar, and meaning. However, **round-robin** techniques, in which children take turns while others follow along, have been criticized for inefficiency and for the embarrassment experienced by some children with limited skills. It is important to help children develop positive attitudes toward reading and other aspects of literacy.

Select and review irregular words

The beginning teacher teaches children to recognize high-frequency irregular words by selecting words that appear frequently in children's books and reviewing difficult words often.

Explicit instruction and modeling can help students master irregular words. Word walls and other lists are also useful. Teachers should keep track of the irregular words that they introduce in class and review these words frequently.

The teaching of irregular words should focus on examples that are most common in elementary-level books and other written materials. Although the introduction of irregular words should be sequenced, teachers should make note of groups involving simple examples (for example, "fight," "tight," "right," and "sight").

Teach children to identify vowel sounds and multisyllabics

The beginning teacher teaches children ways to identify vowel-sound combinations and multisyllabic words.

Vowel-sound combinations should be introduced after children have some facility with consonants and consonant clusters. At first, vowels can be introduced in combination with rimes. For example, the teacher can introduce the word "man" as consisting of the onset "m" combined with the rime "an." Later, the teacher can subdivide the rime into its two phonemes /a/ and /n/.

Multisyllabic words should be avoided until after children have mastered some monosyllabic words. It is helpful if the first multisyllabic words introduced to children are familiar to them, and if these words are constructed out of simpler words, as in the examples "football" and "horseshoe." It is also helpful if the earliest multisyllabic words incorporate affixes, syllables, and/or rimes that the class is already familiar with. For example, if the students have already learned the "-an" spelling pattern (used for words such as "man," "can," and "plan"), then the teacher can introduce words such as "candy" and "candle."

Teach children how to use structural cues

The beginning teacher provides instruction in how to use structural cues to recognize compound words, base words, prefixes and suffixes, and inflections.

One strategy for word recognition is structural analysis. **Structural analysis** consists of the identification of morphemes, the smallest units of meaning in a word. Morphemes include **base words** (also known as roots), which are the primary source of meaning in a word and cannot be further subdivided. Morphemes also include **affixes** (prefixes and suffixes), inflections, contractions, and other grammatical elements.

Teachers can help children use structural analysis to divide words into morphemes. Structural analysis can help in many ways to make word recognition easier. For example, compound words such as "baseball" can be divided into their constituent words. Suffixes that indicate case and tense can be identified and temporarily "removed" so that students can focus on decoding the base word. Generally, the goal of structural analysis is to identify parts of words that are familiar, so that identification of the entire word can be facilitated.

Help children make use of syntax and context

The beginning teacher teaches children to use knowledge of English word order (syntax) and context to support word identification and confirm word meaning.

Syntax is a source of information that supports word identification in the context of individual sentences. A child who has successfully read that "Ricky is going to the . . ." can expect the next word to be a place or an event rather than, say, a color or an action. In other words, the syntax as well as the meaning of this sentence creates an expectation for what the final word will be. Teachers can help early readers notice and make use of syntactic cues that support word identification.

Teachers can also help early readers use syntax as a basis of monitoring their reading. Students can be encouraged to listen to themselves as they read and to make adjustments when the result for a particular word does not seem accurate or sensible. A child who reads the sentence "Mary wants a cookie" as "Mary walks a cookie" can be encouraged to question whether that reading makes sense. Although early readers cannot articulate the underlying grammatical rule that has been violated in this instance, upon reflection they would be able to tell that the sentence does not sound right, and they would know which word seems out of place and requires another look.

Context is another important source of information that can be used to support word recognition and to evaluate the accuracy of a particular word once it has been read. A child who reads about Goldilocks finding three "beads" can be encouraged to think about what happens in the story (and, perhaps, what the accompanying picture shows), and to consider whether they have read the word correctly. Goldilocks may have found three bears or three beds, but it is unlikely, given the context, that she has found three "beads."

Use assessment to plan instruction

The beginning teacher uses formal and informal assessments to plan and adjust instruction based on individual children's word-analysis and decoding skills.

Assessments should be used to evaluate skill levels at particular times, as well as progress in skill levels over time. Informal assessments can be conducted in group as well as individual settings, while formal assessments require one-on-one interaction. Although it is important to monitor each child's progress, teachers should avoid over-testing children.

Running records are written accounts of changes in a specific behavior over time. Running records are a good source of information about progress in word-analysis and decoding skills, in that they allow teachers to track the specific strategies that each child uses at different times, as well as the kinds of mistakes the child makes and the extent of the child's improvement over time.

Oral reading serves as the basis of both formal and informal assessments. The teacher can listen to each child read and make note of tempo, accuracy, omissions, repetitions, and self-monitoring behaviors such as self-correction. In addition, the teacher can make note of specific mistakes or mispronunciations in decoding.

When teachers analyze children's reading, the goal is not merely to quantify accuracy, but to keep track of the kinds of strategies children use and the kinds of words or word elements they tend to struggle with. Often, a given reading behavior can be interpreted in more than one way, depending on the situation and the student. For example, mispronunciations could indicate decoding errors, or they could be attributed to an accent, a difference in dialect, or a speech impediment. Hesitation could indicate difficulty applying a word-analysis skill, or it could show that the child notices an especially difficult word and wants to be very careful about sounding it out. Substitution may occur when the child cannot sound out a word, or it may occur when the child recognizes a word but replaces it with a synonym that is easier to pronounce.

As reading progresses, assessment shifts from emphasis on word-analysis and decoding skills to comprehension. (Assessment of comprehension is discussed at length under Competency 007.) Teachers use standardized and informal test results, reading response notebooks, conversations, and other sources of information to determine how well children understand what they read. With beginning readers, comprehension can be a useful indicator of how well word-analysis and decoding skills are applied.

Assessment also includes keeping track of what each child is reading so that appropriate adjustments can be suggested. As noted earlier, word-analysis and decoding skills are fostered when reading materials are closely matched to the skills that the child has already acquired. The teacher can use the results of assessment to suggest books for independent reading and home use that are more or less difficult than what the child has been reading or represent a closer fit with the child's interests.

Further details about assessment are discussed under Competencies 006 and 011.

Foster collaboration with families and other professionals

The beginning teacher understands how to foster collaboration with families and with other professionals to promote all children's word-analysis and decoding skills.

It is important for teachers to keep parents informed about their children's progress and to suggest home activities that reinforce the word-analysis strategies being taught at school. Parents can be encouraged to engage in shared reading and to work with children on materials they bring home from school. Specific guidance can be given for working with these materials in a positive and supportive way. Parents can also be given lists of books, games, software, and Internet sites that provide decodable text that matches their child's skill level and that can be used interactively to foster the development of word-analysis strategies.

Sample Questions

1. A 2nd grader would benefit most from structural analysis of which of the following difficult words?

   A. jacket
   B. sneaker
   C. underwear
   D. tuxedo

   C Structural analysis allows children to identify morphemic constituents of words. Option C, unlike the other options, contains a word that is composed of two simpler words. By breaking the word down into "under" and "wear" the child may be able to read the entire word more easily. The other words in the list cannot be broken down into simpler morphemic units. Hence, option C is the correct answer.

2. Which of the following lists reflects an appropriate order for the introduction of written vocabulary to kindergarteners as they first begin to read?

   A. match, mad, map, man
   B. rat, run, red, runner
   C. pillow, pot, pear, pond
   D. man, mango, apple, cat

   B Option A is incorrect, because the first word contains a consonant cluster. Option C is incorrect, because the first word is multisyllabic and begins with a stop sound. Option D is incorrect, because the first word contains two visually similar consonants, and because the second word is multisyllabic and may be an unfamiliar term for some children. Option B is the best answer. The first three words are simple consonant-vowel-consonant combinations that are monosyllabic, begin with continuous sounds, and represent words that are familiar to children in oral language. The fourth word builds on the first one in the list.

Competency 006 (Reading Fluency)

The teacher understands the importance of fluency for reading comprehension and provides many opportunities for children to improve their reading fluency.

Review

Understand the role of rate, accuracy, and intonation in fluency

The beginning teacher understands that fluency involves rate, accuracy, and intonation.

Fluent reading is the ability to read quickly, accurately, smoothly, and with expression. The term "smoothly" indicates that fluent readers do not usually hesitate between words, although they may pause in appropriate places (for example, between paragraphs) or for the purpose of emphasis (for example, "Then George saw . . . a *snake*.")

Fluent reading is an automatic and relatively effortless process. Automaticity and effortlessness become possible when the reader can accurately identify many words by sight (rather than having to sound them out). However, reading fluency is not just a matter of accurate word identification. Fluency also depends on the ability to make use of prosodic cues.

Prosody refers to the pitch, loudness, tempo, and rhythm of language. Both the meaning of a written sentence as well as its punctuation are sources of prosodic cues. For example, the passage "Could that be a flower? Here?" should be read with a pause between the sentences, and with emphasis on the key words ("flower" and "here"). Prosodic information is conveyed by the meaning of these sentences as well as the question marks at the end of each one.

One aspect of prosody is **intonation,** or patterns of pitch that contribute to the meanings of phrases and sentences. For example, different intonations should be used for the sentences "Go over there!" and "Go over there?" because the former is a demand while the latter is a question. The last word in the sentence "Go over there?" should be read with a very different pitch from the first two words. (If a tone of amazement is intended, "there" may be read with a rapidly rising pitch. If a tone of complaint is intended, "there" may begin with a high pitch that rapidly drops.) As this example illustrates, correct intonation depends in part on sensitivity to intended meaning as well as punctuation.

Generally, fluent readers are able to read with expression, because they are sensitive to prosodic cues conveyed by textual meaning and punctuation, and because they have had experience with breath control, phrasing, and other contributors to fluency.

Understand how rate and fluency affect comprehension

The beginning teacher understands how children's reading rate and fluency affect their comprehension.

Before children can recognize a word by sight, they must decode the word through phonic analysis. Sounding out words, one by one, is a slow process and tends to result in limited fluency. Because early readers must devote a great deal of attention and energy to the decoding of individual words, they will find it challenging, if not overwhelming, to combine words in order to appreciate the meanings of phrases, sentences, and passages. As children get older, reading rate and fluency increase, and comprehension increases accordingly.

Studies show that children whose reading is slower and less fluent than that of their peers also tend to have poorer comprehension. However, some children who read slowly have good comprehension. Other children may be fairly quick and accurate in decoding words without clearly understanding the content of the text. It is important for teachers to realize that although reading rate and fluency affect comprehension, they are not synonymous.

Fluency is a dimension of oral reading. The discussions of Competencies 007 and 008 provide further detail on reading comprehension.

Understand the development of fluency

The beginning teacher understands how children develop reading fluency.

The emergence of reading is sometimes described in terms of four stages: Pre-reading, initial reading, fluency, and reading to learn.

- Children in the **pre-reading stage** may have alphabetic and graphophonemic knowledge, and they may be in the process of learning word-analysis skills, but they do not yet have the ability to read unfamiliar words. Their ability to "read" is limited to the recognition of a few sight words, such as their own names.

- First and 2nd graders, who must sound out many of the words they read, are typically in the **initial reading stage.** This stage is also known as the **decoding stage,** because children tend to focus on the decoding of individual words. For children at this stage, each word is a problem that must be consciously and deliberately solved. As a result, children's reading has an awkward, halting quality, because they are putting a great deal of effort into sounding words out, one by one, through phonic analysis.

- As children progress through elementary school, they enter the **fluency stage.** During this time, they become more familiar with written language, and their decoding becomes more automatic as a result of learning more sight words. Greater automaticity allows children to pay more attention to combinations of words, to levels of meaning beyond individual words, and to punctuation and other elements of orthography. As a result, children become more fluent and expressive in their reading.

- By the end of elementary school, fluent reading has become relatively easy for most children, and they enter the **reading to learn stage,** in which their attention is focused primarily on content rather than the act of reading itself. This stage points to an important shift that takes place as word recognition and other aspects of fluent reading become even more automatic. It is often said that when children enter the fourth stage, they shift from "learning to read" to "reading to learn." However, it should be kept in mind that readers of any age can learn from the content of a text.

The four stages describe what happens as children learn word-analysis skills and progress from sounding out individual words to reading fluently. Progress toward fluent reading is facilitated by vocabulary development, by the learning of sight words, and by the ability to make use of semantic and grammatical cues. For example, a fluent reader who instantly recognizes the first five words of the sentence, "The hungry lion saw a gazelle" may be able to quickly decode the word "gazelle" if that word is part of her vocabulary and if she makes use of the available syntactic and semantic cues. The syntax of the sentence implies that the last word is a noun, while the semantic context established by the first five words suggests that the last word could be the name for something edible.

Apply norms to monitor fluency

The beginning teacher applies norms to identify and monitor children's fluency levels.

It is important for EC–4 teachers to identify and monitor their students' levels of reading fluency. Fluency can be assessed through informal observation, and in a more formal way through the use of standardized tests, which are based on norms. A **norm** is a typical score or range of scores found within a particular group of individuals. Standardized tests of fluency allow an individual student's score to be compared to the norms that have been identified for a comparison group, such as other students of the same age, grade, or gender.

Norms give teachers a sense of what to expect among students of a particular age, grade, or demographic background. Norms for reading fluency can be used to identify students with learning differences, as well as students who are beginning to fall behind their peers. Norms can also be used as benchmarks, or goals to be achieved by a particular time (for example, the end of an academic year).

Standardized assessments of reading fluency pertain to rate, accuracy, and/or expression. For example, on the **Test of Reading Fluency** (**TORF**), students receive timed reading samples (one minute per sample), and the number of words pronounced correctly is recorded. Most standardized assessments of fluency also record other information such as comprehension. For example, on the **Gray Oral Reading Test-3** (**GORT-3**), students read passages of increasing length and difficulty. Reading rate, accuracy, and comprehension are recorded, along with information about errors and pauses.

Teachers often evaluate reading fluency through informal assessments that are not scored with reference to norms. These assessments are described under Competency 011.

Use instructional approaches to develop fluency

The beginning teacher selects and uses instructional strategies, materials, and activities to develop fluency (for example, reading independent-level materials, reading orally from familiar texts, repeated reading, partner reading, silent reading for increasingly longer periods, self-correction).

Teachers should use a variety of strategies, materials, and activities to foster reading fluency.

- **Effective models:** It is important for EC–4 teachers to model fluent oral reading. Teachers of younger students will naturally do so as part of their daily reading to students. Teachers of older students may need to be more deliberate about identifying difficult passages and reading them out loud. In some cases, more advanced students can model fluent reading for less advanced ones. Whether a teacher or an advanced student is modeling oral reading, each reading should consist of an entire passage rather than one or two sentences, so that the rest of the class can hear the phrasing that is used.

- **Repeated reading:** Repeated reading is a method in which children reread a short, meaningful passage until a degree of fluency is achieved. The assumption underlying this method is that each time the child reads the text, decoding will be quicker and more automatic. As the speed and automaticity of decoding increases, children will be able to devote more attention to prosody, and their reading will become more expressive. The teacher may choose to model the oral reading of a passage before students engage in repeated reading.

- **Oral Recitation Lessons:** An Oral Recitation Lesson (ORL) is a kind of repeated reading exercise based on interactions between teacher and students. At the beginning of the ORL, the teacher models the oral reading of a text. Next, the teacher leads a discussion of the meaning of the text as well as its prosodic features. Students then practice reading the text before engaging in a performance in which individual students read the text for the rest of the class.

- **Partner reading:** Partner reading, also known as **paired reading,** requires students to work in pairs. Each student takes turns reading a passage. If one partner encounters a difficulty, he/she asks the other partner for help. At some point, partners take turns asking each other questions about what was read. Initially, the teacher may choose to model partner reading with the help of a student volunteer. The teacher can model each component of partner reading, including the oral reading of passages, the use of verbal strategies for asking for and giving help, and the use of strategies for asking and answering questions.

- **Familiar texts:** Students will have many opportunities to read familiar texts through repeated reading, oral recitation lessons, partner reading, and other activities. These activities promote reading fluency in part by reducing word-identification and comprehension demands. That is, as texts become familiar to students, their oral reading can focus increasingly on fluency.

- **Independent-level materials:** It is important for students to have texts that match their particular reading level. If a book is too advanced, for example, the student will struggle with word-identification and have little opportunity to read for fluency. The assessment of independent reading level is discussed at length under Competency 011.

- **Silent reading:** Silent reading contributes to fluency by allowing children to familiarize themselves with key vocabulary, so that oral reading of the same passage can be based on a higher proportion of sight words. **Sustained Silent Reading (SSR)** or **Drop Everything and Read (DEAR)** are silent reading activities in which the teacher sets aside a short period of time each day for silent reading. To facilitate a positive response to SSR or DEAR, teachers make a variety of books available for students to choose from. Although there is no assessment at the end of an SSR or DEAR period, these activities have benefits for fluency as well as comprehension.

- **Self-correction and feedback:** Self-correction by the reader, as well as feedback from the teacher, both contribute to greater fluency. In either case, it is important for teachers to help students maintain a positive attitude.

Foster collaboration with families and professionals

The beginning teacher understands how to foster collaboration with families and with other professionals to promote all children's reading fluency.

Oral reading can be frustrating or frightening to students, and they sometimes become reluctant to read out loud. Teachers should encourage parents to be supportive. Parents should understand that it is more important to help young children feel comfortable about reading out loud than it is to try to directly improve their fluency.

Sample Questions

1. In order to promote reading fluency, which of the following is the best approach for introducing a 2nd-grade class to a play that has been written for their grade level?

   A.   paired reading
   B.   Sustained Silent Reading (SSR)
   C.   Oral Recitation Lesson (ORL)
   D.   repeated reading

   C Options A, B, and D all represent useful approaches to the promotion of reading fluency. However, an Oral Recitation Lesson is probably best for introducing a new text to this age group. The ORL would give students guidance in the oral reading of the play, because the teacher would model fluent reading, and then discuss semantic and prosodic issues of pertinence, before students read the play out loud. Thus, option C is the best answer. The other options reflect methods that would be more effectively used after the ORL had been implemented.

2. Stacy is a 3-year-old who is capable of reading and gleaning simple information from 2nd-grade books, although her oral reading is slow and somewhat labored. What stage of reading fluency has she achieved?

   A.   pre-reading
   B.   initial reading
   C.   fluency
   D.   reading to learn

   B Although Stacy is only 3 years old, the fact that she can read and understand elementary-level books indicates that she has surpassed the pre-reading stage. Hence, option A is incorrect. At the same time, it is clear that she is still sounding out words and, thus, options C and D are incorrect too. Option B is the correct answer. Although it is unusual for 3-year-olds to be so advanced, there is considerable variability in the development of reading fluency. Stacy is an extremely precocious child who has already reached the initial reading stage—but not a higher stage, because she is still decoding words one by one.

Competency 007 (Reading Comprehension)

The teacher understands the importance of reading for understanding, knows the components of comprehension, and teaches children strategies for improving their comprehension.

Review

Understand influences on reading comprehension

The beginning teacher understands factors affecting reading comprehension, such as oral language development, prior reading experiences, language background, and characteristics of specific texts (for example, structure, vocabulary, story grammar).

Reading comprehension refers to the reconstruction of the meaning of a written text.

Influences on reading comprehension include characteristics of individual readers, such as world knowledge, life experiences, size of vocabulary, reading ability, logical skills, and schemata. **Schemata** are clusters of ideas about objects, places, and events. Schemata can be very specific and concrete (for example, knowledge of dinosaurs) or relatively abstract (for example, views on democracy). Among the schemata that children develop is a **story schema,** or set of expectations about the internal structure of stories. Story schemata allow readers to appreciate, for example, that the main character in a story has goals, that the character will attempt to achieve those goals, and that the character's actions will influence the outcome of the story. When a story schema is activated, it will enhance comprehension, because the reader will be trying to figure out what the main character's goals are and how they fit into the story.

Reading comprehension is not only influenced by story schema and other characteristics of individual readers, but also by characteristics of the text being read, including its structure, content, and vocabulary. Structural elements include the **story grammar,** which is the set of elements that constitute a story as well as the rules that relate those elements. Experts have described a number of different story grammars. For example, in one of the simpler analyses, the elements of a story consist of the setting, characters, theme, plot, and resolution.

Ultimately, reading comprehension reflects the interaction between the characteristics of the individual reader and the characteristics of the particular text being read. Reading comprehension is facilitated when the background, the interests, and the skills of the reader match the content and other characteristics of the text.

Understand and teach different levels of comprehension

The beginning teacher understands levels of reading comprehension and knows how to model and teach skills for literal comprehension (for example, identifying the stated main idea or recalling details), inferential comprehension (for example, inferring cause-and-effect relationships or making predictions), and evaluative comprehension (for example, analyzing character development and use of language or detecting faulty reasoning).

When reading a text, several levels of comprehension are possible. **Literal comprehension** refers to the understanding of information that is explicitly stated in a written passage. This information includes the main idea of the passage (if explicitly stated) as well as the details and the sequence of events. Literal comprehension of a text is important as a source of information as well as a prerequisite for higher levels of understanding. Teachers can promote literal comprehension by making sure that students have the necessary background information, including knowledge of the vocabulary that is used in a text.

Inferential comprehension is the understanding of information that is not explicitly given but rather implied in a written passage. For example, inferential comprehension is needed to understand **anaphora,** or the use of one word or phrase in place of another one. Pronouns are commonly used in place of nouns without an explicit connection between them, as in the following passage: "Mary jumped into the pool. The water felt cool on her skin." Inferential comprehension allows the reader to understand that "her" in the second sentence refers to "Mary" in the first one.

One of the most common applications of inferential comprehension is the identification of **cause-effect relationships.** A simple example would be the sentence "When the dog barked, the cat ran away." In this example, inferential comprehension is needed in order to understand that the cat ran away *because* the dog barked, because this relationship is implied rather than explicitly stated.

Readers also use inferential comprehension to make predictions. The sentence "The mouse saw the cat" suggests the prediction that the mouse will become afraid and run away. A reader's ability to make inferences depends on the information given in the text as well as the reader's background knowledge and inferential skills. For example, consider the following passage: "It was February in Nome. Cecilia got dressed and went outside." It can be inferred that Cecilia probably put on a warm jacket, gloves, hat, and boots, and that it was very cold and possibly even snowing outside. Making such inferences is dependent on background knowledge, such as the fact that Nome is in Alaska, and that Alaska is very cold and snowy in the winter. These inferences also depend on the ability of the reader to predict that an individual's choice of clothing is likely to match the weather.

As with literal comprehension, inferential comprehension is an important source of information as well as a prerequisite for further understanding. Teachers can promote inferential comprehension by providing children with background knowledge of relevance to a text, and by modeling the kinds of inferences that can be made during the reading. ("It was February in Nome. Let's see, Nome is in Alaska, so it must've been cold. It says that Cecilia got dressed and went outside. What do you think she wore?")

Evaluative comprehension refers to the ability to use critical thinking skills, logical analysis, and aesthetic considerations to evaluate a text. Students need a great deal of direct support from teachers in order to develop evaluative comprehension skills. Following is a list of some of the uses of evaluative comprehension:

- Detecting contradictions and other weaknesses in the way the author develops an argument.
- Judging the accuracy of information in a text based on background knowledge, reasoning, and information obtained from other texts.
- Differentiating facts from opinions, evidence from conclusions, and relevant information from irrelevant information.
- Appreciating mood, foreshadowing, character development, and other literary qualities.
- Recognizing the ideological, moral, and rhetorical intentions of authors.

Facilitate the transition to "reading to learn"

The beginning teacher provides instruction in comprehension skills that support children's transition from "learning to read" to "reading to learn" (for example, recognizing different types of texts, understanding how a text is organized, using textual features such as headings and glossaries).

The transition from "learning to read" to "reading to learn" is described under Competency 006. Teachers can support this transition by helping children appreciate aspects of a text other than the meanings of individual words and sentences. For example, teachers can call attention to the basic purpose of a text. A distinction can be made between **narrative texts** (those that relate a story or sequence of events) and **expository texts** (texts that provide factual information and explanations).

Narrative and expository texts tend to differ in organization as well as purpose. Narrative texts tend to have a story grammar, while expository texts tend to begin with introductory material, followed by topical material and, finally, a summary. Textual features such as the table of contents, headings, and glossaries contribute to the organization of expository texts. (These features are also discussed under Competency 008.)

Use instructional approaches that build comprehension

The beginning teacher selects and uses instructional strategies, materials, and activities that facilitate children's comprehension before, during, and after reading (for example, providing background knowledge for written text, previewing the organization of a text, making predictions, questioning, guiding discussions).

Reading should never be a process of mindless decoding. Teachers should use strategies, materials, and activities that encourage children to actively attempt to make sense out of the texts they read.

Before reading a text, students may need to be provided with background knowledge, definitions of key vocabulary, previews of textual organization and intent, and other information that can help facilitate comprehension. It may be necessary to help children understand the appropriate schemata to use when reading a story. Moreover, the teacher may need to help children understand the purpose of reading a particular text. It is important for students to be clear about whether they are reading for enjoyment, for obtaining specific information, for exploring new ideas, for developing a critical judgment, or for some other purpose(s).

After reading a text, comprehension at all levels can be facilitated by encouraging children to summarize or retell what they have read, either orally or in writing. Interactive activities such as group discussion are extremely useful. In some cases, encouraging children to reread all or part of a text can promote comprehension, particularly when specific information is being sought.

Before, during, and after children's reading of a text, teachers should use questioning strategies that facilitate comprehension. Questions about main ideas, details, and sequences of events can be used to promote literal as well as inferential comprehension. Questions can also be used to facilitate evaluative comprehension. Particularly with younger students, it is important for teachers to model the entire process of understanding and answering questions. That is, teachers should help students understand what a particular question is asking, how a text should be examined to find the answer, and how to phrase the answer in formulating a reply. Four types of **Question-Answer Relationships (QARs)** that students should know are as follows:

- **Right there** questions can be answered from information explicitly given in a text.
- **Think and search** questions require looking at information in a text, and then drawing a conclusion.
- **Author and you** questions require the combination of information in a text and the student's background knowledge.
- **On your own** questions call for evaluative responses.

The suggestions described in this section have been incorporated into a number of instructional methods for enhancing reading comprehension. Some of these methods are described in the following section.

Help children monitor and improve their comprehension

The beginning teacher models and teaches a range of instructional strategies that children can use to monitor and improve their reading comprehension (for example, self-questioning, rereading, mapping, using reading journals, discussing texts).

A commonly used instructional strategy is the **Directed Reading Activity** (**DRA**). At the outset of the DRA, the teacher activates and develops schemata by linking the topic of the text to students' own experiences or by finding ways to get students interested in an unfamiliar topic. It may be necessary at this point for teachers to introduce new concepts and vocabulary that are used in the text. Next, the teacher supports silent and oral reading by providing students with **study-guide questions** (questions that aid comprehension by helping to clarify the purpose, structure, and content of a text). At any point, instruction may be provided in word-recognition and comprehension. After the reading, children are given opportunities to practice the knowledge and skills they have acquired. Finally, enrichment activities are provided in which children can link the topic of the reading to additional reading material or to writing, art, and/or music projects of their own creation.

The DRA is a teacher-directed activity. A widely used alternative is the **Directed Reading-Thinking Activity** (**DR-TA**), which is more student-guided. In the DR-TA, the teacher asks students to examine the title of a story and predict what the story is about. Next, the teacher has students examine an illustration at the outset of the story and check whether initial predictions about the story need to be revised. During silent reading, students continue to check and revise their predictions, while making notes for subsequent group discussion. Following discussion, silent and/or oral rereading may be encouraged, in conjunction with additional discussion and instruction from the teacher. The entire process is repeated after each section of the text.

The **K-W-L** teaching model is a general strategy for supporting comprehension of expository text before and after reading. Each letter in the name of this model represents a self-questioning strategy that teachers should encourage students to use. The "K" stands for "What I *know*," the "W" stands for "What I *want* to learn," and the "L" stands for "What I *learned*." Prior to reading a text, the teacher should help students think about what they know and what they want to learn from the text. After reading the text, the teacher should help students reflect on what they learned. Like the DRA and DR-TA strategies, the K-W-L model can be used with virtually any sort of text.

The K-W-L model relies on the use of **metacognition**, or awareness of mental contents and processes (see Competency 001 for additional discussion). If the term "cognition" refers to thinking, the term "metacognition" refers to thinking about thinking. Knowing the name of the first president is an example of cognition. Metacognition includes your awareness that you know the name of the first president, your realization that you have momentarily forgotten the name of the first president, your understanding that you could learn about the first president by reading a book about him, and your recognition that the more carefully you read, the more you will learn. K-W-L questions promote metacognition, because they encourage students to reflect on their own knowledge.

Metacognition allows readers to monitor their level of comprehension as they read and to appreciate when improvements in comprehension are needed. As a consequence, the use of metacognitive monitoring strategies is associated with good comprehension.

Teachers can facilitate monitoring in a variety of ways. Students can be taught how to self-question to determine whether they understand key concepts and passages. They can be taught how to reread difficult passages or to read such passages more slowly. Discussion is a particularly good method for encouraging students to compare and reflect on different understandings of stories.

It is important for younger students to understand that reading is not simply a process of decoding, but also a process of seeking meaning. Understanding the broader purpose of reading is a form of metacognition that indicates the need for ongoing monitoring. Older students also need support for more specific monitoring activities, such as the need to check for inconsistencies in their understanding.

A general approach to monitoring and improving comprehension is to encourage story mapping. A **story map** is a graphic representation of the elements of a story. A story map for a particular story could consist of a timeline showing the sequence of events in the story. Alternatively, the story map could represent relationships between all the important events, concepts, and characters in a story without following a chronological sequence. The terms "semantic map," "semantic web," and "story web" are often used to describe a story map that depicts these various elements.

Along with story maps, other written and graphic representations of story content can facilitate monitoring and comprehension. For example, as discussed under Competency 010, students can be encouraged to create journals that summarize the content of what they read or that describe their reactions to the content.

Use multicultural instructional approaches

The beginning teacher selects and uses instructional strategies, materials, and activities to guide children to increase knowledge of their own culture and the cultures of others through reading.

As children progress from "learning to read" to "reading to learn," it becomes increasingly important for them to be exposed to information about their own and other cultures. A multicultural approach to reading is essential, owing to the vast cultural diversity reflected in each Texas classroom. Each child needs to have access to reading materials and activities that are related to his or her own particular background. In addition, a better academic experience and classroom atmosphere will result from children being exposed to the cultural backgrounds of their peers.

Use assessments to meet individual needs

The beginning teacher selects and uses a variety of formal and informal procedures for monitoring children's reading comprehension and adjusts instruction to meet the needs of individual children, including English Language Learners.

Formal and informal procedures for monitoring children's reading comprehension are briefly described under this competency and under Competency 011. Often these procedures are appropriate for working with English Language Learners. In addition, there are a number of specific strategies that teachers can use to monitor the progress of ELLs and to adjust instruction accordingly. For example, group activities can provide support for children with limited English skills. Through group discussion, and through the joint creation of story maps, ELLs will be exposed to many channels of information about the meaning of a particular story. More broadly, **sheltered instruction** (also known as specially designed academic instruction in English, or SDAIE) can be used to help children with limited English learn both grade-level content as well as content-related language.

Teach elements of literary analysis

The beginning teacher teaches elements of literary analysis, such as story elements and features of different literary genres.

A **genre** is a category that is used to classify a literary work. Genres can be defined in terms of form, content, or technique. It is important for students to appreciate some of the key distinctions among genres, which include fiction, folklore, poetry, drama, and nonfiction.

Students should also have some appreciation of the story elements in each genre:

- **Setting:** Students should be able to identify the setting of a story, and to think about how the setting influences the events and atmosphere of the story.
- **Characterization:** Students should be able to discuss the motivations and personalities of different characters and to describe any changes that the characters experience during the course of a story.
- **Plot:** Students should be able to see how a story is introduced, developed through a series of events, and then brought to a conclusion. Students should understand how the main events of the story are connected.
- **Style:** Students should be able to understand how certain kinds of word choice and modes of expression give a literary work a particular style.
- **Theme:** As abstract-thinking skills develop, students should be able to identify recurrent themes in a literary work.

Foster collaboration with families and other professionals

The beginning teacher understands how to foster collaboration with families and with other professionals to promote all children's reading comprehension.

Teachers should convey to parents the importance of providing a literate home environment for children, in which children observe their parents reading and have opportunities to participate in meaningful reading-related interactions. Such interactions include storytelling and shared reading, as well as other activities such as reading letters, instructions, and recipes with family members. As children's reading skills develop, parents can be encouraged to have discussions with children about what they are reading or have read. Parents can ask friends and relatives to write notes, letters, holiday cards, and other missives to children. Parents themselves can occasionally leave notes for children.

Sample Questions

1. A 2nd-grade class is asked to read a famous nursery rhyme: "Little Miss Muffet / sat on a tuffet / eating her curds and whey. / Along came a spider / who sat down beside her / scaring Miss Muffet away." After reading the nursery rhyme, the teacher asks students what Miss Muffet sat on. Then, the teacher asks the class what they think a "tuffet" is. What sort of comprehension is the teacher's second question intended to tap into?

   A. literal
   B. inferential
   C. evaluative
   D. all of the above

   B The literal meaning of a tuffet is neither given in the nursery rhyme nor familiar to contemporary American children and, thus, option A is incorrect. Because the question is about the likely meaning of a word, option C is also incorrect. Because options A and C are incorrect, option D could not be correct, either. Option B is the best answer. The teacher's question encourages children to make a simple inference based on the semantic and syntactic context established by the first two lines.

2. After reading "Miss Muffet" and discussing what a "tuffet" may be, the teacher asks students why they suppose the author of the rhyme used such an unusual word. The teacher then leads a class discussion of this question. To help fuel discussion, the teacher intends to inform students that the rhyme was created in England a long time ago. The teacher also intends to say something about the process of creating rhymes. What sort of comprehension is the teacher trying to stimulate through class discussion?

   A. literal
   B. inferential
   C. evaluative
   D. all of the above

   C Students have not been given a direct answer to the teacher's question, so option A is incorrect. If option A is incorrect, option D must be incorrect too. Although one can infer from the teacher's comment that the word "tuffet" reflects the particular time and place of the rhyme's creation, inference is not the sole focus of the class discussion and, thus, option B is not the best answer. That is, option B is not the best answer because it is only partially true. Option C is the best answer. In order to arrive at some sense of why the word "tuffet" was used, students will have to explore the possibility that English speakers from different times and places use different vocabulary, and they will have to consider the role of end rhyme in poetry. Looking at the poem from historical and literary perspectives reflects evaluative comprehension.

Competency 008 (Research and Comprehension Skills in the Content Areas)

The teacher understands the importance of research and comprehension skills to children's academic success and provides children with instruction that promotes their acquisition and effective use of these skills in the content areas.

Review

Teach children how to obtain information from a range of texts

The beginning teacher teaches children how to locate, retrieve, and retain information from a range of content-area and expository texts.

The term **content literacy** is used to describe the ability to use written texts (as well as other forms of communication) as sources of information about a given topic or area. Experts acknowledge the importance of not only teaching young children how to read narratives, but also how to read for comprehension in content areas.

Teachers promote content literacy by showing children how to obtain and retain information from content-area materials and expository texts (texts whose primary intent is to provide factual information and explanations). The teacher's role may range from introducing students to the school library to modeling strategies for using reference materials to providing support for comprehension monitoring during the reading of expository texts to guiding discussion of difficult concepts, and so on.

In the discussion of Competency 007, several comprehension monitoring and facilitating strategies are discussed. Those strategies tended to be at least somewhat teacher-directed. The **SQ3R method** is a student-directed approach in which students are taught five steps for studying content-area and expository texts:

1. **Survey.** The first step is to survey the title, headings, introductory materials, and any pedagogical devices such as figures and tables that may contribute to the understanding of a text.
2. **Question.** The next step is to formulate a list of questions that will hopefully be answered by reading the text. (This is similar to the "W" in the K-W-L model described under Competency 007.)
3. **Read.** After formulating a list of questions, the next step is to try to answer them by reading the text.
4. **Recite.** After reading, the next step is to try to state the answers to each of the original questions, without looking at the text.
5. **Review.** The final step is to reread to verify that the original questions were satisfactorily answered and to make corrections as needed.

Teach the use of text organizers

The beginning teacher teaches children how to use text organizers (for example, headings, tables of contents) to locate and organize information.

In the discussion of Competency 004, it is noted that pre-readers gradually learn about conventions of print, such as the idea that books convey information and that some of the information in books is conveyed through words. As the ability to read emerges, children continue to learn about the conventions of printed texts. Some of these conventions pertain to the way texts are organized.

Content literacy includes the ability to make use of the organizational elements in books and other printed materials. Tables of contents, summaries, headings, page numbers, glossaries, and bibliographies are among the organizers that are intended to help readers obtain information from expository texts. Teachers should help children identify these text organizers and to understand where each one is likely to be found. In addition, teachers should help children understand what kinds of information can be obtained from each organizer and to know when each one should be used.

Help children use graphics

The beginning teacher selects and uses instructional strategies, materials, and activities to help children use graphics (for example, tables, charts, maps, diagrams, timelines) and other sources of information and technologies to acquire information.

Graphics are an important source of information that early readers may disregard, or be distracted by, if they have not been taught how to make use of them. Generally, students need to understand that graphics convey information. Teachers should explain how to use the title of a graphic feature, as well as other information, to determine how the graphic is related to the text. Teachers should also help students understand the features of specific types of graphics and how they can be used. Following are some key examples.

For map reading, teachers should help students follow a sequence of appropriate actions.

1. First, the student should examine the title in order to determine what the map represents.
2. In many cases, the next step is to identify the four directions depicted in the map.
3. Next, the student should identify any legend on the map that would explain the various symbols.
4. Finally, the student should attempt to grasp the scale of the map, to relate the map to a larger area if appropriate, and to return to a consideration of how the map is connected to the text.

For the reading of graphs, teachers should make students aware of the four basic types of graphs and the kinds of information they convey. Specifically, students should know that **picture graphs** illustrate quantities, **bar graphs** use horizontal or vertical bars to contrast quantities, **line graphs** show changes in quantity and other variables over time, and **pie charts** show part-whole relationships.

Teachers should help students understand the specific features of other types of graphics as well, such as the schematics used in a diagram, the rows and columns of a table, and the chronological structure of a timeline.

Encourage the use of multiple sources

The beginning teacher selects and uses instructional strategies, materials, and activities to help children use multiple sources, including electronic texts, experts, and print resources, to locate information.

Children should be encouraged to use multiple sources of information, including printed materials, electronic materials, and expert individuals. One reason for encouraging the use of multiple sources is simply that variety helps maintain student interest. Another reason is that each source of information can be somewhat unique in the learning experience that it sustains. For example, electronic texts differ from printed texts in a number of important respects.

- The control that readers have over the flow of information is greater for electronic texts, given the interactive nature of many software and Internet-based programs currently available.
- Electronic texts are searchable in distinctive and powerful ways that are not possible with printed texts.
- Electronic texts tend to be part of multimedia environments, in which text, illustrations, audio, and video are integrated.
- Electronic texts such as e-mail sustain communication with other writers and readers.

Help children summarize and organize information

The beginning teacher understands how to help children summarize and organize information from multiple sources (for example, by taking notes, outlining, creating graphic organizers).

Note-taking is an important academic skill. Notes can used to paraphrase or summarize information, to keep a record of important details, and to record critical comments or questions. Notes can be recorded in learning logs, on paper or index cards, or on computers. Where appropriate, making annotations to a text serves a note-taking function.

Students need to understand that the general purpose of taking notes is to aid one's memory. Without notes, most students would forget a great deal of what they have read. Students also need to learn specific note-taking strategies. Following are some useful strategies and guidelines:

- Identify the source of the notes.
- Write down key words and phrases.
- Don't focus too much on punctuation, grammar, and so on.
- Include enough information so that the notes will be comprehensible later.
- Distinguish between quotations and paraphrasings.

Like note-taking, the creation of outlines is a way of summarizing information. Outlines also serve an important organizational function. The outline can be structured as sentence format (each point is a complete sentence) or a topic format (each point is a key word or phrase).

A **graphic organizer** is a visual representation of textual content. Graphic organizers can be used before, during, or after reading to summarize a text, to show the relationships between concepts in a text, to relate new concepts to familiar ones, or to assist comprehension in other ways. A simple example would be a series of boxes linked by arrows (that is, a flow chart), each representing a significant event in a historical sequence. (See the discussion of semantic webs under Competency 007).

Foster collaboration with families and other professionals

The beginning teacher understands how to foster collaboration with families and with other professionals to promote all children's ability to develop effective research and comprehension skills in the content areas.

As children's ability to read develops, parents can be encouraged to support research and comprehension skills by taking their children to the library, exposing children to a variety of expository print forms, knowing about and perhaps helping their children with reports and other content area homework, engaging in various activities that support content area reading, and helping introduce children to text features that are pertinent to research and comprehension.

Sample Questions

1. Which of the following instructional strategies most directly supports content literacy?

   A. use of both expository and narrative texts in a thematic unit
   B. use of the K-W-L teaching model
   C. encouragement of comprehension monitoring during reading
   D. all of the above

   B Although option A describes a good instructional strategy, it is not the best option, because it is too broad. It reflects a strategy that would promote literacy development in general, not just in the area of content literacy. Option C is also too general, because it describes a strategy that teachers should encourage during all sorts of reading, not just reading in content areas. Option D is incorrect, because option B is more directly supportive of content literacy than the other options. That is, option B is the best answer. The K-W-L teaching model encourages students to reflect on what they know and want to learn before reading an expository text and to consider what they learned after reading it. (See discussion of Competency 007 for further details.) Option B is the best answer in part because it is the only option that focuses specifically on comprehension of expository texts.

2. Which of the following can a parent do to help a 4th grader research a class project on whales?

   A. Encourage the child to use the school library and to ask the librarian for assistance.
   B. Help the child use the Internet as a resource.
   C. Help the child decide which index selections of a student encyclopedia would be most relevant.
   D. all of the above

   D A is a correct option. Although the parent would not be directly helping the child, encouraging the child to use the library and seek expert assistance would be beneficial. B and C are correct options, because in each case, the parent would be providing expert guidance. Hence, option D is the best answer.

Competency 009 (Writing Conventions)

The teacher understands the conventions of writing in English and provides instruction that helps children develop proficiency in using writing conventions.

Review

Understand the development of writing

The beginning teacher understands that many children go through predictable stages in acquiring writing conventions, including the physical and cognitive processes involved in scribbling, recognition of environmental print, mock letters, letter formation, word writing, sentence construction, spelling, punctuation, and grammatical expression, but that individual children vary in their development of these conventions.

Children begin to recognize environmental print at around age two. In subsequent years, children become more sensitive to the specific characteristics of the words they see, including the shapes of individual letters. At the same time, children gradually develop the ability to produce words through writing. A combination of physical maturation, experience and, in some cases, instruction, allows children to hold writing implements and create marks.

During the preschool years, children begin to produce representational drawings. At this time, there is not a clear distinction between drawing and writing. Children often tell stories or convey information through drawings, scribbles, and other marks that they use to express themselves.

Gradually, children's scribbling becomes more reminiscent of writing. The scribbles may become somewhat linear, and may contain **mock letters** (letter-like forms). At this point, the scribbles are not comprehensible to others, but children may talk about the scribbles as if they are words or even stories. Scribbling and mock letters may accompany pictures or be created separately.

By kindergarten age, most children have begun to write individual letters, followed by letter combinations. At first, children's writing tends to lack conventional left-to-right and top-to-bottom orientation. It is common for children to leave out punctuation as well as spaces between words, and to be inconsistent in the relative size and position of their letters. It is also common for children to generate reversals, or letters that are written with incorrect orientation. Some reversals are made along a horizontal dimension, as when a "b" is written as a "d," or a "p" is written as a "q." Other reversals are vertical, as when an "m" is written as a "w," or an "n" is written as a "u."

Through literacy instruction in school, children gradually learn to form words and sentences that reflect correct spelling, punctuation, and grammar. Although the stages described here are somewhat predictable, individual children differ in the rate at which they progress through the stages, as well as in the kinds of writing and miswriting they most commonly produce at each stage.

Understand how spelling is influenced by phonological awareness

The beginning teacher understands the relationship between spelling and phonological and alphabetic awareness.

Phonological awareness allows children to notice and think about the sounds of language (see discussion of Competency 002). Appreciation of the alphabetic principle allows children to learn graphophonemic correspondences between letters and sounds (see discussion of Competency 003). As children's phonological and alphabetic awareness increase, they become capable of sounding out written words one letter at a time (see discussion of Competency 005). The development of these skills also contributes to spelling. When children spell unfamiliar words, they can also "sound out" the words they intend to write. Phonological and alphabetic awareness help young spellers think about the phonemic constituents of a word and to choose a sequence of letters to represent those constituents. At the same time, practice with spelling also contributes to phonological and alphabetic awareness.

Understand and nurture the development of spelling

The beginning teacher understands the stages of spelling development (precommunicative "writing" [understands the function of writing but cannot make the forms], prephonemic, phonemic, transitional, and conventional) and knows how and when to support children's development from one stage to the next.

Orthography refers to the nature and use of written symbols in a language. Knowledge of orthography includes appreciation of the rules governing spelling and punctuation. Like other aspects of orthography, spelling develops in a somewhat predictable sequence:

1. In the **precommunicative stage,** writing consists of scribbling, mock letters, and other marks that preschoolers use to convey meaning. Any attempt to represent words consists of random letter strings. Thus, spelling is not a characteristic of this stage, although children appreciate the general idea that creating and talking about written marks is a way of telling stories and sharing information with others.

2. Once children learn the alphabetic principle (see Competency 003), they are able to enter the **prephonemic stage,** in which letters are used to represent sounds and words. Writing at this stage contains **phonemic spellings** (also referred to as **invented** or **developmental spellings**). At first, phonemic spellings consist of one or two letters that are intended to represent an entire word. These letters are often consonants and often include the first letter of the word. Thus, a child may write "d" for the word "dog" or "ck" for the word "cake." As children progress to higher stages, phonemic spellings become more complex.

3. In the **phonemic stage,** children tend to represent all the basic sounds in a word. However, their spelling is still frequently incorrect. Short vowel sounds are typically miswritten, as when a child writes "buk" for the word "book." Vowels are often excluded when the basic sound is conveyed by an adjacent consonant. Thus, a child may write "bakr" for the word "baker" or "cak" for the word "cake." In these examples ("buk," "bakr," "cak") it can be seen that all the phonemes of each word are represented, even though the representations are partially incorrect.

4. As children's understanding of orthography increases, they distinguish more clearly between the way words look and the way they sound. This growing attention to the visual appearance of words ushers in the **transitional stage.** Children now appreciate some basic orthographic conventions, such as the principle that every syllable contains a vowel (and/or a "y"). The word "baker," for example, may be spelled "bakur" or "bakor" in the transitional stage. Children are now capable of representing certain vowel sounds with digraphs (pairs of vowels), as when the word "fifty" is written as "fiftee." In some cases, children overuse silent vowels, as when the word "soup" is written as "supe." These examples show that transitional stage children have learned spelling patterns. The double "ee" is incorrect when used to spell the word "fifty," but it is a pattern that frequently occurs in other words. Likewise, the final "e" in "supe" is incorrect, but it is extremely common in English for the final consonant of a word to be followed by a silent "e," as in the words "cape," "broke," and "ride." Phonemic spellings are still frequent during the transitional stage, but the proportion of correct spellings is beginning to increase.

5. In the **conventional stage,** children's knowledge of orthography continues to increase as they make use of a variety of information to guide spelling, including structural cues (prefixes, suffixes, compound words), knowledge about silent consonants, appreciation of stress patterns in oral language, and so on.

Teachers should support development from one stage to the next without discouraging children from expressing themselves through writing.

Base spelling instruction on phonics skills

The beginning teacher selects and uses systematic spelling instruction in common spelling patterns based on previously taught phonics skills.

As discussed under Competency 005, phonics is a method of instruction that focuses on linking phonemes with written letters. Through phonics, children learn how to engage in phonic analysis.

Although English is a highly irregular language (see Competency 003 for further discussion), phonics does provide some support for reading. The same phonics skills that are used to sound out written words can be used to sound out words that the student is attempting to spell.

Use instructional approaches that build fine-motor skills

The beginning teacher selects and uses instructional strategies, materials, and hands-on activities for the development of the fine motor skills necessary for writing (for example, tearing, cutting, puzzles, clay, painting, drawing).

A variety of hands-on materials and activities foster the fine-motor skill development that is needed for writing. These activities include tearing or cutting paper, playing with finger puppets, working with modeling clay, and stringing beads. Games that require a pinching motion (such as pick-up-sticks) and activities that require the use of pencils and other writing implements (such as drawing) are especially helpful.

Teach the mechanics of handwriting

The beginning teacher selects and uses instructional strategies, materials, and activities to teach pencil grip, paper position, and beginning strokes.

Ultimately, the goal of writing is to communicate, whether one chooses to write with a crayon, a pencil, or a computer. Handwriting is not an end in itself but simply a means of conveying information. The purpose of writing fluently (that is, quickly and easily) is to help writers express themselves. The purpose of writing legibly is to facilitate communication between writer and reader. Hence, the mechanics of handwriting should be taught in a meaningful context.

Many variables should be considered when teaching children the mechanics of handwriting. It is important for children to have good posture and support. The lighting should be adequate, the desk at which each child works should be an appropriate height, and the paper should be appropriately positioned. Children should be encouraged to use the dominant hand, and appropriate adjustments should be made for left-handed children. Children's pencil grip should be closely monitored to ensure that it is neither too loose nor too tight. Likewise, the pressure of the pencil on the paper should neither be too light or too heavy.

Teachers should use a variety of instructional approaches to help children master the basic mechanics of handwriting. Some of the activities that are helpful include air-writing, finger-tracing, and writing with one's eyes closed. Patience is especially important in the teaching of good handwriting technique, and teachers should remember that children may be more comfortable about writing with some kinds of implements as opposed to others.

Although the process of writing is important, children's attention should also be directed to the product—that is, the physical appearance of the strokes, letters, and words they are creating.

- Each stroke should begin at the correct position, and the writer should form the correct vertical, horizontal, slanted, and/or curved strokes that form each letter.
- The strokes should be steady and consistent in thickness.
- Each letter should touch the baseline.
- Letters should be uniform in size, and the proportional difference in size between upper- and lowercase letters should be the same.
- Letters should be appropriately oriented. (In printed writing, the letters are vertical. In cursive, letters slant slightly to the right for right-handed students, and slightly to the left or not all for left-handed students.)
- The spacing between letters in words, between words, and between sentences and paragraphs should be consistent.

The preceding list describes ideals of good handwriting. Teachers should not expect students to achieve these ideals in each case. In some cases, it is not desirable for students to even attempt their best handwriting. When students are taking notes or brainstorming, for example, too much emphasis on handwriting is detrimental. In such instances, the goals are merely quickness and minimal legibility.

Help all children use English writing conventions

The beginning teacher selects and uses instructional strategies, materials, and activities to help all children, including English Language Learners, use English writing conventions (for example, grammar, capitalization, and punctuation) in connected discourse.

Literacy development involves the emergence and refinement of multiple, interrelated skills. Writing depends on the ability to comprehend as well as produce oral and written language. Although the writing skills of English Language Learners may be limited owing to weaknesses in oral language skills (such as knowledge of English vocabulary and grammar), these children should receive support for both oral and written English. Some writing activities are appropriate even for English Language Learners who have little or no understanding of English. For example, ELLs can participate in cooperative learning groups in which their contributions match their particular skill level. When working on their own, ELLs can use their native language to do some writing activities, such as journaling.

Recognize differences between spoken and written English

The beginning teacher recognizes the similarities and differences between spoken and written English (for example, in syntax and in vocabulary choice) and uses instructional strategies to help children apply English writing conventions effectively.

Although spoken and written English share basic similarities, writers need to be aware of how they differ in grammar and vocabulary. In particular, spoken English consists of a relatively large number of sentence fragments, informal idioms, and slang. These characteristics are illustrated in the following dialogue:

> **A:** Where'd you go this morning?
>
> **B:** To get a Nintendo.
>
> **A:** Yeah? Where?
>
> **B:** Tucker's. You know, the one at the mall.
>
> **A:** Yeah, that's my favorite. Cool place.
>
> **B:** Yeah. Way cool.

This is an ordinary, natural-sounding dialogue between two native English speakers. Notice that each sentence, except for the first one, is a fragment rather than a complete sentence. The use of the phrase "You know" is highly idiomatic, and the "yeah" and "way cool" are examples of slang.

Students must understand that unless their writing is intended to represent spoken dialogue, their finished products should contain complete sentences and avoid excessively idiomatic or slang words and phrases.

Foster collaboration with families and other professionals

The beginning teacher understands how to foster collaboration with families and with other professionals to promote all children's effective use of writing conventions.

Fostering collaborations to promote effective use of writing conventions, as well as other writing skills, is discussed at the end of Competency 010.

Sample Questions

1. Mark's 1st-grade teacher notices that although he has good handwriting, Mark sometimes complains that his hand hurts when he writes. What should the teacher do first?

   A. Send Mark to the school nurse.
   B. Call Mark's parents to get their feedback.
   C. Observe Mark's pencil grip closely.
   D. Ignore Mark's complaints unless they persist.

   C Option D is clearly incorrect, because a child's physical complaints should not be ignored. Options A and B are not the best initial actions on the teacher's part. Although it is important to refer students to the nurse if a physical problem is suspected and to keep lines of communication with parents open, the first thing to do in this particular case is to simply check whether Mark is holding the pencil too tightly, "hooking" his wrist, or doing something else as he writes that could be easily corrected.

2. Which of the following activities is best for promoting the development of writing among 1st graders?

   A. Each child is encouraged to make a Christmas letter for a family member, describing something special that the child has experienced. The letter contains a mix of artwork and writing that the child creates.
   B. Each child keeps a notebook in which he or she writes each letter of the alphabet ten times. The notebook is assembled over a period of weeks and upon completion, children can see how their handwriting has progressed.
   C. Children are taught how to air-write each letter of the alphabet. Then, the class plays a game in which teacher sings the alphabet song very slowly while the children trace each letter in the air.
   D. Each week, the teacher focuses on the writing of a different letter. Children are encouraged to write, paint, and draw the letter using different media.

   A Options B, C, and D may contribute to improvement in writing, but they focus on handwriting in isolation from a meaningful use of language. Option A is the best answer, because the creation of letters to relatives would allow children to practice writing about topics that interest them, and to incorporate the writing into meaningful communication.

Competency 010 (Development of Written Communication)

The teacher understands that writing to communicate is a developmental process and provides instruction that promotes children's competence in written communication.

Review

Understand the stages of writing development

The beginning teacher knows that many children exhibit predictable stages in developing written language but that individual variation may occur.

The stages through which children develop writing are discussed in several places under Competencies 004 and 009.

Encourage written expression of ideas

The beginning teacher provides materials, activities, and experiences for children to construct an understanding of the writing system in an environment that nurtures the expression of ideas.

Writing is a set of conventions about the formation of letters and words, as well as the use of orthographic strategies such as capitalization and punctuation. Writing is also a means of communication. The role of the teacher is not only to teach the conventions of writing but also to help students understand the relationship between the conventions and the purposes of written text. With the teacher's assistance, students come to realize that using punctuation in a conventional way, for example, helps a reader understand their ideas.

As students learn the mechanics and conventions of writing, it is important that they be nurtured in the written expression of their ideas. Accordingly, EC–4 teachers are encouraged to focus more on the process than the product of children's writing; in other words, teachers are encouraged to place more emphasis on the steps and strategies that students use to generate a piece of writing than the quality of the final product.

Students should be given the opportunity to write every day. Some of the activities that teachers choose should focus primarily on helping students express themselves. One such activity is journal writing, in which students make regular entries in their journals. Journals can focus on personal experiences, as diaries do, or they can serve a variety of other purposes.

- In a **response journal,** the student records his or her thoughts and feelings as a text is read. Students may be given prompts for their response journals, or they may be asked to freely record whatever comes to mind as they read.

- In a **learning log,** the student records what he or she is learning. Students use their own words in learning logs, because these journals are not primarily intended for sharing.

- In a **simulated journal** (also known as a character journal), the student writes journal entries from the perspective of a historical or literary figure.

- In a **dialogue journal,** a written conversation between student and teacher (or between students) takes place in the student's journal as it is passed back and forth between them. Teachers do not provide corrections in the dialogue journal, although they will be modeling correct use of language through their written comments.

Journals can be private or shared with the teacher. When evaluating journal writing, the teacher should keep in mind that the writing is informal and may not have been edited.

Another activity that promotes the expression of ideas is **freewriting,** in which students write their thoughts freely, without concern for mechanics or revision. During freewriting, students are encouraged to write continuously for 5 to 10 minutes without pausing, rereading, making corrections, or worrying about spelling, punctuation, or capitalization. Freewriting helps students express themselves. It can be a particularly useful method for students who freeze at the outset of writing (the blank-page syndrome), for students who are overly concerned about creating perfect sentences, and for students who struggle with spelling and other orthographic considerations to the extent that the expression of their ideas is diminished.

An activity that can be carried out individually or in groups is **brainstorming,** in which students choose a topic and then write down all the words and phrases that come to mind with respect to the topic. As with freewriting, students are encouraged to write whatever comes to mind during the brainstorming process, without concern for whether the words and phrases are "correct" or not. By inspecting the lists that are created through brainstorming, students will often find good ideas for writing.

A variant of brainstorming is **clustering,** in which the words and phrases in the list are circled and linked to the topic word. The result is a diagram that conveys some sense of how the different words and phrases are connected.

Teach purposeful, meaningful writing

The beginning teacher teaches purposeful, meaningful writing in connection with listening, reading, and speaking.

In traditional approaches to writing, students receive a topic from the teacher, and then write a single-draft composition for the teacher to evaluate. Younger students may be asked to copy down passages from the blackboard or a worksheet. Experts now believe that, because writing is a form of communication, traditional activities such as copying down passages are unlikely to benefit writing skills in a meaningful way, while asking students to write about uninteresting topics, or to focus on both mechanics and content simultaneously through single-draft writing, will stifle the written expression of ideas. It is believed that students can obtain sufficient practice with the mechanics of writing through meaningful uses of the skill, such as writing about their own experiences and relating their writing activities to listening, reading, and speaking experiences both in and outside of class.

In a **process writing approach,** students choose a topic and develop a piece of writing for a particular audience (typically not just the teacher). Process writing develops over a period of days as students revise what they have written. In contrast to traditional approaches, the process and not just the product of writing is emphasized. The teacher's role is not only to examine the final product but also to monitor and support the process by which that product is created. By allowing students to choose their topics and by encouraging revisions with a final publication in mind, the teacher helps students appreciate that writing can be a purposeful, meaningful activity.

Monitor and motivate the writing development of individual children

The beginning teacher monitors children's writing development and provides motivational instruction that addresses the strengths, needs, and interests of individual children, including English Language Learners.

Writing development can be monitored formally or informally, in order to provide each student with the best and most engaging instruction. Following are four general methods.

- Teachers can evaluate student writing through **holistic scoring,** in which an overall impression of the writing is formed. Teachers may use holistic scoring to divide student compositions into groups ranging from strongest to weakest.
- **Primary trait scoring** is used to evaluate a specific characteristic of writing. A primary trait is the most important characteristic in a particular form of writing. For example, the primary trait of a story may be level of interest, while the primary trait of a letter to the president may be degree of persuasiveness.
- **Analytic scoring** is used to compare student performance on key dimensions of writing to some standard, typically performance by other students of the same age.
- **Error analysis** is used to identify specific weaknesses in a student's writing.

Students whose writing development is limited, such as English Language Learners, may feel frustrated or incompetent if they see their classmates creating written text that they are unable to produce. If their writing skills in the native language are limited, they may be overwhelmed by the prospect of writing in English. It is important for teachers to encourage English Language Learners to engage in writing, even if in the native language, and to help these students become comfortable with the idea of expressing themselves in this medium. The teacher may need to speak with the child, the child's parents, or other knowledgeable individuals about the child's abilities and interests.

Teach the components of the writing process

The beginning teacher selects and uses instructional strategies, materials, and activities to teach the components of the writing process, including prewriting, drafting, editing, and revising.

The components of the writing process can be distinguished as follows:

1. **Prewriting:** During prewriting, the student chooses a topic, identifies a purpose (whether to instruct, to entertain, and/or to persuade), decides on a format, considers the intended audience, and generates ideas. Some students find prewriting difficult, because they struggle to convey their ideas in writing, even in a preliminary way. The teacher may encourage students to use drawing, conversation with others, and other methods such as brainstorming to help students make prewriting decisions.

2. **Drafting:** During the drafting stage, students write their ideas down. They should be encouraged to do so without worrying about orthographic dimensions such as spelling and grammar or about the quality of their ideas, because the purpose of drafting is to generate text that can be edited later. Students should be encouraged to label their drafts and to leave spaces between lines for revision.

3. **Revising:** When revising, students make changes to the content of what they have written on the basis of rereading their drafts, as well as suggestions from the teacher and/or other students. Writing groups may be formed in which students share their work with classmates. The teacher should help students understand the importance of feedback and should model appropriate feedback, both negative and positive. Suggestions for improvement should be polite and constructive, while positive feedback should be specific.

4. **Editing:** The editing stage focuses on proofreading in order to identify and correct errors in spelling, grammar, punctuation, and capitalization. Students may use checklists to monitor whether each dimension of their writing contains errors.

5. **Sharing:** In the final stage, the student shares his or her work with others. In this stage, the student learns more about the concept of author by playing the authorial role. Books can be created in which the pages have been bound together in some fashion, and the final product can be shared with classmates, parents, and other individuals.

Use technologies that facilitate writing

The beginning teacher provides instruction in the use of appropriate technologies that facilitate written communication.

Along with instruction in the use of writing implements such as pencils and pens, teachers help students understand how to use the computer to write. Word processing is a powerful tool that facilitates revision and editing and frees students from the physical constraints of handwriting. In our society using the computer effectively has also become an important academic skill in its own right.

Teach the differences between drafting and final products

The beginning teacher teaches children the differences between first-draft writing and writing for publication and helps them apply writing conventions to their own written products.

During the revising and editing stages, the teacher helps students understand the differences between drafts and shared products. The teacher plays the role of audience and asks questions when information is ambiguous or insufficient. The teacher may indicate that some aspect of content is unclear or that something about the orthography makes a passage difficult to understand. The teacher may express interest in reading more details about a particular topic or may question the relevance of details that are provided.

Encourage writing in a variety of forms

The beginning teacher provides opportunities for children to write in a variety of forms and modes and for various purposes and audiences.

A distinction can be made between narrative writing, poetic writing, expository writing, and persuasive writing. Each form of writing has a different purpose and may speak to a different audience. Students should have opportunities to engage in each type of writing. Differences in the content and purpose of each type should be discussed.

The audience for student writing can be the teacher, the class or other classes, parents, pen pals, and so on. By exploring each type of writing, the meaningfulness of writing as a form of communication is reinforced.

Teach children to assess their own writing

The beginning teacher teaches children to apply criteria (for example, clarity, comprehensiveness, interest to audience) for assessing their own written work.

Just as early readers are encouraged to monitor and evaluate their own comprehension, so early writers should be encouraged to monitor and evaluate their written work. Students should be encouraged to self-assess drafts as well as finished products. Self-assessment can be informal or carried out by means of checklists. Following are some of the questions students should ask:

- Is my topic interesting?
- Did I stick to the topic?
- Did I cover everything I was supposed to cover?
- Were my ideas organized?
- Was my writing understandable?
- Did I use descriptive words?
- Was my conclusion clear?
- Did I check my grammar, spelling, and punctuation?

Foster collaboration with families and other professionals

The beginning teacher understands how to foster collaboration with families and with other professionals to promote children's development of writing skills.

Teachers should encourage parents to visit the classroom, to look at videotapes of children's writing activities (if available), and to have positive discussions with children about their writing samples that are sent home with them.

Parents may assume that the purpose of writing instruction is to teach children the mechanics and conventions of writing in English. Parents may be concerned that not enough structured activities such as workbooks are used to teach writing. In such cases, teachers should help parents understand the rationale for giving children autonomy and flexibility, for emphasizing the writing process and not just the product, and for encouraging the free expression of ideas.

At home, parents should be encouraged to let children see them write. Space and materials should be made available for children to engage in writing themselves. Criticism should be avoided. Parents should understand that they need to be encouraging and focus on the content of what children write.

Sample Questions

1. In a unit on Texas history, Mrs. Jones asks her 4th graders to work in groups to create written descriptions of the social, military, and political importance of the Alamo. Once each of the groups has generated some ideas to work from, which of the following would be a good strategy for proceeding?

   A. freewriting
   B. brainstorming
   C. revising
   D. drafting

   C Options A, B, and D are useful for generating ideas, but they are not designed to refine existing ideas. Option C is the best answer. Once students have ideas to work from, revision is the next step if the ultimate goal is a finished product that will be shared with others.

2. Which of the following types of writing would most directly help 2nd graders take the perspective of someone from a very different culture?

   A. learning log
   B. simulated journal
   C. response journal
   D. dialogue journal

   B Options A, C, and D could help students take someone else's perspective. A learning log could be used to describe an inhabitant of a different culture, while a response journal could record the student's thoughts and feelings about that person. The exchanges in a dialogue journal could also focus on the life of an individual in a distant culture. However, option B is the best answer, because a simulated journal would require the student to take the other person's perspective throughout the entire writing process.

Competency 011 (Assessment of Developing Literacy)

The teacher understands the basic principles of literacy assessment and uses a variety of assessments to guide literacy instruction.

Review

Understand formal and informal literacy-assessment techniques

The beginning teacher understands characteristics and appropriate uses of a wide range of formal and informal literacy-assessment techniques, including techniques for assessing oral language, and uses assessment results to adapt instruction to address the needs of individual children, including English Language Learners.

A variety of formal and informal assessments are available for evaluating children's literacy as well as their **oracy** (fluency in speaking and listening).

- The **norm-referenced test** is a type of formal assessment that measures a student's performance relative to a large group of individuals, such as other students of the same age across the nation. Scores on such tests can be used to describe a student in terms of grade level, percentile rank, or stanine.

- **Criterion-referenced tests** measure how well a student meets a set of standards or expectations for a particular group, such as age or grade level. Criterion-referenced tests are not usually normed. They indicate what a student can or cannot do, rather than how well the student is performing relative to others of the same age. The TExES EC–4 Generalist test is an example of a criterion-referenced test, because it yields information about how well the test-taker has mastered basic knowledge and principles of EC–4 pedagogy.

Base instruction on children's reading and writing performance

The beginning teacher analyzes children's reading and writing performance and uses it as a basis for instruction.

Teachers use a variety of informal methods to assess and analyze children's reading and writing performance. The purpose of these assessments is not only to record accuracy levels but also to understand the basis of student performance. Tallying errors is not as useful as analyzing the source of the errors, so that instruction can be modified appropriately.

- **Assessing reading level: Informal Reading Inventories (IRIs)** are used to assess general reading level. When administering an IRI, the teacher records how accurately the student pronounces words during oral reading, as well as how accurately the student answers comprehension questions after oral as well as silent reading.

- **Uncovering difficulties with reading:** The **Reading Miscue Inventory (RMI)** can provide specific information about the difficulties students have with reading as well as the specific reading strategies they use. The RMI provides information about **miscues,** or cases in which a student reads a word that is different from the one that is printed. Through an analysis of miscues, the teacher may be able to identify patterns of error. For example, it can be observed whether or not the student makes use of semantic and/or syntactic cues. The student who reads the passage "The plate fell to the floor with a crash" as "The plate fell to the floor with a bang" is making use of semantic cues, because the word "bang" makes sense in the context of this sentence. However, the student who reads the passage as "The plate fell to the floor with a car" is not taking advantage of the semantic context established by the sentence.

- **Tracking reading progress:** Similar to IRIs and RMIs, **running records** are used to track students' reading progress. To create a running record, the teacher examines a passage that a student is reading and places a mark by each word that the student pronounces incorrectly. Miscues and self-corrections are also recorded. One advantage of running records is that they can be made relatively easily in any ordinary classroom situation in which the teacher has a copy of the text that a student is reading out loud.

- **Assessing writing:** Writing can be assessed through a variety of observational methods. Teachers can record student progress **anecdotally.** In addition, teachers can use **checklists** to record student performance on various dimensions, including mechanics, handwriting, spelling, punctuation, revision activities, and content (including vocabulary, grammar, thematic development, and so on). A **portfolio** consists of a collection of materials that shows student progress over time. Portfolio assessment can be done to evaluate progress in reading and/or writing. The portfolio may consist of tests and results of formal and informal assessments, journal writings, illustrations, projects, and writing samples ranging from drafts to final products.

Know TEKS content and performance standards

The beginning teacher knows the state content and performance standards for reading, writing, listening, and speaking that comprise the Texas Essential Knowledge and Skills (TEKS) and recognizes when a child needs additional help or intervention to bring performance up to grade level.

EC–4 Teachers should know that the TEKS provides guidelines for determining whether a child is reading, writing, listening, and speaking at his or her particular grade level. Teachers should be familiar with TEKS content and performance standards that are provided for each grade and should be able to use the standards to determine when a child is functioning below grade level and consequently needs support. Teachers should know where to find the TEKS on the Internet.

Identify and make use of children's reading levels

The beginning teacher knows how to determine children's independent, instructional, and frustration reading levels, and uses this information to select appropriate materials for individual children and to guide children's selection of independent reading materials.

Teachers often use an Informal Reading Inventory (IRI) to assess children's general reading level as well as particular strengths and weaknesses in word identification and comprehension. Typically, the IRI consists of a sequence of paragraphs that are graded in difficulty, and the teacher will analyze oral reading, silent reading, and listening comprehension.

During the administration of an IRI, a sight word test is given first in order to determine which paragraph the student should use to begin the oral reading. Following the oral reading, the teacher asks questions. The student then engages in silent reading, followed by further questions. The questions posed to students typically focus on both literal and inferential comprehension of main ideas, details, sequences of events, cause-effect relations, and key vocabulary. Students' reading performance and responses to the comprehension questions are used to identify different reading levels.

- Material is written at a student's **Independent Reading Level** if the student pronounces 95% or more of the words correctly and shows more than 90% accuracy in response to comprehension questions. As the name suggests, the Independent Reading Level refers to material that the student can read on his or her own, without assistance.

- Material is written at a student's **Instructional Reading Level** if the student pronounces 90 to 94% of the words correctly, and answers 70 to 89% of the questions correctly. The Instructional Reading Level refers to challenging material that the student can read with assistance from the teacher. As the name suggests, the Instructional Reading Level is the level at which instruction can take place. Instruction is not needed for Independent Reading Level materials. At the same time, instruction will not be effective for the Frustration Reading Level, in which material is too difficult for the student.

- Material is written at the **Frustration Reading Level** if the student pronounces less than 50% of the words correctly and answers less than 70% of the questions correctly. Materials at the Frustration Reading Level are too difficult for a student and should be avoided until the student is ready for them.

Teachers should use the results of IRIs to help determine the texts that are appropriate for individual children. Teachers should also monitor students' progress with the texts that the teacher or student chooses, because IRIs provide estimates rather than infallible indicators of children's reading levels.

Use ongoing assessments

The beginning teacher uses ongoing assessments to determine when a child may be in need of classroom interventions or specialized reading instruction and to develop appropriate instructional plans.

Reading assessments can be administered on an ongoing basis to monitor progress and serve as the basis of instructional planning. Interventions and specialized reading activities, which are tailored to individual children, may take into account learning disabilities, differences in learning style, differences in cultural background, or differences in student interests. As with all learners, it is important for teachers who develop such interventions or activities to be positive, to use varied methods, and to provide each student with opportunities for success.

Foster collaboration with families and other professionals

The beginning teacher communicates children's progress in literacy development to parents/caregivers and to other professionals through a variety of means, including the use of examples of children's work.

Parents should be kept informed about their children's progress through oral and written communication from the teacher, as well as through samples of their children's work that are assembled in portfolios, displayed during open house, and sent home with children on a regular basis. The teacher should coordinate efforts with everyone involved in the delivery of an Individualized Education Plan (IEP). Various strategies for conveying information to parents, and for helping parents promote literacy development at home, are discussed under earlier competencies.

Sample Questions

1. A verbal intelligence test such as the Peabody Picture Vocabulary Test (PPVT) exemplifies what type of test?

    A. norm-referenced
    B. criterion-referenced
    C. running record
    D. oracy

A By themselves, intelligence tests do not indicate how well the test-taker meets a set of criteria or standards and, thus, option B is incorrect. Option C is incorrect, because running records are informal assessments obtained by teachers. Option D is incorrect, because oracy is an abstract concept. Option A is the correct answer. Intelligence tests yield scores that indicate each student's ability relative to other students of the same age.

2. Mr. Smith gives each student in his 3rd-grade class an IRI near the beginning of the year in order to determine each student's independent reading level. He then identifies a set of books that each student will be allowed to choose from for free-reading throughout the year. What else should Mr. Smith be doing?

    A. Keeping running records for each student.
    B. Allowing students some input into their choice of free-reading texts.
    C. Sharing information about student progress with parents.
    D. all of the above

D Option A is correct, because each student's reading ability will change over time, and it will be important for Mr. Smith to re-administer IRIs, keep running records, and otherwise monitor student progress in order to adjust his expectations about what each student is capable of reading. However, it is important for students to be able to read what they like during free-reading time and, thus, option B is correct. Option C is correct too, because parents should be kept informed about their student's progress in reading as well as other aspects of academic and social functioning. Thus, option D is the correct answer.

Domain II: Mathematics

Competency 012 (Mathematics Instruction)

The teacher understands how children learn mathematical skills and uses this knowledge to plan, organize, and implement instruction and assess learning.

Review

Plan appropriate activities

The beginning teacher plans appropriate activities for all children based on research and principles of learning mathematics.

Much research has been done on learning mathematics. Understanding Piaget's stages of cognitive development helps teachers develop stage-appropriate exercises for students. Piaget's stages of cognitive development are sensorimotor, pre-operational, concrete operational, and formal operational.

1. The **sensorimotor stage** (usually from birth to about two and one-half years of age), involves making sense of the world through their senses and their motoring abilities. This child begins to grasp the concept that objects and people still exist, even though they are out-of-sight. This is called object permanence.

2. The **pre-operational stage** (from about two and one-half years of age through seven years of age), includes the child's movement away from geocentricism. The child becomes aware of points of view and feelings of others in the world. Symbols begin to make sense to the child. These symbols include words. Blocks can represent trucks or planes. Number and space concepts are developed through the use of concrete objects.

3. The **concrete operational stage** (starting at about age seven and lasting through roughly age twelve) involves gradual development of mental images. This child needs to discover mathematical concepts by playing with attribute blocks, chips, or other manipulatives. This child has achieved conservation of number and mass and is developing conservation of weight. Here again, the use of manipulatives is important. Classification of objects, events, and people becomes possible. The child also can put these objects in order by a specific characteristic, such as size. The child can also think logically about objects and events. In addition, the concrete-operational-staged child can use reversibility in thought. So this child understands the connection between addition and subtraction. The child begins to think about the whole-part relationship. This will help in the development of concepts of fractions and division. This child is expected to understand a situation from another's perspective.

4. The final stage, **formal operational stage** (reached at approximately age twelve), includes increased sophistication of thought. This child is beginning to form hypotheses, draw conclusions, analyze, and develop more formal modes of reasoning.

In order to educate each child, the teacher needs to be ever mindful of the stage of the child's cognitive development.

Instruction should be rooted in the principles of the National Council of Teachers of Mathematics (www.nctm.org). The principles are:

- **The Equity Principle:** Excellence in mathematics education requires high expectations and strong support for all students.

- **The Mathematics Curriculum Principle:** A mathematics curriculum must be coherent, focused on important mathematics, and well-articulated across the grades.

- **The Teaching Principle:** Effective mathematics teaching requires understanding what students know and need to learn and then challenging and supporting them to learn it well.

- **The Learning Principle:** Students must learn mathematics with understanding, actively building new knowledge from experience and prior knowledge.

- **The Assessment Principle:** Assessment should support the learning of important mathematics and furnish useful information to both teachers and students.

- **The Technology Principle:** Technology is essential in teaching and learning mathematics; it influences the mathematics that is taught and enhances students' learning.

These principles provide the foci that ensure excellence in an elementary mathematics program that connects mathematics with other disciplines and with the real world.

Build on diversity

The beginning teacher employs instructional strategies that build on the linguistic, cultural, and socioeconomic diversity of children and that relate to children's lives and communities.

Teachers need to provide instruction to each student in language that the student relates to regarding actual words used, examples given, and experiences to which they can relate. Making the material real for students will encourage students to learn the material and to remember it. Elementary school children develop the ability to follow up to five commands in a row, so multi-step exercises are possible.

In addition, teachers need to be aware of language deficits students may exhibit. These could be due to background or medical issues. Likewise, teachers need to be attentive to students with hearing problems. These will certainly inhibit a child's ability to learn. The savvy teacher knows the background of each child in the class and understands the values that each child's culture embraces.

Provide developmentally appropriate instruction

The beginning teacher provides developmentally appropriate instruction along a continuum from concrete to abstract and plans instruction that builds on strengths and addresses needs.

The teacher must be aware of the stages of learning that the child goes through in order to best educate the child. Developing exercises that move through the sequence from working with concrete objects through abstract reasoning provides the best instruction. As students move through these stages at different rates, the teacher must be able to group the students accordingly to capitalize on each student's current capacity for learning.

Division could first be presented to students concretely by showing students repeated removal of objects from a set. Starting with 12 chips, remove 3 of them, set that group in a pile aside. Now, remove 3 more chips and follow the same procedure. After doing this two more times, the original set is empty. Four sets of 3 chips were removed. This activity could be done with chips being left that do not create another set of the given number. The preceding example could have been done with 14 chips, which would have resulted in four groups of 3 and two leftover chips. This could be used to discuss the idea of the remainder.

Children can also draw pictures of groups of objects and circle sets of objects to demonstrate division.

Use manipulatives

The beginning teacher knows how mathematical learning may be assisted through the appropriate use of manipulatives and technological tools.

The use of **manipulatives** helps teachers move children from the concrete through the abstract stages of reasoning necessary for learning higher-level mathematical concepts. Chips, Cuisenaire Rods, dice, play money, and Unifix Cubes are some examples of manipulatives.

Some tips for incorporating manipulatives into the curriculum include the following:

- Tell students why manipulatives are used.
- Give students opportunities to handle the manipulatives and to discover their characteristics. Students will be curious about these new items. If they are given the opportunity to "play" with them initially, they will be more focused when it is time to use them for work.
- Be sure to have rules about the use of manipulatives. Be sure that students understand that they are used to learn and solve problems. Also, instill in the children the need to keep the manipulatives organized. Have them in a location that they can easily find and reach.
- Inform parents or guardians about the manipulatives being used. In fact, including at-home activities for them to do with their children reinforces the value of their use.

Motivate through a variety of tasks and settings

The beginning teacher motivates children and actively engages them in the learning process by using a variety of interesting, challenging, and worthwhile mathematical tasks and by providing instruction in individual, small-group, and large-group settings.

The teacher will provide instruction to children or groups of children, depending upon the needs of the group. A child may need one-on-one instruction in order to grasp a concept. In other scenarios, students may require group instruction in order to talk about the concepts being taught and learn from each other. So the teacher needs to be aware of these needs. Keep in mind that cooperative learning reinforces the learning of all in the group, provided the teacher ensures that all students are taking part in the activity.

The most effective mathematics classroom experiences allow students to explore different approaches to exercises, to discuss their findings with others both orally and in print, and to learn from their peers and their teachers.

Elementary school children work with right triangles. The elementary school teacher needs to provide opportunities for the students to experience them. **Tangrams** are suitable for the student who needs the tactile experience with the triangle. **Geoboards** also provide the tactile experience of creating right triangles. A geoboard is a block of wood with a rectangular array of pins. These pins are used to hold geobands (rubber bands) in place. These bands are used to form triangles and other polygons. These are activities that children can do with their classmates. The teacher should encourage the children to talk about the "work" they are doing. This is an opportunity for the students to reinforce their vocabulary, such as "hypotenuse" and "right angle."

After enough manipulative work, the students can progress to drawing right triangles so that they are still seeing and creating them. "Please make a right triangle with two equal sides. Please make a right triangle that has a hypotenuse that is double the length of one of its legs." The students can work in small groups or in teams for this activity. Again, talking about their work should be encouraged. These students can move into individual work, in which they find the perimeter of each right triangle given with the lengths of the legs and of the hypotenuse clearly marked.

Use a variety of lifelong tools

The beginning teacher uses a variety of tools (for example, counters, standard and nonstandard units of measure, rulers, protractors, scales, stopwatches, measuring containers, money, calculators, software) to strengthen children's mathematical understanding.

Students need to use a multitude of tools in order to become comfortable with the concepts they are learning. Students will use these tools for a lifetime. These help make the mathematics they learn real to them. The use of nonstandard units allows them to be creative in the real world when standard measuring tools are unavailable. Students need to be able to measure length, capacity, weight, mass, area, volume, time, temperature, and angles. Likewise, students need to be able to approximate these measures.

A favorite activity of elementary school children is using the trundle wheel. This lends itself to team work. One student uses the trundle wheel, while another marks the dimensions found. Then the students switch jobs: measuring the gym, measuring around the school building, measuring the length of the hall. These activities can also be used to develop the children's approximating skills.

Develop appropriate learning goals for students

The beginning teacher develops appropriate learning goals based on the Texas Essential Knowledge and Skills (TEKS) in mathematics and uses these learning goals as a basis for instruction.

The Texas Essential Knowledge and Skills provides guidelines for instruction. Beginning teachers need to follow a plan that has worked for experienced teachers. These guidelines serve to guarantee that every student is exposed to the material necessary to succeed not only in the current grade but also in the following grades. This structure assures that both the teacher is teaching the required material and that each student is being presented the essential grade-specific skills. The creative aspect of teaching comes into play in the methods and materials used by each teacher.

Make connections with the real world

The beginning teacher helps children make connections between mathematics, the real world, and other disciplines.

Students need to see the connection between their learning and the real world. Paying for a meal at a restaurant, telling time, cooking, keeping score, fencing in a garden, buying carpeting for the family room are all examples of connecting mathematics to the real world.

Use a variety of questioning strategies

The beginning teacher uses a variety of questioning strategies to encourage mathematical discourse and to help children analyze and evaluate their mathematical thinking.

Students need to be able to answer questions about the way they think about mathematics, not just to be able to answer questions that require rote memorization. Therefore, the teacher needs to question in a way that allows the student to exhibit the thought process behind the ultimate answer. This questioning technique is important for the teacher to use when helping a child work through a problem. If a student can start an exercise but gets stuck, the competent teacher is able to guide the student through the exercise through a series of questions.

1. Teachers should begin with direct questions, questions that students may know by rote memorization.
2. Then the teacher should move on to a higher level of questioning. Students asked these questions will need to take information that is directly given and "massage" it in some way.
3. After this level, students are ready to bring their own experiences into the answering of these even higher level questions.
4. Finally, students should be able to answer questions that are entirely based upon their own experiences.

The responses to the questions should indicate to the teacher the level of comprehension students have of the material being presented. Students may have misunderstood the lesson completely; that situation provides a "learning moment" for the teacher. See these as opportunities to improve instruction. Delving into the way students are learning awards opportunities for more advanced work with students, too. This could be advancing students who grasp the concepts or reviewing the material with students who are struggling.

The National Council of Teachers of Mathematics describes five categories of questions.

Questions that help students work together to make sense of mathematics:

- What do others think about what Janine said?
- Do you agree? disagree?
- Does anyone have the same answer but a different way to explain it?
- Would you ask the rest of the class that question?
- Do you understand what they are saying?
- Can you convince the rest of us that that makes sense?

Questions that help students rely more on themselves to determine whether something is mathematically correct:

- Why do you think that?
- Why is that true?
- How did you reach that conclusion?
- Does that make sense?
- Can you make a model to show that?

Questions that help students learn to reason mathematically:

- Does that always work?
- Is that true for all cases?
- Can you think of a counterexample?
- How could you prove that?
- What assumptions are you making?

Questions that help students learn to conjecture, invent, and solve problems:

- What would happen if . . .? What happens if not?
- Do you see a pattern?
- What are some possibilities here?
- Can you predict the next one? What about the last one?
- How did you think about the problem?
- What decision do you think he should make?
- What is alike and what is different about your method of solution and hers?

Questions that help students to connect mathematics, its ideas, and its applications:

- How does this relate to . . .?
- What ideas that we have learned before were useful in solving this problem?
- Have we ever solved a problem like this one before?
- What uses of mathematics did you find in the newspaper last night?
- Can you give me an example of . . .?

Use a variety of assessment procedures

The beginning teacher uses a variety of formal and informal assessments and scoring procedures to evaluate mathematical understanding, common misconceptions, and error patterns.

As with questioning, teachers learn about the effectiveness of their teaching by assessing the learning of the students. The teacher should be upfront with the students about the need for assessment. Students should know what concepts are being tested.

Paper-and-pencil tests are only one type of diagnosis. Others are oral tests of understanding and discussion of attitudes about mathematics, project work, one-on-one skill development, compilation of portfolios, and informal assessments. Another possibility is for students to keep journals of their mathematics learning and their attitudes about those learnings. These evaluation results should be charted and used to improve instruction.

Understand the reciprocal nature of assessment and instruction

The beginning teacher understands the reciprocal nature of assessment and instruction and knows how to use assessment results to design, monitor, and modify instruction to improve mathematical learning for individual children, including English Language Learners.

The results of evaluations should be used by the teacher to improve instruction.

- Was more time instructing a topic necessary?
- Were the instructions clear to each student?
- Are students making careless mistakes?
- Have students begun to make mistakes on material that had been considered mastered?

Understand the usefulness of mathematics in careers and professions

The beginning teacher understands how mathematics is used in a variety of careers and professions and plans instruction that demonstrates how mathematics is used in the workplace.

Incorporating real-life applications is important so that students appreciate the value of what they are learning. Having a guest speaker present skills that are used in that person's profession is an excellent technique for showing students that their mathematics really is useful. Integrating problem-solving applications relevant to the speaker's lecture solidifies the work done by the speaker.

Sample Questions

1. Which of the following best indicates to the teacher that Emma can use mathematics to solve a real-world problem?

    A.   Emma writes an essay explaining Roman numerals.
    B.   Emma is able to answer ten multiplication facts in one minute.
    C.   Emma talks for five minutes about a famous contemporary mathematician.
    D.   Emma finds the cost of two notebooks at $0.75 each and three pens at $1.25 each.

    D. The famous contemporary mathematician (choice C) certainly is in the real world, as are the ten multiplication facts (choice B). However, talking about this person does not indicate to the teacher that Emma herself can do mathematics. The explanation of Roman numerals (choice A), while interesting, is not a real-world problem. Choice D indicates to the teacher that Emma understands multiplication, addition, decimals, and money. The correct answer is D.

2. Mr. McCarthy spilled some chips. He asked his students to pick them up and categorize them. The students came up with this chart.

Color/Pattern	Number of Chips
Striped	4
Black	12
Gray	3
Checked	1

Which of the following represents a pie chart that shows the information in the chart?

A.

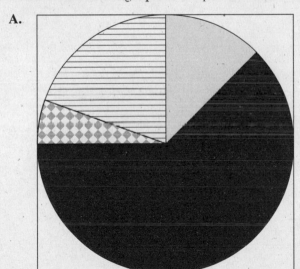

B.

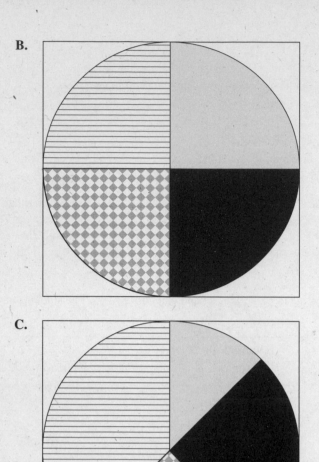

C.

D.

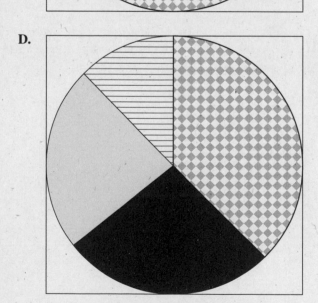

A. Using the process of elimination, first eliminate those that do not show black as the biggest portion of the pie chart. That eliminates B, C, Sund D. The correct answer is A.

3. Twenty students need to be split into teams of five students each. How should the teacher, Miss Abernethy, accomplish this?

    A. Have the students count off by 4s. All of the 1s make up a group, as do the 2s, 3s, and 4s.

    B. Write each month on a piece of paper. Post those pieces of paper around the classroom. Ask the students to go stand by the month in which they were born, and groups are formed.

    C. Put children in groups based upon the number of siblings they have.

    D. Choose five students as leaders. Have them pick classmates, one at a time, until all students are on a team.

A. Choice A describes a method that would evenly split the class of twenty students into four equally-sized groups of five students each. The method described in choice B could create up to twelve different groups, without necessarily the same number of students in each group. The method in choice C would not assure groups of five students each. Choice D would create five equally sized groups. The correct answer is A.

4. The label of a cylindrical soup can is removed from the can and placed flat on a table. The shape of the label is a

    A. circle

    B. quadrilateral

    C. pentagon

    D. rhombus

B. The label is a polygon: The sides are straight, not curved. So choice A is incorrect. Choice B is correct: The label does have four sides. Choice C is incorrect: A pentagon has five sides. Choice D is incorrect, because a rhombus must have four equal sides. A soup label could have four equal sides; however, it does not have to have equal-length sides. The correct answer is B.

5. The best method for determining the way the children in a class think about fractions is to:

    A. Give a short-answer quiz on the concept of fractions.

    B. Give a multiple-choice test on fractions.

    C. Have a conversation about fractions with the students.

    D. Have the class follow a recipe to make peanut butter cookies.

C. The methods described in choices A and B would provide the teacher with information about the knowledge that the children have about fractions. However, such assessments would not necessarily permit the teacher to pursue the line of thinking that each student uses in answering the questions. The method in option C gives the teacher the opportunity to delve into the thought processes that each student uses. The method of choice D provides tasty results and good practice dealing with measurements. However, that choice would not allow the teacher to probe the way method C would. The correct answer is C.

6. The following is a list of activities Mr. Tigeres has planned for his class. Which order is best pedagogically?

A. Groups of up to four children can play this game. The teacher provides one deck of cards that contains blue, green, purple, and yellow 0s, 1s, 2s, 3s, 4s, 5s, 6s, 7s, 8s, 9s, and 10s to each group. Each child draws two cards from the deck. Each student multiplies the values on each of the two cards together. The child with the largest product wins. In the case of a tie, each of the tying children draws two new cards and multiplies them to determine the winner.

B. Children are given a worksheet of 20 multi-digit multiplication exercises to complete.

C. Single-digit multiplication facts that are written on cards are given to a small group of children. The group is also given a set of chips. Using the chips, the children are to figure out the products of these facts.

D. A piece of graph paper is handed to each child. Given an exercise such as $\frac{4}{\times 3}$, the child is to write the exercise on the paper. Then directly below the exercise, the child is to color in four rows of three boxes each. Finally, the child writes the number of boxes colored in under the exercise: $\frac{\begin{array}{r}4\\\times 3\end{array}}{12}$.

A. c d a b
B. d c b a
C. b c d a
D. a b d c

A. The chip exercise, C, is the first activity that should be presented to the children. This exercise provides the children the experience to understand that multiplication is repeated addition. The exercise with the graph paper, D, is a semiconcrete means of "experiencing" multiplication. The method with the cards, A, provides additional practice with the facts. The multi-digit method, B, is more advanced. The correct answer is A.

Competency 013 (Number Concepts, Patterns, and Algebra)

The teacher understands concepts related to numbers and number systems and demonstrates knowledge of patterns, relations, functions, and algebraic reasoning.

Review

Analyze number theory

The beginning teacher analyzes and describes number concepts (for example, off, even, prime), operations and algorithms, and the properties of numbers.

Several concepts of numbers need to be understood by students during their elementary-school years. Examples are even/odd and prime/composite numbers. Even numbers are divisible by two; odd numbers are not. Prime numbers have no factors other than one and the number itself. Composite numbers have factors other than one and the number itself. One is in a class by itself: one is neither prime nor composite.

Operations need to be performed singly and in groups. Algorithms are step-by-step methods for solving arithmetic computations and more advanced mathematical operations. Often, a variety of algorithms lead to the same result. Students should be allowed to use the algorithm that makes the most sense to them. Remember that the goal is for the mathematics taught to make sense to the students. Exercises should be reasoned through for best understanding and long-term retention.

Properties of numbers that the elementary school child learns are:

- **Commutative property of addition:** $5 + 3 = 3 + 5$
- **Commutative property of multiplication:** $7 \times 9 = 9 \times 7$
- **Associative property of addition:** $(4 + 2) + 3 = 4 + (2 + 3)$
- **Associative property of multiplication:** $(6 \times 8) \times 2 = 6 \times (8 \times 2)$
- **Additive identity element:** a number $+ 0 =$ the number
- **Multiplicative identity element:** a number $\times 1 =$ the number
- **Zero property of multiplication:** a number $\times 0 = 0$
- **Distributive property:** $2(4 + 3) = 2 \times 4 + 2 \times 3$ and $2 \times 4 + 2 \times 3 = 2(4 + 3)$

Analyze number operations

The beginning teacher analyzes, explains, and models the four basic operations with whole numbers, integers, and rational numbers.

The relationship between addition and multiplication and subtraction and division is important for students to understand not just for their elementary experiences but for their later learning of higher-level mathematical concepts.

In a classroom, several activities may be going on at the same time. One group of students will be applying addition and subtraction facts and algorithms. Another group will be recalling multiplication and division facts, while a third group will be mastering multiplication algorithms. Division algorithms are being developed by a fourth group.

More specifically, the first group of students may be working on word problems that apply multi-digit addition and subtraction, while the second group plays a card game to practice its multiplication and division facts. The third group may be working with **Dienes blocks** (base-10 blocks) to reinforce multi-digit multiplication. The final group, at the same time, could be just developing their division concepts and vocabulary through the use of chips.

Of course, all operations should first be presented concretely, using manipulatives. Extensive opportunities for drill, including applications of real-life situations, help students comprehend and retain the material, especially if they connect the concepts to the world. Another important avenue to retention is continual chances to utilize the facts and algorithms. Attaining mastery of a concept does not terminate the need to review it. In fact, the students develop new concepts while they continue to review facts and hone skills. The effective teacher is able to balance all of this in the classroom.

Use numbers in applications

The beginning teacher uses numbers to describe and quantify phenomena such as time, temperature, and money.

Applications to the real world are essential to the children's appreciation of mathematics. Such concepts as time, temperature, and money are essential for the children's understanding that the mathematics they learn is useful to them. They also need to develop an appreciation for the use of different units around the world. Although they may never use some units, they should know that other cultures use different units. Discussions about units of currency in different countries present opportunities for connecting mathematics with geography.

Students also need to experience the various mechanisms used to measure time and temperature. Applications in science are useful for this.

Apply number theory

The beginning teacher applies knowledge of place value and other number properties to perform mental mathematics and computational estimation.

Number sense is important for each student to grasp. Especially in applications, students need to be able to determine the appropriateness of an answer. "Is it big enough or too big?" "Does a fractional answer make sense when you are dealing with a number of people?" "Can 120.45 people be at the zoo?"

Students need to have a variety of experiences with approximating. Often, students work to get exact answers when that is unnecessary. Heading to buy an ice cream cone necessitates having enough money to cover that expense. Having the exact change is not required.

Illustrate numerical relationships

The beginning teacher illustrates relations and functions using concrete models, tables, graphs, and symbolic expressions.

Relationships include one-to-one correspondences. Here are some ideas for the classroom:

- Use chips and let each green chip represent a boy in the class, while each yellow chip represents a girl. Use these chips to provide comparisons of more and less.

- Use the chips to develop the concepts of fractional parts. Use different color chips to represent different colors of hair.

- Create a bar graph using the results of chip comparisons. Make this into a paper-and-pencil graph.

- Have children bring in and explain graphs from magazines or newspapers. **Pictographs** are effective in transitioning students from concrete forms of graphs to more abstract forms. A pictograph uses pictures to represent data sets on a graph.

- Use a basic survey as a source of data that can be graphed. Such a survey could be a take-home assignment. Such an assignment will keep the parents or guardians informed of their child's school experiences, while providing personal information that students can use to compare some aspect of their own life to that of their classmates. Questions may be based upon number of children living in the home (female and male), types and numbers of pets, numbers of telephones owned by the family, and so on.

Understand algebraic thought

The beginning teacher understands how to use algebraic concepts and reasoning to investigate patterns, make generalizations, formulate mathematical models, make predictions, and validate results.

Pattern recognition and categorizing, which start at a young age, are basic concepts of algebra. These develop into the ability to write mathematical and algebraic expressions and then equations.

Matching is the beginning of pattern recognition. Students advance from basic matching exercises to comparing and contrasting objects. How are the items in a group the same? What makes them different? What object does not fit with the others? **Attribute blocks** are useful manipulatives for this objective.

The concept of order is important. Students need to practice ordering objects by size, color, or some other attribute. A sequence has a specific order based upon an attribute, perhaps time. Breakfast is followed by lunch, which is followed by dinner. The daily schedule of a class is a sequence of events. Those events are done in a predetermined order.

Seriation occurs when changes are gradual. Height of each student in the class is an attribute that would exhibit seriation.

Know how to use patterns

The beginning teacher knows how to identify, extend, and create patterns using concrete models, figures, numbers, and algebraic expressions.

Pattern recognition and categorization begin with objects. Blocks can be arranged by color: yellow, blue, red, purple, yellow, blue, red, purple, yellow, blue, red, purple, and so on until the blocks are all used. People can be put in a pattern: girl, boy, girl, boy.

Musical sounds can make patterns, too. Allowing the students to use instruments to mimic sound patterns is a fun method of reinforcing this skill. Once students can mimic patterns, they should develop their own patterns. The rest of the class can figure out the pattern.

Body movements can be used to express patterns: hop, clap, turn around, stomp, hop, clap, turn around, stomp.

Understanding how changing one value in an expression alters the result of the expression lays the groundwork for the algebra work the child will encounter later in life. Several hands-on examples should be offered to reinforce the concept of change.

Use relationships in real-world applications

The beginning teacher uses properties, graphs, and applications of relations and functions to analyze, model, and solve problems in mathematical and real-world situations.

Making a graph of the amount of money it costs to buy more textbooks, for example, illustrates a linear relationship. Students can see that as the number of textbooks purchased increases, so does the price. The line rises as the number of textbooks increases.

Such representations encourage the development of mathematical vocabulary. The rising line illustrates a positive slope. Students can come up with their own examples of other real-world applications that can be illustrated with a similar line.

Translate real-life applications to algebraic expressions

The beginning teacher translates problem-solving situations into expressions and equations involving variables and unknowns.

Initially, boxes are used to represent missing values in expressions and equations. Very young students of mathematics can recognize that replacing the box with a number creates a true mathematical statement. "Six girls are in a room. How many boys must join them in order to have ten children present?" "T-shirts are on sale for $9 each. Marjorie has $19. How many shirts can she buy?" Eventually, variables, such as *x* and *y,* take the place of boxes.

Model problem-solving

The beginning teacher models and solves problems, including proportion problems, using concrete, numeric, tabular, graphic, and algebraic methods.

Problem-solving begins with exercises that students can **act out.** An example from the preceding section is such a problem: "Six girls are in a room. How many boys must join them in order to have ten children present?" The students in the class can demonstrate this exercise.

A next level of problem-solving is **using blocks** to represent the students. Although the point is just to demonstrate that something is added to six to make ten, different colored blocks can be used to represent girls and boys.

Next, have the students **draw** the situation. The students will draw six girls, then four boys to get the total ten children.

Tables and graphs often are useful in solving problems. In more complicated algebra problem-solving, charts are frequently used to organize the information. Do you remember motion problems: rate times time equals distance? Such exercises lend themselves to organization by charting.

Although a "sloppy" way to approach a problem, **trial and error** often works. This method is also known as **guess and check.**

Students eventually represent problems with equations. The girl/boy example could be written as the equation: $6 + b = 10$. Later in their schooling, the children will represent it as: $g = 6$, $b = ?$, $g + b = 10$. Substitution will be used to solve this type of equation.

Sample Questions

Ella, Molly, Sal, and Theo each went shopping. Ella bought a book for $4.95, a pencil for $0.95, and a toothbrush for $1.14. Molly spent $6.00 for a book, $0.95 for a pencil, and $2.10 for a toothbrush. Sal paid $2.25 for a book, $5.35 for a pencil, and $2.94 for a toothbrush. Theo spent $5.20 on a book, $1.04 on a pencil, and $5.89 on a toothbrush.

Ella spent approximately _____ dollars.

Molly spent approximately _____ dollars.

Sal spent approximately _____ dollars.

Theo spent approximately _____.

1. Who spent about $10.00?

   a. Ella

   b. Molly

   c. Sal

   d. Theo

1. The preceding exercise would be useful for the teacher to use in determining if students can:

   A. multiply multi-digit numbers

   B. make change

   C. order quantities

   D. estimate sums

D In order to answer the question, students need to round off each value to the nearest dollar. Ella spends about $5 + 1 + 1 = 7$ dollars. Molly spends about $6 + 1 + 2 = 9$ dollars. Sal spends about $2 + 5 + 3 = 10$. Theo spends about $5 + 1 + 6 = 12$ dollars. So, Sal is the person who spends about $10.00. No multiplication was required, so answer A is out. No making of change was necessary; eliminate option B. Although quantities are calculated, they are not put in order, so you can eliminate answer C. Totals were estimated. The correct answer is D.

2. Midge is doing some online shopping. She picks out a $75 dress, a pair of shoes for $52, a sweater for $23, and a bracelet for $42. If the store is having a tax-free sale, how much will Midge get back from the two hundred dollars she gives the shopkeeper?

   A. $8

   B. $18

   C. $92

   D. $192

A By subtracting the total of $75 + 52 + 23 + 42$ from the $200 given to the shopkeeper, the difference is $8. The correct answer is A.

3. Steps to an algorithm follow:

Step I: $(5 \times 4) \times 2 = (4 \times 5) \times 2$

Step II: $(4 \times 5) \times 2 = 4 \times (5 \times 2)$

Which of the following correctly identifies each step?

A. I: associative; II: distributive
B. I: associative; II: commutative
C. I: commutative; II: distributive
D. I: commutative; II: associative

D The first step demonstrates a change of order. That is the commutative property of multiplication. The correct answer, then, is either C or D. The second step shows a change of grouping. That is the associative property of multiplication. The correct answer is D.

4. Mr. Hammer wants to reinforce the concept of various patterns using different modes. He asks Miss April to help him. Because she teaches music, she brings some instruments with her. They develop a pattern. Then, they come up with a code so that they can easily communicate to each other that pattern and other patterns they create. This is their legend.

Instrument	Symbol
Cymbals	C
Drum	D
Triangle	T

The pattern they created goes like this:

CDTCDDTCDDDTCDDDDT...

What instrument would next be listed in the pattern?

A. cymbals
B. drum
C. triangle
D. No pattern exists.

A Notice in the pattern that the order of the letters is C, D, T. However, each time, one more D appears. One D, then two Ds, then 3 Ds, then four Ds. Because the pattern ends with T, the next letter should be C. (C represents the cymbals.) The correct answer is A.

5. Mr. Ned, the gym teacher, asks for seven volunteers. Amy, Brad, Dean, Georgia, Inez, Mario, and Pauline step forward. He then asks for one of them to volunteer. Mario volunteers. Mr. Ned pulls over a portable white-board and hands Mario a marker. He asks the remaining six volunteers to follow his commands. He asks the girls to walk away from the group. So, the group of six loses the four girls. He asks Mario to write an equation to describe what occurred. Mario writes $6 - 4 = 2$. Mr. Ned praises the group of volunteers and asks each one to choose a replacement. Amy chooses Zach, Brad chooses Dave, Dean chooses Eva, Georgia chooses Gwen, Inez chooses Martha, Mario chooses Marco, and Pauline chooses Claude. The new group is Claude, Dave, Eva, Gwen, Marco, Martha, and Zach.

Again, Mr. Ned asks for one of those seven to volunteer. Eva steps forward. Mr. Ned asks the volunteers to follow his new command. His new command is that each person whose first name begins with a vowel should sit down on the floor. Now, of the six people, one sits down on the floor. He asks Eva to write an equation expressing that. She writes $6 - 1 = 5$. Mr. Ned then poses this question, "Using t for the total number in the group, s for the number of students who sat down on the floor, and u for the number of students still standing up, please write an equation representing what happened." Eva wrote the correct equation. Which of the following did she write?

A. $s - u = t$
B. $t + u = s$
C. $s - t = u$
D. $t - s = u$

D This scenario has a group of students (the total, t). Then, a sub-group (s) sits down on the floor. Some students (u) remain standing. So, $t - s = u$. The correct answer is D.

6. Mrs. Dutch ended class today with a review activity. She asked students to raise hands when they knew the answer. She assured them that she would call only on students who raised their hands. Her questions got progressively more difficult. "What is 5 times 6?" Jimmy correctly answered 30. "How many inches are in a foot?" Claudia was right with her answer of 12. "How many quarters make two dollars?" Eight was Liza's correct answer. "Some number is multiplied by 5. The result is 45. What is the number?" Clementine correctly answers this question. What did she answer?

A. 4
B. 9
C. 225
D. 2,025

B This could be expressed as follows: $n \times 5 = 45$. The number that has to replace n is nine, because $9 \times 5 = 45$. The correct answer is B.

Competency 014 (Geometry, Measurement, Probability, and Statistics)

The teacher understands concepts and principles of geometry and measurement and demonstrates knowledge of probability and statistics and their applications.

Review

Apply knowledge of geometrical concepts

The beginning teacher applies knowledge of spatial concepts such as direction, shape, and structure.

Understanding geometry helps to organize the world and to move about it. Spatial sense, stages of comprehension of geometrical concepts, and the four systems of geometry should be understood by the beginning teacher.

Spatial sense is comprised of seven skills. Body-eye coordination is the ability to connect what is seen with various body parts. Ground-figure perception is the ability to identify a figure surrounded by a complicated background. Perceptual constancy is the ability to recognize objects in space, regardless of their size, location, or position. Position-in-space perception is the ability to compare location of oneself with an object in space. Perception of spatial relationships is the ability to relate objects in space to one another and to oneself. The ability to compare and contrast objects is called **visual discrimination.** Remembering objects that cannot be seen is visual memory. All of these are important for spatial sense.

Children move through five stages of learning geometry. The first stage is **visualization.** In this stage, children recognize and name figures. Stage two is **analysis.** In this stage, children describe figures and objects. The third stage, **informal deduction,** involves classification of figures and objects. These three stages are noticeable during the elementary school. Children need to receive instruction in order to reach each stage.

Children typically are taught after elementary school the skills that enable them to move on to the last two stages of geometrical development. These stages are deduction and rigor. **Deduction** involves writing proofs from definitions, postulates, and theorems. **Rigor** is the stage in which students work in several geometrical systems.

The four systems of geometry are topological, Euclidean, coordinate, and transformational. **Topological geometry** deals with locations of objects relative to each other. **Euclidean geometry** involves the descriptions of figures and objects. **Coordinate geometry** places two-dimensional shapes and three-dimensional objects into a grid system. Finally, **transformational geometry** is sometimes known as **motion geometry,** because it involves moving shapes throughout space.

Identify and use geometrical formulas

The beginning teacher identifies and uses formulas to find lengths, perimeters, areas, and volumes of basic geometrical figures.

Various units of measure are used, starting with non-standard units. Examples are length of a child's stride or length of a child's hand span. Using these non-standard units, children can measure the length of a desk or the dimensions of the classroom. Children could then compare these results with those found using rulers or tape measures.

The perimeter of the classroom, playground, or school, could be measured using both non-standard and standard units of measure. These activities could be followed by measuring units of length and perimeters on blueprints of the school. Informing the parents or guardians of these activities will keep the learning alive for the children. Measuring at home would provide opportunities for parents or guardians or older siblings to reinforce the child's learning.

Areas can also be measured informally: How many yoga mats does it take to cover a portion of the classroom floor? How many sheets of construction paper must be used to cover the bulletin board?

Area can be used as an example of multiplication: Five sheets of construction paper fit across the bottom of the bulletin board. Six such rows, one row on top of the other, will cover the board. Six times five is 30 sheets of construction paper.

Of course, moving from this hands-on approach to working with a diagram representing this situation then to a diagram showing that the bulletin board is five feet by six feet builds the concept of area.

Similarly, volume can be measured with objects initially: How many beans does it take to fill the jar?

Use mathematical reasoning in geometrical applications

The beginning teacher uses mathematical reasoning to prove geometric relationships.

One such relationship is **congruence.** Two figures are congruent if they match up exactly in size and shape. Another relationship is **similarity.** Similar figures have sides that are proportional from one figure to the next. All corresponding angles in similar figures are congruent. Attribute blocks are excellent manipulatives to use to compare and contrast shapes. Children should be questioned about the relationships among these blocks: "Are all of the circles in the set congruent?" "If not, why not?" "Are all of the rectangles congruent?" "Are all of the rectangles similar?"

Geoboards (see Competency 012) should be used with children when comparing shapes. The children should be able to produce two right triangles that look very different to determine that all right triangles are neither congruent nor similar.

Understand process and accuracy of measurement

The beginning teacher understands measurement as a process, methods of approximation and estimation, and the effects of error on measurement.

Measuring is an important skill. Children need to be able to measure discrete objects and continuous properties. Discrete object counting allows students to compare sets of objects. On the other hand, also useful is comparing properties: heavier, longer, older.

Although exact values are important at times, approximates often provide enough information. In fact, measurements truly are always approximations. The way to improve precision in measurement is to use a smaller unit. Of course, more of those units will be required. However, this does improve the accuracy of the measurement. Students need to understand the importance of precision.

Children also need to appreciate the different degrees of accuracy depending upon the project. The level of accuracy varies from situation to situation. Measuring the length of material for an outfit, the length of a board for a bookshelf, the amount of sugar in a recipe, or the weight of a package all require degrees of accuracy.

A trundle wheel is fun to use with children. Children enjoy using this wheel to measure lengths. Measuring the length of the gym floor would be an excellent exercise.

Understand units of measurement in applications

The beginning teacher understands the use of numbers and units of measurement for quantities related to temperature, money, percents, and speed.

Understanding the relationships among the units of measure and the accuracy of the instruments used to find measurements is of paramount importance for elementary school children. These skills are crucial for survival. Ask: "What units should be used to measure temperature?" "Which are used to measure speed?" "What instrument should be used to measure temperature?" "Do you know what an instrument used to measure speed is called?"

The cultural aspect of units should be presented to students. Although students need not know the value of different systems of currency than their own, they should be aware that many other countries use different forms of currency than what is used in Texas. The peso is used just across the border in Mexico. Likewise, units of measures of speed differ from area to area. The speed limits for Texas roads generally are measured in miles per hour. However, in Mexico, speed limits are usually measured in kilometers per hour. Children need to have a clear understanding that different units of measure are used around the world.

Illustrate geometrical properties

The beginning teacher uses translations, rotations, reflections, dilations, and contractions to illustrate similarities, congruencies, and symmetries of figures.

Translations are sliding motions, **rotations** are turning motions, **reflections** are flipping motions, **dilations** are expansions, and **contractions** are reductions.

Similar figures have the same shape, while **congruent figures** have exactly the same size. **Symmetry** occurs when perfect matching occurs. A figure is symmetric around a line, for example, if when the figure is folded on that line, the halves exactly correspond.

Attribute blocks are ideal for working on congruence and similarity. All of the large squares are congruent; all of the little squares are congruent. The large squares and little squares are similar. Similar figures have congruent corresponding angles and proportional corresponding sides.

A set of **counting bears** also illustrates congruence and similarity. A set of counting bears contains small, medium, and large bears that all have the same shape and proportions, just different sizes. Children should be allowed to play with them and group them. Asking the child how the groups were formed reinforces the language of geometry.

Geoboards are also useful for demonstrating congruence and similarity. Right triangles are easily made. Congruence in right triangles works, provided the lengths of the corresponding sides are equal. The concept of proportion, as easy as doubling the size of the corresponding sides, can be demonstrated with the right triangles on a geoboard.

Several corporate **logos** exhibit symmetry. A good at-home assignment is to have children find examples of symmetry in magazines or on computer Web sites. Children can bring those to school and describe the symmetry to the class.

Tessellations, or tiling patterns, are repeating a shape in a systematic pattern in order to completely fill a space. Tessellations exhibit congruence. Also, the concepts of translation, rotation, reflection, and symmetry can be discussed relative to such an arrangement of shapes.

Apply knowledge of measurement conversions

The beginning teacher applies knowledge of conversions within and between different measurement systems.

Measurements within the metric system are easier to convert, because only multiplication or division by powers of ten is required. The following list of prefixes is used in the metric system.

Prefix	Meaning
milli	$\frac{1}{1,000}$
centi	$\frac{1}{100}$
deci	$\frac{1}{10}$
deka (or deca)	10
hecto	100
kilo	1,000

In fact, here is a mnemonic that helps students work within the metric system: "Kyle hurriedly drew mandolins during class Monday."

- k stands for kilo
- h stands for hecto
- d stands for deka (or deca)
- m stands for meter, the standard unit of length in the metric system
- d stands for deci
- c stands for centi
- m stands for milli

Converting from one unit to another is relatively easy, because the decimal point moves as many places as the movement in this sentence is, in the same direction. Here is an example.

$$63.45 \text{ cm} = \underline{\hspace{1cm}} \text{ km}$$

The move from *class* to *Kyle* is five places to the left. So, 63.45 cm = 0.0006345 km.

The English system of measure is more difficult. Converting from one unit to another requires knowledge of the equivalencies. The main reason for the increased difficulty of the English system is the multitude of equivalents: twelve inches equal a foot, three feet equal a yard, and 5,280 feet equal a mile.

Experiences with both systems must be provided for students to feel comfortable measuring. Children must realize that although the metric system is easier to deal with generally, our country tends to use the English system of measurement. As early as the 1800s, attempts have been made to adopt the metric system in this country. The changeover has occurred in some areas of government, industry, and science in this country. However, much of the country still uses the English system. Therefore, students must be able to work with the more difficult conversions.

Understand techniques for describing mathematical representations of data

The beginning teacher understands how to use graphical and numerical techniques to explore data, characterize patterns, and describe departure from patterns.

Tracking data begins with tallying. Simple hash marks can be used to indicate the occurrence of an event. Upon completion of this task, the hash marks are counted. This information can then be converted into a frequency table before putting the information into graphical form.

Stem-and-leaf plots provide an organized arrangement of values. Height could be easily represented in such a fashion. The stem is the left-hand column. This represents each ten's place digit of the numbers. The right-hand column, so-called the leaf, represents each unit's digit of the numbers. So, such a plot would look like the following.

2	8,9
3	0,5,5,6,7,9
4	0,1,1,1,2,4,7,9,9
5	0,0,1,1,2,3
6	0,0,1

The graphs can be **line plots,** in which each entry is represented on the graph by an x. The result is a form of a bar graph. (A graphing board is useful here.) The **bar graph** illustrates which event occurred most frequently and least frequently. It also shows any events that occurred an equal number of times. A **histogram** is the next step in presenting graphing to students. A histogram is used when data is continuous, such as ages of children in a class. A **line graph** connects the top points of each bar in a bar graph. Line graphs are most effective for showing trends in data.

Understanding the axes on a graph is important. Not only does the student need to know what each axis represents, but the student must also be aware of the units being used. Children must have a number of experiences with line graphs before they internalize the relationship portrayed in these graphs.

Circle graphs, or **pie charts**, represent the relationship that each part has to the whole. A simple circle graph can be produced by taking a circle and dividing it into equal-sized portions, each portion representing a student in the class. Eye color could be used as the attribute.

Understand probability

The beginning teacher understands the theory of probability and its relationship to sampling and statistical inference and knows how statistical inference is used in making and evaluating predictions.

Probability comes in two forms. **Mathematical probability** is based upon chance: the likelihood of an event occurring. **Historical probability** is based upon data accumulation over time.

Beginning with concepts of more likely and less likely, students begin to develop the concept of probabilities of events occurring. Weather units are useful for developing these concepts: "What is the probability of snow in July?"

A fraction is used to represent probability: $\dfrac{\text{number of times the successful event occurs}}{\text{number of attempts that were made}}$. A simple example of

probability is tossing a coin. The probability of tossing a head is $\frac{1}{2}$. The child needs to understand that there are two possible outcomes: head or tail. There is one of each. So, on one toss, the probability of tossing a head is $\frac{1}{2}$, as is tossing a tail.

Use statistics to analyze data

The beginning teacher supports arguments, makes predictions, and draws conclusions using summary statistics and graphs to analyze and interpret one-variable data.

Collected data needs to be organized. Organizing data makes it easier to make comparisons. Data can be used to back up an argument: "We need more textbooks, because the population in each grade in our elementary school is growing, as is indicated by this data set." Data can be analyzed in different ways, depending upon the question to be answered. Such terms as mean, median, mode, range, and outlier are used in descriptive statistics.

- The **mean,** or **arithmetic mean,** is the average of the values. Adding up the values and dividing by the number of values gives the mean. This number uses every value in the data set.
- The **median** is the middle value in the set. In order to determine the median, the values must first be put in order from smallest to biggest. Then, the middle value is selected. If there is not a middle value, the average of the two middle values is taken to be the median.
- The **mode** is the value that occurs most frequently. The number of times that an event occurs is called its **frequency.** A set may not contain a mode, if no value occurs more than the others. On the other hand, a set may have more than one mode. If more than one value shares the highest frequency, then each of those values is considered a mode.
- The **range** is found by subtracting the smallest value in the data set from the largest value in that set.
- An **outlier** is a data value that is far from the other values in that particular set. A score of 10% on a test that others scored above 70% on would represent an outlier.

A graph is a picture of data. Comparisons are readily made by viewing graphs. The most frequently occurring value is easily seen, for example.

Looking at trends in data, an individual is able to make predictions. Although one must take care in using data as a predictor, one can tentatively plan for the future. Care must be taken to assure that any trend is likely to continue.

Apply probability to situations

The beginning teacher knows how to generate and use probability models to represent situations.

A **probability tree** represents all of the possible combinations of outcomes. Options for sandwiches (choices of meats, breads, cheeses, vegetables, condiments) can be illustrated with a probability tree.

Samples are used to draw conclusions about an entire population by investigating a portion of the population. Surveys are taken using a sample. Because survey results are used to make decisions about the entire population, the sample must be representative of the entire population. The people selected to complete the survey must be representative of the entire population: males/females, city-dwellers/country-dwellers/suburbia-dwellers, families with children/families without children, pet-owners/non-pet-owners. The uses of the survey results dictate the guidelines used to create the sample.

Simulations can be used to determine the probability of an event. Care must be taken to represent the actual event as accurately as possible.

Use a normal distribution graph

The beginning teacher uses the graph of the normal distribution as a basis for making inferences about a population.

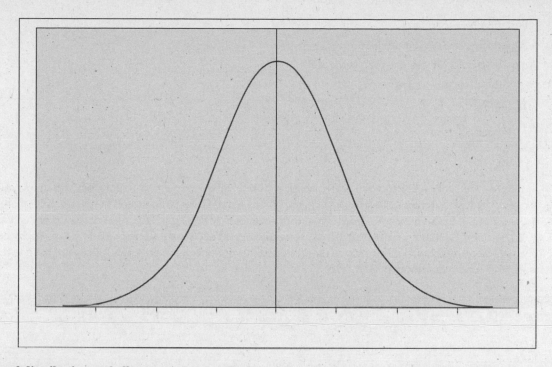

The **normal distribution,** or **bell curve,** is a representation of a norm-referenced event. The curve is highest in the middle, where the values have the greatest frequency. The midpoint of the curve is the mean of the data set. It is also the median. The values away from the center are determined by the calculated standard deviation. All of the values within one standard deviation of the mean, below and above, represent approximately 68% of all of the values in the normally-distributed data set. The values within two standard deviations approximate 95% of all of the values in the normally-distributed data set. Approximately 99.7% of all values in the normally-distributed data set fall within three standard deviations of the center.

The mean represents the 50th percentile, which means that one-half of the students scored below this value and one-half of the students scored above this value. It is generally agreed that students scoring between the 16th and 84th percentiles are performing within the average range. Although below average is below the 16th percentile, it is generally assumed that students performing below the 35th percentile actually would benefit from extra help. These students have not demonstrated adequate competency with the material being evaluated.

The height of the curve decreases as one moves away from the center. The curve is symmetric about the mean.

Sample Questions

1. Which of the following statements is/are true?

    I.   All rectangles are squares.
    II. All quadrilaterals have four sides.
    III. A parallelogram always has four equal sides.
    IV. Every rhombus is a square.

    A. I, II, and IV
    B. II only
    C. I and IV only
    D. IV only

    B Statement I is false. Some rectangles are squares; not all rectangles have four equal sides, which is required of a square. So, because statement I is false, eliminate choices A and C. Answers B and D remain. Statement II is true. A quadrilateral has to have four sides. Therefore, statement II belongs in the final answer. That is it; choice B is right. By the way, statement III is incorrect. A parallelogram need not have four equal sides. Statement IV is also false. A square has four right angles. A rhombus may have four right angles, but it does not have to have four right angles. The correct answer is B.

2. The temperature at a given location in the south at 2 p.m. each August 10th for ten consecutive years was measured to be (in degrees Celsius) 33, 38, 34, 29, 31, 29, 28, 39, 29, and 30. What is the mean?

    A. 29
    B. 30
    C. 32
    D. approximately 33

    C The mean, or arithmetic mean, is the average. The average is calculated by dividing the sum of all values in the set by the number of values in the set. In this case, $\frac{33 + 38 + 34 + 29 + 31 + 29 + 28 + 39 + 29 + 30}{10} = \frac{320}{10} = 32$. The correct answer is C.

3. Daphne is trying to decide which sweater to wear today. She has narrowed down her selection to her favorite pink sweater, the light blue sweater with pockets, her navy sweater with the loon pattern, and the green sweater she bought in Iceland. What is the probability she will choose the loon sweater?

    A. $\frac{1}{3}$
    B. $\frac{1}{4}$
    C. 1
    D. 3

    B The probability is represented by a fraction. The bottom number, the denominator, is the total number of choices. In this case, she has a choice of four sweaters from which to choose. The top number, the numerator, is the number of desired choices. The loon sweater is what is desired: There is one such sweater. The answer, then, is $\frac{1}{4}$. The correct answer is B.

4. The following normal distribution curve represents the graph of the scores on Mr. Zepter's first test on division facts. The highest score on the test was 99%; the lowest grade was 52%. The average was 82%. What score belongs in place of the A on the graph?

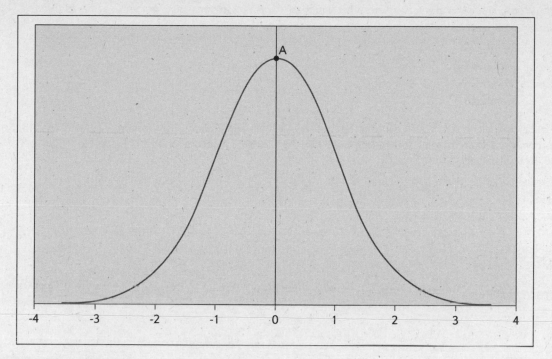

A. 52%
B. 75%
C. 82%
D. 99%

C The normal distribution is highest in the middle of the graph. That high value occurs at the mean of the data set. The mean is the average. Therefore, the A on the graph should be 82%. The correct answer is C.

5. This is the stem-and-leaf plot for a data set. What is the median of the set?

2	8,9
3	0,5,5,6,7,9
4	0,1,1,1,2,4,7,9,9
5	0,0,1,1,2,3
6	0,0,1

A. 33
B. 40
C. 42
D. 43

D The median is the middle value in the set of data, when that set is put in order from smallest value to largest value. The values in this set are: 28, 29, 30, 35, 35, 36, 37, 39, 40, 41, 41, 41, 42, 44, 47, 49, 49, 50, 50, 51, 51, 52, 53, 60, 60, and 61. The set includes 26 values. Because there is no middle value, the median is the average of the two middle values: $\frac{42+44}{2} = \frac{86}{2} = 43$. The correct answer is D.

161

6. Baxter is helping Mr. Emerald, the principal, get ready for the Mayflower Elementary School Annual Carnival. Baxter measured a desk and found it to be about 22 inches long. Mr. Emerald told Baxter that he wanted the measurement in centimeters instead of inches. Mr. Emerald told Baxter that every inch contained about 2.54 centimeters. He asked Baxter to determine which of the following answers best approximated the desk's measurement in centimeters.

A. 11 centimeters
B. 25 centimeters
C. 56 centimeters
D. 66 centimeters

C Every inches contains 2.54 centimeters, and 2.54 is between 2 and 3. Multiplying 22 by 2 gives 44. So, choices A and B are too small. Multiplying 22 by 3 gives 66. Therefore, choice D is too big. ($22 \times 2.54 = 55.88$) The correct answer is C.

Competency 015 (Mathematical Process)

The teacher understands mathematical processes and knows how to reason mathematically, solve mathematical problems, and make mathematical connections within and outside of mathematics.

Review

Understand applications of reasoning

The beginning teacher understands the role of logical reasoning in mathematics and knows methods and uses of informal and formal reasoning.

Informal reasoning is done via hands-on activities. Observing the world and manipulating objects is the first step in reasoning. Reasoning becomes more formalized as the steps in the reasoning process are noted.

Reasoning is crucial in problem-solving. Students spend a lifetime using their problem-solving skills. Even babies "figure out" how to achieve their goals. Granted, they cannot communicate specifically what they want. However, they do communicate that they need something.

Making connections between attributes and shapes is an exercise young children accomplish. If it has three sides, they reason, it is a triangle. As they get older, children are able to fine-tune their reasoning in order to more specifically describe triangles placed before them. An equilateral triangle is three-sided, with all three sides equal.

Discussing mathematics with children allows the teacher to get a sense of how the children are thinking about and reasoning through the exercises placed before them. As an elementary-school child writes down his thought processes for the mathematics he does, he is preparing for the more formalized proofs he will do during his high school years. Teachers should ask open-ended questions to encourage this reasoning. Communication about mathematics supports this learning and should be both written and spoken. Group work necessitates communicating about mathematical processes. One-on-one time with individual students allows the teacher the opportunity to determine how each child is thinking about the mathematics the child is learning.

During class, when asking questions, remember to wait for responses. Students need time to think through what they want to say and how to say it. If students know that they will be expected to explain their rationale for an answer, they will put thought behind it. Also appropriate is the request for different approaches. This will remind students that more than one approach works. If a child answers incorrectly, give credit for the portion of the answer that is correct. Then, gently ask others to continue the explanation. Also, teachers should talk through their own thought processes when working through exercises in class so that students can witness thought processes.

Discourse in the written form is also important. Students need to be able to express their thoughts on paper.

Apply reasoning to derive conclusions

The beginning teacher applies correct mathematical reasoning to derive valid conclusions from a set of premises.

The validity of an argument is based upon its form. A conclusion must be drawn from accurate premises in order to form a valid argument.

Paying attention to the thought process a child goes through is one way in which teachers utilize their own reasoning skills. Teachers need to understand the process students use to come up with correct answers. Therefore, teachers need to know how each step in the learning process is approached and mastered. Building on the strengths of the students and taking time to review their weaknesses provides lasting positive results.

Apply principles of reasoning

The beginning teacher applies principles of inductive reasoning to make conjectures and uses deductive methods to evaluate the validity of conjectures.

Exploring mathematics and providing justification is part of learning mathematics. Induction involves combining pieces of information to form conclusions. Induction flows from specific tidbits of information to general rules. Categorizing shapes is an excellent activity for induction.

Deduction, on the other hand, requires the student to go from a rule to specifics. Some informal deductive vocabulary includes "all," "some," and "none." If all quadrilaterals have four sides, then using deductive reasoning, the student recognizes that a square is a quadrilateral.

Evaluate arguments and recognize fallacious reasoning

The beginning teacher evaluates mathematical arguments and recognizes examples of fallacious reasoning.

Mathematical arguments must be formed from true premises and organized logically. A fallacy is an error in reasoning, the structure of the argument.

The teacher must understand the importance of mapping the reasoning each child uses to make conclusions. Understanding the errors in reasoning helps the teacher determine the best way to help the student. Students may need to work on supplemental exercises in order to correct their errors in reasoning. An astute teacher will recognize patterns of errors and provide remediation accordingly.

Understand connections among areas of mathematics

The beginning teacher understands connections among concepts, procedures, and equivalent representations in areas of mathematics (for example, algebra, geometry).

Students need to be able to communicate an understanding of a concept in addition to being able to perform its corresponding procedure. Unless a student understands the theory behind the concept, the procedure is meaningless. The goal is for students to grasp the meaning behind the procedure, and then to use the procedure for problem-solving. In addition, students need to appreciate that more than one approach will result in the correct answer.

Furthermore, concepts may be presented using several different approaches. Multiplication can be presented as repeated addition: four 7s means seven added four times. However, geometrically, four 7s could be represented as 4 rows of 7 each. This could be demonstrated concretely with blocks or semiconcretely with pictures or Xs.

The teacher needs to keep in mind the developmental level of each child in order to optimize learning.

Understand applications of mathematics in other areas

The beginning teacher understands how mathematics is used in other disciplines and in daily living.

The connection between mathematics and some disciplines is obvious: measuring in science, studying shapes and lines in art. However, the connection to other disciplines may not be as clear. The following chart outlines some connections.

Subject	Mathematics-Related Activities
Art	Draw to scale rooms in a house
	Produce tessellations
	Use *Turtle Math* and *Logo* to produce artwork
Health	Keep a chart of height and weight
	Graph calorie intake for a week
Language Arts	Find words that display symmetry: eye, radar, redder
Life Skills	Use units of measure in cooking
	Measure board length in construction
Physical Education	Chart numbers of push-ups each day for a week
	Graph times for students in a running race
	Convert units of speed: feet per minute to yards per second
Science	Track outdoor temperatures at 10:00 AM for a week
	Measure quantity of rain in one month
	Convert quantity of rain from inches to feet and to centimeters
Social Studies	Draw a map from home to school
	Chart/graph/compare distances from each child's home to school

Know how to use manipulatives and technological tools

The beginning teacher knows how to use mathematical manipulatives and a wide range of appropriate technological tools to develop and explore mathematical concepts and ideas.

Manipulatives are compulsory in the elementary classroom. Teachers need to know how to most effectively utilize these manipulatives. The teacher must be sure that the manipulatives support the lesson, that the students know how to correctly use the manipulatives, that every student is actively involved with the materials, and that evaluation of the development of reasoning skills is undertaken.

Although several manipulatives are available for purchase, many items commonly found in an elementary classroom can be used in mathematics instruction. Blocks and chips are useful in many lessons.

One of the advantages of commercial manipulatives is the inclusion of sample class exercises. Also, many manipulative sets offer manageable storage units that allow easy, organized access to the students.

Examples of commercial manipulatives are abacus, attribute blocks, Dienes (base-10) blocks, chip trading materials, compasses, Cuisenaire rods, dice, double-arm scale, geoboards, graphing boards, measuring cups and spoons, number scale, pan balance, pattern blocks, play money, playing cards, protractors, rulers, spinners, tangrams, thermometers, trundle wheel, and Unifix cubes.

Technology should also be used to support learning in the elementary classroom. The use of technology is a powerful means of demonstrating many of the concepts presented to youngsters. Computer software can be used for drill, games, problem-solving, remediation, and simulation. Of course, calculators have their place in the elementary classroom, provided teachers do not allow their use as a substitute for mental arithmetic. If a calculator is used as a tool for exploration of patterns and relationships, it fills a need in the elementary classroom. Also, its use in problem-solving is valuable.

Any use of manipulatives or technology should not stand alone. The use of these important tools should complement the teacher's effort.

Demonstrate knowledge of the development of mathematics

The beginning teacher demonstrates knowledge of the history and evolution of mathematical concepts, procedures, and ideas.

Understanding the development of mathematics aids the teacher in developing effective learning units. Hand-in-hand with this is the teacher's comprehension of theories of learning. Use of this combined knowledge paves the way for a successful teaching/learning experience.

Mathematics was once taught as a series of steps to be memorized. It was presented as a single entity, without concern for connections to other disciplines. The focus was arriving at the correct answer, without all that much concern for process.

This approach was gradually combined with the use of manipulatives and of applications to real-life and to other areas of study. Connecting mathematics to problem-solving in other disciplines and to the real world gave mathematics a purpose.

Now, combining historical perspectives and teaching/learning theory, teachers are able to develop lessons that students enjoy, that build on student skills, that involve other areas of study, and that show the importance of mathematics in the real world.

Psychologists have spent over a century observing people master skills and create new concepts. Theories of learning have arisen from these observations.

- **Behaviorism** is the study of learning theory as a mental discipline. These psychologists espoused the theory that the mind is a muscle that needs to be exercised. This school of psychology studied the connection between stimulus and response without any reference to conscious experience. Behaviorists include Edward Thorndike, Ivan Pavlov, and Burrhus Frederic Skinner.

- **Cognitive psychology,** on the other hand, takes into account the mental processes that occur during the stimulus/response connection. These mental processes involve imagining, learning, memorizing, perceiving, reasoning, remembering, and thinking. Jerome Bruner, Jean Piaget, and Richard Skemp were cognitive-development theorists.

- **Meaning theory,** William Brownell's brain-child, focuses on the belief that learning has to be understood in order for it to be permanent. Marilyn Burns and Zoltan Dienes also focused on meaning.

- **Information-processing** is another approach to studying learning. This theory compares a human's learning with a computer's inner workings. Information transferred into the human's long-term memory from short-term memory is similar to saving information from a computer's RAM.

- **Brain-based learning** is rooted in the concept that the brain discovers patterns and builds relationships among concepts. In addition, the brain allows for adaptations in previously learned concepts as new relationships develop.

Understanding the development of mathematics and the methods used to present it to students should assist the teacher in presenting material most effectively to students.

Recognize contributions to and the impact of mathematics

The beginning teacher recognizes the contributions that different cultures have made to the field of mathematics and the impact of mathematics on society and cultures.

Today's mathematics has its roots in other cultures. As well, advances in mathematics around the world enhance not only the study of mathematics but also its application.

Studying the history of mathematics helps make mathematics come alive for some students. What mathematics history can be studied in the elementary classroom? The following list offers some suggestions:

- Algebra of the Tehranians
- Geometry of the Greeks
- Number systems of the Arabs, Babylonians, Egyptians, Romans, and Welsh
- Pi work done by the Chinese
- Practical arithmetic of the Egyptians
- Trigonometry of the Greeks

The world has progressed to the extent that it has due, in large part, to the contributions of mathematics. The competitive nature of humans has accelerated us several times in history. Take the Soviet Union's Sputnik, for example. That event sparked curriculum change in this country, and similar events have motivated us to increase the extent and depth of our curriculum in order to keep up with, or surpass, that of other countries.

Sample Questions

1. An elementary school teacher is trying to determine whether his students can give approximate descriptions of the dimensions of large shapes: a rectangular room, a circular pond. Which of the following manipulatives would be the most sensible to use?

   A. geoboards
   B. trundle wheels
   C. attribute blocks
   D. Cuisenaire rods

   B Choices A, C, and D are too small to use. A trundle wheel, however, is ideal. The students can walk around the shape, listening to the clicking sound. Trundle wheels usually click every yard (36 inches), or every meter (100 centimeters). The correct answer is B.

2. Miss Fitz wants to know whether her students understand the chronology of the development of these forms of technology: abacus, calculator, laptop, Palm Pilot, slide rule, adding machine. Which of the following would illustrate best this ordering?

   A. calculator
   B. calendar
   C. timeline
   D. stopwatch

   C The focus is on time, so a calendar, timeline, or stopwatch should be used. Because one of the forms of "technology" dates as far back as 300 B.C., something that illustrates years is needed. A calendar typically shows a year's time. A stopwatch most frequently is used for minutes and seconds, certainly not years. A timeline should be used. The correct answer is C.

3. Miss Plebo asks each of her students to take a book from the bookshelf and to open it to any page. They are then to list any word that displays symmetry. Which of the following display(s) symmetry?

   I. bob
   II. map
   III. deed
   IV. motor

   A. III only
   B. I and II
   C. I and III
   D. I, III, and IV

   C Imagine slicing down the center of the o in "bob." Each half would have a b and one-half an o. Therefore, the word in I exhibits symmetry. The answer is B, C, or D. The word "map" does not exhibit symmetry, so II should not be in the answer. Choice B is not correct. Both remaining choices include III, which is correct, because "deed" exhibits symmetry, evidenced by slicing it right down the middle, between the two e's. Check "motor." That word does not exhibit symmetry, so do not include IV. The answer must be I and III. The correct answer is C.

4. You and your pals go out for lunch. You decide that leaving a 20% tip is appropriate. The bill comes to $97.56. Which of the following represents an easy way to calculate the tip without a calculator?

   A. Divide $98 by 2.
   B. Multiply $98 by 2.
   C. Multiply $98 by 10, then double it.
   D. Multiply $100 by 10, double it, and divide by 100 by moving the decimal point twice to the left.

D Although choice D has several steps, that method is the easiest approach to calculating the correct tip. The real way to do the calculation is to convert 20% to a decimal, by dividing by 100, then multiplying $97.56 by that. (The efficient way to convert a percent to a decimal is to move the decimal point twice to the left.) Another way to officially solve this problem is to use the proportion: $\frac{\text{percent}}{100} = \frac{\text{part}}{\text{whole}}$. The setup would be $\frac{20}{100} = \frac{\text{tip}}{97.56}$.

Setting the products of the diagonals equal results in

$$100\,(\text{tip}) = 20\,(\$97.56)$$

$$100\,(\text{tip}) = \$1951.20$$

$$\frac{100\,(\text{tip})}{100} = \frac{\$1951.20}{100}$$

$$\text{tip} = \$19.5120$$

Because the tip is to be *approximate*, rounding the bill amount to $100 will be close enough. So, multiplying by 10 would result in $1,000. Doubling it gives $2,000. Finally, dividing by 100 ends in a tip of approximately $20. Clearly, the method in option A, dividing $98 by 2, $49, would result in a tip that is too generous. The method in option B, resulting in $196, would definitely be far too generous. The method in option C would result in a tip of $1,960. That is far too large. Answers to real-life exercises must make sense. The correct answer is D.

5. Paba wants to compare, using Roman numerals, the ages of everyone who lives in his house. He knows the following table of equivalents.

Roman	Hindu-Arabic
I	1
V	5
X	10
L	50
C	100
D	500
M	1,000

Mr. Ladis shows him examples of different numbers:

3 = III

4 = IV

9 = IX, Paba's age

43 = XLIII

97 = XCVII

Paba comes up with the following:

Cherie, his baby sister, is II.

Denver, his older brother, is XVI.

Mama is XXXVIII.

Papa is XLV.

Gramma is LXXVIII.

Grampa is LXXXIV.

What is the difference between Grampa's age and Denver's age?

A. LXII
B. LXX
C. LXVIII
D. CXXII

C One approach to this is to convert each age to our system. Denver is 16, while Grampa is 84. The difference between them, 84 – 16 = 68. Now, converting 68 to Roman numerals: LX is 60 and VIII is eight. The answer is LXVIII. The correct answer is C.

6. Which of the following is true?

A. No parallelograms are squares.
B. Some squares have four equal sides.
C. All squares have four acute angles.
D. A rhombus could be a square.

D Choice A is incorrect, because although not all parallelograms are squares, some are. Choice B is not correct, because all squares have four equal sides. Choice C is incorrect, because all squares have four right angles. (An acute angle measures less than the 90° that are required in a right angle.) Choice D is correct, because a rhombus by definition has four equal sides. If that rhombus had two adjacent sides that were perpendicular, that shape would be a square. The correct answer is D.

Competency 016 (Social Science Instruction)

The teacher uses social science knowledge and skills to plan, organize, and implement instruction and assess learning.

Review

Know state content and performance standards

The beginning teacher knows state content and performance standards for social studies that comprise the Texas Essential Knowledge and Skills (TEKS) and understands the vertical alignment of the social sciences in the TEKS from grade level to grade level including prerequisite knowledge and skills.

There are many ways to define social studies. The TEKS was developed on the basis of the following definition: "Social studies is the integrated study of the social sciences and humanities to promote civic competence." Several aspects of this definition are important.

First, the content of social studies is **integrated,** in the sense that it draws together a variety of disciplines in a coherent way. The primary disciplines are history, geography, economics, government (political science), and culture (which includes anthropology, psychology, and sociology), although other disciplines such as philosophy and law influence the content of social studies.

Second, the purpose of social studies is to promote **civic competence**—that is, helping young people develop the ability to make informed and reasoned decisions for the public good as citizens of a culturally diverse, democratic society in an interdependent world. Social studies is not just abstract or theoretical knowledge; rather, it consists of knowledge, skills, and values that help create productive and engaged citizens. In short, good citizenship is a major goal of social studies education.

The TEKS for social studies are organized around eight strands: history; geography; economics; government; citizenship; culture; science, technology, and society; and social studies skills. The first five strands represent the disciplines mentioned earlier; the sixth and seventh strand are themes, and the eighth strand consists of skills that are informed by the other seven strands. The eighth strand covers a broad range of skills, including the correct use of social studies terminology, the identification of different perspectives on an issue, and the effective use of problem-solving strategies. All of the strands are important at each grade, although some are emphasized more than others depending on grade level or class. An important development in social studies education in recent years, reflected in the TEKS, is increased emphasis on helping students consider multiple perspectives on historical events.

The TEKS for social studies is horizontally aligned across a range of interdisciplinary knowledge and skills. Vertical alignment is also reflected, in that the social studies curriculum is meant to be consistent and cumulative across grade levels. The vertical alignment of the TEKS for social studies can be simplified as follows:

- Kindergarten: Self, family, classroom
- 1st grade: Classroom, school, and local community
- 2nd grade: Local community, Texas, nation
- 3rd grade: Communities past and present, including Texas and the nation
- 4th grade: Texas in the western hemisphere

The vertical organization of the TEKS reflects the expanding horizons curriculum model. To a great extent, the content is sequenced so that children learn about social studies in an increasingly broad range of settings, beginning with themselves, their family, and their classroom, and then incorporating their school and community, other communities, Texas, and its relationship to the nation and to other countries.

Understand the stages of childhood growth and development

The beginning teacher understands the implications of stages of child growth and development for designing and implementing effective learning experiences in the social sciences (for example, knowledge of and respect for self, families, and communities; sharing; following routines; working cooperatively in groups).

Teachers should be aware of the stages of growth and development that distinguish students of different ages. Between kindergarten and 4th grade, a number of important changes take place in knowledge and skills. Reviewed here are four of the most fundamental types of change during this time period:

- First, as children get older, they become increasingly able to grasp abstract ideas. Young children tend to be concrete thinkers. Concepts such as society, democracy, and citizenship are difficult for young children to grasp and should be introduced as simply and concretely as possible. For example, the concept of good citizenship may be defined in terms of how children interact with their classmates in the context of sharing materials, taking turns, and other concrete activities. To take a different example, younger students will be very attuned to the physical details of national symbols such as the flag, but they may find it difficult to grasp the symbolic meaning of the details without considerable support from the teacher.

- Second, over time, children become increasingly good at perspective-taking. Young children are somewhat egocentric, in the sense that they find it difficult to view the world from other perspectives. However, the ability to adopt and evaluate multiple points of view is an essential goal of social studies instruction. Teachers should create learning experiences that have immediate personal relevance to the lives of individual students. Discussions of society, for example, should be solidly grounded in discussions of the classroom and family. Likewise, the motives of historical figures are more easily grasped when framed in terms of classroom or family interactions. By doing so, the ability to take the perspectives of other people can be advanced.

- Third, as children get older, their spatial skills improve. Younger students struggle with the spatial relationships depicted in visual representations such as maps. Mapping can be introduced to younger students by helping them describe objects on a wall or table with positional terms (near/far, above/below, left/right, in front of/behind, far/near). As children become more sensitive to position and positional terms, they acquire basic mapping skills through the creation and use of maps that represent familiar places, such as the classroom and the playground.

- Fourth, as children get older, their knowledge base gradually increases. Part of the difficulty younger children have with maps, for example, is their lack of familiarity with conventions of representation such as keys, symbols, lines of latitude and longitude, and so on. Owing to their greater knowledge and experience, older students can interpret keys and other features of maps with less support from their teachers.

Each instructional activity should be responsive to these and other kinds of differences between younger and older students. Learning experiences that are concrete, personally relevant, and responsive to each student's cognitive level help make social studies material more accessible, and scaffold the development of more abstract and less egocentric thinking. For younger children, that means classroom-based activities (for example, creating maps of the classroom), personally directed activities (for example, the construction of personal genealogies to help students understand chronological time), and other practices that are sensitive to each student's knowledge and skills.

Select effective, developmentally appropriate materials

The beginning teacher selects effective, developmentally appropriate instructional practices, activities, technologies, and materials to promote children's knowledge and skills in the social sciences.

EC–4 teachers should make use of a variety of practices, activities, technologies, and materials in teaching social studies. The goals of social studies instruction are extremely diverse: Teachers attempt to convey factual knowledge, concepts, principles, values, perspective-taking, research skills, and the capacity for critical thinking, problem-solving, and decision-making.

Following are just a few components of an effective teacher's repertoire.

- Along with **direct instruction,** teachers should promote **interactive and collaborative learning experiences,** including class discussion, reciprocal teaching, and cooperative learning activities such as partnering and jigsaw techniques. Cooperative learning activities are important to the teaching of any subject; they are especially relevant for social studies instruction, because they allow children to make use of social skills, they illustrate social interdependence in a concrete way, and they can help students appreciate multiple perspectives on situations and events.

- **Role-play** is particularly useful in helping students learn about historical figures, consider other points of view, and obtain hands-on insight into social interactions. Role-play can be relatively simple, or it can involve the development of formal plays, **sociodramas** (dramatizations centering on emotional or social dilemmas), and other complex activities. Role-play is particularly relevant to social studies instruction given the consistent focus of this field on people and social issues.

- **Simulations** (realistic settings that call for realistic decision-making) also engage students in hands-on experience dealing with practical scenarios and interactions. Simulations may consist of games organized by the teacher or computer software programs that simulate realistic situations. An advantage of simulations is that they permit exploration and experimentation that may not be possible, or wise, in real-life situations. For example, economic concepts can be conveyed by simulations in which students play roles such as shopper, business owner, and producer.

- **Field trips** to museums, historical sites, and interesting geographic settings provide students with learning experiences outside the classroom, along with opportunities to relate classroom learning to real-life experiences.

The materials that social studies teachers use should consist of not only textbooks but also a variety of primary and secondary sources. Written materials may include biographies, folk tales, historical fiction, myths, legends, and other literary genres. Written materials may also include articles from news media, official documents, transcribed speeches, letters, journals, diaries, and other nonfiction sources. Visual materials such as posters, transparencies, maps, photographs, political cartoons, videos, charts, figures, tables, graphs, and timelines are integral to social science instruction. Visual arts, songs, and dance can also play an important role. Multimedia presentations, such as news reports, videos, and simulations can be presented by means of TVs, VCR or DVD players, and/or PCs, and the use of computer technology, ranging from CD-ROMs to Web sites, has become essential in recent years.

The use of a variety of activities and materials presents content while stimulating student interest and providing accessible and engaging material for students who represent a variety of learning styles and ability levels. At the same time, regardless of activities and materials used, it is important for social studies teachers to discuss current events and recent advances in knowledge. The state of knowledge in social studies is continually changing. As a result, it is sometimes necessary for the teacher to extend or update information in textbooks and other materials. The National Council for the Social Studies (NCSS; see www.ncss.org) is an important resource for helping teachers keep up with recent developments in this field.

Select and use appropriate technology

The beginning teacher selects and uses appropriate technology as a tool for learning and communicating social studies concepts.

Technology plays a dual role in social studies instruction. Technology is a tool that contributes to the learning of social studies. In addition, the development of technology and its impact on human cultures is one of the topics that is covered in social studies units.

Along with the print and visual media discussed earlier, a variety of computer-related technologies are available for communicating social studies concepts.

- Interactive software actively engages students in both instruction as well as in problem-solving and decision-making activities. Tutorial programs function like interactive textbooks and can be used to learn a variety of different kinds of content and skills. Problem-solving programs encourage students to make use of problem-solving and other analytical skills (for example, for locating a missing person) in the context of social studies content such as map-reading. Simulation programs create—or allow students to create—situations that are as realistic as possible. Students make decisions in these situations and observe the practical consequences of their decisions.

- Word processing and related software allow students to generate reports, presentations, spreadsheets, and other products. Database software helps students organize data and generate calculations.

- Internet access opens the door to a variety of resources, including news reports, archival materials, databases, maps, videos, virtual tours, educational games, newsgroups, listservs, and blogs, as well as e-mail. A number of Internet sites for children focus exclusively on social studies.

Teachers should make use of a variety of technologies when teaching social studies concepts. The particular technologies used should be appropriate to each child's level, and should be accompanied by technological support when needed. For example, younger students may need guidance in the operation of a PC in order to make effective use of interactive software.

Select and use instructional strategies, materials, and activities

The beginning teacher selects and uses instructional strategies, materials, and activities, including appropriate technology, to promote children's use of social science skills and research tools.

Some of the instructional strategies, materials, activities, and technologies for teaching social studies are particularly useful for promoting social science skills and research capabilities. A few of the instructional approaches of particular relevance to research-related skills are discussed here.

Through **inquiry teaching**, teachers ask and then help students answer questions by proposing hypotheses, gathering and evaluating data, and generating conclusions. Inquiry teaching is essential to the development of critical thinking, as well as to an appreciation of the scientific method (discussed in detail in Competency 020). In social studies instruction, inquiry teaching becomes increasingly important in helping students solve problems and make decisions about real-life issues.

The classroom should contain resources that promote research skills. Maps, globes, atlases, reference books, audiovisual materials, and computer software are among the resources of relevance to social studies instruction.

Through the use of reference materials in the classroom, and through trips to the library, students develop their research skills. These activities help students learn basic distinctions in the kinds of information available from different sources. Some of the distinctions mastered at the elementary level include the distinction between fact and opinion, between relevant and irrelevant information, and between primary and secondary sources. Students also learn where to find different sources, and how to use features such as tables of contents, indices, appendices, references, and so on. Finally, students learn how to formulate questions, obtain and evaluate data, and generate useful conclusions.

Provide instruction that relates skills, concepts, and ideas

The beginning teacher provides instruction that relates skills, concepts, and ideas in different social science disciplines.

Social studies is fundamentally interdisciplinary. Although some strands of the TEKS are emphasized more than others at particular grade levels, EC–4 teachers at each grade cover material that reflects the different content areas of social studies inquiry.

Thematic units play an important role in social studies instruction, because they promote the interdisciplinary approach that is essential to the field. A thematic unit is an extended instructional plan organized around a central idea. For example, a teacher may develop a thematic unit on China and Chinese customs. Such a unit would have multiple objectives. By locating China as well as individual Chinese provinces on a map, students would obtain practice using map skills. By seeing pictures and videos from China, reading stories about Chinese children, and learning how to write a Chinese character, students would learn about similarities as well as differences between cultures, as well as some of the ways that culture influences how people talk, think, and meet their basic needs. By discussing differences in the customs of different regions of China, students could learn about the relationship between geographic conditions and cultural adaptations. These are just a few of the activities that could be incorporated into a thematic unit.

Help children make connections between knowledge and methods

The beginning teacher helps children make connections between knowledge and methods in the social sciences and in other content areas.

As with any other content area, social studies will be integrated with the language arts curriculum. There are many opportunities for teachers to promote literacy through social studies instruction. New vocabulary will be taught. Children will be exposed to different linguistic styles and written genres. And teachers will have students respond to primary sources in their journals, written reports, and class discussions.

When students explore the cultural and historical meaning of specific works of art, music, and literature, and when they create art projects, songs, stories, and poems, social studies is integrated with the study and practice of fine arts.

Discussions of economic topics such as business, industry, and trade often require the incorporation of mathematical skills, as do discussions of geography, political science, and related disciplines.

There is substantial interplay between the social and natural sciences. Scientific research and theory informs our understanding of human behavior. Historical discussion often requires consideration of both the context for scientific and technological innovations, as well as the impact of scientific and technological advancement on human societies. Discussions of geography often rely on research in areas such as geology and meteorology. Discussions of economics are frequently grounded in basic mathematics. Pollution, STDs, genetic engineering, and overpopulation are just a few of the specific topics that inevitably concern both science and social studies.

Use a variety of assessments

The beginning teacher uses a variety of formal and informal assessments and knowledge of the TEKS to determine children's progress and needs and to help plan instruction for individual children, including English Language Learners.

Teachers must consider individual differences when designing and implementing learning experiences within a particular class. Differences in learning styles and other cognitive dimensions, in cultural background, in family belief systems, and in experiences with siblings and peers are among the factors that have important implications for how teachers create and implement learning experiences.

Teachers must be sensitive to diversity among students in order to provide the best possible academic and social environment for individual students. At the same time, diversity is part of the focus of social studies instruction. The social studies curriculum includes attention to various cultures, as well as the influence of those cultures on Texas and U.S. history. Cultural diversity in the classroom provides an opportunity for teachers to make the curriculum more personally relevant by encouraging individual students to share their unique cultural heritage and by modeling respect for and interest in different cultural backgrounds.

Knowledge of TEKS performance standards, as well as both formal and informal assessments, can be used by teachers to determine whether an individual student needs extra support. Along with tests, performance assessments that teachers can use include reports, projects, portfolios, and demonstrations of specific skills. In the case of the English Language Learner, social studies instruction can be integrated with instruction in English. (See Competency 001 for further discussion.)

Sample Questions

1. A 1st-grade teacher introduces a unit on geology by explaining, in very simple terms, the differences between the three types of rocks (igneous, metamorphic, and sedimentary), and then helping students memorize a simple definition associated with each type. What change to the teacher's instructional approach would benefit children most?

   A. Because young children are concrete thinkers, they would benefit from learning new vocabulary and academic content on separate occasions rather than simultaneously.

   B. Because young children have poor perspective-taking skills, they would benefit from a prior explanation of why scientists want to distinguish between different types of rocks.

   C. Because young children are concrete thinkers, they would benefit from hands-on experience with different types of rocks.

   D. Because young children are visual thinkers, they would benefit from a visual representation, such as a drawing, of different types of rocks.

   C Option A is incorrect. Although young children are relatively concrete thinkers, it is not necessarily difficult for them to learn new vocabulary and academic content simultaneously. In fact, integration of social studies and language arts is an important part of the elementary curriculum. Option B is also incorrect. Although young children do have relatively poor perspective-taking skills (and would probably not know why scientists distinguish between types of rocks) simply expanding the teachers' introduction would be counterproductive, because it consists entirely of verbal explanation. Option D is incorrect, in spite of the fact that it would better for the teacher to present a drawing of rocks, as opposed to no visual image at all, while discussing them. Although option D reflects an improvement, it is not the best option, because children still have no opportunity to experience actual rocks. Option C is the correct answer. Because young children are relatively concrete thinkers, it would be essential for them to be able to look at and actually handle rocks as part of their introduction to geology.

2. What is the focus of social studies curriculum at the 4th-grade level?

   A. the student's local community
   B. the state of Texas
   C. the United States
   D. the world

   B Option A is incorrect, because the local community is the focus of instruction at earlier grades. Options C and D are incorrect owing to their breadth. Although the vertical organization of the TEKS reflects increasing breadth of topic across grade levels, the primary focus of 4th-grade social studies instruction is the state of Texas in the context of the western hemisphere and, thus, option B is the correct answer.

Competency 017 (History)

The teacher demonstrates knowledge of significant historical events and developments and applies social science skills to historical information, ideas, and issues.

Review

Know major reference points in Texas, U.S., and world history

The beginning teacher knows traditional points of reference in the history of Texas, the United States, and the world.

History is the study of the material record of the past. By studying the past, students gain insight into their present lives. Knowing the choices and decisions that have been made by their predecessors helps students make wise choices and decisions in response to contemporary situations.

One approach to the organization and teaching of historical material is chronological. For example, Texas history from the 16th through the 19th centuries can be divided into the following periods:

- Spanish Texas (1519–1821)
- Mexican Independence (1821–1835)
- Texas Revolution (1835–1836)
- Republic of Texas (1836–1845)
- Antebellum Texas (1846–1861)
- Civil War (1861–1865)
- Reconstruction (1866–1877)

Each of the periods listed contains one or more traditional points of reference. To take one example, Spanish Texas begins with the first exploration and mapping of the Texas coastline in 1519 and includes Spanish exploration and settlement of Texas, as well as the period of Spanish rule that lasted from 1716 until 1821.

In a similar way, chronological divisions can be used as the basis for organizing United States and world history along traditional points of reference.

Historical material can also be organized by thematic rather than chronological divisions. For example, the Bradley Commission on History in Schools identifies six essential themes in the study of history:

- **Conflict and cooperation:** This theme concerns international and domestic relations, causes and effects of war, policies on isolation and interdependence, and related topics. In a unit on international conflict, for example, a teacher may discuss the War for Independence from Mexico as an example of a conflict that stemmed in part from a clash between colonists and established residents.

- **Comparative history of major developments:** This theme concerns the characteristics of political systems, periods, and practices across time and place, such as revolutionary, reactionary, and reform periods; systems of feudalism and centralization; and so on. In a unit on slavery, for example, the role and treatment of African-American slaves in the cotton industry in Texas may be compared and contrasted to the role and treatment of slaves in other agricultural industries in America, as well as in other countries at different points in time.

- **Patterns of social and political interaction:** This theme concerns shifting patterns of ethnicity, race, social class, and gender, including patterns of immigration, migration, and social mobility, forms of multiculturalism, and the relation of women, minorities, and poor people to political power. For example, in a unit on the history of Texas government, the stories of prominent female politicians such as Ma Ferguson, Barbara Jordan, and Ann Richards may be discussed and compared.

- **Civilization, cultural diffusion, and innovation:** This theme concerns the development and spread of skills, technologies, scientific advances, artistic achievements, political systems, cities, and other manifestations of culture. For example, a discussion of the central role of petroleum in the world economy of the 20th century may begin with a discussion of the rapid development of the oil industry in Texas at the turn of the century.

- **Human interaction with the environment:** This theme concerns the relationship between geography and culture, including the cultural effects of different climates and regions, and the roles of technology, agriculture, and disease in economic, social, and political change. For example, in a unit on Native Americans in Texas prior to Spanish colonization, the adaptations of each tribal group to their particular geographic region of Texas could be compared and contrasted.

- **Values, beliefs, political ideas, and institutions:** This theme concerns the origins and spread of religious beliefs, ideologies, political systems, and social institutions, with some emphasis on democratic societies and the particular tensions they experience. For example, in a unit on Texas government, parallels could be drawn between the challenges addressed by the development of the Texas and U.S. Constitutions, such as the need for a Bill of Rights in each document in order to protect citizens from the power of the central government.

Know individuals, events, and issues in Texas history

The beginning teacher demonstrates knowledge of the individuals, events, and issues that shaped the history of Texas.

Following is a brief chronology of some of the individuals, events, and issues that shaped Texas history from the 16th through the 19th centuries. This is not meant to be a complete or representative list but rather a sketch of what a representative list may be like:

1519: Alonso Alvarez de Pineda explores and maps the Texas coastline.

1528: Cabeza de Vaca is among the first Europeans to explore the Texas interior.

1682: Corpus Christi de la Isleta, the first of many Spanish missions, is established near El Paso.

1821: Mexico gains independence from Spain.

1821: Stephen F. Austin establishes the first Anglo-American colony, the "Old Three Hundred."

1830: Mexico forbids the entry of further U.S. settlers into Texas.

1835: The struggle for the independence of Texas begins with the Battle of Gonzales.

1836: The Texas Declaration of Independence is created and signed.

1836: At the Battle of the Alamo, losses include David Crockett, Jim Bowie, William Travis.

1836: Santa Anna is routed by General Sam Houston at the Battle of San Jacinto.

1836: Sam Houston is elected first President of the Republic of Texas.

1839: The Texas Congress meets for the first time in Austin, the new capital of the Republic.

1845: Texas is admitted to the Union as the 28th state.

1846: The current Lone Star flag is flown for the first time.

1846: The Mexican-American War is fought over claims to the southern boundary of Texas.

1850: In the Compromise of 1850, Texas relinquishes territory and acquires its present shape.

1861: Texas secedes from the Union and joins the Confederacy.

1870: Texas rejoins the Union.

1876: The current Texas State Constitution is ratified.

1901: Oil is discovered at Spindletop oil field, initiating the modern petroleum industry.

Understand the history of pre-colonial Native-American groups

The beginning teacher understands similarities and differences among Native-American groups in Texas and the Western Hemisphere before European colonization.

Estimates of when the first native peoples came to Texas are frequently revised in light of new evidence. Currently, it is believed that at some point between 10,000 and 12,000 years ago, migrants from Asia crossed the land bridge formerly connecting Asia to America and eventually settled in areas such as modern-day Texas. These nomadic peoples were foragers and hunters of large game, and they developed a variety of simple weapons and tools.

During the Archaic period, extending from roughly 6,000 B.C. to 500 A.D., several groups of Native American tribes occupied Texas. (Competency 018 contains a description of the regions described here.)

- On the Coastal Plains were **Coahuiltecans,** hunters and gatherers who lived in temporary huts but often moved in search of food. The Coahuiltecans appeared to have lived in small family groups rather than tribes.

- Along the Texas coast were **Karankawas,** who also lived in family groups and had a somewhat nomadic lifestyle. Both the Coahuiltecans and the Karankawas ate roots and bulbs of wild plants, deer, rabbits, birds, and other wildlife. In addition, the Karankawa ate fish, turtles, and oysters.

- The peoples of the **Trans-Pecos** region lived in rock shelters. Unlike the Coahuiltecans and the Karankawas, who each created distinct shelters using sticks, poles, animal skins, and reed mats, the peoples of the Trans-Pecos built houses that were relatively permanent. Their houses reflected the relatively extreme desert climate in which they lived. Half of each house was typically underground and walled with adobe, in order to provide a cooler environment. The people of the Trans-Pecos were farmers, but also fished in nearby rivers and traveled to the plains to hunt bison.

- The **Caddos** lived in the Coastal Plains, in an area known as the Piney Woods. Owing to the greater rainfall and richer soil of this region, the Caddos were able to grow crops such as beans, squash, corn, pumpkins, melons, and tobacco. Their main crop was corn, which they boiled, roasted, or ground into meal that was used to make bread. Hunting and fishing were an additional source of sustenance for the Caddo. Like the peoples of the Trans-Pecos, the Caddo built houses that were relatively permanent. Their houses were constructed out of cedar frames, with willow poles and grass fastened to the frames as covering. The Caddos worshipped in large, wooden temples built on flat-topped earthen mounds. The Caddo word for friends or allies is *Tejas*. It is from this word that the name of our state is derived.

At the time of the Spanish exploration of Texas in the 16th century, a variety of other Native American tribal groups existed. Some of these groups were clearly identified by European settlers. For example, the **Tonkawas** were nomadic buffalo hunters and gatherers who lived in central Texas. Other groups, such as the **Atakapans** and **Jumanos,** were not clearly identified. In some cases, the label used to identify a group represented a language rather than a specific tribe.

During the 18th and 19th centuries, many of the Native American groups in Texas were displaced or destroyed by Spaniards advancing from the south, Apaches retreating from the northwest, and conflict with other Native American tribes. European diseases such as smallpox, diphtheria, and measles sometimes moved ahead of the Spanish settlers, decimating many of the Native American groups. Hostilities with Republic of Texas and Texas State governments led to additional destruction and displacement of tribal peoples. Although some tribes were being driven to extinction, others such as the **Shawnee** and the **Kickapoo** migrated to Texas during this time as a result of pressures experienced elsewhere. In the 1850s, provisions were made for the establishment of the first reservations.

Among the tribal groups in Texas who were not driven to extinction during the 18th and 19th centuries were the **Apache,** the **Cherokee,** the **Comanche,** the **Kiowa,** the **Pueblo,** the **Wichitas,** and many others.

Understand European exploration and colonization

The beginning teacher understands the causes and effects of European exploration and colonization of Texas, the United States, and the Western Hemisphere.

The 15th and 16th centuries are often referred to as the **Age of Exploration.** Although this is not the only time that European countries engaged in exploration and colonization, for many countries, it was a period of intense and more or less sustained exploratory activity in the Western Hemisphere. For example, the Spanish established colonies in South America, Mexico, Texas, and Florida; the French established colonies in Canada and along the Mississippi River; and the English colonized the east coast of the United States.

The motivation for exploration and colonization varied from country to country and time to time. For example, the earliest European contact with modern-day Texas was the mapping expedition of **Alonso Alvarez de Pineda,** who sailed along the Gulf Coast in 1519 in search of a strait to the Pacific Ocean. Other Spanish expeditions came to Texas in search of gold and other material resources, trade routes, or a suitable place to establish colonies.

Among the first French explorers in America, **Rene-Robert Cavelier, Sieur de La Salle** came to present-day Texas by mistake in 1685 while attempting to establish a colony that would aid France in the war against Spain. In the early 18th century, French explorers came to Texas in order to establish overland trade routes with the Spanish in Mexico. In the 19th century, French immigrants came to the Republic of Texas in search of more favorable political and economic conditions.

The effects of Spanish, French, and English exploration of Texas were extensive and multifaceted, particularly in areas where colonization took place. Some of the effects of colonization were clearly positive, in that many of the early colonies formed the basis of prosperous communities and significant cultural exchange. However, the alienation, displacement, and/or destruction of indigenous peoples were among the clearly negative effects of colonization in Texas and elsewhere.

Understand the historical importance of geography and diffusion

The beginning teacher knows how geographic contexts and processes of spatial exchange (diffusion) have influenced events in the past and helped to shape the present.

Both physical environments as well as cultural exchange have had a major impact on history. These general concepts are readily applied to analyses of historical trends. The ongoing interaction between Hispanic and Anglo cultures in Texas over the past five centuries provides numerous examples of the exchange of ideas, language, and cultural practices. (See Competency 018 for further details on diffusion, acculturation, and the relationship between geography and culture.)

Know about major discoveries in science, math, and technology

The beginning teacher demonstrates knowledge of the origins and diffusion of major scientific, mathematical, and technological discoveries and the effects of discoveries throughout history.

Through individual creativity and cultural transmission, major scientific, mathematical, and technological discoveries and inventions have gradually spread throughout much of the world.

For example, a few of the important discoveries and inventions during the first half of the 20th century are as follows:

1903: The Wright Brothers make the first powered flight.

1906: William DeForest invents the vacuum tube.

1908: Henry Ford begins mass production of the automobile.

1920: KDKA-Pittsburgh becomes the first commercial radio station on the air.

1922: Insulin is created by Canadian researchers.

1927: The first successful television transmission takes place in New York.

1928: Alexander Fleming discovers penicillin.

1932: Wallace Carothers invents nylon.

1935: Radar is developed by Robert Watson-Watt.

1936: Significant oil fields are discovered in Saudi Arabia.

1947: Researchers at Bell Labs invent the transistor.

The scientific and technological advances that most significantly affect our lives often reflect complex and interrelated developments. For example, the concept of electricity developed gradually and reflected contributions by Plato, William Gilbert, Benjamin Franklin, Luigi Galvani, Alessandro Volta, and many others over a period of millenia. In 1831, Michael Faraday figured out how to generate electric current on a practical scale. Four decades later, Thomas Edison invented the direct current generator, as well as the phonograph and one of the first incandescent light bulbs. Since Edison's time, our lives have been profoundly altered by electrical devices ranging from light bulbs to refrigerators, televisions, and computers. At the same time, major industries such as transportation and communication have come to rely heavily on electronic devices.

Relate historical content to other disciplines

The beginning teacher relates historical information and ideas to information and ideas in other social sciences and in other disciplines.

The teaching of history involves numerous points of connection with other disciplines. For example, the development of political systems such as socialism and capitalism over the past three centuries cannot be understood without reference to concepts of government, basic principles of economics, and influential ideas in the history of philosophy.

The teaching of history also involves significant attention to scientific and technological progress. The causes and effects of the industrial revolution, for example, must be understood in the context of 18th-century science and technology, just as the historical importance of the computer requires a consideration of 20th- and 21st-century science and technology.

Finally, the teaching of history involves discussions of geography, mathematics, art, and social sciences such as psychology, sociology, and anthropology. For example, Napoleon's unsuccessful invasion of Russia in 1812 reflects the influence of geography on warfare, the sociology of military organization, and the role of personal charisma, and other psychological variables, in the decision-making of political leaders.

Know how to formulate and answer historical research questions

The beginning teacher knows how to formulate historical research questions and use appropriate procedures to reach supportable judgments and conclusions.

Through contact with historical materials such as textbooks, photographs, journals, letters, artifacts, historical sites, museums, and other sources, EC–4 teachers formulate—and help their students formulate—historical research questions. Teachers and students then obtain and examine historical data, note gaps in the data, and evaluate the data from both a contemporary perspective as well as the perspective of the original time and place. Based on qualitative and perhaps also quantitative analysis, teachers and students form judgments and conclusions that are carefully reasoned and based on the available evidence.

Understand how historical research is carried out

The beginning teacher understands historical research and knows how historians locate, gather, organize, analyze, and report information using standard research methodologies.

As noted, historians make use of scholarly books and articles, autobiographies, eyewitness accounts, letters, diaries, official documents, news reports, databases, artifacts, historical sites, and works of art as sources of historical information.

Know characteristics and uses of primary and secondary sources

The beginning teacher knows characteristics and uses of primary and secondary sources used for historical research (for example, databases, maps, photographs, media services, the Internet, biographies, interviews, questionnaires, artifacts), analyzes historical information from primary and secondary sources, and evaluates information in relation to bias, propaganda, point of view, and frame of reference.

Primary sources of information consist of actual records and first-hand accounts of events and experiences. For example, primary sources of information about the creation of the Declaration of Independence include letters written by Thomas Jefferson and other members of the Continental Congress, Jefferson's autobiography, eyewitness accounts of exchanges between key delegates, and, of course, the actual Declaration itself.

A key advantage of primary sources is that they bring history to life. Primary sources include real objects and records, as well as the personal accounts of historical figures. Through primary sources students can encounter the lives of significant individuals, including their manner of speaking, attitudes, dilemmas, social relationships, and responses to the events and situations that are summarized in textbooks and other secondary sources. Another advantage of primary sources is that they are often useful in helping students appreciate differences in point of view, bias, rhetorical intent, and frame of reference.

Secondary sources of information consist of descriptions and explanations that are created after a historical event has already taken place. Secondary sources of information about the creation of the Declaration of Independence, for example, would include history textbooks currently in use, scholarly analyses of how the Declaration of Independence evolved, and other sources created after the fact.

Secondary sources of information rely on primary sources. Although secondary sources are, by definition, created after the fact, a key advantage of these sources is that authors can often present a more complete description of events than provided in primary sources. Secondary sources can present background information, commentary, and analysis that are indispensable to an understanding of primary sources. In addition, secondary sources can sometimes provide a more balanced or diversified set of perspectives on historical events than could be found in a primary source, because authors of secondary sources often attempt to be as impartial and/or inclusive as possible.

Apply evaluative skills to historical content

The beginning teacher applies evaluative, problem-solving, and decision-making skills to historical information, ideas, and issues.

Social studies skills include the ability to use problem-solving strategies for identifying problems, gathering information, generating options, weighing the pros and cons of specific options, and evaluating the effectiveness of solutions. Likewise, social studies skills include the ability to use decision-making processes to identify situations that require decisions, to gather information, evaluate options, predict consequences, and take action.

The EC–4 teacher uses a variety of evaluative, problem-solving, and decision-making skills in the evaluation as well as teaching of historical content. Following are some examples:

The teacher evaluates historical materials on dimensions such as completeness, coherence, authenticity, authority, and credibility.

The teacher evaluates the values, motives, perspectives, and positions of key contributors to historical events, analyzes the problems and situations they faced as well as their responses, and considers the alternative courses of action that were available to them.

The teacher distinguishes between relevant and irrelevant historical antecedents to an idea or event, considers multiple causes, and traces the influence of the idea or event forward in time.

The teacher distinguishes between fact, inference, interpretation, and opinion, addresses debates and other differences of opinion, and identifies levels of confidence in conclusions drawn from historical materials.

Know how to communication historical content

The beginning teacher knows how to communicate and interpret historical information and ideas in written and graphic form.

It is essential that teachers know how to interpret and communicate historical content to their students effectively. For example, teachers should be able to understand, create, and explain graphic representations such as charts, figures, maps, and timelines.

One of the challenges that is particularly important for teachers of history is to instill a sense of historical change. Although even the youngest students have some sense of time and sequence, their ability to appreciate the chronological order of events is limited, especially when the events in question are not personal ones but rather part of general history. Helping students acquire chronological thinking is thus an important goal at the early elementary level.

Graphic aids for chronological thinking include calendars, timelines, and visual representations of historical periods, changes over time, and genealogies. Young children learn about time and how to structure events chronologically through the creation and examination of calendars and timetables for class events, through the process of learning how to tell time, through the construction of genealogies of their own families, and through a variety of other concrete, personal means. As with other aspects of social studies instruction, fostering the development of chronological thinking should begin with the students' own lives.

Another challenge of particular importance to the teaching of history is to help children appreciate historical patterns and trends. Because patterns and trends tend to be abstract and somewhat removed from children's immediate concerns, it is important for teachers to ensure that the material is presented in a concrete and relevant way. For example, when introducing the Civil War, it would be helpful to discuss the life, interests, and motives of key figures such as Abraham Lincoln, so that the historical trends leading up to the war can be understood in concrete, human terms.

Understand how to analyze historical data

The beginning teacher analyzes historical data (for example, population statistics, patterns of migration, voting trends and patterns) using appropriate analytical methods.

In some cases, historical data is presented in mathematical or graphic form, and cannot be understood or interpreted without the use of simple analytical methods. These methods are discussed in the corresponding sections of Competencies 018 and 019.

Sample Questions

1. Which of the following would be a primary source of information about the Texas Constitution?

   A. a description of the Texas Constitution found in a textbook
   B. an excerpt from the Texas Constitution
   C. an editorial, written this year, calling for an additional amendment to the Texas Constitution
   D. all of the above

   B Option A is an incorrect option, because the textbook contains a summary written after the fact. Likewise, option C is incorrect, because it contains reference to the Constitution long after its creation. (An editorial may be a primary source of information about current opinions among Texas residents, but it is not a primary source of information about a document that is over a century old.) Because A and C are incorrect, option D must be incorrect as well. Option B is the correct answer. An excerpt from the actual Constitution is a primary source.

2. Which of the following would be the best approach to defining the term "colony"?

   A. The teacher could write a simple definition on the board, ask students to memorize the definition, and then introduce some examples of the colonization of Texas in the 16th and 17th centuries.
   B. The teacher could ask students for a definition, and then lead a discussion of any responses that children provide.
   C. The teacher could read the class a story about a family in one particular colony, such as Jamestown, and discuss the meaning of terms such as "colony" as they arise.
   D. The teacher could describe the material conditions in a particular country, such as 16th-century Spain, in order to illustrate the purpose that the establishment of colonies would serve.

   C The term "colony" denotes a relatively complex, abstract concept. Option A is incorrect, because it is not particularly engaging, and because it would not provide children with a very concrete description of the concept. Likewise, options B and D would not result in a very concrete description. Option C is the correct answer, because it would present children with a narrative context in which the concept of a colony would take on a concrete and personal meaning.

Competency 018 (Geography and Culture)

The teacher demonstrates knowledge of geographic relationships among people, places, and environments in Texas, the United States, and the world; understands the concept of culture and how cultures develop and adapt; and applies social science skills to geographic and cultural information, ideas, and issues.

Review

Know and apply key concepts in geography

The beginning teacher applies knowledge of key concepts in geography (for example, location, distance, region, grid systems) and knows the locations and characteristics of places and regions in Texas, the United States, and the world.

Geography is the study of the earth and its inhabitants. **Physical geography** concerns the physical environments of the earth, while **cultural geography** focuses on the relationships between people and their physical environments. Thus, physical geography incorporates information from fields such as geology and meteorology, while cultural geography includes information from sociology, anthropology, and other social sciences.

The Committee on Geographic Education has identified five interrelated themes that organize the teaching of geography: location, place, relationships within places, movement, and regions.

- **Location** includes concepts of absolute and relative location with respect to people and places on the earth. Locations can be described by means of **grid systems,** or sets of lines that cross each other at right angles. There are many types of grid, or coordinate systems. For example, **geographic coordinate systems** use degrees of latitude and longitude to describe location. One of the most commonly used grid systems on world maps is the **universal transverse mercator system,** which preserves the shapes of land masses (at the expense of distortions in size at the periphery of the map).

- **Place** includes physical and cultural characteristics that distinguish and give meaning to each place on the earth. **Topography** refers to descriptions of the physical characteristics of land masses, including elevation, slope, and orientation. The topography of a region is determined to a great extent by tectonics, weathering, and erosion.

- **Relationships within places** are about relationships between humans and their particular environments. Each environment on the earth poses distinct challenges to its human inhabitants. The way people adapt to their surroundings reflects a unique interaction between the characteristics of their environments and their particular cultural beliefs and practices. Thus, in extreme desert conditions, one may expect to find relatively sparse populations as well as shelter, clothing, and water management practices that are adapted to extremely hot and dry conditions. In a more temperate environment, one would expect to find a greater population density, and adaptations to a different set of conditions.

- **Movement** concerns interactions between humans through migration, communication, trade, and other forms of contact, each of which may result in interdependence, cultural diffusion, and/or acculturation.

- **Regions** include subdivisions of the world on various political, cultural, and geographic dimensions. Identification of countries, linguistic preferences, and biomes would be some examples of the kinds of regions that can be identified.

Understand geographic patterns and processes

The beginning teacher understands geographic patterns and processes in major historical and contemporary societies and regions of Texas, the United States, and the world.

According to the Texas Almanac for 2004–2005, Texas is 268,581 square miles in size, making it the second largest state with about 7% of the total area of the United States. The highest point in Texas is Guadalupe Peak (8,749 feet) while the lowest point is found in all the coastal counties, which are at sea level. The largest city in Texas is Houston, with a population of nearly 2 million inhabitants. Major Texas rivers include the Rio Grande, the Red River, and the Brazos River.

Texas consists of four geographic regions.

- The **Great Plains** region is in the Texas Panhandle, the northernmost part of the state. The Great Plains region, which is generally flat and treeless, includes the High Plains, the Edwards Plateau, and the Hill Country (Llano Basin).

- Directly below the Great Plains, extending to the Gulf of Mexico and along the east coast of Texas is the **Gulf Coast Plains.** The Gulf Coast Plains region includes Piney Woods, the Post Oak Belt, the Blackland Prairie, the Gulf Coast Plain, and the South Texas Plains. This relatively humid region is a lowland area that contains pine forests, extensive agriculture, and the port of Houston, one of the largest in the world.

- To the west of the Great Plains is the **Trans-Pecos** region (sometimes called **Big Bend Country**), which occupies the southwestern part of the state. This region is dry and, unlike the rest of the state, quite rocky and mountainous.

- Between the Great Plains and the Gulf Coast Plains, but not extending as far as the Gulf of Mexico, is the **North Central Plains.** The North Central Plains region includes Cross Timbers, Grand Prairie, Rolling Plains, and Prairies and Lakes. This region also contains the Edwards Aquifer, the most productive aquifer in the U.S. and a major source of water for drinking as well as agriculture and industry.

Just as there are other ways to subdivide the geographic regions of Texas, so North America and the world can be divided in different ways. For example, North America can be divided into eight geographic regions based on topographic features. Proceeding in a roughly west-to-east direction, these regions are as follows:

- Coastal Range (rugged Pacific Coast mountains)
- Basin and Range (isolated mountains and Death Valley)
- Rocky Mountains (rugged, high mountains)
- Great Plains (relatively flat grasslands)
- Interior Lowlands (rolling flatlands and hills)
- Canadian Shield (eroded hills and glacial lakes)
- Coastal Plains (broad lowlands)
- Appalachian Mountains (old, eroded mountains)

The physical geography of the world can be categorized by oceans, continents, countries, hemispheres, and/or **biomes,** or bioclimatic zones. There are many ways to categorize biomes. A simple approach is represented by the distinction between marine, desert, forest, grassland, and tundra environments. A more elaborated approach includes the following regions:

- **Tropical rainforest:** Rainforests are characterized by year-round high temperatures, relatively great precipitation, and highly diverse plant and animal life.

- **Tropical dry forest:** Tropical dry forests are characterized by year-round high temperatures, a dry season, and more deciduous tress than found in tropical rainforests.

- **Savanna:** Savannas (or savannahs) are characterized by year-round high temperatures, highly seasonal rainfall, and mostly tropical grasslands with scattered trees.

- **Desert:** Deserts are characterized by generally high temperatures (although they may be cold during nights and winters), low precipitation, and many adaptations to drought conditions.

- **Steppe:** Steppes are characterized by temperate environments, seasonal variation in precipitation, vegetation dominated by grasslands, and relatively little diversity in plant and animal life.

- **Temperate forest:** Temperate forests are characterized by temperate environments with seasonal variation in precipitation, rich soils, and primarily deciduous trees.

- **Taiga:** Taigas are characterized by cold winters with considerable snow, less diversity in plant and animal life than other forested areas, and primarily coniferous trees.

- **Tundra:** Tundra is characterized by long winters, severe winds, limited sun, permanently frozen ground, poor soils, and relatively little diversity in plant and animal life.

Know physical processes and their environmental effects

The beginning teacher demonstrates knowledge of physical processes (for example, erosion, weather patterns, natural disasters) and their effects on patterns in the environment.

Tectonics is the branch of geology that concerns the structure of the earth's crust, as well as changes that take place in the crust over time as a result of folding and faulting. The theory of **plate tectonics** holds that the earth's crust consists of about 20 plates that drift, collide, and separate over long periods of time. The edges where plates meet experience intense geological activity, including mountain building and earthquakes. The theory of plate tectonics accounts for **continental drift** (change in the positions of continents over long periods of time) as well as **sea-floor spreading** (the creation and movement of new oceanic crust at mid-ocean ridges).

To a great extent, the topography of a place reflects tectonic processes. Weathering and erosion are also responsible for a variety of topographic features. **Weathering** is the breaking down of physical material. **Erosion** is the breaking down and removal of physical material. Sources of erosion include wind, water, ice, and gravity. Erosion can result from solution (as when water dissolves minerals in rock), hydraulic forces (as when wind beats against a cliff), abrasion (as when ice scrapes against a rock), attrition (as when a river drives pebbles into its bank), and other agents. Erosion that results from human activity is referred to as **accelerated erosion** and constitutes a major source of topographic change.

Topography concerns the characteristics of land above water as well as on the ocean floor. **Meteorology** is the branch of earth science that concerns **climate** (average weather conditions over relatively long periods of time), **weather** (atmospheric conditions over a short period of time) and the earth's atmosphere more generally.

The earth's atmosphere is composed primarily of nitrogen (78%), oxygen (21%), and argon (1%), and consists of five main layers.

- The **troposphere** extends from the surface of the earth to about 5 to 9 miles above the surface. This is the most dense layer of the atmosphere, and it is the location of almost all weather.

- The **stratosphere** extends from just above the troposphere to about 31 miles above the earth's surface. This layer, which is drier, hotter, and less dense than the troposphere, contains the ozone layer. (**Ozone** is a form of oxygen that absorbs harmful ultraviolet radiation from the sun.)

- The **mesosphere** extends from just above the stratosphere to about 53 miles above the earth. Although the troposphere and stratosphere are referred to jointly as the lower atmosphere, the mesosphere is sometimes called the middle atmosphere.

- The **thermosphere** extends from just above the mesosphere to about 372 miles above the earth's surface. Auroras are found in this layer. Owing to the energy of the sun, the temperatures here can exceed 400 degrees Fahrenheit.

- The **exosphere** is the thinnest and most remote layer of the atmosphere, extending from just above the thermosphere to about 40,000 miles above the earth. Together, the thermosphere and exosphere are referred to as the outer atmosphere.

Because no landform on earth is higher than the troposphere, most human activity takes place in that level of the atmosphere. One exception is commercial air traffic, much of which occurs in the lower part of the stratosphere. Other exceptions include weather balloons, which may travel into the stratosphere; satellites, which are found at more than one level; and NASA's space shuttle, which orbits in the thermosphere.

Understand the effects of human adaptation to the environment

The beginning teacher knows how humans adapt to, use, and modify the physical environment and knows how the physical characteristics of places and human modifications to the environment affect human activities and settlement patterns.

Humans depend on their immediate physical surroundings for air, water, food, and mineral resources. We alter the environment through the construction of houses and commercial buildings; through irrigation and the planting of crops; through the building of roads, bridges, and tunnels; through the use of fossil fuels; and through many other cultural practices. In the process of meeting our basic needs, we damage the environment in many ways, and then we often take steps to heal the damage we create. Reforestation, environmental clean-up efforts, conservation of animal and plant life, responsible agricultural practices, and governmental regulations on emissions are just a few of the ways we attempt to reverse some of the damage the environment has sustained.

The characteristics of the particular environment in which we live influence our interactions with the environment as well as the specific ways we meet our basic needs. Cross-cultural comparisons, analyses of migration, and other anthropological methods can reveal how human activities and settlement patterns are influenced by the physical geography of specific environments.

Understand concepts of culture, diffusion, and exchange

The beginning teacher understands the concept of culture and the processes of cultural diffusion and exchange.

Cultural diffusion is the transmission of objects, ideas, and behaviors from one society to another. The effects of diffusion can be seen in language, architecture, clothing, cuisine, religious beliefs, and many other cultural phenomena.

Cultural diffusion results from migration, trade, visitation, cross-cultural marriages, and written communication. In some cases, diffusion is highly specific. The adoption and widespread use of a foreign word would be an example of a highly specific cultural diffusion. In other cases, a more general set of beliefs, skills, or practices is transmitted. For example, writing, agriculture, the smelting of iron, and computer technology are among the most important forms of cultural diffusion in the history of human civilization.

Cultural diffusion can be distinguished from **acculturation,** in which one society adopts a great deal of another society's culture. (The term acculturation is also used to describe how a child acquires the cultural beliefs and practices of his or her own culture.)

The difference between diffusion and acculturation is largely a matter of degree. The relationship between the cultures of England and France, for example, or the cultures of China and Japan, reflects processes of cultural diffusion, because each culture has incorporated elements from the other one while maintaining a separate identity In contrast, some Native American groups have experienced acculturation, as a result of being forced to give up their land, language, and cultural practices.

As the Native American example illustrates, one cause of acculturation is political or military dominance. However, it is not always the case that the dominant society imposes its culture on a society that it has overpowered. In some cases, the dominant society becomes acculturated. For example, after the Mongols occupied China in the 13th century A.D., they quickly adopted many aspects of Chinese culture.

Recognize multicultural contributions to different cultures

The beginning teacher understands the contributions of people of various racial, ethnic, and religious groups to Texas, the United States, and the world and demonstrates knowledge of the effects of race, gender, and socioeconomic class on ways of life in the United States and throughout the world.

As in other parts of the United States and the world, males and females of various racial, ethnic, religious, and socio-economic backgrounds have had a significant impact on the development of Texas.

The phrase **six flags over Texas** refers to the fact that the flags of six governments have flown over Texas. These are Spain (1519–1685; 1690–1821), France (1685–1690), and Mexico (1821–1836) as well as the Republic of Texas (1836–1845), the Confederate States of America (1861–1865), and the United States of America (1845–1861; 1865–present). Along with the contributions of Spanish, French, and Mexican people and cultures, African-Americans have had a significant influence since first coming to Texas as part of the 16th century Spanish expeditions. Predating all of these groups are the influences of the various Native American tribes (discussed under Competency 017).

Standing alongside the important males in Texas history are a number of prominent women, including Jane Long (1798–1880), referred to as the **mother of Texas,** because she is reputed to have been the first Anglo to bear a child in Texas (in 1821).

Other firsts among Texas women include Ma Ferguson (1875–1961) and Barbara Jordan (1936—1996).

- Ma Ferguson was the first of only two women to serve as governor of Texas. Ma Ferguson served as governor from 1925 through 1927 and then again from 1933 to 1935. Although she was not the first woman to serve as a U.S. governor, she was the first woman to achieve that position by election. (The only other woman to be elected governor of Texas was Ann Richards, a former social studies teacher and public official who served as governor from 1991 through 1995.)

- Barbara Jordan was the first African-American woman from a southern state to serve in Congress when she was elected to the House of Representatives in 1973. In 1974 she played a prominent role in the Watergate hearings, and in 1976 she became the first woman to deliver the keynote address at the Democratic National Convention.

Understand cultural similarities and differences in adaptation

The beginning teacher understands similarities and differences in how various peoples at different times have lived and met basic human needs, including the various roles of men, women, children, and families in past and present cultures.

The basic human needs are often defined as food, clothing, and shelter. Different peoples have met these basic needs in different ways, as a result of the interplay between their physical environments and their cultural beliefs and practices. For example, climate and other aspects of local geography influence what people eat, what kinds of clothing they wear, and how they construct their houses and other forms of shelter.

The size and structure of families, as well as the roles played by various family members, vary widely across time and place and reflect the influence of geographic conditions. For example, at the turn of the 19th century, the majority of Americans lived in rural areas and worked the land with their families. School was not compulsory at this time, and as a result, most children joined their parents in agricultural work as soon as they were able.

In the 19th and 20th centuries, industrialization resulted in the rapid expansion of cities as well as shifts in the roles of family members. The majority of men began to work outside the home in factories, businesses, and other organizations. Public education became compulsory, so that the majority of children were now educated outside the home. However, women were rarely employed during this time and, consequently, their primary role became the maintenance of a domestic life for their families.

In the past half-century, the roles of women in particular have changed and become more diverse as a result of their entering the work force in increasing numbers, along with other factors such as the increasing incidence of single motherhood.

Relate geographic content to other disciplines

The beginning teacher relates geographic and cultural information and ideas to information and ideas in other social sciences and in other disciplines.

The study of geography is inherently interdisciplinary. For example, physical geography is informed by sciences such as geology, meteorology, and astronomy. Cultural geography is informed by social sciences, such as psychology, sociology, anthropology, history, as well as by the study of architecture and the arts. The history of Texas, for example, was molded by interactions between diverse cultures; contact between particular cultures and particular geographic regions; the development of natural resources such as cotton, cattle, and oil; the decisions of talented and ambitious individuals; and many other factors.

Know how to formulate and answer geographic research questions

The beginning teacher knows how to formulate geographic and cultural research questions and use appropriate procedures to reach supportable judgments and conclusions.

A variety of approaches and materials can be used to formulate and answer questions about physical and cultural geography.

For example, the teacher should know how to interpret maps and other visual aids in order to measure the distance between two places, to decide which of two countries has a proportionally larger area of rainforest, to document migratory patterns over time, and to make other kinds of informed judgments.

The teacher should know how to use observational strategies to identify landforms, cloud types, biomes, and other geographic patterns.

The teacher should also be able to summarize and apply quantitative information, such as information about climate and weather reported in an almanac, which can be used to make predictions about the kinds of clothing and shelter preferred in a particular region at particular times of the year.

Understand how geographic research is conducted

The beginning teacher understands research relating to geography and culture and knows how social scientists in these fields locate, gather, organize, analyze, and report information using standard research methodologies.

Social scientists who study geography and culture make use of a variety of both quantitative and qualitative research methodologies.

Direct observation is essential to the description of topographic features, cultural practices, and social behaviors. Through observation, social scientists may create case studies, or develop **ethnographies,** which are detailed descriptions of other cultures. Both physical and cultural geography are grounded in a variety of structured as well as informal observational methodologies.

Through **remote sensing,** geographic information about an object, region, or event can be acquired without being in direct contact with it. For example, **seismographs** are used to measure the movement of seismic waves through the earth, as when an earthquake occurs.

Other specialized methods of gathering and analyzing data in physical and cultural geography include discourse analysis, migration research, cartographic research, and statistics.

Understand features and uses of primary and secondary sources

The beginning teacher knows characteristics and uses of primary and secondary sources used for geographic and cultural research (for example, databases, maps, photographs, media services, the Internet, interviews, questionnaires, artifacts); analyzes information from primary and secondary sources; and evaluates information in relation to bias, propaganda, point of view, and frame of reference.

In geography, the landscape itself may be a primary source of information. Other primary sources about the physical features of a region include photographs, eyewitness descriptions, globes, maps, and databases. Primary sources of information about the cultural features of a region include autobiographies, diaries, letters, and interviews. Travelogues, documentaries, and almanacs can be interesting sources of information about both physical and cultural features of a region. Secondary sources of information about geography include textbooks, summaries of historical processes, and so on.

Bias and other aspects of perspective are especially important to consider in cultural geography. Ethnographic reports, for example, must be carefully evaluated in light of the possibility that the members of the culture and/or the anthropologists themselves may be biased.

Apply evaluative skills to geographic content

The beginning teacher applies evaluative, problem-solving, and decision-making skills to geographic and cultural information, ideas, and issues.

The teacher should be able to apply background knowledge when using different types of globes, maps, figures, charts, and other graphic representations to obtain information on physical characteristics of a region such as climate, elevation, and population density. The teacher should be comfortable with the use of specialized representations such as aerial photographs, satellite images, and topographic maps to identify elements of natural and human environments.

The teacher should be able to apply quantitative skills in order to tally landforms, cities, or lakes, to summarize population characteristics, to measure distances, and to make pertinent comparisons among physical features.

The teacher should be able to apply spatial skills in order to determine compass directions, to understand how to use latitude and longitude to identify location, to understand methods of orientation, to recognize systematic distortions on different types of maps and globes, and to create maps and other visual representations that preserve scale.

Regardless of the specific cognitive skills that are used, the teacher should be able to collate different sources of information in the process of evaluating and answering basic geographic questions, such as how a particular culture reflects the environmental conditions in which it developed, whether a particular area of land is being effectively managed, or how a dispute between two groups over a key resource can be most effectively resolved.

Know how to communicate geographic information

The beginning teacher knows how to communicate and interpret geographic and cultural information and ideas in written and visual forms, including maps and other graphics.

The teacher should be able to understand, create, and explain how to interpret maps of different types. Among the types of maps that teachers may create and explain to students are **outline maps** (maps that contain outlines of geographic regions, such as states, without additional detail), **relief maps** (maps that contain raised features representing the topography of a region), **puzzle maps** (maps that the teacher cuts into shapes for students to reassemble), and **topographic maps** (maps that use different colors and symbols to represent various geographic characteristics).

The teacher should be able to understand, create, and explain diagrams of geographic processes, such as the hydrologic cycle.

The teacher should know how to read, create from tabular data, and explain pie charts, bar graphs, and other kinds of visual representations.

The teacher should be able to interpret drawings and photographs and to create drawings of different geographic features such as waves, clouds, and land masses.

The teacher should be able to use materials such as sand, water, modeling clay, and various props in order to help children create and manipulate geographic features.

Understand how to analyze geographic data

The beginning teacher analyzes data related to geography and culture using appropriate analytical methods.

A variety of analytical methods are needed when studying, as well as teaching, geography.

Simple mathematical procedures are often used, as when the average precipitation of two regions is calculated and compared or the standards of living of two countries are contrasted. Other mathematical techniques are needed when trends such as population growth or rates of consumption are predicted from historical data. A summary of some simple descriptive statistics is given near the end of Competency 019.

Simple graphic skills are needed in order to understand tally sheets, bar graphs, pie charts, diagrams, and other visual representations.

A variety of analytical skills are used to evaluate maps in order to acquire information, draw comparisons, or make decisions. Representational skills may be needed to interpret symbols. In some cases, it may be important to realize that a particular map is based on a set of inferences, such as the likely migration pattern of a group of people over time. In other cases, it may be important to recognize systematic distortions, or missing information, in the representations of geographic features on a map.

Sample Questions

1. Which region of Texas contains the rockiest and most mountainous terrain?

   A. Great Plains
   B. Trans-Pecos
   C. Gulf Coast Plains
   D. North Central Plains

B Texas is a relatively flat state. Options A and C are incorrect, because these areas are relatively flat (and in the case of the Gulf Coast Plains, much of the land is at or near sea level). Option D is incorrect, in spite of the fact that the North Central Plains does contain hills and some low mountains. Option B is the correct answer. The Trans-Pecos region is far rockier and more mountainous than other regions of the state.

2. A kindergarten teacher invites her students to talk about what their parent(s) or guardian(s) do for a living. After each student shares, the teacher helps the class compare and contrast the different occupations. What idea does the teacher hope to illustrate?

   A. the idea that every member of society is employed
   B. the idea that the occupations people choose are reflective of their particular environments
   C. the idea that different individuals play different roles in society
   D. the idea that work is central to the economy of a society

C Option A is incorrect, because not everyone is employed, and it is likely that at least some children in class will have a parent or guardian who does not work. Option B is also incorrect, because kindergarteners' discussions of various occupations is unlikely to include much reference to the environment. Likewise, option D is incorrect, because children at this age are unlikely to refer to the economy. Option C is the correct answer. As children compare and contrast the different occupations—as well as the roles of parents or guardians who do not work— the idea that each person plays a different role in society will be illustrated.

Competency 019 (Government, Citizenship, and Economics)

The teacher understands concepts and processes of citizenship; knows how people organize economic systems to produce, distribute, and consume goods and services; and applies social science skills to information, ideas, and issues related to government and economics.

Review

Understand rules, laws, rights, and responsibilities

The beginning teacher understands the purpose of rules and laws; the relationship between rules, rights, and responsibilities; and the fundamental rights of American citizens guaranteed in the Bill of Rights and other amendments to the U.S. Constitution.

Civics is the study of how society maintains order through government institutions and the political process. Civics focuses on the structure and function of government, the nature and importance of democratic values, and the meaning of citizenship. Civics includes an understanding of laws, rules, rights, and responsibilities, which define appropriate and desirable behavior from the perspective of the local community, the state, and the nation.

The fundamental rights of U.S. citizens are guaranteed in the Bill of Rights and subsequent amendments to the Constitution. At the same time, the Ninth Amendment holds that the Constitution does not contain all fundamental rights. The Ninth Amendment is based on the practical consideration that not all rights could be explicitly described in a single document, even though provisions for those rights may be made elsewhere. The purpose of the Ninth Amendment is to prevent certain rights from being violated simply because they are not explicitly mentioned in the Constitution.

Broadly, our rights as citizens reflect the **rule of law.** The rule of law is fundamental to a democratic society. In contrast to the rule of men, the rule of law embodies the idea that all people should receive fair, equal, and consistent treatment under the law. According to this idea, individuals should answer primarily to a set of laws rather than the desires of one or more authority figures. The rule of law reflects a variety of interrelated principles, including the need for an independent judiciary and a transparent judicial process, among other things.

Understand fundamental democratic concepts

The beginning teacher understands fundamental concepts related to life in a democratic society (for example, importance of voluntary participation, the expression and tolerance of differing points of view, roles of public officials).

The teaching of democratic values is central to social studies instruction. Students are taught the characteristics and importance of values such as patriotism, equality, tolerance for diversity, the rule of law, and the right to vote. Ultimately, the goal of social studies instruction is to instill good citizenship—that is, to create students who are informed, engaged, active participants in the democratic process.

Know the structure and function of Texas government

The beginning teacher knows the basic structure and functions of local, state, and national governments and their relationships to each other and knows how people organized governments during the early development of Texas.

In 1836, a constitution was created for the newly formed Republic of Texas. Nine years later, when Texas became a state, the first state constitution was developed. Several more versions were written prior to the Constitution of 1876, which remains in force today.

The 1836 and 1876 Constitutions were both patterned on the U.S. Constitution, and consequently share many similarities. At the same time, there were important differences. For example, the 1836 Constitution legalized slavery and made provisions for a President of the Republic, who would serve a term of three years. The 1876 Constitution prohibited slavery and made provisions for a governor.

Among its other functions, the Texas Constitution outlines the structure of state government and its relationship to the federal government. For example, the Texas Constitution stipulates that the governor of Texas is elected to a four-year term, with no term limits. The lieutenant governor is also elected to a four-year term but runs for office on a separate ticket. The lieutenant governor serves as the president of the Texas Senate. The 31-member Senate and a 50-member House of Representatives together constitute the Texas Legislature. The Legislature convenes during odd-numbered years for a 140-day regular session, and the governor has the power to call additional 30-day special sessions.

The Texas Constitution also describes the relationship between the Texas government and the U.S. government. For example, in compliance with both state and federal rules, Texas elects 2 senators to the U.S. Senate and 30 representatives to the U.S. House of Representatives. In the presidential election, Texas has 32 electoral votes.

Understand significant Texas and U.S. political documents

The beginning teacher understands the key principles and ideas of the U.S. and Texas Declarations of Independence, Constitutions, and other significant political documents.

The American political system is grounded in two important 18th century documents, the Declaration of Independence and the Constitution.

- **The United States Declaration of Independence:** The Declaration of Independence consists of four parts: introduction, preamble, body, and conclusion. The introduction states the necessity for the American colonies to break from the British Empire. The preamble describes "self-evident" principles of democracy. The first part of the body describes the "abuses and usurpations" perpetrated on the colonists by King George III, while the second part of the body indicates that the colonists had previously appealed in vain to the British for relief. Finally, the conclusion states that the colonies are free and independent, with no further political connection to Britain.

- **The United States Constitution:** The Constitution contains our nation's fundamental laws. The Constitution establishes the structure of our government and describes the rights and liberties of the American citizens.

The precursor to the Constitution was the **Articles of Confederation,** which was ratified by all states in 1781. This document, our first national constitution, made provisions for a federal government, and formally changed the designation of the colonies to states. In terms of providing a foundation for a national government, the Articles of Confederation were incomplete and otherwise problematic on various points of procedure as well as practice. As a result, the Constitutional Convention gathered in 1787 to create a more adequate and permanent constitution. The U.S. Constitution was created in 1787 and took effect in 1789.

The Constitution consists of seven articles and 27 amendments. The first three articles of the Constitution establish the **separation of powers** that prevents any single branch of the government from becoming too powerful. The three main branches of government defined in the Constitution are the **legislative, executive,** and **judicial branches,** which are represented by the Congress, the President, and the Supreme Court, respectively.

- The first three articles outline the rules, responsibilities, and rights associated with each branch of government.
- The fourth article of the Constitution describes the relationship between states and between individual states and the federal government.
- The fifth article identifies the procedure by which the Constitution can be amended.
- The sixth article promises to honor debts and obligations made by the United States prior to the adoption of the Constitution. The sixth article also establishes the primacy of the Constitution by stating that all laws must be consistent with it, that all federal and state officials should give allegiance to it, and that it is superior to state laws in the event of a conflict.
- The seventh article states that ratification by nine states would be sufficient for the establishment of the Constitution.

The first ten amendments to the Constitution are referred to as the **Bill of Rights,** because they describe the rights and other protections granted to individual citizens. Following the Bill of Rights are 17 additional amendments, the most recent being the 27th Amendment, ratified in 1992, which prevents Congress from passing salary increases for itself until after the next congressional election.

The political system of Texas, like that of the United States, is based on a declaration of independence and a state constitution.

- **The Texas Declaration of Independence:** The Texas Declaration of Independence was created overnight at the Convention of 1836 and signed on March 2, 1836. The urgency of its creation stemmed from the fact that while it was being prepared, the Alamo was under siege by the Mexican army of Santa Anna (see Competency 017 for further details on Texas history). The structure of the Texas Declaration of Independence, written primarily by George C. Childress, is similar to that of the United States. It contains principles of government, followed by a list of grievances and a statement that Texas is a free and independent republic.

- **The Texas State Constitution:** The Texas State Constitution, ratified on February 15, 1876, remains in force today. In some respects, it resembles the U.S. Constitution. For example, the Texas Constitution guarantees freedom of speech and press, the right to trial by jury, and the right of citizens to bear arms. The Texas Constitution also contains some uniquely Texan characteristics, many of which pertain to land law. Analogous to the U.S. Constitution, the Texas Constitution defines the structure of government, outlines the rights of citizens, and serves as the basic law of the state. It is one of the longest state constitutions and contains hundreds of amendments.

Understand basic economic concepts

The beginning teacher understands basic economic concepts (for example, economic system, goods and services, free enterprise, interdependence, needs and wants, scarcity, roles of producers and consumers), knows that basic human needs are met in many ways, and understands the value and importance of work.

Economics is the study of how people produce, distribute, and use resources to satisfy their wants and needs. Following are some of the basic economic concepts that would be important for an EC–4 teacher to understand; other economic concepts are discussed in later sections of this competency.

- **Barter:** Direct exchange of goods and services without use of money.
- **Business:** An activity through which goods and services are exchanged for profit. A business may be a **sole proprietorship** (owned by a single person), a **partnership** (owned by two or more people), or a **corporation** (licensed by the government and owned by stockholders). A corporation that owns many businesses is a **conglomerate.**
- **Capital:** Wealth that can be used to generate more wealth. Capital can be material objects, such as tools, or money itself, which can generate more wealth through investment.
- **Choice:** What occurs when someone is faced with two or more alternative uses for a resource. The second best alternative that is given up when a choice is made is called **opportunity cost.**
- **Circular flow:** The model of an economy that shows how consumers and businesses interact in the context of a market.
- **Consumption:** The use of goods or services. A **consumer** is the person whose wants and needs are met through use of goods and services. The dependence of a consumer, business, or government on others for at least some goods and services is called **interdependence.**
- **Demand:** Extent of interest in purchasing a particular good or service. Demand may be **elastic** (greatly increased when the price falls) or **inelastic** (not strongly influenced by price).
- **Division of labor:** The process through which each worker or group of workers performs only a single task or a few tasks.
- **Distribution:** The way that goods or services are made available to consumers.
- **Economic system:** The way the production, consumption, and distribution of goods and services is organized in a society. The major types of economic systems are capitalism, socialism, and communism.
- **Exchange:** The movement of goods or services between producer and consumer. Exchange may take place by means of money, bartering, or some other medium.
- **Goods:** Physical objects that can satisfy wants or needs.
- **Labor:** Any human activity that produces goods or services.
- **Market:** Any setting where buyers and sellers exchange goods, services, currencies, and other resources.
- **Market economy:** An economic system in which goods and services are typically exchanged in private markets, and in which prices tend to be determined by buyers and sellers.
- **Money:** A physical medium of exchange that can be used to buy goods and services.
- **Price:** The value of a good or service in monetary terms. The price at which consumers will purchase exactly the amount of goods or services supplied by a producer is the **equilibrium point.** A general increase in prices is referred to as **inflation.**
- **Production:** The creation of goods or services. Overproduction creates a **surplus,** while underproduction results in a **shortage. Scarcity** occurs when individuals do not have all the goods and services they desire.
- **Productivity:** The ratio of the quantity or quality of goods and services to the input required to create them.
- **Public goods:** Goods and services provided by the government.
- **Resources:** Aids to the production of goods and services. Resources can be natural, human, or capital.
- **Services:** Activities that can satisfy wants or needs.
- **Specialization:** A situation in which the goods and services that people produce is narrower than what they consume.
- **Supply:** Quantity of available goods or services.

Know the characteristics and development of free enterprise

The beginning teacher understands the characteristics, benefits, and development of the free-enterprise system in Texas and the United States and knows how businesses operate in the U.S. free-enterprise system.

Capitalism is an economic system in which the means of production, distribution, and exchange are privately controlled, and in which personal profit can be obtained through labor and capital investment. Capitalism is based on the concept of **free enterprise,** which holds that the interests of society are best served by free markets, which are based on supply and demand, with minimal intervention from the government and minimal influence of coercion or theft. The industrial revolution and the philosophy of Adam Smith were two important influences on the development of modern free enterprise systems that began in the late 18th century in the United States and other countries.

The free-enterprise system in the United States is not completely free, in the sense of reflecting no governmental influence whatsoever:

- The government owns and operates significant enterprises, including the Postal Service and public schools.
- The government regulates a variety of industries, in order to prevent fraud, monopolies, and other abuses.
- The government influences the economy through monetary policy. The **Federal Reserve System** is a regulatory agency that can adjust the supply of money as well as the interest rates, thereby influencing the availability of money for loans to individuals and businesses.
- The government may impose **embargos** (bans on trade with other countries) or **tariffs** (taxes on foreign goods that encourage the consumption of domestic products).
- The government also provides subsidies, tax credits, incentives, and otherwise exerts a variety of other influences on individuals and businesses.

Although federal and state governments influence American businesses on a variety of levels, free enterprise does characterize the economic system of the U.S. in many important respects. Individuals are free to choose the type of business they go into. Individuals are free to own private property. Individuals are free to make a profit from their business and to compete with others for profit. And individual consumers are generally free to patronize whatever business they choose.

Know patterns of work and the measurement of economic level

The beginning teacher demonstrates knowledge of patterns of work and economic activities in Texas and the United States. past and present, and knows how a society's economic level is measured.

There are many ways to measure the economic level of a society.

- The **standard of living** can be thought of as the overall financial health of a society. One way to measure standard of living relies on the **Gross National Product (GNP)**, or the total value of goods and services produced in a year. The GNP per capita—in other words, the GNP divided by the size of the population—is one indicator of standard of living.

- A similar way of defining standard of living is based on the **Gross Domestic Product (GDP)**. The difference between GNP and GDP is that the GDP is restricted to goods and services produced within the geographic boundaries of a country, regardless of the nationality of the producer. The GNP does not include goods and services produced by a foreign company, but it does include goods and services produced by a domestic firm operating in a foreign country. Put simply, GDP is defined in geographic terms, while GNP is defined by nationality.

- Another way to measure standard of living is to calculate the **Gross National Income (GNI)** per capita, or the total income obtained by a country during a year divided by the total population of the country. There are several ways to calculate these figures, and several other measurements of standard of living used by economists.

  One shortcoming of indicators such as the GNP, GDP, and GNI is that they do not take into account all variables that may be important in determining a society's standard of living. Other economic and quality of life variables that have been measured include employment rate, incidence of poverty, literacy rates, levels of education, and life expectancy.

- Along with standard of living and quality of life measures are indicators that focus on specific economic variables. For example, the **Consumer Price Index (CPI)** is the average price of essential goods and services, such as food and housing, over a one-month period. The CPI is an indicator of the value of the dollar, so it provides information about inflation over a period of time.

Periodic changes in the economic activity and economic level of a society are known as the **business cycle.** When business activity significantly decreases, the result is a **recession.** A recession is commonly defined as a decline in the GDP for at least two consecutive quarters. A severe recession is referred to as a **depression.**

Understand the links between Texas, U.S., and world economies

The beginning teacher understands the interdependence of the Texas economy with that of the United States and the world.

From the 17th century through the present, cotton has been central to the Texas economy. At the time of the Republic, **cotton** was shipped from the Gulf of Mexico to other states and to European countries and was the leading export. The primacy of cotton in the Texas economy diminished somewhat during the late 19th century, as sharecropping replaced the slave plantations and as the cattle industry began to expand. During the early 20th century, extensive damage to cotton crops from the boll weevil as well as the discovery of significant petroleum reserves further diminished the role of cotton in the Texas economy. However, cotton remained a major cash crop, and even now, about a third of all cotton produced in the United States originates in Texas.

Cattle ranching was an important but largely domestic business in Texas for about a century prior to the establishment of the Republic. During the second half of the 19th century, the production of cattle expanded and gradually supplanted cotton as the largest Texas export. The ascendancy of the cattle industry reflected a number of factors, including the expansion of the American population as well as increasing interdependence among the states. The cattle industry has developed cyclically, with periods of success interspersed by significant downturns, but it remains a major part of the Texas economy.

The modern **petroleum industry** was marked by the discovery of the Spindletop oil field near Beaumont, Texas, in 1901. Texas quickly became a major producer of oil, and the state experienced a large and rapid influx of human and capital resources. By 1946, oil had replaced coal as the most widely used energy source in the world, and the rapid ascendance of the petroleum industry in Texas alone had a profound impact on local, national, and world economies. The petroleum industry experienced several booms and busts following World War II, but it still plays a significant role in the Texas economy.

Currently, Texas leads all other states in the production of cotton, cattle, oil, and natural gas. However, the largest export from Texas is now **electronic products,** including technology related to communications and the computer industry. The development of each of these industries reflects various levels of interdependence with national and world economies.

Relate government and economics content to other disciplines

The beginning teacher relates information and ideas in government, citizenship, and economics to information and ideas in other social sciences and in other disciplines.

Discussions of government, citizenship, and economics are inherently interdisciplinary. These topics are naturally approached from a historical perspective. Psychology provides a lens through which the motives and behaviors of political leaders can be interpreted. Sociology and anthropology sustain comparisons between different cultural groups and their concepts of government and leadership, as well as their economic systems. Philosophy and political science provide insights into the ethical bases of governments and their authority.

For example, economic interdependence is a concept that naturally calls for an interdisciplinary instructional approach in EC–4 classrooms. The topic of interdependence may be introduced by having children think about the basic needs in their lives, such as food and shelter. As children think about how these needs are met, the teacher can introduce different kinds of businesses and industries, with some emphasis on the kinds of products that are imported from other communities, states, or countries. A variety of instructional strategies could be used, including classroom visits from parents and others from the local community to discuss their particular jobs. The teacher may then arrange role-play activities in which groups of children form communities, with each "community" consisting of business owners, employees, shoppers, bankers, and a unique set of natural resources (which may consist of pictures of natural resources drawn by the children). During interactions within and across communities, the concept of interdependence could be illustrated in a concrete and interdisciplinary way. Economics concepts such as profit, as well as basic mathematical skills, would be used to guide financial transactions within and across communities. The influence of geographic conditions on interdependence would be illustrated by the reliance of each community on others for natural resources. Concepts of citizenship would be learned in the context of developing cooperative relationships within and across communities.

Know how to formulate and answer research questions

The beginning teacher knows how to formulate research questions related to government, citizenship, and economics and use appropriate procedures to reach supportable judgments and conclusions.

Some of the important research questions that can be framed about a particular government are as follows:

- How did this government originate?
- What is the structure of this government?
- How is power allocated?
- Is there a system of checks and balances?
- What is the relationship between national and local governments?
- What rights are conferred upon citizens?
- How are the rights of citizens protected?
- What is the nature of the political process?
- What roles can individuals play in the government?

Some of the important questions that can be framed about a particular economic system are:

- What is the nature of the system?
- What is the standard of living in the society?
- What is the quality of life in this system?
- What patterns of work are common in this system?
- In what ways are this system interdependent with others?

The EC–4 teacher should know how to examine primary sources such as key documents, as well as secondary sources such as databases, to formulate judgments and conclusions with respect to questions such as these, and to guide their students in the formulation of judgments and conclusions.

From a pedagogical perspective, good questions are ones that are formulated in terms that students can understand, and that engage students in a meaningful way, while good judgments and conclusions are ones that are evidence-based, carefully reasoned, and relevant to the original questions.

Know how research in government and economics is carried out

The beginning teacher understands research in government, citizenship, and economics and knows how social scientists in these fields locate, gather, organize, analyze, and report information.

Social scientists in the fields of government, citizenship, and economics make use of a variety of primary and secondary sources for obtaining information. Sources of pertinent information include:

- Scientific books, journals, technical reports, and Web sites
- News reports, editorials, political cartoons, satires
- Publications and Web sites sponsored by U.S. government agencies, such as the Department of Education and the National Institute of Health
- Documents, databases and statistics made available by U.S. government organizations such as the Federal Reserve Bank
- Publications and Web sites sponsored by international agencies such as the United Nations and the World Bank

The research that is based on, or reported in, these sources may be quantitative or qualitative. The methodologies used range from simple observation to highly specialized econometric and statistical techniques.

Know features and uses of primary and secondary sources

The beginning teacher knows characteristics and uses of primary and secondary sources used for research in government, citizenship, and economics (for example, databases, maps, media services, the Internet, biographies, interviews, questionnaires); analyzes information from primary and secondary sources; and evaluates information in relation to bias, propaganda, point of view, and frame of reference.

Some of the primary and secondary sources used for research in government, citizenship, and economics are noted in the preceding section and in discussions of prior competencies. Also discussed in earlier competencies is the idea that because the examination, evaluation, and teaching of values is critical to social studies, it is essential for teachers to be able to identify the point of view, rhetorical intent, and other aspects of communication involving government, citizenship, and economics.

Apply evaluative skills to government and economics content

The beginning teacher applies problem-solving, decision-making, and evaluation skills to information, ideas, and issues related to government, citizenship, and economics.

Discussions of this topic with respect to history (Competency 017) and geography (Competency 018) apply equally well to the study of government, citizenship, and economics. Citizenship issues in the classroom tend to be the focus of considerable problem-solving and decision-making on the part of both teachers and students. In addition, economic issues such as value are often at the heart of student concerns. Because these are among the issues of most immediate personal relevance to elementary students, they are the issues that students have most probably addressed already by means of problem-solving, decision-making, and evaluation skills.

Know how to communicate government and economics content

The beginning teacher knows how to communicate and interpret information and ideas related to government, citizenship, and economics in written and graphic forms.

Discussions of this topic with respect to history (Competency 017) and geography (Competency 018) apply equally well to the interpretation and teaching of government, citizenship, and economics. In terms of communicating these topics to elementary-level students, political cartoons can be a particularly good resource, because each cartoon tends to express a relatively simple idea and a relatively clear point of view or bias.

Understand how to analyze government and economics data

The beginning teacher analyzes data related to government, citizenship, and economics using appropriate analytical methods.

In some cases, data of relevance to government and economics are presented in mathematical form and cannot be understood or interpreted without the use of simple mathematical techniques. For example, descriptive statistics such as the mean, the median, and the mode are often helpful in understanding such data.

- The **mean** is the average of a set of continuous data. One may be interested in the average population of a particular region over time, the average number of voters representing a particular demographic group, or the average income of workers in a particular occupation. In such cases, the mean may provide useful information.

- The **median** is the middle point in a set of continuous data. The median is often a different number than the mean. For example, the mean income for a particular group may be higher than the median income for that group, if a small number of people in the group have extremely large incomes. In this instance, the "average" income for the group may be more accurately reflected by the median than by the mean.

- The **mode** is the most frequently observed number in a set of continuous data. The mode provides useful information when questions are asked about the typical or most common observation in a particular group. For example, consider a small tribal group consisting of eight families. The number of children in each family is as follows: 2, 2, 2, 2, 2, 4, 8, 10. The mean number of children per family is 4. Although the mean conveys useful information, it would be misleading to say that the "average" or "typical" family in this tribe contains 4 children. It would be more accurate to say that the "typical" family contains 2 children, because more than half of the families do. This is an example in which the mode is the most pertinent source of information.

The corresponding discussion of geographic data analysis under Competency 018 also applies to government, citizenship, and economics.

Know how to foster good citizenship

The beginning teacher knows how to apply skills to foster good citizenship (for example, negotiation, conflict resolution, persuasion, compromise, debate).

In a sense, all social studies instruction is intended to foster good citizenship. The teaching of factual information, principles, critical-thinking skills, and decision-making skills all foster good citizenship by giving students a basis for making informed decisions about political, social, and family issues. However, the EC–4 teacher should be aware of specific instructional approaches and strategies that can be used to directly foster good citizenship in the classroom.

Good classroom management naturally promotes good citizenship. Teaching children appropriate conflict resolution strategies, as well as the importance of taking turns, sharing, and being polite can make children better classroom citizens. Being a better classroom citizen in turn provides the foundation for being a good citizen generally. Concepts such as compromise, cooperation, and tolerance are best introduced to children in the context of classroom interactions. Through role-play and other activities, parallels can be drawn between interactions among children in the classroom, and interactions among individuals, groups, communities, and nations in other places and times. Teachers can also convey good classroom citizenship through modeling, explicit discussion, and other activities.

Teachers can also promote good citizenship at home and in the local community. Encouraging students to give away things that they do not use, to be kind to neighbors, to conserve water, to keep a trash bag in a parent's car, or to do a good deed are just a few examples. Generally, the older the student, the more readily the teacher can engage in explicit discussion of the concept of citizenship.

Sample Questions

1. Which of the following implies that two countries have an interdependent relationship?

   A. Each country's economy reflects the basic principles of free enterprise.

   B. Each country lacks a key natural resource that the other one possesses.

   C. One country has recently imposed tariffs on the other one.

   D. One country has recently established diplomatic relations with the other one.

   C Option A is incorrect, because the fact that each country has a free enterprise system does not necessitate any contact between them. Likewise, option B is incorrect, because each country may obtain the needed resource from some other country. Option D is incorrect, because diplomatic relations do not necessarily imply economic relations (even if this is often the case in practice). Option D is the correct answer. The creation of tariffs implies that the two countries already engage in trade.

2. How may the teaching of social studies contribute to good citizenship?

   A. Students may use facts about other political systems to develop their own opinions about politics.

   B. Teachers may illustrate good citizenship by means of classroom examples.

   C. Students may use principles of economics to make wise decisions about money.

   D. all of the above

   D Options A, B, and C each reflect one way that social studies can promote good citizenship.

Domain IV: Science

Competency 020 (Science Instruction)

The teacher uses knowledge of science content and methods to plan effective, engaging, and safe instruction and to assess learning.

Review

Prompt student engagement in scientific inquiry

The beginning teacher plans and implements instruction that prompts all children's engagement in processes of scientific inquiry (for example, asking a scientific question; formulating a testable hypothesis; selecting appropriate equipment and technology to gather information related to the hypothesis; making observations and collecting data; organizing, analyzing, and evaluating data to find data trends and patterns and make inferences; communicating and defending a valid conclusion).

Scientific inquiry, the instructional process of acquiring information and learning through asking questions, is embodied within the well-established process of the **scientific method.** The scientific method is a widely recognized series of steps that a scientist undertakes to answer a question and acquire knowledge about nature. Although theories differ slightly on the actual text and the number of steps involved, it is generally accepted that the scientific method includes the steps discussed in this section.

The student begins by **asking a question**—a question about why a process occurs or why/how a specific factor influences a process. It is a question to which the student does not readily know an answer, which means that the student has to develop and strategize a procedure for finding the answer.

As the student begins to ponder about posing such a question, questions that a teacher may encourage the student to consider to guide the process include:

- What am I interested in learning about and finding more information about?
- What specifically would I like to know about my topic of interest?

The student then **formulates a hypothesis.** A **hypothesis** is an *educated* guess as to what the student thinks the answer will be. Notice the word "educated" is italicized. It is important for the teacher to emphasize to the students that a hypothesis is not a pie-in-the-sky guess regarding the answer to the question but is a guess based on past experiences, initial observations, inferences, and predictions. Instructing the student to formulate a hypothesis demonstrates the in-depth thought and reasoning skills required to truly understand the scientific principles involved in the topic of interest and, more importantly, in answering the question.

As the student defines a hypothesis, questions that a teacher may encourage the student to consider include:

- What do I think the answer to the question will be?
- Based on my past experiences, can I logically deduce what I think the end result or answer to my question may be?

The student must now create a plan in search for an answer to the question or develop an experiment to **test his/her hypothesis.** This is the most important and involved step of the scientific process. The student must lay the framework on how to answer the question. In this step, the student must decide:

- What materials are required?
- What steps or procedures are involved in the experiment?
- Which data or information best supports the hypothesis?
- How will the data be measured and reported?
- How can any competing variables be eliminated, so that any trends or relationships between the two variables of interest from the data are not subject to error or bias from other variables?

As the student develops an experiment, questions that a teacher may encourage the student to consider include:

- What can I do to try and answer my question?
- What steps can I take to find an answer to my question?

As students conduct experiments, they will **seek data or scientific information** that help address the hypothesis. The data can be either quantitative in the form of numerical values presented in tables or in graphs or qualitative in the form of observations recorded in the student's science log or notebook. Both forms of data are important in the scientific process. The teacher, however, should understand the potential for graphs in this context, particularly for the student that needs to step back and see the big picture.

The data that the student collects depends on the variable of interest, the instrument used to measure the variable, and the appropriate unit associated with the value. If the experiment involves the measurement of length or distance, the student must use an instrument that provides length data such as a ruler or meter stick. Each length measurement should be recorded as accurately as possible and with appropriate units (centimeter, meter). If a student is involved in an investigation involving heat, the student will use a thermometer to make temperature measurements, either in units of Fahrenheit or Celsius. Regardless of the variable or the measurement, the student should be instructed to organize the data collected from an experiment in a table with properly labeled columns.

As the student observes and collects data, questions that a teacher may encourage the student to consider include:

- What data from my experiment(s) will best help me to answer my question?
- Have I used the appropriate instruments to make measurements in my experiment?
- Have I properly reported my measurements with correct units?

The students have made observations and collected data from their experiment. In order for the data to be useful to the scientist, the **data must be graphed.** Graphs allow the student to visualize the data where trends between the graphed variables become clearly visible. A graph is a scientific way to demonstrate a relationship between two variables.

The three most common types of graphs used to illustrate scientific information are line graphs, bar graphs, and pie charts.

- **Line graph:** A line graph is generally used to demonstrate a change in a variable over time. Consider an experiment in which the student would like to investigate the growth of a bean sprout exposed to sunlight over a period of one week (7 days). After each day (including the starting day, Day 0), the student will use a ruler to measure the length of the sprout. Because the size of the sprout is the variable of interest, the most appropriate unit for length measurement would be centimeters. The result of this experiment is displayed in the following graph.

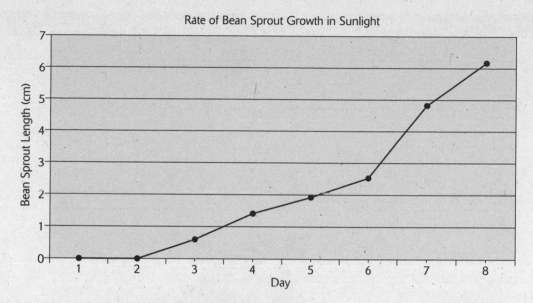

Notice that the line graph has a descriptive title of the data presented in the line graph (rate of bean sprout growth in sunlight), a properly labeled *x*-axis (day) and *y*-axis (bean sprout length), units noted with each label (day, which is unitless, because it refers to the number of days since the beginning of the experiment, and bean sprout length, measured in centimeters).

- **Bar graph:** A bar graph is generally used to demonstrate a comparison between variables in an experiment. Following from the same experiment, the student can now use a bar graph to show the rate of growth of the bean sprout on a daily basis, where the length recorded each day is represented by the bar associated for that particular day.

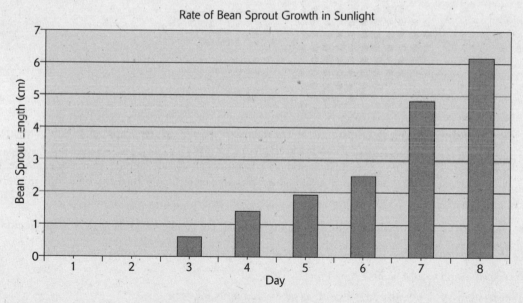

Notice that the bar graph has a descriptive title of the data presented in the bar graph (rate of bean sprout growth in sunlight), a properly labeled *x*-axis (day) and *y*-axis (bean sprout length), units noted with each label (day, which is unitless, because it refers to the number of days since the beginning of the experiment, and bean sprout length, measured in centimeters).

- **Pie chart:** A pie chart is used to demonstrate the associated parts of a complete or entire entity. A possible application of a pie chart may be to show the distribution of colors of M&Ms in a package. Of the 35 candies counted in a particular package, the student records the information in the table and then graphs the information in the pie chart:

Distribution of Colors in a Package of M&Ms	
Color	*Number*
Blue	5
Brown	5
Green	7
Orange	6
Red	4
Yellow	8

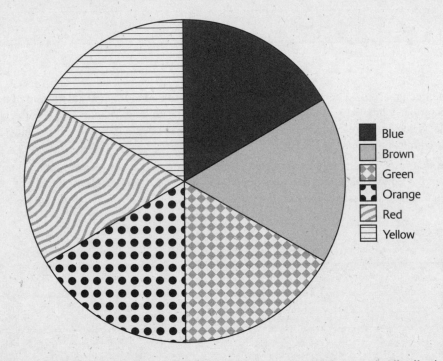

Notice that the pie chart has a descriptive title of the data presented in the bar graph (distribution of colors in a package of M&Ms) and a legend that identifies each piece of the pie and its representative color (or shade) in the pie chart. These graphs can easily be created on most computer spreadsheet applications (for example, Microsoft Excel), but care must be taken to make sure that the graphs are scientifically correct with a title, properly labeled axes, and appropriate units for each axis.

As the student develops an experiment, questions that a teacher may encourage the student to consider include:

- How can I best understand the data obtained from my experiment?
- Which type of graph would be best suited for my data?
- Did I construct my graph with a title as well as labels and units for each axis?

After the experiment has been completed and all of the data (tables, graphs, observations) has been recorded, a student must now try and determine what all of the data means. As the student **analyzes the data,** he/she must review all of the forms/types of data recorded from the experiment and begin to look for substantive meaning from this information. For each type of data, questions/issues that a student must raise during the process vary according to the type of data.

For data listed in tables:

- Is there a sufficient number of data points recorded from the experiment?
- Are there any trends noted in the variables of interest, or is there no change?

For data provided in graphs:

- Was the appropriate graph used to display the data?

For data noted by observations:

- Did the observations follow a trend as the experiment progressed?
- Did the observations note a potential error in the experiment or identify another factor that may potentially influence the results of the experiment?

After the experiment is completed, the student can now **develop a conclusion;** that is, determine what the answer to his/her question posed in the first step of the scientific method is and, more importantly, whether the reasoning used to generate the hypothesis was correct. If the hypothesis was correctly formulated, the student clearly reasoned through the processes involved in the topic of interest and developed an experiment that successfully added to the student's knowledge of the topic. The important thing to emphasize to the students is that, even if the hypothesis was not correct, the scientific method still constructively added to the student's body of knowledge about the topic of interest.

As the student develops conclusions, questions that a teacher may encourage the student to consider include:

- Did my experiment agree with my hypothesis and answer my question?
- If not, was my experiment not done properly or is there something else I need to investigate?

Use situations from students' daily lives to develop instruction

The beginning teacher uses situations from children's daily lives to develop instruction that investigates how science can be used to make informed decisions.

Many of the students in a teacher's classroom come with different life experiences, but chances are very good that many (if not all) of the students will have shared experiences, too. It is from these life experiences that students draw links to new concepts and, therefore, construct knowledge. For example, a teacher interested in teaching a physical science lesson on motion may introduce the concept by tossing a ball up in the air or throwing the ball to a student. Almost every student has either owned a ball or played with a ball with friends. It is also likely that each classroom allows the children to play with balls during recess. Using balls of different sizes (such as a golf ball, baseball, softball, soccer ball, and basketball), the teacher may use these experiences to ask the students to investigate the following questions:

- Which ball will bounce the highest when released from the same height?
- How long will each ball take to reach the ground when dropped from the same height?
- Which ball can be thrown the highest?
- Which ball can be thrown the farthest?

As another example, a teacher interested in teaching a life science lesson may incorporate common insects such as crickets or pill bugs (also known as doodle bugs). These insects are usually found during backyard investigations under rocks or in moist areas but are just as easily found during walks to the park or nature field trips. Using small numbers of crickets or pill bugs, the teacher may use these experiences to ask the students to investigate the following questions:

- How do the insects interact with one another and what types of behavior do they exhibit?
- What are the eating/sleeping habits of the insects during the day?
- If studied in a terrarium environment, what kind of soil do these insects prefer?

Create, implement, and enforce a safe environment

The beginning teacher creates, implements, and enforces rules and safety procedures to promote and maintain a safe learning environment during laboratory and field activities.

It is very important that teachers understand the importance of conducting any scientific investigation safely and responsibly. In general, the teacher should:

- Know and understand all levels (federal, state, district, school) of rules and regulations requirements regarding science laboratory safety.

- Develop, distribute, and require student and parent signatures on a **laboratory safety contract,** which concisely summarizes the rules and regulations required to safely participate in science laboratory investigations.

- Know where the following safety devices are located and instruct the students as to their location as well their purpose: safety goggles, fire blanket, fire extinguisher, and eyewash station.

- Know where the first-aid kit is located and notify students of its location in the event of a minor emergency. Should any emergency occur, the teacher should be prepared to notify the school nurse and the parent/guardian of the student and, in the event of a major emergency, to call 911.

- Ensure that each student, working in small groups, has sufficient space to perform his or her lab experiment responsibly, with no horseplay or joking around.

- Go over the lab experiment, making sure that each student has the proper materials and equipment and understands the instructions for safely performing the experiment.

- Provide each student/working group with the following: clear and detailed procedures for the experiment; the proper materials, instruments, and equipment; and instructions to never touch or taste any substance or compound used in the investigation.

- Require students to clean up their work areas after the experiment, return all equipment and materials to their proper places, and wash their hands after the experiment.

Provide laboratory space and equipment

The beginning teacher provides laboratory space and equipment for all students, including those with special needs.

In order to safely perform science investigations, each student or work group must have adequate space and sufficient equipment, as required by state regulations. Minimum space requirements for all laboratory investigations in an elementary laboratory classroom are 1,200 net square feet for no more than 22 students. Students should be given their own safety devices such as goggles, gloves, masks, and aprons. In addition, students should have their own supplies, materials, and equipment to conduct individual or group experiments. Having to share materials, chemicals, and equipment increases the likelihood of a spill or glass breakage and, hence, the likelihood of injury or an accident.

Design multicultural instruction

The beginning teacher designs science instruction that includes the contributions of individuals from a variety of cultures.

Among the challenges faced by a classroom teacher are the varied background, learning styles, and past experiences of his or her students. These differences arise in large part due to the cultural diversity of the students. By recognizing their cultural diversity and incorporating scientific achievements and accomplishments from scientists of different cultures into science classroom instruction, the teacher does the following:

- Broadens the scientific base of the entire class of students
- Celebrates the past experiences of these scientists while reinforcing and building upon the past experiences of the students
- Encourages each student that they can perform science and make significant contributions to science, regardless of their background, learning style, and past experiences

Examples of the cultural diversity of scientists include African-American scientists, such as the following:

- George Washington Carver (1864–1943) was known for his inventions and scientific contributions to agriculture, particularly with regard to the ability to successfully plant crops of peanuts, soybeans, and sweet potatoes (yams). In fact, Dr. Carver is credited with developing more than 300 uses for peanuts.
- Charles R. Drew (1904–1950) made significant contributions to science and medicine in the field of human blood, spearheading the creation of blood banks or facilities that stored blood as plasma until needed for transfusions into injured patients. He was the first director of the American Red Cross blood banks.
- Mae C. Jemison (1956–present) was a doctor who had the desire to become an astronaut. In 1987, she began taking special engineering classes and was admitted into the NASA (National Aeronautics and Space Administration) astronaut training program. The following year, Dr. Jemison successfully completed her training, becoming the fifth black astronaut and the first black female astronaut in NASA history.

Teachers also want to include Hispanic scientists, such as the following:

- Santiago Ramón y Cajal (1852–1934) made significant contributions to the study of the nervous system and how nerve impulses are transmitted. Originally from Spain, Santiago Ramón y Cajal was awarded the Nobel Prize in 1906 for his work on the structure of the nervous system.
- Antonia Novello (1944–present) is a doctor trained as a pediatric nephrologist (kidney specialist for children). In 1990, she became the first woman and the first Hispanic to become the surgeon general of the United States (1990–1993).
- Ellen Ochoa (1958–present), having received degrees in physics and electrical engineering, was selected by NASA to become an astronaut in 1991, making her the first female Hispanic astronaut. She has participated in four space flight missions and is currently deputy director of flight crew operations at Johnson Space Center.

The achievements of and contributions from these scientists and many others just like them can be incorporated into a variety of science lessons under a number of different circumstances to reflect the cultural diversity in science and to broaden science instruction to address the cultural diversity in the classroom.

Relate scientific ideas and explanation with observations and experiments

The beginning teacher promotes children's understanding that scientific ideas and explanations must be consistent with observational and experimental evidence.

In introducing a science concept or engaging the students in a discussion about a science topic, a teacher will most likely either make a scientifically based statement (such as, "All objects, regardless of mass, will strike the ground at the same time if dropped from the same height") or be asked a scientific question (such as, "Why do some objects float and some sink?"). In either case, it is very important that these two learning opportunities are addressed not by an explanation in words, but by **demonstrations** or **experiments** in action. In order for a child to truly understand a concept, he or she must have proof either through a demonstration (by the teacher) or through an experiment (by the student).

In addressing the first statement ("All objects, regardless of mass, will strike the ground at the same time if dropped from the same height"), the teacher could follow the statement with a demonstration in which she drops two similar objects, say golf balls, at the same time from the same height. Then the teacher could do the same demonstration using objects of different sizes and masses, say a golf ball and a baseball, then a golf ball and a softball, and finally a golf ball and a basketball. The students should see that all of the objects, if dropped at the same time from the same height, will reach the ground at the same time. Why did this happen? The teacher could use this opportunity to discuss gravity as the force that attracts all objects to the Earth's surface. When an object is dropped, it falls because a force due to gravity is pulling it toward Earth and, in doing so, the object accelerates or changes its speed. Because gravity is constant (acts with the same strength everywhere on the Earth's surface), all objects will fall with the same acceleration and, therefore, hit the ground at the same time. An astute student may note that if a piece of paper wadded up and an unfolded piece of paper are dropped at the same time, they do not hit the ground at the same time. This is an excellent opportunity to discuss air resistance and explain that air resistance is why skydivers use parachutes.

For the scientific question ("Why do some objects float and some sink?"), the teacher could engage his or her students in a laboratory experiment in which the students could place objects of different sizes, shapes, and masses into a tub of water. The students would be trying to identify features and characteristics of those objects that sink when placed in the tub and those that float. The teacher should be prepared to discuss the concept of density and how density depends on the nature of the object and not on the size or amount of the object.

Use a variety of assessments

The beginning teacher uses a variety of formal and informal assessments and knowledge of the Texas Essential Knowledge and Skills (TEKS) in science to determine children's progress and needs and to help plan instruction for individual children, including English Language Learners.

Each teacher is charged with instructing their students according to the TEKS, the state-mandated curricular objectives appropriate to the grade level. The teacher must continually assess students on the content incorporated into the lesson, in order to have an indication as to whether the students are learning the major concepts represented by the TEKS. An assessment describes any means by which a teacher gains information about student knowledge or performance. Assessment of student's knowledge can occur either through formal assessments or informal assessments. Formal assessments, usually developed at the national or district levels, include standardized tests, unit tests, and comprehensive tests. Informal assessments, usually developed or constructed by the classroom teacher, include chapter tests, quizzes, homework, laboratory experiences, student projects, portfolios, and discussion sessions.

Assess understanding of the inquiry process

The beginning teacher develops procedures for assessing child participation in and understanding of the inquiry process.

The **inquiry process** embodies a means of instruction that is not teacher-centered but rather learner-centered. In learner-centered instruction, the student assumes responsibility and becomes actively involved in his or her learning, while the teacher serves as a facilitator of the learning process. In the inquiry process, the student should do the following:

1. Ask a meaningful question.
2. Collect information and design an experiment to answer the question.
3. Conduct the experiment.
4. Perform measurements and interpret the data.
5. Assess the results from the experiment and determine whether the question was answered.

As the student is actively engaged in the inquiry process, questions will be asked and discussions will occur between students, working groups, the entire class, and the teacher. Assessment of child participation in the inquiry process is not objective, but subjective. There are no right or wrong questions to be asked and answers to be offered or suggested. Instead, assessment can be performed based on whether questions are asked, how many questions are asked, what type of questions are asked and the extent of the discussion that ensues as a result of these questions, and how many students are participating in the process. However, the learning that occurs as a direct result of the inquiry process can be assessed objectively with a quiz, test, or written report of the experience.

Understand the stages of childhood growth and development

The beginning teacher understands the implications of stages of child growth and development for designing and implementing effective learning experiences in science and selects effective, developmentally appropriate instructional practices, activities, technologies, and materials to promote children's scientific knowledge and skills.

Before teachers can sufficiently accommodate the learning abilities of children, they must first understand the stages of child development. The stages of child development are well-defined periods of time during which a child develops, possesses, or exhibits certain characteristics, abilities, or patterns related to learning. These stages are often the work of many years of observations by child psychologists and generally tend to hold true for children of similar age groups in the classroom. Perhaps the most noted and referred to child psychologist in this regard is Swiss psychologist Dr. Jean Piaget. His interests in child behavior led to the identification and classification of four stages of child development. These stages can help you identify the abilities of EC–4 children in the science classroom.

Piaget's Stages of Cognitive Development for Children		
Stage of Cognitive Development	**Age Span**	**Characteristics**
Sensorimotor stage	Birth – 2 years	The child: • Begins to develop language • Coordinates senses with motor function to learn about himself and his environment • Proceeds from simple reflexive behaviors to the beginnings of early reasoning • Is aware that an object continues to exist even if it is hidden in various places.
Preoperational stage	2 – 7 years	The child: • Exhibits the ability to represent objects and events with words, gestures, objects, and mental images. • Is egocentric (for example, views the world according to his own perspective, because of the fact that he is highly perception-bound). • Experiences rapid increases in the development and ability of spoken language. • Uses symbols (for example, pictures and words) to represent an idea, object, or event.
Concrete operational stage	7 – 11 years	The child: • Performs mental operations but needs concrete objects to operate on. • Classifies objects and events using organized thought structures. • Exhibits **seriation** or the sequencing of objects, for example, arranging ten objects from longest to shortest.
Formal operational stage	11 years and above	The child: • Begins to think like an adult • Incorporates principles of logic • Can reason contrary to fact

Sample Questions

1. Ms. Dempsey, a 1st-grade teacher, would like to introduce her students to genetics by engaging her students in a discussion of the similarities and differences of each student. Because hair color is a trait that is inherited, she sought to find out the different hair colors represented in class. As she noted the hair color of each student, she made a large table on the blackboard of each student and his/her hair color. In order to demonstrate the proportion of students with a particular hair color, what graph would be appropriate to display the data?

   A. pie chart
   B. bar graph
   C. line graph
   D. all of the above

   A Any time scientific data involves proportions or percentages, the pie chart is the most appropriate type of graph to visualize the data. The pie chart shows, through various pieces or slices of the pie, the different percentages that make up the whole (in this case, the entire class).

2. Mr. Bennett introduces a lesson on motion and forces to his 3rd-grade class by posing the following question: Does the size of a paper airplane affect the flight distance? The next step that would be most appropriate for the students would be to:

   A. Search the Internet for an answer.
   B. Make a paper airplane.
   C. Propose a hypothesis.
   D. Wait for Mr. Bennett to give them the answer.

   C This question pertains to the major steps of the scientific method. If the teacher expects his students to conduct a scientific investigation to address his question, the next step is for each student to propose a hypothesis. The hypothesis or an educated guess helps them to establish a framework by which to conduct an experiment to answer the question.

3. Ms. Wade is teaching a lesson to her 2nd-grade class on the environment and focuses on the adaptation and habitat of frogs. She wants her students to learn about the life cycle of frogs, what they require in order to thrive, what they eat, and how they interact with other wildlife. Which activity would have the most instructional impact on the students?

   A. Read a book about frogs.
   B. Conduct a field trip to the zoo.
   C. Construct a terrarium with frogs.
   D. Watch a scientific movie about frogs.

   C Although all activities do have some instructional benefit in this lesson, the activity with the most benefit would be to construct a terrarium with frogs. By constructing a terrarium, the students will be modeling the environment of frogs, allowing students to make careful observations and obtain useful information that will help answer their questions about frogs and their habitat.

Competency 021 (Physical Science)

The teacher understands the fundamental concepts, principles, and processes of physical science.

Review

Understand properties of objects and materials

The beginning teacher understands properties of objects and materials and selects appropriate procedures and tools for observing and recording them (for example, size, shape, temperature, hardness, mass, construction, density.)

A fundamental ability of scientists is to accurately describe pertinent features and characteristics of an object in both a qualitative and quantitative manner. This is the first step in gaining information toward answering the question according to the scientific method (see Competency 020). Several features and characteristics that can be used to identify the properties of objects and materials include the following:

Size: A student may ask the following questions about the size of an object:

- How big or small is the object?
- Is the object two-dimensional or three-dimensional?
- What are the lengths of each dimension and in what units are they measured?
- If a student knows the lengths of two dimensions, what is the area of the object?
- If all three dimensions are known, what is the volume of the object?

Shape: A student may ask the following questions about the shape of an object:

- If the object is two-dimensional, is it in the shape of a circle, square, rectangle, triangle, or is it an irregular shape?
- If the object is three-dimensional, is it in the shape of a sphere, cube, rectangular prism, triangular prism, or is it an irregular shape?

Temperature: Temperature is an indication as to how hot or cold an object or material is. A student may ask the following questions about the temperature of an object:

- What is the temperature of the object under normal room conditions?
- How was the temperature measured and in what measurement scale?

Hardness: Hardness is a material property that indicates how hard it is to deform or change the form of the material by bending, scratching, or cutting. The hardness of an object is generally related to the strength of the chemical bonds of the material of the object. The material with stronger bonds or atoms that are more tightly-bound are generally the hardest, while those materials with weaker bonds are the softest. The hardness of a material, generally used to analyze rock and mineral samples, can be determined by scratching the surface, which either breaks bonds or displaces atoms. It can be measured according to the Mohs' hardness scale, a scale developed by German mineralogist, Friedrich Mohs. The scale ranks the hardness of ten common minerals on a scale of 1 (softest) to 10 (hardest). The hardest material is diamond, while the softest mineral is talc.

Mohs' Hardness Scale	
1.	Talc
2.	Gypsum
3.	Calcite
4.	Fluorite
5.	Apatite
6.	Feldspar
7.	Quartz
8.	Topaz
9.	Corundum (Ruby & Sapphire)
10.	Diamond

A student may ask the following questions about hardness of an object:

- How does the object react when its surface is scratched?
- Does it react differently when scratched with different objects (for example, fingernail, penny, paper clip, and so on)?

Mass: Mass is the amount of substance that an object has. (Mass is often confused with **weight,** which is the effect of gravity on mass.) Mass is measured using a triple-balance beam and is reported in units of kilograms or grams. A student may ask the following questions about the mass of an object:

- What is the mass of the object?
- How accurate is my measurement of the mass of the object?
- How many times should I measure the mass of the object before I am comfortable with its accuracy?

Construction: Construction refers to the nature of the object or material being studied. A student may ask the following questions about the construction of an object:

- Is the object constructed out of man-made materials or are the materials naturally occurring in nature?
- Is the object constructed out of wood, plastic, steel, or some other material?

Density: The density of a material is another characteristic of an object that describes the amount of mass per unit volume. Mass is generally expressed in units of grams and volume in units of cubic centimeters (cm^3); therefore, density is expressed in units of g/cm^3. The density of several common substances is listed in the following table.

Density of Common Substances	
Substance	*Density (g/cm³)*
Air	0.0013
Aluminum	2.7
Gold	19.3
Ice	0.93
Lead	11.3
Water	1.00
Wood (oak)	0.85

A student may ask the following questions about the density of an object:

- What is the density of the object being investigated?
- How may I determine the density of an object if I don't know what material it is made of?
- Is the object constructed out of wood, plastic, steel, or some other material?

Describe concepts of force and motion

The beginning teacher understands concepts of force and motion and describes the motion of an object subject to an unbalanced force (for example, a push or a pull).

All children have to do is look out the classroom window and they will see many examples of **motion.** Whether it is cars driving down the street, people walking down the sidewalk, trees moving in the breeze, or birds flying in the sky, motion is an integral part of nature and in the past experiences of all of the students. Motion is the science of movement.

The motion of an object begins by defining its position, say Point A. This can be demonstrated in class by having a student stand at the front of the classroom, where his position will be referred to as Point A. Now, suppose he walks to the back of the classroom, now considered to be Point B. The student's change in position from the final position (Point B) to the starting position (Point A) is known as **displacement.** The displacement of the object is defined as the distance and direction between the final position (Point B) and the starting position (Point A) or

$$\text{displacement} = \text{position at point B} - \text{position at point A}$$

where displacement or distance is measured in units of length, for example, meters. The difference between displacement and distance is that displacement also requires a specific direction or, in other words, displacement is a distance in a given direction.

Now consider the time it takes for the student to travel from Point A to Point B, or the rate of change of displacement of the student. This is known as the **velocity** of the student, or $\text{velocity} = \dfrac{\text{displacement}}{\text{time}}$, where velocity or speed is measured in units of length/time, for example, meters/second. Just like the difference between displacement and distance, the difference between velocity and speed is that velocity requires a specific direction.

Yet another quantity of motion that is important is the time rate of change of velocity known as **acceleration.** Acceleration can be calculated by determining the change in velocity of an object over a time interval or $\text{acceleration} = \dfrac{\text{velocity}}{\text{time}}$.

Forces are physical quantities that cause motion. A force is a push or a pull and is measured in units of Newtons (1 Newton = 1 kg m/s^2). Examples of forces can be found in a person standing, walking, or running or a ball being thrown, kicked, or hit with a bat—in short everything that is in motion, and even in things that are stationary. It makes sense that exerting a push or a pull on an object will cause the object to move, but how could a force be involved in an object that doesn't move? Only when that force is balanced with another force that is equal in size but acting opposite in direction. Consider a person standing still. The person is exerting a force on the floor due to gravity. However, the floor is exerting an equal and opposite support force on the person. Because these forces are balanced, the person does not move.

A force exerted on an object causes motion, or more precisely, causes the object to accelerate. In equation form, a force can be described by:

$$\text{force} = \text{mass} \times \text{acceleration}$$

In explaining this concept, a teacher can apply the same force or push to objects of various masses (a marble, a book, a student desk, and a teacher's desk). Because the force is the same, the student will find that, as the mass of the object becomes larger, the slower it will move (accelerate). If the student investigates the concept of force on a single object, say the book, the student will find that the larger the force applied to the book, the faster it will move (accelerate).

Understand basic concepts of heat, light, electricity, and magnetism

The beginning teacher understands basic concepts of heat, light, electricity, and magnetism.

Heat

Heat is closely associated with temperature but they are very different quantities. Temperature is a measure of how hot or cold an object is. Temperature is measured with a thermometer and is typically expressed in units of degrees Fahrenheit (°F) or degrees Celsius (°C). Temperature values expressed in degrees Fahrenheit can be converted to units of degrees Celsius by the following conversion formula:

$$T_F = \frac{9}{5} T_C + 32 \qquad \text{or} \qquad T_C = \frac{5}{9}(T_F - 32)$$

Heat (that is, **thermal energy**) is a form of energy that depends on the change of temperature. Because heat is a form of energy, it is measured in units called Joules. When heat is applied to an object in its solid state (for example, ice), the heat transfers its energy to the molecules of the object, which gain kinetic energy and begin to move. As a result of the added energy, the solid object now becomes liquid. As heat continues to be added to the object in its liquid state, the heat transfers more of its energy to the molecules, increasing their kinetic energy. The object now becomes a gas.

If two objects at different temperatures are placed in contact with one another, **heat energy** is transferred between the two objects. The hotter object loses its heat energy to the colder object. Heat energy is transferred between two objects depending on the states of matter of the object.

- **Conduction** is the method of heat energy transfer that occurs in solids (for example, the warming of a spoon when stirring cream in the coffee).
- **Convection** is the method of heat energy transfer that occurs in liquids (for example, the cooling of coffee after pouring cream).
- **Radiation** is the method of heat energy transfer that occurs in space (for example, the Earth's surface being warmed by the sun).

Light

Light is a form of energy that travels as waves in space. But light described in this context is much more than just the visible light that you can see emitted from a light bulb. Visible light is a small part of the electromagnetic spectrum, a collection of waves that travel at the same speed (speed of light in a vacuum = 3×10^8 m/s) but have different wavelengths. A wavelength of a wave is defined as the distance between successive peaks of the wave.

The **electromagnetic spectrum** is arranged with the larger wavelengths (radio waves) to the left and the smaller wavelengths (gamma rays) to the right. The entire spectrum of waves is (from larger wavelengths on the left to smaller wavelengths on the right) represented in the following graphic:

- Radio waves
- Microwaves
- Infrared waves
- Visible light
- Ultraviolet waves
- X-rays
- Gamma rays

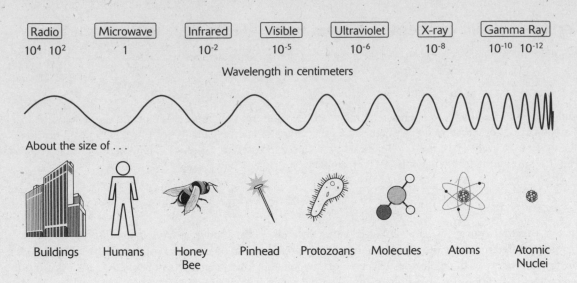

The **primary colors** of visible light are red, green, and blue. When these colors are mixed together in sufficient proportions, white light is produced. The **complementary colors** of visible light are cyan, magenta, and yellow. When these colors are mixed together in sufficient proportions, the color black is obtained.

Light moves in a straight line through a medium until it encounters a different medium. At that point, the path of light will change depending on the nature and surface of the medium.

- If light strikes a material with a smooth surface, light is **reflected** in such a manner that the angle of the incident light is equal to the angle of the reflected light. This is how light displays images seen when you look into a mirror.

Reflection from a flat mirror

Butterfly is
really here . . .

But it looks
like it is here

Mirror

P

Normal

θ_i

θ_r

O

Q

Actual
light path
to eye

The eye thinks this
is the light path

Flat
mirror

- When light moves between two transparent media (such as from air to water or from water to glass), the incident light wave changes its speed (albeit slightly) and, hence, its direction when it strikes the surface of the second medium. The change of direction of the light wave in this scenario is called **refraction.**

Refraction at surface of water

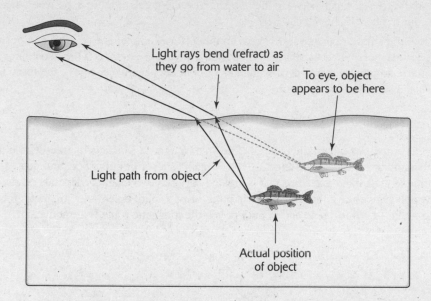

Electricity

Electricity is based on the physical properties of the electron. One of three particles of an atom (**proton, neutron,** and **electron**), the electron is the smallest and lightest. In addition, the electron moves outside of the nucleus and is negatively charged.

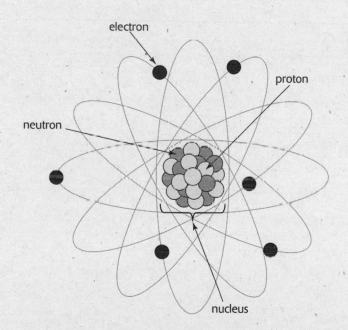

Electric charge is a conserved quantity. In other words, electric charge can not be created nor destroyed, only transferred. Electric charge moves easily through materials known as conductors. Examples of conductors include most metals such as copper and aluminum. The opposite of conductors is insulators or materials through which electric charge does not move easily. Examples of insulators include glass, rubber, plastic, and paper.

Electric charges can have one of two signs: a **positive sign** (indicating positive charge) or a **negative sign** (indicating negative charge). Two electric charges exert a force between themselves, the strength of which depends on the size, distance of separation, and sign of the charges.

- **Size:** The greater the size of the charge, the greater the force exerted between them.
- **Distance:** The shorter the distance between the two charges, the greater the force between them. The farther apart the charges are, the weaker the force becomes.
- **Sign:** If the two charges have opposite signs between them (for example, one positive charge and one negative charge, the force is **attractive** and the charges are pulled toward one another. If the two charges have like charges between them (for example, both are positive charges or both are negative charges), the force is **repulsive** and the charges are pushed away from one another.

Magnetism

Magnetism refers to the properties of certain materials known as magnets. Magnets interact with other magnets by exerting forces on one another. A magnet can exist in shapes, such as a bar or horseshoe, and possesses two poles—a north pole and a south pole. The magnetic force that is created between two magnets depends on the poles that are in close proximity. If the poles are alike—that is, two north poles or two south poles—the magnetic force is repulsive. If the poles are not alike—that is, a north pole and a south pole—the magnetic force is attractive.

Apply properties of fundamental forces to everyday situations

The beginning teacher applies properties of fundamental forces (for example, push or pull, friction, gravity, electric force, magnetic force) to analyze common situations and objects (for example, toys and playground equipment).

A **force** is a push or a pull and occurs in various forms in nature. General examples of forces include pulling a chair back or pushing a book across the desk. However, forces also occur in nature in different capacities within common situations and objects. Specific examples of force are:

- **Weight** is the force exerted on an object by the pull of gravity. A person can measure his/her own weight by stepping on a scale. In fact, the weight of any object can be measured by using a scale.

- **Friction** is the force that exists between the surface of an object as it moves along another surface. If a force is applied to a book, the book will move and eventually come to a stop. The reason it comes to a stop is that **friction,** a force that occurs when two surfaces are in contact, opposes motion and eventually causes the book to stop.

- **Electric force** is the force that exists between two electric charges. For like charges (either two positive charges or two negative charges), a repulsive (pushing) force will be exerted on each charge. For unlike charges (one positive charge and one negative charge), an attractive (pulling) force will be exerted on each charge. A striking example of electric force is the Van De Graaf electrostatic generator. A Van de Graaf electrostatic generator looks like a large aluminum sphere placed on a clear plastic pipe that is mounted to a platform. When it is turned on, positive charge accumulates on the surface of the sphere. When a person places his hand on the sphere (before it is turned on), charge that accumulates on the sphere begins moving onto the person, because he is a conductor. Because the charge is of the same sign, they exert a repelling force between each other. The most visual evidence of this phenomenon is in the person's hair. The repelling force between the charges in the hair causes the hair to stand straight up.

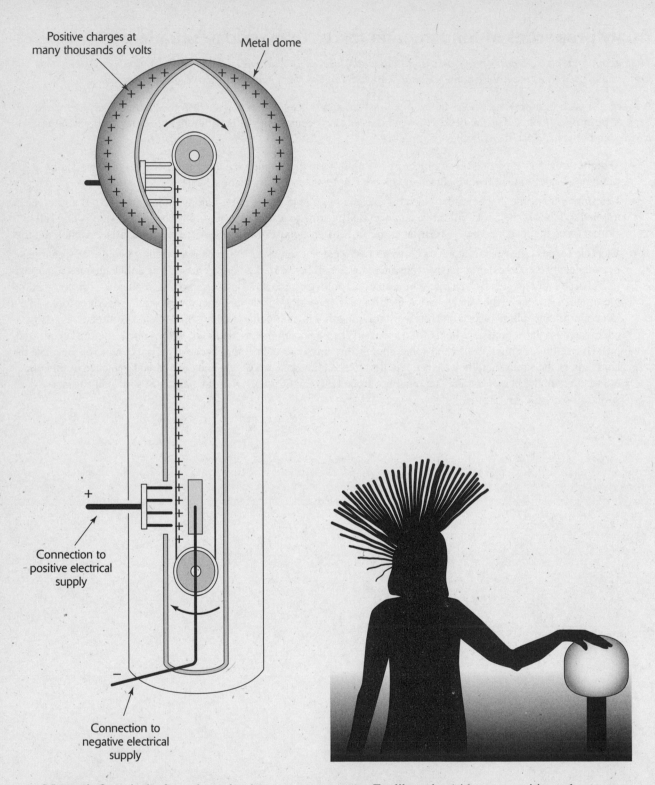

Positive charges at
many thousands of volts

Metal dome

Connection to
positive electrical
supply

Connection to
negative electrical
supply

■ **Magnetic force** is the force that exists between two magnets. For like poles (either two positive poles or two negative poles), a repulsive (pushing) force will be exerted on each magnet. For unlike poles (a north pole and a south pole), an attractive (pulling) force will be exerted on each magnet. An example of the use of magnetic force in common applications is the compass. A compass consists of a small, lightweight magnet, often referred to as a needle, balanced atop a frictionless pivot. At either end of the needle are letters: "N" representing north and "S" representing south. A compass, which is used to indicate general direction, works because of the magnetic field of the Earth. If one considers the Earth's magnetic field represented by a large bar magnet that runs through the center of the Earth, then the South end of the magnet aligns with the North end of the needle (because opposite poles attract) and vice versa.

Describe and analyze changes in the states of matter

The beginning teacher describes and analyzes changes in the states of matter caused by the addition and removal of heat energy.

There are three recognized **states of matter: solid, liquid,** and **gas.** Plasma or ionized (charged) gases are sometimes mentioned as a fourth state of matter, however, a fourth state is not universally accepted by the science community as a definite state of matter. The following table summarizes the characteristics and properties of the three states of matter: solids, liquids, and gases.

Changes in States of Matter	
Change in the State of Matter	*Descriptive Term*
Solid state → Liquid state	Melting
Liquid state → Solid state	Freezing
Liquid state → Gas state	Boiling
Gas state → Liquid state	Condensation
Solid state → Gas state (bypassing the liquid state)	Sublimation
Gas state → Solid s tate (bypassing the liquid state)	Disposition

Changes in the states of matter depend on the addition or removal of heat energy from the substance. The temperature at which changes in the state of matter occur depends on the substance and their freezing points or boiling points. For example, water will change its state from liquid to solid at a freezing point of 0°C or 32°F, while water will change its state from liquid to gas at a boiling point of 100°C or 212°F. The temperature values for the freezing and boiling points described pertain only to water. Each substance has a specific temperature at which it changes states of matter.

Characteristics of the Three States of Matter: Solids, Liquids, and Gases		
Solid	*Liquid*	*Gas*
Substance that retains a fixed volume and shape (for example, ice)	Substance that fills the shape of the container that it occupies (for example, water)	Substance that assumes the shape and volume of its container (for example, steam)
Molecules are rigid and particles locked into place.	Molecules can move/slide past one another.	Molecules can move easily past one another.
By increasing temperature and decreasing pressure, it becomes liquid.	By decreasing temperature and increasing pressure, it becomes solid; by increasing temperature and decreasing pressure, it becomes gas.	By decreasing temperature and increasing pressure, it becomes liquid.

Understand conservation of energy and energy transformations

The beginning teacher understands conservation of energy and energy transformations and analyzes how energy is transformed from one form to another (for example, mechanical, sound, heat, light, chemical, electrical) in a variety of everyday situations.

When physics is applied to the world outside, all objects have the ability to change. For example, a ball is thrown into the air, and its position is changing. One also notes that in addition to its changing position, its speed is changing as well. Any time change occurs, it occurs as a result of energy. Energy is required to facilitate change. There are various forms of energy that exist in nature but are similar in that they all result in change. These forms of energy include:

- **Kinetic energy** is the energy of an object in motion. Any moving object, regardless of its mass, has kinetic energy.
- **Potential energy** is the stored energy of an object. The stored energy can be a result of position or height above the Earth's surface (**gravitational potential energy**), the amount of stretching or compression of an elastic object like a spring or rubber band (**elastic potential energy**), or the number and type of chemical bonds (**chemical potential energy**).
- **Mechanical energy** is the sum of the kinetic energy and potential energy of an object.
- **Chemical energy** is the energy that occurs as a result of the bonds of chemicals. An excellent source of chemical energy is food.
- **Thermal energy,** also known as heat, is the energy that occurs as a result in temperature difference.
- **Sound energy** is the energy that occurs as a result of sound.
- **Light energy** is the energy that occurs as a result of light.
- **Solar energy** is the energy that occurs as a result of the sun.
- **Electrical energy** is the energy that occurs as a direct result of moving electric charges.

Regardless of the particular form, energy is a conserved quantity. According to the **law of the conservation of energy,** energy can neither be created nor destroyed, only transformed. Examples of conservation of energy are evident everywhere in nature and include:

- **Potential energy → kinetic energy:** An object held at a certain height above the ground contains potential energy. However, when the object is dropped, the potential energy is dropping as the object gets closer to the floor but also the speed of the object is increasing. So the potential energy that the object originally had is quickly becoming transformed into kinetic energy.
- **Solar energy → chemical energy:** Energy from the sun is important in the production of chemical energy or food for plants. This is the basic principle behind photosynthesis.
- **Electrical energy → thermal energy + light energy:** An example of this type of energy transformation is when a light bulb stand is plugged into a wall outlet. The wall outlet supplies electrical energy that is used to light the light bulb. When the bulb is lit, the electrical energy has been transformed into light energy as well as thermal energy.

Know how the systems model can be used to understand common themes of physical science

The beginning teacher understands how the systems model can be used as a conceptual framework to organize, unify, and connect the common themes of physical science to other sciences and technology.

Even though the major branches of science are presented and taught separately in their own context, there are many instances in which physical science, life science, and earth and space science are interrelated and, in fact, rely on each other to truly explain a particular concept or phenomenon. Consider the major concepts taught in physics and chemistry:

- Laws of motion
- General forces
- General forms of energy and conservation of energy
- Law of gravitation
- Law of thermodynamics
- Atomic theory
- Conservation of mass
- Chemical bonds/reactions
- Stoichiometry principles

Each of these concepts can be applied to and integrated within other sciences such as many chemical and physical systems, the human body, the solar system, and the cycles of the Earth.

Analyze systems in physical science by applying the systems model

The beginning teacher analyzes systems in physical science (for example, the interactions of the parts of a toy car or a simple pendulum) in terms of constancy, change, cycles, structure, and processes.

Although they may seem elementary at first, many simple demonstrations in physical science provide an opportunity for teachers to discuss major concepts in depth. For example, consider the simple pendulum. A simple pendulum consists of a mass (known as a bob) attached to one end of a string and allowed to swing freely about a fixed pivot.

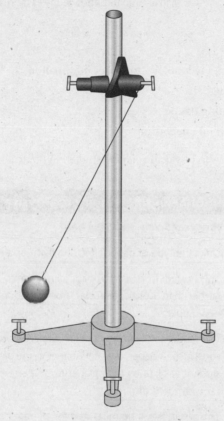

The five features of a system—constancy, change, cycles, structure, and processes—can be applied to a simple pendulum.

- **Constancy:** When the bob is suspended a certain angle (known as amplitude angle) from its equilibrium point (vertical line in which the bob is not moving but rather hanging from its pivot), the bob has potential energy. When released, the bob gains speed as it approaches the bottom. As the bob is released, the potential energy is transformed to kinetic energy. The kinetic energy at the bottom is then lost as the bob rises on the other side, thereby gaining stored potential energy. This process will continue as a result of conservation of energy unless another form of energy interferes with the constancy of the system.

- **Change:** In a simple pendulum, the position of the bob changes during its cyclic trip. Because the position changes, the pendulum bob has velocity and acceleration. If the pendulum bob accelerates, there must be force(s) acting on the bob. The changes observed during a cycle of a pendulum allow the teacher and the student to discuss important features of the pendulum.

- **Cycles:** As the pendulum bob is released, it continues back and forth in a periodic or cyclic nature. Two characteristics of a simple pendulum that are used to describe the cyclic nature of the pendulum are period and frequency. **Period** is the time required for the pendulum bob to complete one cycle or one round trip. **Frequency** is defined as the number of cycles or round trips that the pendulum bob makes per unit of time.

- **Structure:** The structure of a pendulum consists of a mass and a string. The object can be of any mass, size, or shape, and the string can be of any type or length.

- **Processes:** This feature of describing the pendulum refers to the processes by which the elements of the system interact with others in the system. The processes allow for interesting laboratory investigations, including the effects of string type, string length, object mass, object size, object shape, and amplitude angle on the period.

Engage in the process of scientific inquiry

The beginning teacher engages in the process of scientific inquiry in physical science (for example, asking a scientific question; formulating a testable hypothesis; selecting appropriate equipment and technology to gather information related to the hypothesis; making observations and collecting data; organizing, analyzing, and evaluating data to find data trends and patterns and make inferences; communicating and defending a valid conclusion).

In physical science, as in all branches of science, the process of scientific inquiry (also called the scientific method—see Competency 020) is vital and integral to science instruction and knowledge. The major steps of scientific inquiry are:

1. Asking a scientific question
2. Formulating a testable hypothesis
3. Selecting appropriate equipment and technology to gather information
4. Making observations and collecting data
5. Organizing, analyzing, and evaluating data
6. Communicating and defending a valid conclusion

An example of applying scientific inquiry to physical science is noted in the following table.

Application of Scientific Inquiry to Physical Science	
Major Step in Scientific Inquiry	**Physical Science Experiment**
Asking a scientific question	Does the type of paper affect the flight distance of paper airplanes?
Formulating a testable hypothesis	The student believes that paper airplanes constructed from poster board will fly farther than those constructed from notebook paper, construction paper, and newspaper.
Selecting appropriate equipment and technology to gather information	The student will construct paper airplanes out of poster board, notebook paper, construction paper, and newspaper in the same design and of the same size. The student will launch all airplanes from the same place in the same manner with the same amount of push.
Making observations and collecting data	The distance will be measured for all paper airplanes by the same student for several trials using a meter stick. The flight distance will be defined as the distance between the starting line and the point of the nose of each airplane.
Organizing, analyzing, and evaluating data	The student will conduct and record the measurements of the flight distances for all airplanes included in the investigation. The data should be recorded in a table in the student's laboratory notebook and should be graphed in order to visualize the data and make comparisons between airplanes.
Communicating and defending a valid conclusion	Based on the findings of the experiment presented in the table and graphs, the student should easily determine whether his/her hypothesis was correct. If the hypothesis was incorrect, the student should now be able to revise the hypothesis, conduct a different experiment, and begin to search for an explanation or reasons why the hypothesis is now correct.

Use a variety of tools and techniques to gather and use data

The beginning teacher uses a variety of tools, equipment, technology, and techniques to access, gather, store, retrieve, organize, and analyze data in physical science.

In order to successfully investigate physical science, a student must have access to and understand how to use a variety of tools and equipment to collect data or scientific information. These tools are described in the following table:

Measurement Tools Used in Physical Science Investigations		
Type of Measurement	*Measurement Tool*	*Unit of Measurement*
Length	Ruler, meter stick, measuring tape	meters, m centimeters, cm yard, yd feet, ft inches, in
Area	Ruler, meter stick, measuring tape	square meters, m^2 square centimeters, cm^2 square yards, yd^2 square feet, ft^2 square inches, in^2
Volume (length)	Ruler, meter stick, measuring tape	cubic centimeters, cc cubic feet, ft^3 cubic inches, in^3
Volume (liquid)	Measuring cups, beaker, graduated cylinder	milliliters, mL cubic centimeters, cc cubic feet, ft^3

(continued)

Measurement Tools Used in Physical Science Investigations (continued)		
Type of Measurement	Measurement Tool	Unit of Measurement
Mass	Balance/scale	grams, g kilograms, kg
Time	Stopwatch	seconds, s
Temperature	Thermometer	degrees (°F, °C)

Understand the concepts of precision, accuracy, and error

The beginning teacher demonstrates knowledge of the concepts of precision, accuracy, and error with regard to reading and recording numerical data from a scientific instrument in the context of physical science investigations.

Accuracy refers to how close a measurement is to the standard or accepted value and depends upon the quality of the measuring device. For example, if a student places a 200.0 g object or sample on a balance, the student should observe a reading of 200.0 g. A reading of 200.1 g is more accurate of a measurement than 210 g. The error of a measurement refers to the variance between the experimental measurement and the standard or accepted value and can be calculated by:

$$\text{percentage error} = \frac{\text{observed value} - \text{accepted value}}{\text{accepted value}} \times 100\%$$

Precision is the ability of a measurement to be consistently reproduced. If the student placed the 200.0 g object or sample on a balance five times and each time recorded a measurement of 200.1 g, the measurement would be both accurate and precise. If the student placed the 200.0 g object or sample on a balance five times and each time recorded a measurement of 210.0 g, the measurement would be inaccurate but precise. The goal of a scientist is to obtain both accurate and precise measurements in an experiment.

Communicate data in a variety of ways

The beginning teacher organizes, displays, and communicates physical science data in a variety of ways (for example, collections, graphs, tables, written reports) using appropriate technology.

An important facet of scientific inquiry is the ability of the scientists to not only record information from a scientific experiment but also to present the results of their experiment and defend or support their hypothesis. There are a variety of forms of communication of scientific data including tables, graphs (line graph, bar graph, pie chart), maps, diagrams, physical science formulas, mathematical equations, and conceptual demonstrations. A student must be knowledgeable of these various forms of communication and be adept at creating most, if not all, of these forms of communication for their particular investigations. Furthermore, a student should also be instructed on the different types of media used for creating these forms of communication such as graph paper, a calculator, a computer, and various software programs such as Microsoft Word, Microsoft Excel, and Microsoft PowerPoint.

Understand procedures for using and disposing of chemicals

The beginning teacher understands procedures for the appropriate storage, handling, use, disposal, care, and maintenance of chemicals, materials, and equipment in physical science.

Safety should be of utmost importance to a teacher in any physical science investigation performed by the students. Teachers must understand and instruct their students on the appropriate storage, handling, use, disposal, care, and maintenance of chemicals, materials, and equipment used in all physical science investigations.

Sample Questions

Ms. Fielding, a 3rd-grade teacher, was teaching a physical science lesson on gravity and its effect on objects. She explained that gravity is a pulling force that keeps all of us on the surface of the Earth. To demonstrate gravity, she held up a heavy backpack and a pencil at the same height. She asked the class which object would hit the ground first when dropped at the same time: the backpack or the pencil. Ms. Fielding decided to have the students participate in an investigation to help answer their question. Working in small groups, the students were given various types of balls: golf ball, baseball, and softball.

1. As the students dropped the golf ball, baseball, and softball at the same time from the same height, they found that all balls hit the ground at the same time. These results indicate that which characteristic is influenced by gravity:

    A. mass
    B. density
    C. shape
    D. none of the above

    D Comparison of the three different balls (golf ball, baseball, and softball) yields objects that differ in mass, density, and shape, yet when all three are dropped from the same height at the same time, they all hit the ground at the same time. Thus, none of the variables (mass, density, and shape) is influenced by gravity, and D is the correct response.

2. As the students observed all of the balls reaching the ground at the same time when dropped from the same height, Ms. Fielding then dropped the backpack and the pencil at the same time from the same height, and those objects also hit the ground at the same time. She asked the students to explain why this was the case. A plausible explanation would be:

    A. Gravity acts on all objects with the same force.
    B. Gravity acts on all balls with the same force.
    C. Gravity acts on all objects with an increasing force.
    D. Gravity acts on all objects with a decreasing force.

    A Because all of the balls landed at the same time when released from the same height, it is clear that gravity acts on all balls with the same force. However, because Ms. Fielding also went on to drop the backpack and the pencil (two objects very different from the balls) at the same time, and they also reached the ground at the same time, one must infer that the force of gravity is constant for all objects, not just balls. Thus, A is the correct response.

3. Based on the results from the golf ball, baseball, and softball, Ms. Fielding asked the students to predict what would happen if the same objects were dropped from the top of the school building. A viable prediction of this experiment would be that the three balls would

    A. still strike the ground at the same time and in the same amount of time.
    B. still strike the ground at the same instant but would require a longer time to do so.
    C. not strike the ground at the same time with the larger object striking the ground first.
    D. not strike the ground at the same time with the smaller object striking the ground first.

    B All of the objects, when released from a larger distance, will strike the ground at the same time, because gravity acts with the same force on objects at the larger distance as it does at the smaller distance. However, because the objects must travel a larger distance, they will require more time to reach the ground. Thus, B is the correct response.

Competency 022 (Life Science)

The teacher understands the fundamental concepts, principles, and processes of life science.

Review

Understand that each structure performs a different function

The beginning teacher understands that living systems have different structures to perform different functions.

All living systems are composed of cells, the smallest unit of life.

- The inside of the cell consists of **organelles** or little organs; the cell is enclosed by a border known as a **membrane,** which protects structures of a cell, separates its interior from the surroundings, and strictly controls what moves in and out.

- Cells contain the hereditary information necessary for regulating cell functions and for transmitting information to the next generation of cells.

- **Unicellular organisms** (for example, bacteria) have one cell; **multicellular organisms** (for example, plants, animals, and humans) have more than one cell.

- In multicellular organisms, the level of organization involving cells can be summarized as follows:

Cells	$\rightarrow$	Tissues	$\rightarrow$	Organs	$\rightarrow$	Organ Systems
neurons		nerves		Brain/spinal cord		nervous system
(nerve cells)				(nervous tissue)		

- **Cells:** Basic structure of living things that represents the primary level of organization in a multicellular organism
- **Tissues:** Groups of similar cells that perform specific functions
- **Organs:** Groups of tissues that perform specific functions
- **Organ systems:** Groups of organs that work together to perform specific functions

Describe the stages of the life cycle

The beginning teacher understands and describes stages in the life cycle of common plants and animals.

The life cycle describes the general process of how an organism lives and grows.

The major stages in the **life cycle of common plants** can be summarized by:

seed   →   germination   →   stems and roots   →   flower

The major stages in the **life cycle of common animals** can be summarized by:

egg   →   caterpillar   →   pupa   →   butterfly

egg   →   chicks   →   chicken

egg   →   tadpole   →   frog

Recognize that organisms have basic needs

The beginning teacher understands that organisms have basic needs.

Organisms must be able to perform the following necessary functions in order to survive: feeding, respiration, circulation, excretion, response to internal and external stimuli, movement, and reproduction.

- **Feeding:** Animals must be able to find, ingest, and digest food and the needed nutrients required for the organism to sustain life at the cellular level. The organs and features of a digestive system vary according to species to accommodate the different feeding habits of an organism. For example, carnivores (meat eaters) have a digestive system equipped with fast-acting, meat-digestive enzymes to break down the proteins and make it easier for the body to use the smaller components of the proteins. Herbivores (plant eaters), on the other hand, generally have large intestines lined with colonies of bacteria to help break down plant tissues.

- **Respiration:** In addition to the nutrients supplied by food, the cells of an organism also must be able to take in or inhale oxygen and impart or exhale carbon dioxide. This is the primary function of an organism's respiratory system.

- **Circulation:** The previous processes involve the need for food and oxygen by an organism to survive. The use for food and oxygen occurs at the cellular level. The circulatory system of an organism is designed to not only ensure the delivery of food and oxygen to the cells but also remove cellular waste products. In humans, the circulatory system consists of a heart connected to a complex arrangement of blood vessels, with arteries transporting oxygenated blood to the organs of the body and veins carrying deoxygenated blood from the organ back to the heart.

- **Excretion:** As an organism utilizes the food and water to sustain cell growth, waste products are formed that must be removed or excreted from the body. Some waste products, for example ammonia, contain nitrogen and can be potentially dangerous if allowed to build up in the body. In humans, liquid waste products are usually eliminated through the kidneys, while solid waste products are eliminated through the intestines.

- **Response:** In order to survive, an organism must be able to respond to external and internal stimuli in its environment. This is accomplished through the nervous system, consisting of nerve cells. Nerve cells are responsible for receiving information from stimuli such as sounds or light, transferring this information to the brain (where the information is received and processed), and followed by a coordinated response of the organism.

- **Movement:** A response to any external or internal stimulus often causes an organism to move. Movement in the human is accomplished through the muscular and skeletal systems. Electrical impulses received by the brain through the nerve cells are also sent out to all parts of the body as the brain coordinates its response to the stimulus. If movement is required in response to the stimulus, the electrical signals sent from the brain are transmitted to the muscles of the body, which are connected to the skeletal system. The signals cause the muscles to move, which in turn moves the desired part of the skeletal system. This is particularly important for an organism to avoid potentially dangerous situations.

- **Reproduction:** In order for a species to survive, it must be able to reproduce or create offspring. If a species cannot reproduce, it will become extinct.

Demonstrate knowledge of adaptive characteristics

The beginning teacher demonstrates knowledge of adaptive characteristics and explains how adaptations influence the survival of populations or species.

All species possess unique, inherited characteristics or features, known as **adaptations,** that aid in their ability to survive in their environment. It is a species' adaptations that account for the large amount of diversity in nature. Adaptive characteristics can relate to features about the anatomy (the structure of the body) or physiological processes (how the body works). Examples of species and their unique adaptive characteristics are described in the following table.

Adaptive Characteristics of Species	
Anatomical Features	
Organism	*Adaptive Characteristic*
Chameleons	**Coloration:** These lizards can change color to blend in with the colors of their environment for protection/defense.
Birds	**Waterproof wings:** Birds have wings that are either waterproof or dry easily after swims or in inclement weather (rain).
Ducks	**Webbed feet:** Ducks can easily swim (navigate in water) because of their webbed feet.
Lions, alligators, sharks	**Sharp teeth:** Lions, alligators, and sharks all have sharp teeth to help them kill their prey and eat it.
Rhinos	**Horns:** The horn of a rhino allows it to dig through dirt and use it as a defense mechanism.
Physiological Processes	
Organism	*Adaptive Characteristic*
Cactus	**Covering and spines:** The cactus has a thick waxy covering to protect it against water loss.
Bats	**Nocturnal nature:** Bats sleep in cool caves during the day and are active at night, enabling them to search for food, primarily insects, at night.
Brown bear	**Ability to hibernate:** The brown bear possesses the ability not only to hibernate over prolonged periods of food shortage but also to store large amounts of fat.
Polar bear	**Ability to withstand exposure to extreme cold:** A polar bear, whose living environment is the extreme cold conditions of Antarctica, can survive because of its coat. The hairs of its coat are hollow, not only helping the polar bear to maintain body warmth but also helping the bear float while swimming.
Jack rabbits	**Ability to dissipate heat:** These desert mammals use their long ears, equipped with many blood vessels, to release heat when they are upright, thus providing a means for cooling the jack rabbit. When a jack rabbit is in cold weather, its ears retract or lie close to the body to provide warmth.

Know that organisms respond to stimuli

The beginning teacher understands that organisms respond to internal or external stimuli and analyzes the role of internal and external stimuli in the behavior of organisms.

In order to survive in an environment, a species must be able to recognize, interpret, and respond to stimuli. A **stimulus** is an action, agent, or condition that initiates a response. The stimulus can be either internal (occurring from within the organism) or external (occurring from outside the organism). Examples of internal stimuli include a species' search for food in response to hunger and a species' search for water in response to thirst. Examples of external stimuli include a species' shivering and search for warmth in response to cold temperatures and a species' search for a safe haven in response to a threatening or unfamiliar sound.

Regardless of the type, the body recognizes the stimuli through **receptors,** which are then transmitted to the brain as an electrical impulse through the nervous system. Once the impulse reaches the brain, the organism interprets the stimulus, decides on the appropriate actions to take to address the potential impact or effect of the stimuli, and then sends impulses back through the nervous system to the various parts of the body that will be required to successfully carry out the intended actions of the organism.

Describe plant and animal reproductive processes

The beginning teacher describes the processes by which plants and animals reproduce and explains how hereditary information is passed from one generation to the next.

All living things (organisms) can reproduce, a process that is critical for species survival. Reproduction between two individuals of the same species will produce offspring of the same species. The physical features or traits of the offspring will occur as a direct result of the combination of genetic information from both parents, referred to as heredity.

The basic molecule involved in heredity is DNA (deoxyribonucleic acid), found in the nucleus of the cell. DNA, a molecule in the shape of a double helix or twisted ladder, consists primarily of three major components: a sugar (deoxyribose), a phosphate molecule, and nucleotide bases of which there are four: adenine, thymine, guanine, and cytosine. The portion or segment of DNA that transfers the instructions of a trait from parent to offspring is called a **gene,** which is found in the chromosomes of each cell.

Compare and contrast inherited traits and learned characteristics

The beginning teacher compares and contrasts inherited traits and learned characteristics.

Traits are specific characteristics that are unique to an individual. An inherited trait is a specific characteristic of an offspring expressed as a physical feature or ability inherited from the parents through their DNA (deoxyribonucleic acid). Examples of inherited traits in humans include eye color, earlobes, blood type, skin color, and height. Examples of inherited traits in other species include the scaly exterior of a snake, the feathers of a bird, and the fruit borne by a particular plant. Although an inherited trait can result from either a single gene or many genes, it is also possible for a single gene to be responsible for the expression of more than one inherited trait.

Acquired traits or learned characteristics are those characteristics that an individual acquires as a result of his or her environment. Examples of acquired characteristics include hair length, nutrition, and exercise. Some major diseases or disorders such as high blood pressure, diabetes, and heart disease are believed to be caused as a result of both inherited traits, such as family history, as well as acquired characteristics or conditions, such as poor nutrition, obesity, lack of exercise or physical activity, and smoking.

Understand the relationships between organisms and the environment

The beginning teacher understands relationships between organisms and the environment and describes ways in which living organisms depend on each other and on the environment to meet their basic needs.

In order to survive as a species, an organism must engage in relationships between other organisms of the same species and with the environment. An organism depends on other organisms of the same species if they are to flourish as a species. Their dependence on each other is demonstrated through several types of behavior:

- **Cycles of behavior:** Many cycles occur in nature including the cycle between night and day as well as the cycles of the seasons. Any naturally occurring cycles can induce behavior changes in animals such as hibernation and migration.

- **Courtship:** The success of a species depends on the ability of organisms to reproduce. However, on a social level, rituals of courtship occur in which organisms identify and attract potential mates for reproduction through certain stimuli in the form of sounds, visual displays, or chemicals.

- **Social behavior:** Because members of the same society often share many of the same genes, they form a bond that often helps them in many of the vital functions required to survive, such as working together to search for food and banding together as a means of defense and protection. However, this type of behavior has potential pitfall. Members of the same species may compete for the same territory with its limited resources, often resulting in aggressive behavior.

- **Communication:** Yet another important ability of organisms in their dependence on each other involves the ability to communicate in a language understandable between all organisms of the same species. The language can be as complex as the various tongues spoken by humans and as simple as a sound, visual signal, or touch that conveys thoughts.

An organism must be able to maintain a constant or stable environment necessary for life. This ability for an organism to maintain constant conditions or equilibrium is referred to as **homeostasis**, which literally translates to "stay the same." Regardless of the environment, an organism must have access to food, water, and shelter.

Identify organisms, populations, or species with similar needs

The beginning teacher identifies organisms, populations, or species with similar needs and analyzes how they compete with one another for resources.

In environments containing organisms, populations, or species, particularly those confined to a specific area or region, there are limited available resources to accommodate the needs of these organisms. These limited resources include food, water, shelter, nesting sites, and potential mates—all necessary for an organism's survival and reproduction. This often leads to the definition of territories and a competitive behavior that often involves aggression.

Know how the systems model can be used to understand common themes of life science

The beginning teacher understands how the systems model can be used as a conceptual framework to organize, unify, and connect the common themes of life science to other sciences and technology.

Even though the major branches of science are presented and taught separately in their own context, there are many instances in which the physical sciences, life sciences, and Earth sciences are interrelated and, in fact, rely on each other to truly explain a particular concept or phenomenon. Consider the major concepts taught in physics and chemistry:

- Laws of motion
- General forces
- General forms of energy and conservation of energy
- Law of gravitation
- Law of thermodynamics
- Atomic theory
- Conservation of mass
- Chemical bonds/reactions
- Stoichiometry principles

Each of these concepts can be applied to and integrated within other sciences, such as many chemical and physical systems, the human body, the solar system, and the cycles of the Earth.

Analyze systems in life science by applying the systems model

The beginning teacher applies the systems model to analyze systems in life science (for example, the interactions of the parts of a plant or an animal) in terms of constancy, change, cycles, structure, and processes.

An example of an application of the systems model to life science is the circulatory system. The circulatory system, consisting of the heart and blood vessels, is responsible for pumping blood and hence transporting oxygen and nutrients to all organs of the body and removing cellular waste. The five features of a system—constancy, change, cycles, structure, and processes—can be applied to the circulatory system of the human body.

- **Constancy:** In order for a human being to survive, the cells must receive a constant, sufficient supply of oxygen and nutrients through blood in order to maintain the high level of energy needed to carry out its life-sustaining functions. Depending on the age and overall health of the person, the heart beats at a typical rate of 70 beats per minute, about 1.1 beats per second, with each beat providing the constant supply of blood to the cells of the body.

- **Change:** As the heart beats, it is causing a change in the position of blood, moving it through an array of blood vessels, which become progressively smaller, entering the smallest vessels in the body (capillaries) and exiting through veins, which become progressively larger, until reaching the heart. Changes also occur with the pumping force of the heart or blood pressure. The systolic blood pressure—the pressure of the heart while it is beating—is about 120 mm Hg in a normal person. The diastolic blood pressure—the pressure of the heart in its resting state—is about 80 mm Hg in a normal person.

- **Cycles:** The circulatory system is, in essence, a closed circuit or loop. As blood is ejected from the heart at the onset of each heartbeat, blood flows through the aorta, and then enters arteries, which become progressively smaller as the blood gets closer and closer to the organ. Once in the organ, blood passes through the smallest vessels of the body, the capillaries, before exiting through small veins, which become larger and larger until blood reaches the heart again to become oxygenated by the oxygen in the lungs. The route of blood through the circulatory system is one cycle. Yet another cycle is the heart beat itself, which continues at a cycle of about 1.1 beats every second.

- **Structure:** The structure of the circulatory system consists of a heart—a 300 g organ with four chambers or openings in it. The two upper chambers are referred to as atria while the two bottom chambers are referred to as ventricles. The blood vessels are long, thin, flexible tissues in the shape of cylinders with a hole through the center similar to the shape of a long straw. The structure varies between the arteries, veins, and capillaries.

- **Processes:** This feature of describing the circulatory system refers to the processes by which the elements of the system interact with others in the system. The processes allow for interesting laboratory investigations. One may be interested in looking for a relationship between exercise and blood pressure or the effects of age and/or gender on the pulse rate of a person.

Engage in the process of scientific inquiry

The beginning teacher engages in the process of scientific inquiry in life science (for example, asking a scientific question; formulating a testable hypothesis; selecting appropriate equipment and technology to gather information related to the hypothesis; making observations and collecting data; organizing, analyzing, and evaluating data to find data trends and patterns and make inferences; communicating and defending a valid conclusion).

In life science, as in all branches of science, the process of **scientific inquiry** (also called the scientific method—see Competency 020) is vital and integral to science instruction and knowledge. The major steps of scientific inquiry are:

- Asking a scientific question
- Formulating a testable hypothesis
- Selecting appropriate equipment and technology to gather information
- Making observations and collecting data
- Organizing, analyzing, and evaluating data
- Communicating and defending a valid conclusion

An example of applying scientific inquiry to life science is noted in the following table.

Application of Scientific Inquiry to Life Science	
Major Step in Scientific Inquiry	*Life Science Experiment*
Asking a scientific question	How does light affect the growth of plants?
Formulating a testable hypothesis	The student believes that plants (for example, bean or radish) will grow better in sunlight than in artificial light. The indication of growth will be studied through the measurement of the length of the sprout.
Selecting appropriate equipment and technology to gather information	The student will conduct an experiment in which the same seeds will be placed in the same containers with the same amount of soil watered in the same intervals but exposed to different types of light: sunlight, white light, green light, blue light, and no light (total darkness).
Making observations and collecting data	The length of the sprout will be measured for all types of lights after a predetermined time interval (for example, one week following planting of the seeds).
Organizing, analyzing, and evaluating data	The student will record the measurements of the sprouts exposed to all types of light. The data should be recorded in a table in the student's lab notebook and should be graphed, in order to visualize the data and make comparisons between the sprouts.
Communicating and defending a valid conclusion	Based on the findings of the experiment presented in the table and graphs, the student should easily determine whether his/her hypothesis was correct. If the hypothesis was incorrect, the student should now be able to revise the hypothesis, conduct a different experiment, and begin to search for an explanation or reasons why the hypothesis is now correct.

Use a variety of tools and techniques to gather and use data

The beginning teacher uses a variety of tools, equipment, technology, and techniques to access, gather, store, retrieve, organize, and analyze data in life science.

In order to successfully investigate life science, a student must have access to and understand how to use a variety of tools and equipment to collect data or scientific information. These tools are described in the following table:

Measurement Tools Used in Life Science Investigations		
Type of Measurement	*Measurement Tool*	*Unit of Measurement*
Length	Ruler, meter stick, measuring tape	meters, m centimeters, cm yard, yd feet, ft inches, in
Area	Ruler, meter stick, measuring tape	square meters, m^2 square centimeters, cm^2 square yards, yd^2 square feet, ft^2 square inches, in^2
Volume (length)	Ruler, meter stick, measuring tape	cubic centimeters, cc cubic feet, ft^3 cubic inches, in^3
Volume (liquid)	Measuring cups, beaker, graduated cylinder	milliliters, mL cubic centimeters, cc cubic feet, ft^3

(continued)

Measurement Tools Used in Life Science Investigations (continued)

Type of Measurement	Measurement Tool	Unit of Measurement
Visual magnification	Microscope	centimeters, cm inches, in square centimeters, cm^2 square inches, in^2
Acidity/basicity of a substance	Litmus paper	pH (numerical scale:1–14) Low values: Acidic High values: Basic

Understand the concepts of precision, accuracy, and error

The beginning teacher demonstrates knowledge of the concepts of precision, accuracy, and error with regard to reading and recording numerical data from a scientific instrument.

Accuracy refers to how close a measurement is to the standard or accepted value, and depends upon the quality of the measuring device. For example, if a student places a 200.0 g object or sample on a balance, the student should observe a reading of 200.0 g. A reading of 200.1 g is more accurate of a measurement than 210 g. The error of a measurement refers to the variance between the experimental measurement and the standard or accepted value and can be calculated by:

$$\text{percentage error} = \frac{\text{observed value} - \text{accepted value}}{\text{accepted value}} \times 100\%$$

Precision is the ability of a measurement to be consistently reproduced. If the student placed the 200.0 g object or sample on a balance five times and each time recorded a measurement of 200.1 g, the measurement would be both accurate and precise. If the student placed the 200.0 g object or sample on a balance five times and each time recorded a measurement of 210.0 g, the measurement would be inaccurate but precise. The goal of a scientist is to obtain both accurate and precise measurements in an experiment.

Communicate data in a variety of ways

The beginning teacher organizes, displays, and communicates life science data in a variety of ways (for example, collections, graphs, tables, written reports) using appropriate technology.

An important facet of scientific inquiry is the ability of the scientists to not only record information from a scientific experiment but also to present the results of their experiment and defend or support their hypothesis. There are a variety of forms of communication of scientific data including tables, graphs (line graph, bar graph, pie chart), maps, diagrams, life science formulas, mathematical equations, and conceptual demonstrations. A student must be knowledgeable of these various forms of communication and be adept at creating most if not all of these forms of communication for their particular investigations. Furthermore, a student should also be instructed on the different types of media used for creating these forms of communication such as graph paper, a calculator, a computer, and various software programs such as Microsoft Word, Microsoft Excel, and Microsoft PowerPoint.

Understand procedures for using chemicals and treating specimens

The beginning teacher understands procedures for the appropriate storage, handling, use, disposal, care, and mainte-nance of chemicals, materials, specimens, and equipment and demonstrates ethical care and treatment of organisms and specimens.

Safety should be of utmost importance to a teacher in any life science investigation performed by the students. A teacher must understand and instruct their students on the appropriate storage, handling, use, disposal, care, and maintenance of chemicals, materials, and equipment used in all life science investigations. Students must also understand that any living organism or animal that is involved in a life science demonstration, even one as elementary as observing or petting a pet hamster in the classroom, must be treated in an ethical and responsible manner.

Sample Questions

In preparing a two-week-long unit on the human body, Mr. Garcia began by speaking to his 2nd-grade students about the circulatory system and its major parts: the heart and the blood vessels. The heart is a pump that pushes blood through the blood vessels of the body. The heart makes sure that all parts of the body have the food and oxygen they need in order to grow and work properly. He then asked his class, "How do we know our heart is working?" "By placing my hand over my chest," a student replied. Working off of this response, Mr. Garcia decided to conduct a classroom investigation in which students, working in small groups, were to determine the effect of exercise on the heart. He asked them to walk, hop on one foot, and then run down the classroom hallway. After each type of exercise, the students were to measure their heart rate or to count the number of beats in 10 seconds, and then multiply by 6 to give them beats per minute.

1. Before the students begin to work on their investigation and collect data, it is important that they:

   A. Make several measurements and average the values.
   B. Have more than one student participate and measure their heart rate as well.
   C. Measure their heart rate at rest.
   D. Have stopwatches that measure to within 0.001 accuracy.

   C It is important that, in any laboratory investigation, a baseline measurement be performed as a basis for comparison. Walking, jogging, and running will elevate the heart rate but to measure the extent of the elevation, there must be a baseline value for comparison. Option A is a true statement but is something that should be done during the experiment, not before the experiment is started. Option B is not correct, because having the measurement from two or more different students does not improve the quality of data and, in fact, reduces it. Stopwatch accuracy for this type of experiment is not necessary to this degree and, thus, option D is not a viable answer.

2. Mr. Garcia pointed out to each group that, as they completed each exercise and measured their heart rate, it was important for them to rest about five minutes before performing the next exercise. The reason for this would be:

   A. to prevent the students from tiring out over this activity
   B. to minimize bias in the data
   C. to give students a chance to get a drink a water
   D. to prevent the student from hurting themselves

   B Although safety is an important issue in any scientific investigation, the correct response is B. Each activity the students are performing elevates their heart rates. If sufficient time is not allowed after each activity, their heart rates will be artificially elevated for the next physical activity, making the results and the experiment biased. Thus, in order to eliminate the potential for bias, asking the students to rest five minutes will lower their heart rate back to a normal (resting) value making it a more representative value when it is collected after the next activity.

3. A possible extension to this activity may be for Mr. Garcia to have the students

   A. Engage in their activity for longer periods of time.
   B. Try different types of exercise activities.
   C. Compare the results between boys and girls.
   D. Make measurements of the pulse rate by placing two fingers over the wrist.

   A The key word in this problem is "extension." Although each option poses an interesting investigation in its own right, the activity that follows from the investigation just completed would be to engage in their physical activity for longer periods of time. All of the other options would involve different experiments altogether.

Competency 023 (Earth and Space Science)

The beginning teacher understands the fundamental concepts, principles, and processes of earth and space science.

Review

Describe the properties and uses of earth materials

The beginning teacher understands and describes the properties and uses of earth materials (for example, rocks, soils, water, and atmospheric gases).

In order to perform meaningful investigations in Earth and space science, a scientist must first begin by studying features and components found on the Earth's surface and in the surrounding environment. Specific features and components that are particularly important to the surface of the Earth are rocks, soils, water, and atmospheric gases.

Of all of the materials readily available and in abundance on the Earth's surface, **rocks** are the most common. Rocks are objects composed primarily of naturally occurring minerals and can be classified according to three separate categories based on how they were formed: igneous, sedimentary, and metamorphic.

- **Igneous rock:** Igneous rocks are formed when melted rock, known as **magma,** cools. Igneous rocks can form underground when the magma becomes trapped in small pockets and cools slowly. These types of rocks can also form on the Earth's surface when magma rises to the Earth's surface as a result of volcanic eruption and cools quickly. Examples of igneous rocks include mica, feldspar, and quartz.

- **Sedimentary rock:** Sedimentary rocks are formed when sediments or tiny particles and pieces of other rocks that have been eroded over time by wind and water are deposited along layers, compacted together, and hardened over time by the pressure exerted by existing sediments above them. Examples of sedimentary rock include sandstone, limestone, and shale.

- **Metamorphic rock:** Metamorphic rocks are either igneous or sedimentary rocks that have **morphed** or changed shapes under intense heat or pressure at significant depths under the Earth's surface. Examples of metamorphic rocks include schist and gneiss.

The formation and relationship between the three types of rocks are described by the **rock cycle.** In fact, any of the three types of rocks can transform themselves into either of the two remaining types of rock—that is, igneous rock can transform itself into sedimentary rock or into metamorphic rock; sedimentary rock can transform itself into metamorphic rock or into igneous rock; and metamorphic rock can transform itself into igneous or sedimentary rock. The rock cycle is illustrated in the following figure.

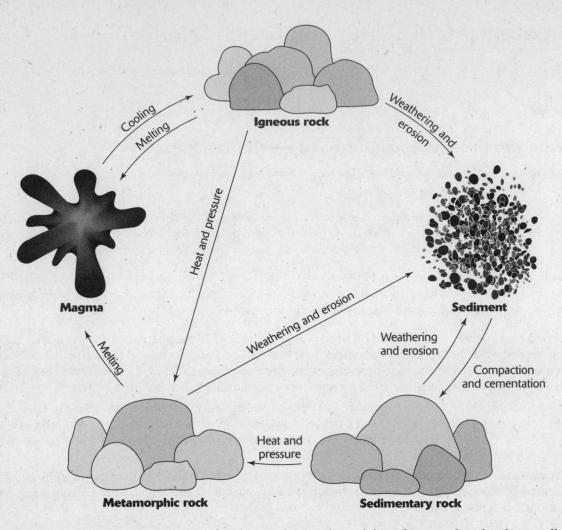

Soils, a natural resource that serves as nutrients for plants and vegetation, originate from weathered rocks as well as organic material produced from decaying plants and animals. The process of soil formation is affected by several factors, including rock type and structure, climate, animals, and time.

Water is very important in many of the geological processes that occur on the Earth's surface. Because water exists in all three states of matter—solid (ice), liquid (water), or gas (water vapor)—it is always changing. The constant changing of the states of matter of water is the basis for the water cycle.

The Earth's surface is always subjected to variations in temperature, which result in the addition or subtraction of heat. The gain or loss of heat results in the changing of the states of matter, a continual process described by the **water cycle.** According to the water cycle, either of the states of matter can transform to either of the other two states of matter, depending on the nature of heat transfer. For example, ice can transform to water or water vapor; water can transform to ice or water vapor; and water vapor can transform to water or ice. The water cycle is illustrated in the following figure.

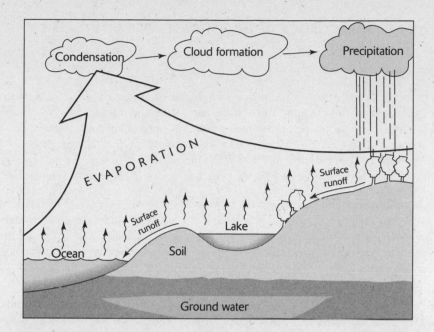

Atmospheric gases are the gases that comprise the surrounding air of the Earth's atmosphere. Although many gases are present, the two major gases found in air are nitrogen and oxygen, which account for 78% and 21% percent of air, respectively. The remaining 1% of the gases found in the atmosphere is referred to as trace gases and includes in small amounts: argon, hydrogen, methane, nitrous oxide, water vapor, ozone, and carbon dioxide.

Understand the characteristics of and measures for weather

The beginning teacher demonstrates knowledge of characteristics of weather, changes in the weather, and tools for making weather measurements.

Weather refers to the phenomena that naturally occur as a result of the lower atmosphere. The weather differs according to the geographical location and time of the year. The five elements of weather that are used to describe the condition of the Earth's lower atmosphere are: air temperature, precipitation, sunshine/cloud cover, wind speed/direction, and air pressure. All of these elements combined can help the weather forecaster to predict the type of day or week in a certain region and to prepare a community or region for any potentially dangerous weather that could develop (tornados and hurricanes). Changes in the weather result primarily from the consequences of changes in air temperature and air pressure.

- **Changes in air temperature:** The Earth's surface is heated by the sun unevenly. When molecules are subjected to heat, they gain kinetic energy and expand, becoming less dense than the cooler air surrounding them, causing them to rise. The cooler air has less kinetic energy and hence greater density, and as a result moves closer toward the Earth's surface. The warmer air rises, spreads out in the atmosphere above, becomes cooler, and then descends toward the Earth's surface. This is a method of the transfer of heat energy known as convection.

- **Changes in air pressure:** A change in air pressure is a strong indicator of changes in weather. As a low pressure area approaches a high pressure area, a difference in pressure is created, resulting in the formation of winds. The strength of the winds increases as the pressure difference between the two areas increases. If the air pressure drops a significant amount in a rapid manner, severe weather such as tornados and hurricanes can develop.

Common weather instruments include the following:

- **Rain gauge:** A rain gauge is an instrument consisting of an open container that measures the amount of rain (liquid precipitation) in units of centimeters (cm), millimeters (mm), or inches (in) that falls in a particular area over a particular time interval.

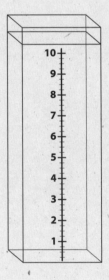

- **Thermometer:** A thermometer is an instrument that measures the temperature. A thermometer is usually a long, thin glass tube filled with mercury or alcohol (although mercury thermometers are no longer made because of the toxicity of mercury and the safety dangers that arise if the thermometer is broken). The liquid inside the glass tube is chosen such that it rises for higher temperatures and lowers for cooler temperatures. The units of temperature are degrees Celsius (°C) or degrees Fahrenheit (°F).

- **Hygrometer:** A hygrometer is an instrument used to measure the humidity or amount of water in the air. The relative humidity, expressed in units of percent (%), is generally an indication of impending rain.

- **Wind vane:** A wind vane is an instrument that measures the direction of the wind. Measurements of the wind direction are expressed in units of direction [that is, N (north), S (south), E (east), W (west), NE (northeast), NW (northwest), SE (southwest), SW (southwest)].

■ **Barometer:** A barometer is an instrument that measures the air pressure or amount of force exerted by the air in the atmosphere on the Earth's surface. Air pressure is measured in units of Barr, Torr, millimeters of mercury (mm Hg), or kilopascals (KPa). Pressure systems generally reveal information about the type of day with high pressure systems resulting in sunny days, while low pressure systems result in rainy and cloudy days.

■ **Anemometer:** An anemometer is an instrument that measures wind speed in units of miles per hour (mph).

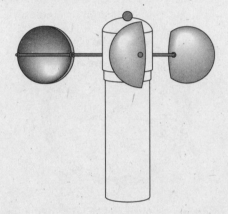

Know the forces and processes that change the Earth's surface

The beginning teacher understands forces and processes that change the surface of Earth (for example, glaciers, earthquakes, weathering).

The Earth is constantly in motion (as it rotates about its axis and revolves about the sun) and, as a result, is subjected to forces and processes that change the surface of the Earth. To understand the processes that change the surface of the Earth, students must first understand the four major interior layers of the Earth: crust, mantle, outer core, and inner core.

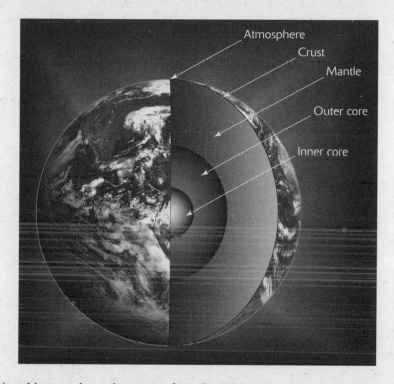

- **Crust:** The crust is a thin outer layer that ranges from 5 to 35 km (3.1 miles to 22 miles) in thickness. It consists primarily of sand and rock and comprises about 0.5% of the total mass of the Earth. The temperature of the crust is about 0°C (32°F).

- **Mantle:** The mantle is a thick layer of rock about 2,900 km (1,800 miles) in thickness and extends to half the distance to the center of the Earth. The primary elements found in the mantle include silicon, oxygen, aluminum, and iron and comprise approximately 68% of the total mass of the Earth. The temperature of the mantle is much higher than the crust with an approximate temperature of about 1,000°C (1,800°F).

- **The outer core:** The outer core is a thick layer of liquid or molten rock about 2,200 km (1,360 miles) in thickness. The primary elements found in the outer core include iron and nickel (in their liquid state) and comprise approximately 32% of the total mass of the Earth. The temperature of the outer core is much higher than the mantle of the Earth with an approximate temperature of about 2,500°C (4,500°F).

- **The inner core:** The inner core is a layer of solid rock about 1,220 km (745 miles) in thickness. The primary elements found in the mantle include iron and nickel (in their solid state) and comprise approximately 1.7% of the total mass of the Earth. The temperature of the inner core is much higher than the outer core with an approximate temperature of about 5,000°C (9,000°F).

Examples of the forces and processes that change the Earth's surface include glaciers, earthquakes, and weathering.

- **Glaciers:** Glaciers are large thickened masses of ice that evolve over many years. Glaciers occur in areas where snow has accumulated for periods of time long enough to transform into ice. Glaciers cover approximately 10% of the Earth's land area and account for about 75,000 square kilometers or 29,000 square miles in the United States, mostly located in Alaska.

- **Earthquakes:** An earthquake is a sudden movement (shaking, rolling, or trembling) of the Earth's surface. The Earth's surface or crust consists of a rigid, outer layer known as the **lithosphere.** The lithosphere consists of an irregular pattern or mosaic design of plates, which are in constant motion and can slide. As these plates move and interact with other plates, stresses can occur, resulting in a buildup or storage of energy. Because energy is a conserved quantity, the energy built up by the plate movement can only be released through transformation. In other words, the mechanical energy stored within the Earth's crust will be transformed in the mechanical (seismic) energy of the plates as well as sound energy.

- **Weathering:** Weathering refers to the processes involved in the breakdown of rocks. Weathering is influenced by many factors such as rock type/structure, climate, slope, animals, and time. The two general categories of weathering are physical weathering and chemical weathering. **Physical weathering,** the involvement of physical or mechanical forces in the disintegration of the rocks and minerals, can occur through several different processes, including crystal growth, heat (extreme temperatures), and plant/animal activity. **Chemical weathering** is the decomposition or alteration of rocks and minerals through chemical processes, primarily through oxidation (exposure to water) and dissolution by weak acids. The most common weak acid responsible for chemical weathering is carbonic acid [H_2CO_3], which is produced in rain water by the reaction between water with the CO_2 gas in the atmosphere.

Describe the characteristics of the sun, moon, and stars

The beginning teacher understands and describes characteristics of the sun, moon, and stars.

Located at the center of our solar system, the **sun** is a medium-sized star of approximately 1.4 million kilometers (865,400 miles) in diameter and approximately 93,000,000 miles from Earth. In comparison to the Earth, the sun's volume is greater by 1.3 million times, the sun's mass is greater by about 700 times, and the sun's surface gravity is greater by approximately 28 times.

The **moon** is a satellite of the Earth and is 3,476 kilometers in diameter. The moon is about 240,000 miles from Earth and can be clearly seen with the naked eye. The major features visible on the surface of the moon are craters, some caused by impact with meteors and some caused by volcanic activity on the moon.

Stars, consisting primarily of hydrogen and helium gases, can be extremely hot (between 180 and 1,080 million degrees Fahrenheit) and number in the hundreds of trillions. Stars are located 20 trillion miles away and farther from Earth and will burn for about 10 billion years.

Demonstrate knowledge of objects in the sky

The beginning teacher demonstrates knowledge of objects in the sky and their characteristics (for example, the sun as Earth's major energy source, position of the planets in relation to the sun).

The solar system consists of nine known planets and their moons that orbit around the sun. The nine planets (starting closest to the sun and extending outward) are Mercury, Venus, Earth, Mars, Jupiter, Saturn, Uranus, Neptune, and Pluto.

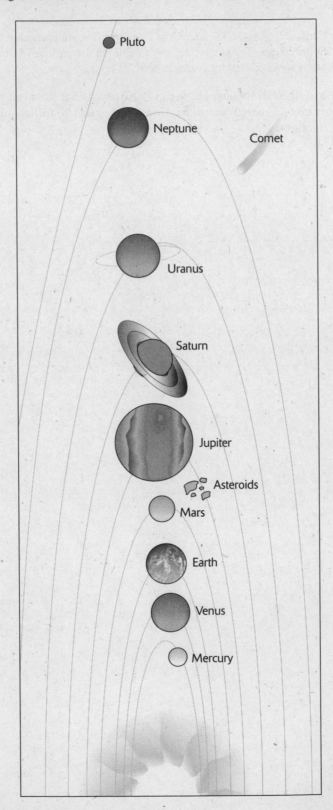

The sun provides the necessary amounts of light and heat required to sustain life on Earth. The temperature at the surface of the sun is between 5,500 – 6,000°C (10,000°F); the temperature at the center of the sun is much hotter, reaching temperatures of 10 million°C and greater.

Analyze the consequence of the moon's orbits and the Earth's orientation and movement

The beginning teacher analyzes the consequences of the moon's orbits around the Earth (for example, phases of the moon) and Earth's orientation and movement around the sun (for example, day and night and the seasons).

The solar system and the planets are in constant motion. All of the planets and planetary objects are spinning about their axis (rotation) and are moving in an elliptical orbit or path (revolution) around the sun.

The moon requires 27.3 days to complete one rotation about its axis. The moon also takes 27.3 days to complete one revolution or full cycle around the Earth, covering an average distance of 384,000 kilometers. The moon can always be seen during its revolution about Earth, but exactly how much of the moon is seen depends on the amount of sunlight reflected from the moon to the Earth's surface. The moon's cycle is divided into several stages or phases, described in the following table.

Phases of the Moon's Cycle (Cycle Duration: 29.5 Days)		
Phase	**Time Duration**	**Orientation of the Moon**
New moon	Day 0 to Day 7	The new moon occurs when the moon is between the sun and the Earth.

Phase	Time Duration	Orientation of the Moon
First quarter 	Day 8 to Day 14	At the first quarter phase, the moon has completed one fourth or one quarter of its revolution around the Earth and one half of the illuminated part of the moon is visible.
Full moon 	Day 15 to Day 22	The full moon occurs when the Earth is between the sun and the moon.

(continued)

Phases of the Moon's Cycle (Cycle Duration: 29.5 Days) *(continued)*

Phase	Time Duration	Orientation of the Moon
Last (third) quarter	Day 23 to Day 29	At the last (third) quarter, the moon has completed three-fourths or three quarters of its revolution around the Earth and one half of the illuminated part of the moon is visible.

The Earth completes one rotation about its axis in 24 hours (1 day) and completes one revolution or full cycle about the sun in 365 days. As the Earth revolves around the sun, the sun's rays strike different areas or regions of the Earth's surface, causing the Earth's temperature and atmosphere to change. The changes in the temperature and atmosphere are responsible for the different seasons. Winter occurs in the Northern Hemisphere and summer in the Southern Hemisphere when the North Pole is tilted away from the sun. The Northern Hemisphere experiences summer and winter occurs in the Southern Hemisphere when the North Pole is tilted toward the sun.

Know how the systems model can be used to understand common themes of earth and space science

The beginning teacher understands how the systems model can be used as a conceptual framework to organize, unify, and connect the common themes of earth and space science to other sciences and technology.

Even though the major branches of science are presented and taught separately in their own context, there are many instances in which physical science, life science, and Earth and space science are interrelated and, in fact, rely on each other to truly explain a particular concept or phenomenon. Consider the major concepts taught in physics and chemistry:

- Laws of motion
- General forces
- General forms of energy and conservation of energy
- Law of gravitation
- Law of thermodynamics
- Atomic theory
- Conservation of mass
- Chemical bonds/reactions
- Stoichiometry principles

Each of these concepts can be applied to and integrated within other sciences such as many chemical and physical systems, the human body, the solar system, and the cycles of the Earth.

Analyze systems in earth and space science by applying the systems model

The beginning teacher applies the systems model to analyze systems in earth and space science (for example, the ocean, the atmosphere) in terms of constancy, change, cycles, structure, and processes.

An example of the systems model applied to earth and space science is the Earth's (as well as all of the planetary objects that make up the solar system) position and movement around the sun. The five features of a system—constancy, change, cycles, structure, and processes—can be applied to the Earth's rotation around the sun.

- **Constancy:** The motion of the Earth about its own axis and in orbit about the sun is caused by the gravitational forces that exist between the Earth and the sun. Because the size (mass) of the Earth and the sun remains constant, so does the gravitational force that exists between them, as well as the motion of the Earth.

- **Change:** The movement of the Earth both about its axis and in orbit about the sun results in a change in position. The change in Earth's position in the rotation about its axis determines the time of the day, with 24 hours required to complete one rotation. The change in the Earth's position in its orbit about the sun determines the changes in the seasons, with 365 days required to complete one revolution.

- **Cycles:** The continuous motion of the Earth, whether the motion refers to the Earth's rotation about its axis or revolution about the sun, occurs in cycles. The Earth's rotation about its axis requires 24 hours and represents how we define a day. Once one rotation has passed, another begins that starts the next day, or 24 hours later, and so on. The Earth's revolution about the sun is similar: One complete revolution marks a time period of 365 days or one year. Once a revolution is complete, another one begins, marking the beginning of the following year.

- **Structure:** The structure or geometry and location or position of the Earth remains constant, so the times required for the Earth to complete one rotation about its axis or one revolution in orbit about the sun will remain the same.

- **Processes:** This feature of describing the Earth's motion refers to the processes by which the elements of the system, in this case, the Earth and the sun, interact with others in the system (the other planets in the solar system). This is not a situation in which a student can manipulate variables for further study as one could do with the investigations in physical science and life science; however, it is possible for one to collect and analyze data with regard to weather and climate on Earth for a given day, week, or month and compare such data with the location of the Earth within its own rotation about its axis and in orbit about the sun.

Engage in the process of scientific inquiry

The beginning teacher engages in the process of scientific inquiry in earth and space science (for example, asking a scientific question; formulating a testable hypothesis; selecting appropriate equipment and technology to gather information related to the hypothesis; making observations and collecting data; organizing, analyzing, and evaluating data to find data trends and patterns and make inferences; communicating and defending a valid conclusion).

In earth and space science, as in all branches of science, the process of **scientific inquiry** (or scientific method—see Competency 020) is vital and integral to science instruction and knowledge. The major steps of scientific inquiry are:

- Asking a scientific question
- Formulating a testable hypothesis
- Selecting appropriate equipment and technology to gather information
- Making observations and collecting data
- Organizing, analyzing, and evaluating data
- Communicating and defending a valid conclusion

An example of applying scientific inquiry to earth and space science is noted in the following table.

Application of Scientific Inquiry to Earth and Space Science	
Major Step in Scientific Inquiry	*Earth and Space Science Experiment*
Asking a scientific question	Does angle of inclination of a river bed affect the rate of erosion?
Formulating a testable hypothesis	The student believes that the larger angle of inclination has more of an effect on the rate of erosion of a river bed than smaller angles.
Selecting appropriate equipment and technology to gather information	The student will construct a river bed out of garden soil using a long, thin rectangular cardboard box. The student will pour the same amount or volume of water at the top of the river bed and pour the water from the same location down the center of the river.
Making observations and collecting data	The student will first pour water down the river bed held at a rather small angle of inclination (for example, 5°), and then measure the amount of erosion or soil displaced from the river bed. The student will then conduct the same experiment keeping the same variables constant except for angle of inclination of the river bed, which will vary in intervals of 5° (for example, 10°, 15°, and 20°)
Organizing, analyzing, and evaluating data	The student will conduct and record the measurements of the amount of soil erosion for all angles of inclination of the river bed.
Communicating and defending a valid conclusion	Based on the findings of the experiment presented in the table and graphs, the student should easily determine whether his or her hypothesis was correct. If the hypothesis was incorrect, the student should now be able to revise the hypothesis, conduct a different experiment, and begin to search for an explanation or reasons why the hypothesis is now correct.

Use a variety of tools and techniques to gather and use data

The beginning teacher uses a variety of tools, equipment, technology, and techniques to access, gather, store, retrieve, organize, and analyze data in earth and space science.

In order to successfully investigate physical science, a student must have access to and understand how to use a variety of tools and equipment to collect data or scientific information. These tools are described in the following table:

Measurement Tools Used in Earth and Space Science Investigations		
Type of Measurement	*Measurement Tool*	*Unit of Measurement*
Length	Ruler, meter stick, measuring tape	meters, m centimeters, cm yard, yd feet, ft inches, in
Area	Ruler, meter stick, measuring tape	square meters, m^2 square centimeters, cm^2 square yards, yd^2 square feet, ft^2 square inches, in^2
Volume (length)	Ruler, meter stick, measuring tape	cubic centimeters, cc cubic feet, ft^3 cubic inches, in^3
Volume (liquid)	Measuring cups, beaker, graduated cylinder	milliliters, mL cubic centimeters, cc cubic feet, ft^3

Type of Measurement	Measurement Tool	Unit of Measurement
Visual magnification	Magnifying glass, telescope	magnification (%)
Visual magnification	Magnifying glass, telescope	magnification (%)

Understand the concepts of precision, accuracy, and error

The beginning teacher demonstrates knowledge of the concepts of precision, accuracy, and error with regard to reading and recording numerical data from a scientific instrument in the context of earth and space science investigations.

Accuracy refers to how close a measurement is to the standard or accepted value, and depends upon the quality of the measuring device. For example, if a student places a 200.0 g object or sample on a balance, the student should observe a reading of 200.0 g. A reading of 200.1 g is more accurate of a measurement than 210 g. The error of a measurement refers to the variance between the experimental measurement and the standard or accepted value and can be calculated by:

$$\text{percentage error} = \frac{\text{observed value} - \text{accepted value}}{\text{accepted value}} \times 100\%$$

Precision is the ability of a measurement to be consistently reproduced. If the student placed the 200.0 g object or sample on a balance five times and each time recorded a measurement of 200.1 g, the measurement would be both accurate and precise. If the student placed the 200.0 g object or sample on a balance five times and each time recorded a measurement of 210.0 g, the measurement would be inaccurate but precise. The goal of a scientist is to obtain both accurate and precise measurements in an experiment.

Communicate data in a variety of ways

The beginning teacher organizes, displays, and communicates data in a variety of ways (for example, collections, graphs, tables, written reports) using appropriate technology.

An important facet of scientific inquiry is the ability of the scientists to not only record information from a scientific experiment but also to present the results of their experiment and defend or support their hypothesis. There are a variety of forms of communication of scientific data including tables, graphs (line graph, bar graph, pie chart), maps, diagrams, earth and space science formulas, mathematical equations, and conceptual demonstrations. A student must be knowledgeable of these various forms of communication and be adept at creating most, if not all, of these forms of communication for their particular investigations. Furthermore, a student should also be instructed on the different types of media used for creating these forms of communication, such as graph paper, a calculator, a computer, and various software programs such as Microsoft Word, Microsoft Excel, and Microsoft PowerPoint.

Understand procedures for using and disposing of chemicals and other materials

The beginning teacher understands procedures for the appropriate storage, handling, use, disposal, care, and maintenance of chemicals, materials, and equipment in earth and space science.

Safety should be of utmost importance to a teacher in any earth and space science investigation performed by the students. Teachers must understand and instruct their students on the appropriate storage, handling, use, disposal, care, and maintenance of chemicals, materials, and equipment used in all earth and space science investigations.

Sample Questions

Mrs. Ramos, a 2nd-grade teacher, was interested in supplementing her unit in earth science with teaching a lesson on volcanoes. She introduced the students by explaining to the kids what a volcano was, how it was formed, and what the major features of a volcano were. She then read them a story about a scientist who studied volcanoes. To show the kids what a volcano may look like when it erupted, she gathered the kids around her table when she took an inverted funnel, wrapped it in brown construction paper, and placed it over an open jar with baking soda and vinegar. Shortly after mixing the baking soda and vinegar, the volcano erupted.

1. In referring to a previous discussion on the types of rocks, Mrs. Ramos asked the class, How would volcanic rocks be classified?

   A. igneous rocks
   B. sedimentary rocks
   C. metamorphic rocks
   D. they fall under all three categories

   A Through a discussion of the properties of volcanic rocks and a search on the Internet about the rocks that evolve from volcanoes, the students will realize that volcanic rocks are igneous rocks.

2. What is the best follow-up activity for students to do to understand more about volcanoes?

   A. Have them write about their thoughts of the story.
   B. Show them a movie about volcanoes.
   C. Invite a guest speaker who is a geologist who can talk in more depth about volcanoes.
   D. Have them create a paper mâche model of a volcano.

   D Although all of the options offered are viable, the teacher should look for the one that is student-centered and allows them the opportunity to construct or model the scientific nature of volcanoes. Creating a paper mâche model of a volcano allows the student to learn by doing.

3. When the students gathered around the table to witness the demonstration of the volcano, what should Mrs. Ramos do first to guarantee the demonstration is safely performed?

   A. Have each student wear safety goggles.
   B. Make sure a fire extinguisher is located near by.
   C. Make sure the eye wash station is working properly and is nearby.
   D. Make sure the first aid kit is nearby and readily available.

   A Ensuring student safety should be a top priority in any classroom science demonstration or laboratory investigation. The options presented are all important in ensuring student safety. However, options B, C, and D are all safety considerations used in response to a lab accident. Option A is used to prevent a lab accident. Furthermore, because baking soda and vinegar react vigorously, it is possible that the "lava" that is created could reach the eyes of a student who may be too close. It is important to protect the eyes in these types of science demonstrations.

Domain V: Fine Arts, Music, Health, and Physical Education

Competency 024 (Visual Arts)

The teacher understands concepts, processes, and skills involved in the creation, appreciation, and evaluation of art and uses this knowledge to plan and implement effective art instruction.

Review

Understand how perception is developed

The beginning teacher knows and understands how perception is developed.

Perception is developed through several processes.

- **Observation** is the act of noting and recording. Children learn to draw by study, practice, and observation. Teachers should encourage watching and closely examining the subject matter.

- **Prior knowledge** (or **schema**) consists of information and experiences a learner has and uses to relate to new information. Prior knowledge enhances comprehension. Most students learn and retain new information best when it is linked to relevant prior knowledge. When teachers connect classroom instruction to prior knowledge, they are able to build on their students' experiences. The connections to the curriculum help children link to their own backgrounds and cultures. Teachers should link new information to the students' prior knowledge, because it helps to activate interest and curiosity.

- **Imaginative process** refers to the use of creative drawing, painting, collage, photography, and other art forms to help explore the possibility of understanding the world through its images and symbols. Teachers should encourage children's creativity through exploration, examination, and expression. The ability to identify a problem or need, use one's knowledge and skills to analyze, test new ideas, and find a solution are all components of imaginative process.

- **Cognitive process** refers to the ways of processing information and developing self awareness as it relates to the exploration of the environment through movement, sight, sound, and taste. Art education should help develop a child's literacy in all symbol systems. Art should also encourage various modes of thought and all means of inquiry. In early childhood, perception—more than logic—governs a child's sense of reality. Children use art as a media for communication and expression at a time when they have not fully developed their communication skills. Art provides experiences that will help to develop problem-solving skills and higher-level reasoning.

- **Multisensory experiences** in the arts can make a powerful combination. Teachers should look for ways to combine music, movement, and art. Sensory and kinesthetic experiences can be used across the curriculum. Multisensory experiences provide opportunities to explore and create an environment where children use their senses to learn aesthetically. Teachers must nurture young artists' sensory and kinesthetic development through the incorporation of multisensory experiences.

Deepen students' perception and reflection of the environment

The beginning teacher selects and uses instructional strategies, materials, and activities to deepen perception and reflection of the environment.

Teachers must nurture children's creative and artistic potential. The art that children produce is a result of an active process of exploration and inquiry. Art activities should be developed and taught across the curriculum. Teachers should introduce the practice of guided discovery and the use of **realia** (real objects) as ways to engage and motivate their students.

Teachers should provide multisensory and interactive activities. Children learn best when sensory, visual, and spatial modalities are combined. Teachers need to provide hands-on art activities that stimulate the senses.

Teachers should create an enriched environment where children can examine, touch, and explore. The teacher should also provide children with adequate time to work, a maximized work space, a variety of real art materials, and consistent encouragement.

Know the elements of art

The beginning teacher demonstrates knowledge of the elements of art.

- **Color** is the surface quality of an object or a substance as revealed by the light that reflects off it and that is seen as a hue in the spectrum. Children love the bright colors of red, blue, and yellow. Make sure children have access to a range of media with a wide variety of colors.

  Color has three properties or components. **Hue** is the name of the color. **Value** is the lightness or darkness of the color. **Intensity** (saturation) is the brightness or dullness of the color.

- **Texture** is the visual or actual feel of a surface. Examples of texture include the feel or visual appearance of sandpaper, bark on a tree, and fur on an animal. Textures, including smooth, rough, bumpy, and jagged, are found in all artwork and are integral to collage and modeling activities. Children should compare textures and find words to describe textures in their environments.

- **Shape** is described as a two-dimensional area defined by lines, colors, or values. The shapes created by intersecting, merging, or touching lines may take many forms, and everything has a shape. A two-dimensional shape has height and width and may be geometric, organic, symbolic, or free-form. Teachers should encourage children to play games that involve finding shapes and should talk about the quality of shapes. This includes descriptors such as big, small, short, tall, colored, or textured.

- **Form** is the three-dimensional quality of objects. Forms have depth, height, and width. Examples include cylinders, cubes, spheres, pyramids, and rectangular solids. Teachers should expose children to a wide variety of forms and encourage students to touch and examine many forms. These activities allow children to visually recognize the nature of forms as they grow and develop.

- **Line** is a mark made by a tool moving across a surface. A line can be straight or curved or wiggly or zigzag. Lines can be thick, thin, long, or short. Children can use lines to make shapes, symbols, letters, and numbers. Lines are found in all forms of art media and are an important element of children's artwork.

- **Space** is the area that surrounds shapes and forms. Children see not only shapes and forms but also the spaces that surround them. Teachers need to help young children see space in their artwork. Encourage young artists to examine and identify shapes and space within the environment.

- **Value** in color terminology is the lightness or darkness of a hue. When examining a composition, value represents the light and dark elements of the composition. The value includes the range of lights and darks of the colors. Children should be encouraged to examine the use of color and the mixing of colors to create and explore the complete range of lights and darks in their compositions.

Know the principles of art

The beginning teacher demonstrates knowledge of the principles of art.

- **Emphasis** is a principle of design. Important elements in a composition are emphasized. The center of interest in a picture can also be called a **focal point.** When creating a piece of artwork, an artist may designate the most dominant element of the work by using other principles of design to emphasize the most important part.

- **Contrast** is an unlikeness in quality. The degree of difference between colors, tones, shapes, or other elements is referred to as contrast. Teachers should emphasize terms like light/dark, big/small, top/bottom/ thick/thin, and so on when teaching about contrast in works of art.

- **Pattern** is a design made by repeating a motif or symbol. Some patterns occur naturally, as in the designs on a zebra's skin, while others are invented by artists. Children should be encouraged to identify patterns in nature and to find patterns in works of art. Patterns are important in art, so the ability to identify and understand patterns is important. Understanding patterns is also a prerequisite for mathematical understanding.

- **Rhythm** is the way in which repeating, varying, and spacing elements can create the equivalent of notes and pulses in music. Rhythm is the repetition of a visual element, such as lines, spaces, and shapes. Visual rhythm creates a sensation of movement as one observes a work of art.

- **Balance** is a principle of design. Balance may be formal, informal, symmetrical, asymmetrical, or radial. Balance contributes to the arrangement of the elements in a work of art.

- **Proportion** is the relation of one thing to another in size, degree, or amount. Teachers should encourage observation and comparison of objects when developing lessons on proportion.

- **Unity** is a principle of art. When everything in a composition falls into place through the use of fundamental principles of art, unity is achieved.

Select appropriate techniques

The beginning teacher selects appropriate techniques used to create art in various media.

- **Drawing** is the process of creating a picture using any linear art materials. Materials that can be used to create drawings are pencil, markers, charcoal, ink, and chalk. Contour drawings trace the outside edge of an object.

- **Paintings** are usually more color intensive than drawings. Paintings can be created using tempera paint, water-soluble acrylics, or watercolors.

- **Printmaking** is a picture made by using any technique that produces multiple copies, including woodcut, seriograph (silk screen), etching, and lithography.

- **Construction** is the act of creating or building a piece of artwork. The construction of pottery, sculpture, clay, and ceramics are art activities that can be taught in the elementary classroom.

- **Ceramics** is an art media that allows children to use clay and other media to form shapes and other art objects. Ceramics can be fired in a kiln. Glaze firing can also be used when teaching the ceramic process.

- **Fiber art** includes art forms such as weaving, appliqués, and embroidery. This art form uses fibers or materials created from fiber to produce art objects. Fiber activities can be used as part of the thematic study of texture, pattern, and line.

- **Electronic media** is where images are created through the use of technology. This art form may include the use of computer software programs that range from simple draw and paint programs to more sophisticated programs like Adobe Photoshop. When using this media, teachers should teach about legal issues such as copyright laws.

Promote multicultural awareness

The beginning teacher selects and uses instructional strategies, materials, and activities to promote cultural awareness and appreciation of multiple cultures and the Western tradition.

Teachers should recognize art as an international language. Art provides a mirror for cultural groups, which reflects the group's values, identity, and heritage. Art is a primary way to translate cultural identity. It is a way cultural identity is examined, transmitted, and perpetuated.

Using art to promote cultural awareness is a way to help children understand the connection between the content and form of a work of art and the culture and period of time when it was created.

Children should understand the characteristics of a variety of art forms from many cultures. The art forms should represent both the Western and non-Western traditions. The teacher should understand and explore the roles of history and culture and their relationship with art. One of the most important relationships that should be stressed in the curriculum is the relationship between art and culture. Teachers should help children to reflect on the aspects of their own culture and help them to relate to artwork from other cultures.

Promote the development of visual literacy

The beginning teacher applies the skills and knowledge required for visual literacy and provides instruction that promotes the development of visual literacy.

Visual literacy can be achieved through the development of skills necessary to analyze, interpret, and evaluate works of art as well as make informed judgments about personal artworks and those of others. Visual literacy is the ability to make meaning from what is seen or observed. Children need to develop a keen sense of observation and develop higher-order thinking skills in the visual realm. Teachers should engage students in conversations about their art and common objects in their environment. In this way, teachers help children articulate their own value systems and their own criteria for evaluating art.

Integrate visual arts across the curriculum

The beginning teacher integrates instruction in the visual arts across the curriculum.

Art should be integrated into the different subject areas across the curriculum, yet also taught as a curricular basic. The integration of art across the curriculum encourages children to construct knowledge and become active learners. Art experiences are essential for cognitive development. As thought becomes more complex, teachers should encourage children to be self-motivated learners who are responsible for their own learning. Teachers can foster children's thinking by designing lessons that include hands-on art experiences, allowing children to explore and develop their own understanding.

The art curriculum should foster children's cognitive, social, physical, emotional, and perceptual growth. Art and other curriculum areas are interrelated. Activities in other curriculum areas can extend learning in art and art can enhance learning in other subjects.

Understand cognitive and artistic development

The beginning teacher understands cognitive and artistic development and implements effective art instruction and assessment.

Piaget (1959) describes how children developed their knowledge of the world. His findings help us to understand cognitive and artistic development. Children are active learners who are curious and who enthusiastically seek information that helps them make sense of their environments. Children construct knowledge based on their experiences. Children have different and unique experiences, all of which influence their understanding. A child's understanding changes continually based on new experiences. The experiences are essential to cognitive development.

Teachers can foster cognitive development by providing hands-on art experiences that allow children to explore and create. Through the experiences, children develop their own understanding. Open-ended art materials that encourage many creative possibilities should be available to children. Teachers can encourage logical thought by asking children to explain why they used the materials they did. This questioning also helps them to discover cause and effect.

When teachers understand how children create art, they can use a child's art as a means of assessing a child's cognitive learning and artistic development.

Develop age-appropriate art instruction

The beginning teacher applies knowledge of the visual arts, content, curriculum, and the Texas Essential Knowledge and Skills (TEKS) for developmentally appropriate art instruction for early childhood to 4th grade.

The art curriculum should foster children's social, emotional, physical, cognitive, and perceptual growth. Teachers should design developmentally appropriate practices that are based on children's abilities, interests, and needs. Teachers should nurture creativity by incorporating activities that are open-ended. Teachers should find ways to create a balance between perception, response, and creativity that fosters affective, physical, and cognitive growth.

The Texas Essential Knowledge and Skills (TEKS) are requisite knowledge for each grade level in all subjects. TEKS are not curriculum, nor how to teach the content for art, but they are the content knowledge required for all students at all grade levels.

Sample Questions

1. Mrs. Jones teaches 2nd-grade art. She has planned a lesson that includes a field trip around campus to identify objects that the children can feel. She wants the children to take pencils and paper and do rubbings of trees, leaves, and other surfaces. Which element of art is Mrs. Jones emphasizing with this activity?

   A. space
   B. form
   C. texture
   D. shape

   C The art element of texture refers to the visual or actual feel of a surface. The texture can be actual or implied (as in rubbings of multiple surfaces). The other answer options do not address the element of texture.

2. Mr. Taylor is working with his 4th-grade students on the elements of art. He has selected several objects to display on a table in the front of the room. The class has already discussed the element of shape. They know that shape is a two-dimensional area defined by lines, color, or values. Today he wants the students to concentrate on the area that surrounds shapes and forms. Today's lesson is emphasizing what element of art?

   A. shape
   B. hue
   C. space
   D. texture

   C Space is the area that surrounds shapes and forms. The children have studied shape and now must be able to identify space. The other answers would not apply to this element of art.

3. The children in Mrs. Gomez's 1st-grade classroom are examining the designs on some animal hides that are displayed in the library. What principle of art would be obvious to an observer?

   A. form
   B. pattern
   C. space
   D. contrast

   B Pattern is a design made by repeating a motif or symbol. The teacher wants to examine patterns and has chosen the exhibit to demonstrate examples of pattern. The other response options do not describe the principle found in this activity.

4. Students in a 1st-grade class have been offered various papers, magazine pictures, and small objects to glue onto their pictures. The children are creating

   A. a block print
   B. a collage
   C. a painting
   D. a weaving

   B Collage is an art form where children arrange or randomly place collage materials on paper or other surfaces. Answers A, C, and D describe other art techniques.

Competency 025 (Music)

The teacher understands concepts, processes, and skills involved in the creation, appreciation, and evaluation of music, and uses this knowledge to plan and implement effective learning experiences in music.

Review

Promote lifelong enjoyment of music

The beginning teacher knows how to involve children in activities that promote lifelong enjoyment of music and provides children with a wide range of opportunities to make and respond to music.

As with all other areas of the curriculum, music activities should involve gross motor movement, regardless of age. Music activities should also include unstructured activities (for example, asking children how else they could sing a song—slow, fast, loud, soft) and structured activities (for example, playing a non-tuned percussion instrument to add a sound effect when a character in a story appears). Music can be an excellent opportunity for children of other cultures to share their heritage with their classmates. Similarly, children who study music outside of the classroom should have opportunities to share their musical talents with the class. In general, good pedagogy brings the children's world into the classroom. Approaching instructional design in this way makes learning meaningful, moving the children from known experiences to unknown experiences.

Another important aspect of best practice is the use of concrete experiences that allow children to kinesthetically interact with new concepts, vocabulary, ideas, and so on. With regard to music, younger children should be allowed to explore music with hands-on manipulation of classroom instruments (for example, tambourines, cymbals, drums, shakers, and so on). Older children should have access to tuned percussion instruments (for example, xylophones, bells) as well as non-tuned percussion instruments (for example, drums, claves, cowbell). Older children should be allowed to create music based on an element or several elements of music (for example, tempo, dynamics, timbre, form, rhythm, and so on).

Use standard terminology to describe and analyze musical sound

The beginning teacher applies knowledge of standard terminology for describing and analyzing musical sound (for example, rhythm, melody, form, timbre, tempo, pitch, and meter) and standard music notation.

The elements can be arranged and manipulated to make music. Children need to understand these elements so that they can create their own music. They probably have experienced each of these but possibly do not know the technical terms for each.

- **Beat:** Most music has a steady beat, something that you can dance to. Once a steady beat or pulse has been established, rhythms can be added. When we listen to pop music and say "I like the beat" what we really mean is that "I like the rhythms in the music."

- **Meter:** In mathematics we often group objects together so that it is easier to see an entire pattern. We try to help children group things together so that they can learn to manipulate more information more easily. In music, steady beats are grouped together so that there are aurally identifiable patterns. The meter signature of any piece of music communicates how many steady beats are grouped together. The most common groupings of steady beats are sets of 2s, 4s, and 3s. Each group of steady beats is called a measure. Most melodies that we sing with on the radio are 8 measures long and are in a meter of 4. Following are examples of meter signatures. The top number indicates if the meter is a walking meter (that is, 2 or 4) or a skipping/swaying meter (that is, 3 or 6).

- **Dynamics:** How loud or soft music is played or sung. Common dynamic markings are *f* = *forte* = loud and *p* = *piano* = soft. Dynamic markings are found throughout musical compositions.

- **Tempo:** How fast or slow music is played or sung. Common tempo markings are *andante* (walking), *allegro* (fast), and *adagio* (slow). Tempo markings most often appear at the beginning of a composition or song.

- **Melody:** The tune of a song or piece. A sequence of notes that can move up or down, or repeat. This up and down movement is called **contour.** In a pop song, melodies are usually sung.

- **Pitch:** This relates to the exact placement of a note on the staff. The higher the note (ball at the end of the stick), the higher its corresponding pitch. Looking at standard notation, the pitch is indicated by the circle or ball at the end of the stick.

Pitch: This example has five pitches.

- **Key signature:** The key signature tells the performer what "black notes on the piano" to play or sing. Key signatures can have flats (♭) or sharps (#).

Key signature: Sharps

Key signature: Flats

- **Harmony:** The accompaniment of a song. In a pop song, harmonies are often played by guitar or keyboard. The types of chords used can add to the dramatic effect of a piece.

- **Timbre and instrumentation:** Different styles of music (for example, jazz, pop, classical, and so on) can be recognized by the types of instruments used by the composer. Depending on what is desired, a composer can choose from a wide variety of instruments to communicate to the audience a specific emotion or feeling. Instrumentation can also be called timbre. Each instrument has a different quality of sound. Similarly, every person has a different quality of vocal sound.

- **Clef:** Music is usually written in either the treble clef or the bass clef. Men sing in the **bass clef,** which denotes lower sounding pitches, and women sing in the **treble clef,** which denotes higher sounding pitches. The following example illustrates both of these clefs.

- **Rhythm:** Rhythm is analogous to how the syllables in a sentence sound. It's like the long and short sounds of the words. Composers can choose fast or slow rhythms to communicate to their audience. If you clap the syllables of any word or sentence, you are clapping rhythm. Rhythmic clapping equals clapping syllables.

Rhythm: The "sticks" of printed notation identify the rhythm of a song.

If you clap the words and syllables of "Twinkle, Twinkle Little Star," "Baa, Baa Black Sheep," and the "Alphabet Song," you notice that they all have the same number of short and long claps. Similarly, if you clap the words and syllables of "Happy Birthday" and the "Star Spangled Banner," you notice that they sound the same and have the same number of short and long claps. This is because they have the same rhythms. In the second example, the rhythms are identical but the tunes are different.

- **Form:** The big pieces of a song or work. Take, for example, *Twinkle, Twinkle Little Star.* It has three distinct sections. The melody heard in the first part of the song ("Twinkle, twinkle little star, how I wonder what you are") is repeated at the end of the song with the same lyrics. The middle section of the song uses a different melody and lyrics ("Up above the world so high, like a diamond in the sky"). The form of this song would be ABA, because the outside melodies are identical (for example, A) and the middle of the song is different (for example, B).

Show how music reflects elements of society and culture

The beginning teacher demonstrates an understanding of the purposes and roles of music in society and how music can reflect elements of a specific society or culture.

Music is an important part of every society and every culture. Because there is diversity in the peoples of the world, you can also expect that there is diversity in their music as well. In some cultures, music and dance bring people together for celebrations and rituals. In other cultures, music is used for political purposes or as a commentary on current social events. In general, social and political issues, along with where people live in the world, influence what they create musically and how they make music. It is difficult in a short review to cover all the music of the world. However, here are a few examples of how music is used in several different cultures.

- **A region's natural resources dictates what can be made into musical instruments.** In other words, location, location, location. For example, it would be difficult for Native Americans who lived at the beginning of the 19th century on the plains of North America to build and create music on a rosewood xylophone; they didn't have access to rosewood, because it is not native to that area of North America. Additionally, rosewood is rather heavy. Nomadic peoples who followed the animals they needed to survive would most likely not make things that were unduly heavy. Another example may be that the same people would not have used whale skins to make drums. When answering any question related to culture and society, always think about the times and the place in which they lived and rule out answer choices that are obviously wrong.

- **In many cultures, music is tied to religious rituals.** This is true of both traditional main-line churches in Western cultures and in polytheistic cultures.

- **Secular music has also served as a vehicle for social commentary.** Regardless of when they were written, popular songs reflect the times in which they were written. For example, the lyrics of one pop song written during the Great Depression used "Buddy can you spare a dime?" as its refrain. More recent instances of social commentary or protest songs include music of the Civil Rights movement, Vietnam protests, and the anti-apartheid movement in South Africa.

Identify and describe how music reflects the heritage of the United States and Texas

The beginning teacher identifies and describes how music reflects the heritage of the United States and Texas.

Folk songs and ballads are a way of remembering and recounting history in the early days of our nation and state. Songs were used as work songs and protest songs. (Songs that tell a story are called **ballads.** Most country and western songs that tell a story are ballads.) For example, the song "I've Been Working on the Railroad" relates to westward expansion in the mid- to late-19th century. This work song provides us with an aural snapshot of the life and times of railroad workers during this period in our nation's history. Similarly, the gospel-singing tradition was borne out of a time in our nation's history when slavery was a common practice on southern plantations. The music slaves created as they worked reflects their individual and collective struggles for freedom. This same idea can be seen in the songs of the Civil Rights movement of the 1950s and 1960s, and also in the South African anti-apartheid movement of the 1990s. Songs were also used to communicate noble qualities of larger-than-life characters. Some of these were factitious (for example, Pecos Bill, Paul Bunyan) but others were based on real people (for example, Johnny Appleseed, Davy Crockett).

Apply knowledge of criteria for evaluating and critiquing music

The beginning teacher applies knowledge of criteria for evaluating and critiquing musical performances and experiences.

In any teaching setting evaluation is important. This competency is simply a musical version of any good assessment. When children begin to evaluate and critique performances, they first need a common musical vocabulary, including the elements of music. Next, they need to construct a rubric that reflects the elements of music they plan on evaluating. As with all areas related to the EC–4 Generalist exam, look for answers that have children explaining their evaluation. Answers such as "It was great!" do not provide an explanation as to why the performance was "great." Answers such as, "It was great, because they used a fast tempo that contrasted with the slow tempo they used at the beginning of the song" provide specific information about the performance (lower levels of Bloom's Taxonomy) and show critical-thinking skills (higher levels of Bloom's Taxonomy). See the Introduction for additional information on Bloom's Taxonomy.

Applying predetermined criteria is useful at the completion of a creative musical assignment, such as making up a sound piece with found instruments and asking children to use different timbres, fast/slow, and loud/soft. When you get to the evaluation portion of the lesson, the criteria are already determined because they were part of the original assignment that everyone was to follow.

Integrate musical instruction across the curricula

The beginning teacher integrates instruction in music with instruction in other subject area.

Music by its very nature pervades all areas of the curriculum. The rhythms in music are similar to the rhythms in language. Vocal music transmitted stories via folk idioms and was a vehicle for setting poetry. The properties of sound are based on hard science. Music is not created in a vacuum and, therefore, embodies cultural and societal values. In the past, musical instruments were made with the natural resources close to a specific society. And, above all, music is aesthetic. It is a primary means of expressing emotion.

- Traditionally, music has been used to augment social studies lessons as a way to bring children into the mind-set of a people. Music and dance are also important ways to get children actively engaged in a lesson.

- Music can be integrated into language arts. Words and sentences of poems can add rhythmic vitality to a lesson. You can clap the syllables of different words to make rhythmic patterns.

- Science can be integrated with music by highlighting the relation of sound to materials used in making an instrument (for example, metal, wood, shakers, and drums).

- Music is mathematical because of the relation between length of an object and the sound that is produced. There is also proportion in relation to subdividing a steady beat. Musical form and pattern also has a corollary to patterns in mathematics.

Plan and implement developmentally appropriate instruction

The beginning teacher applies knowledge of music content and curriculum, including the Texas Essential Knowledge and Skills (TEKS), and of children in early childhood through 4th grade to plan and implement effective, developmentally appropriate instruction, including instruction that promotes children's creativity and performance skills and their ability to use critical-thinking and problem-solving skills in music contexts.

Early childhood classrooms should focus on musical exploration, unstructured musical choices (for example, "How should we sing the song now?" "Fast!"), and gross motor play and dances. Every classroom should have rhythm band instruments (for example, tambourines, sticks, drums, and so on).

Middle childhood classrooms should focus on creating music based on the elements of music. Lessons move from an early childhood exploration focus to a task-specific focus. For example, children in 3rd grade may be asked to create a sound piece using two different timbres of instruments. Once everyone has completed the task, the teacher helps the children see the similarities and differences between and among all the students' compositions. Every classroom should have rhythm band instruments and world percussion instruments. Some lessons should also include gross motor movement activities (for example, multicultural dances).

Note: The TEKS site is one of the best for reviewing all the fine arts: http://www.cedfa.org.

Sample Questions

1. If you are trying to teach a song to children, what is the best way get them to learn it?

   A. Listen to a recording of the song and have the children sing along.

   B. Have the children memorize the words first and then learn the music.

   C. Sing the entire song for the children several times. Then have them learn individual phrases, and then have them sing the entire song.

   D. Sing the entire song everyday for two weeks. Make sure that the children are quietly listening so that they can memorize the words and the music.

   C The most appropriate way to get children to learn/memorize a longer poem, chant, or song, is to present the entire song/chant/poem to them several times. This helps the children grasp the whole of the song/chant/poem which will help them learn how the individual phrases/sentences relate to one another. Once the children have the big picture of the song/chant/poem (for example, saying/singing it several times while the children listen), they will be able to relate the individual phrases/sentences to the whole, thereby increase their retention and memorization. The next step is to have the children echo each phrase/sentence, adding one phrase onto the previous one until the entire song/chant/poem can be sung/said without assistance. The general pedagogical principle being employed is whole/part/whole learning.

2. A kindergarten class is beginning to learn movements to a new song. The movements include walking, jumping, clapping, stopping, and hopping. Unfortunately, the children cannot reproduce the sequence of movements accurately. What should the teacher do so that the children can reproduce all movements? Choose the best answer.

   A. Simplify the movements by using fewer movements.

   B. Simplify the movements by slowing the tempo of the entire song so that the children spend several minutes with each movement.

   C. Simplify the movements by having the children sit and practice the movements with their hands.

   D. Simplify the movements by having the children watch the teacher several times.

   C For this question, you are to select the *best* answer. Each choice may appear to be appropriate, but there are several things that will lead you to the best choice. First, try to eliminate all choices that are questionable. Answer choice D is not appropriate, because it has the children watching passively. In most instances, look for answer choices that have children actively involved. Answer choice A can also be eliminated, because the question stem asked "What should the teacher do so that the children can reproduce all movements?" The first answer reduces the number of movements, which is an appropriate strategy, but it does not address the question asked. The best answer is C. The children are asked to sit still and use their hands to practice the sequence. While the children are actively involved in the learning process, the task is simplified because they are not moving around the room. This will help them focus on learning the sequence rather than simply enjoying a gross motor activity.

3. A 3rd-grade teacher is using tuned percussion instruments to enhance his children's experiences with story-telling. To highlight the differences between the three bears in *Goldilocks and the Three Bears,* which of the following tuned percussion instruments should he use?

   A. drum, tambourine, and wood block

   B. xylophones and bells

   C. xylophones, tambourine, and wood block

   D. bass drum, tympani, and snare drum

   B This questions addresses not only your knowledge of tuned and non-tuned percussion instruments but also your knowledge of developmentally appropriate instruments. Answer choice D is not the best choice, because these instruments are typically associated with band programs and not generally used by classroom teachers but by music specialists. Answer choice A is incorrect, because there are no "tuned percussion" instruments. Remember, tuned percussion instruments must be able to play a tune, like *Twinkle, Twinkle.* You can't hear the tune of a song when you beat it on a drum. What you're attending to is the rhythm, not individual pitches or notes. Answer choice C is also incorrect, because it has non-tuned percussion instruments in the list.

4. In the following example, what element of music is represented by the higher and lower notation?

Like the dawn of a new day your eyes are so bright.

    A. harmony
    B. steady beat
    C. melody
    D. rhythm

C This question assesses your knowledge of musical notation and music. In the example, note that there are chord symbols above the printed notation (for example, Fmaj7). These symbols specify to the performer what chords should be played to accompany the melody. As you recall, accompaniment pertains to harmony, not melody. The question specifically asks about "higher and lower notation" which, in this example, means the printed music or notes to be played and sung. The chord symbols are related to the music but are not the notation.

5. A 4th-grade class is reciting a long poem together. The classroom teacher wants to make sure that they begin and end at the same time, and that they say all the words at the same time with an unchanging tempo. For this to happen, which of the following must remain constant?

    A. the words
    B. the rhythm
    C. the syllables
    D. the beat

D This question assesses your knowledge of music. Specifically, the idea is that if children say any poem or chant at the same time without speeding up or slowing down (that is, "remains constant" or "unchanging tempo") they must have a constant steady beat. The other choices all relate to the rhythm of the poem. Children can say any poem together, but the rate at which they say the words may vary. They may speed up or slow down. It is the beat, the underlying pulse, that keeps chants and poems from speeding up or slowing down.

6. A 4th-grade class is studying 20th-century history. The teacher brings to class several recordings of music written during the 1950s. The recordings feature novel sound sources for their time (for example, electronically produced sounds, synthesizers, sine waves, square waves, and so on). What may the teacher have the students understand about this music in relation to science and technology?

    A. Music was created to reflect the influences of the 1950s.
    B. Music created during this decade was influenced by technological advances made in science and physics.
    C. Composers used many novel sounds while composing in the 1950s and enjoyed pushing musical boundaries.
    D. Science and technology influenced the music of the 1950s.

B The question assesses your ability to recognize how areas outside of music influence compositions. The answer choices A and C restate information presented in the question. The last choice is a good choice, but not the best. If you compare B and D, note that the correct answer provides more information related to connecting music and technology.

7. A 3rd-grade teacher shows his class a DVD with several selections of music on it: One selection is a concert performance of a popular song off the radio; one selection is music performed for a wedding celebration by a community from a small remote village in Western Africa; and one selection features community singing, announcing the birth of an infant from a village on a small island in the Pacific Ocean. The teacher asks the children to compare and contrast the three examples and to compare them to music in their own lives. What may the teacher want his students to understand about the three different performances?

    A. That music in many non-western cultures is performed by everyone in a community.

    B. That there are performers in each of the musical examples.

    C. That music in our culture tends to have fewer performers and focuses on entertainment.

    D. That all cultures enjoy music and that music is an important part of all cultures and societies.

C One of the challenging things about the exam is that most of the answer choices are plausible and you are to look for the *best* choice. In this question, each answer is viable; that is, they all make sense in the context of the question. Another important thing to recognize is that while question stems may be very long, there will be one sentence or a part of a sentence that provides key information about how to select the best answer. In this question, the important sentence is, "compare and contrast the three examples and compare them to music in their own lives." Only answer choice C relates the music of the DVD examples to the music of the children's world. The remaining choices are correct, but are not specific to what the question asked.

8. A teacher plays "The Streets of Laredo," "Git Along Little Doggies," and "Camping on the Chisholm Trail." How may these selections relate to children in Texas public schools?

    A. They retell important places and occupations of 19th-century Texas.

    B. They retell specific occupations and places.

    C. They are songs sung each year during a Texas celebration festival.

    D. They are songs sung and enjoyed by millions of people in Texas and the Southwest United States.

A As you look for the best answer, remember that it may not be readily apparent. All of the answer choices will likely relate to children in some way. Yes, these songs are probably sung by millions of people (choice D), and they are possibly sung each year during a Texas celebration (choice C), and they retell specific occupations and places (choice B); however, these choices are not the best. Answer A provides specific information about when and where the selections were written. This choice would lead the class toward discussions of Texas history and how this history was recorded in song.

9. During an activity in which small groups of students were asked to create short sound pieces with non-tuned percussion instruments, one of the children noted that another group's sound piece used the same instruments but a different order of sounds. In an effort to help all the children begin to discuss the similarities and differences in an objective way, what may the classroom teacher do? Select the best answer.

    A. Provide the children with a rubric that specifies all the various elements of the composition assignment.

    B. Use the music TEKS to create a rubric for the children to use as they assess their peer's compositions.

    C. Discuss the overall objective of the assignment with the children, ask them for input as to what choices may be possible, and ask them to create an assessment rubric.

    D. Discuss the overall objective of the assignment with the children, ask them for input as to what choices may be possible, and create an assessment rubric that uses the music TEKS for the children to use as they assess each other's compositions.

C Many *best* answers on the exam are child-centered, so look for answer choices that have the students actively involved in decision making, creating, and exploring. This question assesses whether you can recognize the importance of authentic assessment and a child-centered way to involve children. Choices A and B could easily be eliminated, because they are teacher-centered when compared to the last two choices. Think carefully about any answer in which the teacher presents something to the children. In the last two choices (C and D), the children are given the opportunity to think and discuss. What makes answer choice C better than D is that the children create the assessment rubric.

10. Reading music will not assist children in which of the following other disciplines?

    A. Math, because there are patterns in music and math.

    B. Reading, because children are practicing tracking from left to right.

    C. Language development, because children must listen to the rhyme scheme of a song or chant.

    D. Science, because children must watch notation.

    D The first three answers show how music reading does enhance reading skills, in general. Watching music notation has nothing to do with science. There are correlations between science and music, but reading is not one of them.

11. A 1st-grade class is preparing for a PTO presentation. As the children sing and chant their parts, the teacher tells them that their parts cannot be heard. To what element of music does the teacher refer?

    A. steady beat

    B. dynamics

    C. tempo

    D. rhythm

    B To answer this question correctly you are called upon to use your knowledge of the elements of music. The children could not be heard, and this relates to how loudly they sing and chant. Loudness or softness of singing and chanting relate to dynamics. Steady beat relates to whether the children are chanting or singing together. Tempo refers to whether the children are rushing or slowing the chant or song as they perform. Rhythm does not relate to the question.

Competency 026 (Health)

The teacher uses knowledge of the concepts and purposes of health education to plan and implement effective and engaging health instruction for all children.

Review

Understand health-related behaviors and strategies for enhancing wellness

The beginning teacher understands health-related behaviors, ways in which personal health decisions and behaviors affect body systems and health, and strategies for reducing health risks and enhancing wellness throughout the life span.

The nation has begun to focus resources on health education and preventative practices in order to close the gap between optimal health knowledge and actual health behaviors. In the 1900s, life expectancy was under 50 years of age; infectious diseases took the greatest toll. Babies born now can expect to live 25 years longer, but the major causes of death are chronic diseases (heart disease, cancer, and stroke). Behavioral aspects (tobacco use, dietary practices, amount of physical activity, sexual behavior, and unnecessary injuries) are major contributors to death rates today.

To combat the problems, Texas—along with many other states—is implementing Coordinated School Health Programs (CSHPs) at the elementary level; it is more successful to begin healthy behaviors during childhood than to alter unhealthy behaviors in adults. The program organizes physical activity through the school's physical education program, health education, nutritional services, and parental involvement. The classroom teacher is the prime health educator for elementary-level school health instruction and is responsible for the preparation of units and individual lessons related to the curriculum. The teacher also is responsible for using teachable moments for the delivery of health information and, ultimately, for being a **role model,** with powerful impact on student's health. Therefore, it is vital for the teacher to deliver health instruction with a sound philosophy and broad understanding of 21st-century health risks and wellness considerations.

Health risk factors are associated with the potential for developing illness or disease; **health behaviors** are undertaken for the purpose of preventing disease. Many risk factors are personally manageable, including controlling cholesterol (lowering bad LDL and raising good HDL), not using tobacco, controlling high blood pressure, monitoring body weight, and keeping physically active. Risk factors not within a person's control include age, sex, and genetic predisposition. Positive, informed changes in health behaviors related to controllable factors are the ultimate aim of school health education programs.

Wellness is the term generally used to mean optimal health. It entails constant and deliberate choices to achieve the highest level of well-being. Involving more than just physical care of the body, wellness also includes dimensions related to emotional, social, environmental, and intellectual growth and development. By advocating personal health behaviors related to this all-encompassing approach to health, teachers can influence students to become health literate, even at an early age, and develop the foundation for a lifetime of biological and psychological well-being.

Demonstrate knowledge of major areas of health instruction

The beginning teacher demonstrates knowledge of major areas in health instruction, including body systems (for example, structures and functions of various body systems), illness and disease (for example, types of disease, transmission mechanisms, defense systems, disease prevention), nutrition (for example, types of foods and nutrients, maintenance of a balanced diet), stress (for example, effects of stress, stress-reduction techniques), and fitness (for example, components of fitness, methods for improving fitness).

Understanding the body and how it functions is a fascinating subject for young children due to their innate egocentric nature. Instruction should focus on the **systems of the body** including basic information related to skeletal, muscular, integumentary (skin), cardiorespiratory, digestive, and sensory systems. The sensory system will branch into information related to the **five senses:** sight, hearing, taste, smell, and touch. After establishing this foundation, more information can be shared with other body structures including the nervous, endocrine, lymphatic, urinary, and reproductive systems. The skeletal and muscular systems are particularly fascinating to children at this age; even kindergarten students can master the names and identify locations for major bones and muscles. The EC–4 TEKS for health education encompasses vertical alignment from grade level to grade level, including understanding of the basic structure and functions of the human body and how they relate to personal health throughout the life span.

Diseases are abnormal conditions of the body or mind that cause discomfort or distress to a body part, an organ, or the entire system. Diseases result from various causes and are characterized by an identifiable group of signs or **symptoms. Illness,** although often used to mean disease, also refers to perceptions of health, regardless of whether the person has a disease. There are many types of diseases, including: congenital (inherited from parents), dietary (deficiency or over-nutrition), infectious (due to the invasion of germs), environmental or occupational (related to conditions such as heavily polluted air or poor hygiene), and mental illness. **Chronic** diseases, those that progress slowly and continue for a long time, are distinctively different from **acute** conditions, which end quickly.

With EC–4 students, an excellent basis for the study of diseases involves infectious diseases and those that require vaccination to attend school. This leads to understanding of transmission mechanisms, defense systems, and disease prevention through essential sanitation practices (thoroughly cleaning hands, covering sneezes/coughs, avoiding insect/animal bites, caring for wounds, and consuming safe water and food). Research substantiates the prevention of many diseases by reducing unsafe behaviors. Strategies to develop constructive health behaviors will help students become critical thinkers and problem solvers.

Nutrition is the science dealing with food and nourishment for growth, energy, and replacement of tissues. The nutritional successive stages include digestion, absorption, assimilation, and excretion. Teachers must have knowledge about the nutritional process, beginning with food selection. A sensible diet comes from careful selections from the four basic food groups (dairy, meat, vegetables, and fruit), and from all three energy nutrients (carbohydrates, fat, protein).

- **Carbohydrates,** the main energy source, can be obtained by eating bread, pasta, cereal, vegetables, fruits, and milk products. Indigestible carbohydrates, also called **fiber,** are important to health in the regular elimination of wastes.
- **Fats,** or lipids, provide a significant fuel source; but because they contain more than double the number of calories per gram as carbohydrates, high-fat foods are high in calories. There is also a dangerous relationship between fat intake and high cholesterol, particularly with saturated fat (which is solid at room temperature) and trans fat (formed during the manufacture of processed foods).
- **Proteins,** from such sources as dairy products, poultry, meat, fish, and eggs, are the third energy source. Their purpose is to maintain, repair, and grow muscle and other tissue. Vegetarians are able to get enough protein if they eat the proper combination of plant proteins.

Vitamins, minerals, and water are also important to a balanced diet, because they regulate body processes.

Nutritional information is vital to attack the disastrous results of today's fast-food emphasis. According to the Center for Disease Control (CDC), less than 40% of children and adolescents in the United States follow the recommended U.S. dietary guidelines for saturated fat (less than 10% of total calories), while almost 80% of young people do not eat the recommended number of servings of fruits (2–4) and vegetables (3–5). MyPyramid, released by the United States

Department of Agriculture in 2005, is an updated version of the comprehensive U.S. food guide pyramid. The new image emphasizes physical activity and a proper mix of food groups in one's diet. **Junk foods,** those that have little nutritional value, but high caloric content, are extremely problematic. Junk foods may include high quantities of sugar, margarine/butter/lard, oils, or alcohol.

The national prevalence of overweight among children in kindergarten through 4th grade more than doubled in the past 20 years, going from 7% to 16%. A CDC study estimated that one in three American children born this decade would develop diabetes in their lifetime. **Caloric expenditure** (through basal metabolism related to body functions, along with added physical activity choices) and caloric intake (through eating) must be balanced to maintain a healthy weight. Weight reduction plans must include a decrease in caloric intake and an increase in physical activity in order to be safe and effective.

Stress involves physical or psychological stimulus that can produce mental tension or physiological reactions that may lead to illness. Stress can affect anyone, even young children, who feel inundated with pressures from outside sources—including family, school personnel, and friends—and from internal ones. Adults who force youngsters to excel or who push children's participation in an influx of activities may cause excessive stress, because children often do not experience these dreams and drives as their own. Even though the types of stressors affecting children are similar to those of adults, the major difference for children is they do not have the ability to control the situations that cause them stress. Grade-school children go through the phases of stress response—general alarm, resistance, and exhaustion—in dealing with fears such as toilet mishaps, abandonment, punishment, being ridiculed, not completing assignments, failure to comprehend new material, and peer disapproval. Prudent teachers will look for extreme stress responses and provide appropriate coping mechanisms including altering perceptions, revising expectations, teaching relaxation, providing physical activity breaks, and surrounding students with ample laughter and fun.

Physical fitness encompasses a state of well-being that allows a person to perform daily activities with vigor. It reduces the risk of health problems relating to lack of exercise and is a sufficient fitness base to provide energy for daily participation in recreational physical activities and for handling emergencies. There are eleven different components of physical fitness.

- Six of these are **skill-related** and include agility, balance, coordination, speed, reaction time, and power. Although these can enable optimal work or sport performance—and can be improved with proper instruction and training—participants are genetically limited in their ability in these areas mostly due to the body's predisposed percentage of slow- and fast-twitch muscle fibers.
- **Health-related fitness** comprises those components of fitness that exhibit a relationship with health status and include cardiorespiratory endurance, body composition, muscle strength, muscle endurance, and flexibility.

Physical activity is a process that involves accumulating a wide variety of movements. Many teachers feel that if physical activity is sufficient, fitness will be addressed. Participating in regular physical activity is beneficial in reduction of cardiovascular diseases, depression, adult-onset diabetes, and some cancers, while increasing bone density, improving mental health, and assisting in weight control.

Overweight (excess body weight for one's age, height, and build) and **obesity** (often defined as a body mass index, or BMI, of 25 or higher, or being 20% above national recommended weight for height) are significantly associated with health problems such as high blood pressure, high cholesterol, asthma, and arthritis. **Body composition** (a comparison of lean mass to fat mass) can be assessed with a variety of techniques including bioelectrical impedance and hydrostatic weighing. For practicality, two measures are frequently used in elementary schools.

- An experienced person can use calipers to measure **skinfold** thickness at strategic body sites and convert the data to a percentile using standardized charts.
- **Body mass index** (BMI), a much simpler approach, is a calculated number using height and weight to assess underweight, overweight, and risk for overweight with others of similar gender and age.

Understand substance use and abuse

The beginning teacher understands substance use and abuse (including types and characteristics of tobacco, alcohol, and other drugs and of herbal supplements).

Drugs are substances, other than food, intended to affect the structure or function of the body. **Over-the-counter** (**OTC**) drugs may be sold without a prescription and without a visit to a medical doctor, unlike prescription only medicine (**POM**). A **street drug** is taken for non-medical reasons, usually for mind-altering (psychoactive) effects. In most cases, street drugs are illegal. The "goodness" or "badness" of drugs, even OTCs, depends on their use; some can be life-saving, such as antibiotics, and some can be life-threatening, like poisons. The Food and Drug Administration (FDA), which oversees the safety of food and drugs sold in the United States, uses the term **dietary supplement** for herbal, vitamin, and mineral products. Even though **herbal medicine** supplements are derived from natural sources, they, too, can cause medical problems if taken inappropriately. Drug use, whether good or bad, is complicated and relevant to each individual. Therefore, students must learn that good drugs should be used with care and concern; bad drugs should not be used at all.

The TEKS for health in kindergarten include knowledge of harmful effects of tobacco, alcohol, and other drugs. By 4th grade, students are expected to understand and engage in behaviors that reduce health risks by identifying the use and abuse of prescription and non-prescription medication, short-term and long-term harmful effects of tobacco and alcohol, and other ways to avoid drugs, and list alternatives for the use of drugs.

Misuse and abuse can lead to drug dependence and addiction. **Drug addiction** can affect its victims both physically and psychologically. **Physical dependency** happens when a drug is used habitually and the body adapts to its effects. In order to feel normal, the person must then continue to use the drug or experience resultant withdrawal consequences. **Psychological dependency** occurs when a drug has been used habitually and the mind has become emotionally reliant on the effects of the drug.

Teachers should concentrate on this vital component of health information and teach the impact of abuse on strong bodies and healthy minds. **Legal consequences** should also be taught. Texas law prohibits the sale of alcohol and tobacco to minors but, despite some of the best efforts, tobacco abuse continues to plague school-aged children. The Texas Department of Health estimates that over 20% of youth become smokers by age 13, according to recent statewide surveys. Alcohol continues to be the most widely used substance among Texas students in 7th through 12 grades, with 71% of students reporting use. Marijuana is the most commonly used illegal substance among Texas students after alcohol and tobacco.

Understand types of violence and abuse

The beginning teacher understands types of violence and abuse (including causes and effects of violence and abuse and ways to prevent and seek help in dealing with violence and abuse).

Abuse is causing harm to a person or thing; it ranges from simple damage to a piece of equipment to critical mistreatment of a person. Abuse may be overt (direct and obvious) or covert (disguised). There are various forms of abuse. **Sexual abuse** involves the unacceptable use of another person for sexual purposes, generally without consent or with physical or psychological threats. It is often inflicted on children. **Physical abuse** occurs when one person inflicts physical violence or pain on another. **Emotional abuse** may involve coercion, humiliation, or intimidation to force another to do something not in their best interests; it also involves one person's manipulation of another's emotional or psychological state for their own ends. **Verbal abuse** is the use of foul language, obscenities, or demeaning talk directed at another.

Violence is abusive or unjust exercise of power. Children today are exposed to increasing levels of violent acts, either as witnesses or victims. Schools play a significant role in reducing the occurrence of violence in our society by implementing violence prevention and intervention programs involving many facets of the community (home, social service agencies, religious institutions, law enforcement and judicial systems, civic organizations, and the media). Furthermore, caring teachers who create a safe school environment, and who consistently apply behavioral standards for students, play an integral part in reduction of violence.

Teachers must be alert to signs of abuse and violence. Children may be victimized by caregivers (**child neglect**), by bullies at school, or in other situations. Arming children with appropriate information includes instruction of basic concepts about personal safety (appropriate and inappropriate touching, trusting their intuitions and feelings, learning to say no emphatically with verbal and nonverbal emphasis, having an adult confidant, as well as assistance from professional agencies and organizations). Teachers must report and prevent abuse and violence.

Teach principles and procedures of safety, accident prevention, and emergency response

The beginning teacher selects and uses instructional strategies, materials, and activities to teach principles and procedures related to safety, accident prevention, and response to emergencies.

Various aspects of home, school, and recreational safety are prescribed by the TEKS for EC–4. Safety development begins with information related to personal safety in a variety of settings. Knowing and implementing the use of protective equipment—protective gear, appropriate dress, sun protection—as well as the ability to identify safe and unsafe places to play, prepares children for appropriate recreation. Youngsters become health literate when they understand the positive role of water, bicycle and fire safety, and the dangers associated with certain items (poisons, knives, scissors, weapons, and so on). Once this basis for personal safety has been established, students are prepared to learn about the larger scope of emergency preparation.

First aid is a series of simple, life-saving techniques performed by non-medical personnel—even children—to assist others in distress. In addition to learning the rudimentary skills of the **Heimlich maneuver** (choking) and care for bleeding and burns, children can master skills associated with **cardiopulmonary resuscitation** (**CPR**) when first aid is necessary for an unconscious person with no breathing and pulse. Activation of the **emergency medical services** (**EMS**), usually through a 911 call, is a vital strategy for all children.

Apply critical-thinking, goal-setting, problem-solving, and decision-making skills

The beginning teacher applies critical-thinking, goal-setting, problem-solving, and decision-making skills in health-related contexts and understands the use of refusal skills and conflict resolution to avoid unsafe situations.

Critical thinking, decision making, and **goal setting** are indispensable lifelong attributes needed to implement and uphold healthy behaviors. By developing these vital skills, children are able to change health knowledge into healthy actions. Although goals provide a sense of direction and purpose, decision making is the cognitive process of selecting a course of action from many options. **Critical thinking** is a mental process of evaluating facts for their truth. Critical thinking involves reflection, reasoning, and forming judgments about the facts.

Refusal skills involve the emphatic use of the word "no" when facing pressure in a decision-making setting. Children who are prepared to use refusal skills are less likely to make poor choices and engage in risky health behaviors that could lead to lifestyle diseases, substance abuse, and teen pregnancy. Children with good refusal skills end discussions quickly and proceed to something else.

Conflict resolution is a process of resolving a dispute in such a way as to provide a diplomatic solution that meets the interests of both parties. Conflict resolution aims to end conflicts before they start or before they lead to physical confrontations. It may be possible to avoid conflict without actually resolving the underlying dispute, by getting the parties to recognize that they may need to agree to disagree, and that no other resolution is feasible.

Help children build healthy, respectful interpersonal relationships

The beginning teacher selects and uses instructional strategies, materials, and activities to help children build healthy interpersonal relationships (for example, communication skills) and demonstrate consideration and respect for self, family, friends, and others (for example, practicing self-control).

The TEKS related to personal and interpersonal skills emphasize communication and respect in early childhood through 4th grade. **Communication skills,** involving both verbal and nonverbal behavior, should be developed for the sharing of information and expression of basic physiological and safety needs, as well as attitudes of love, belonging, and self-esteem. Communication consists of many components: the message, the sound/tone of the voice, facial expression, and body gestures.

Communication skills are not innate; they are learned. Cooperative learning situations greatly foster communication skills, as do **role-playing** and **journaling.** Teachers can role model the outstanding traits of good communicators by creating a learning environment focused on active listening. Good teachers will convince children that they are interested in what they have to say, while listening to the hidden meanings of the discourse. In communicating with students, quality instructors will provide meaningful feedback while accentuating the positive and showing respect for student opinion. When necessary to reprimand, the instructor focuses on the behaviors of students, not on their personal characters.

The study of family dynamics also provides links to communication patterns. Culture, gender, and socio-economic class affect communication models within families. Regardless of these factors, healthy families contribute to high self-esteem within their members.

It is this mutual interaction that expands health education from a personal matter to a societal matter. Health education promotes the acquisition of communication skills in each individual student in order to build stronger relationships with family members, friends, and others. There are risks involved; children may become critical of their parents, caregivers, and authorities. This is where the concept of respect for authority (again through good communication and listening) is vital. By learning and practicing **self-control** (the act of controlling your own impulses), students are better equipped to cope with uncertainties; to show consideration and respect for parents, grandparents, and friends; and to find suitable ways to respond to acts of disrespect by others.

Understand the influence that affect health

The beginning teacher understands the influence of various factors (for example, media, technology, peer and other relationships, environmental hazards) on individual, family, and community health.

To a large degree, the longer life expectancy of children today is due to medical technology that eliminated infectious diseases that once plagued the populace a century before. Citizens no longer worry about deaths from influenza and pneumonia. However, the same technology that brought such medical advances also has contributed to a high standard of sedentary living in the United States. **Hypokinetic** diseases (associated with decreased physical activity), such as heart disease, high blood pressure, and obesity, are the main causes of death.

The health education TEKS for 1st graders includes the identification of how television, computers, and video games can affect health behaviors. Children are developing in media-saturated surroundings. Research indicates US children, on the average, spend over five hours daily with **electronic media** and less than one hour daily with print media. Television/videotapes are the predominant mode, followed by other forms including movies, music, computers, and video games. The latter has received a great deal of publicity, particularly because there has been a steady increase in the number of video games with violent themes. The main health problem associated with prolonged use of electronic media is the time spent in sedentary activity. Thus, health behaviors related to media use need attention, including limiting time and monitoring game selection according to developmental level.

The list of **environmental hazards** is extensive and includes such topics as air pollution, asthma, extreme weather conditions, ultraviolet rays, no-smoking laws, poisons, and water-related public health. Teachers following the TEKS for 2nd through 4th graders will notice a significant emphasis on aspects of environmental health and should personalize instruction in these standards to the community/area where children attend school.

Help students find sources of information to make health-related decisions

The beginning teacher demonstrates knowledge of sources of health information and ways to use information to make health-related decisions.

The TEKS for EC–4 site several sources of health information (parents/guardians, physicians, teachers, nurses). Underlying throughout the TEKS are the many other school and community **health helpers** available for specific health information: firefighters and law enforcement officers, meteorologists, and volunteers representing community health agencies such as the American Heart Association, American Cancer Society, American Red Cross, Texas Bicycle Coalition, Texas Department of State Health Services, and others.

Accessing valid health information and health products is important in the development of good health behaviors. With the refinement of critical thinking comes the ability to identify valid health information and to analyze, select, and access health-promoting services and products. EC–4 teachers must prepare students to apply skills of information analysis and comparison.

Help students become health-wise consumers

The beginning teacher selects and uses instructional strategies, materials, and activities to help children understand the roles of healthcare professionals, the benefits of health-maintenance activities, and the skills for becoming health-wise consumers.

Health behaviors include regular medical and dental assessments. Because the first experience many students have in healthcare is in the school, it is vital for the classroom teacher to work with the **school nurse** to expand each child's health behaviors. The school nurse assumes a major responsibility in a comprehensive school health program, as he or she strives to develop health behaviors in children. This relationship will ultimately improve student academic performance and protect health. The nurse appraises and interprets the health status of children and serves as a consultant and resource person for the total school health program.

According to the TEKS for health education, kindergarten children should be able to name people who can provide helpful health information (parents, doctors, teachers, nurses) and to explain the importance of health information. In one possible lesson, a dentist or dental hygienist could visit the class to teach about tooth care and the function and development of teeth.

Consumer issues related to health behaviors can easily be integrated into units related to other subjects such as math (cost of purchases, measurements of foods), creative arts (important helpers puppet show), language arts (writing an advice column), science (sorting trash and litter), and social studies (creation of a phone list of health helpers).

Integrate health education across the curricula

The beginning teacher applies knowledge of health content and curriculum, including the Texas Essential Knowledge and Skills (TEKS), and of children in early childhood through 4th grade to plan and implement effective, developmentally appropriate health instruction, including relating the health-education curriculum to other content areas.

Because there are limited textbooks available for delivery of EC–4 health instruction, teachers must be creative in planning to meet the standards outlined in the TEKS. Health instruction can be delivered as a separate subject area with unique lesson plans, but also has potential for numerous **integrated learning** opportunities with other subject areas.

Methods for health instruction can span the spectrum, from very teacher-centered activities to those that are extremely student-centered. Selection of a method is dependant on a number of variables, including the objectives of the lesson, characteristics of the learners, size of the class, availability of equipment and facilities, and unique skills of the teacher. Within every class are students with a wide range of learning styles, and because there is no evidence to support a single best teaching style, the wise EC–4 teacher develops a cadre of teaching methods in order to provide learners with ample opportunity to achieve educational outcomes and develop appropriate health behaviors.

- **Lecture,** the most direct teacher-centered approach, involves talking to students in the EC–4 setting. A good rule to follow is the 30/70 rule in which 30% (or less) time is devoted to instructor or media presentations and 70% or more to leaner practice and integration activities. Assessment can be done through planned questions that stimulate thought and discussion.

- **Media presentations** are available from health agencies, including the American Heart Association, American Cancer Society, the American Red Cross, and others. Many of these organizations send speakers to elementary classrooms and provide substantial developmentally appropriate materials for dissemination.

- Another approach using direct methodology may involve presentations by a **guest speaker.** Because health instruction includes the introduction of a variety of health professionals to children, such speaking opportunities can accomplish multiple goals.

- **Interactive groups** give participants an opportunity to discuss ideas and ask questions in greater detail than is possible in a large group format. Such group activities also aid in the clarification of material.

- Interaction and **collaborative experiences** (small groups of students working together in a structured process to solve an academic task) can be effectively used in conjunction with lectures.

- If the students and teacher feel confident with mastery or individualized methodology, **games** (many are available online) and **creative artwork** can be utilized to promote student retention of health knowledge. **Worksheets** allow children to think for themselves without influence from peers.

- When classes are not too large and children do not appear to be self-conscious, **role-play and simulations** are extremely effective. This method allows children the opportunity to assume roles of others and appreciate other viewpoints. It also allows for exploration of various solutions.

- **Field trips** can range from simple tours of the school nurse's office to a neighborhood walking tour to practice pedestrian safety skills or elaborate tours at health fairs and health facilities.

Sample Questions

1. Mr. Perez had his 4th graders engaged in a health assignment. Each student cut a cigarette advertisement out of a magazine or newspaper and wrote a paper which addressed the following question: "What do you think the cigarette company is trying to say to you about smoking?" What was the primary goal of this lesson?

   A. to integrate health with language arts
   B. to stimulate critical thinking
   C. to teach about chronic disease
   D. to teach conflict resolution

   B Although the assignment does utilize a writing component and, thus, integrates with language arts, the primary goal involved each student using mental processes to actively and skillfully analyze and evaluate the messages in cigarette advertisements. Therefore, the stimulation of critical thinking is the best response. Although cigarette smoking is a controllable risk factor and does affect incidence of chronic disease, disease was not the goal of this lesson, making C an incorrect answer. Conflict resolution involves two parties. Because Mr. Perez asked students to write about their own interpretations of the smoking advertisement, answer D would not be correct.

2. Mrs. Bradley teaches health to kindergarten students. She prepared boxes with colored confetti to represent germs, and labeled them as follows: a friend's house, the playground, a pet, and so on. Her students lightly moistened their hands, and then dipped them into each of these boxes representing their travels throughout the day. One group was instructed to not wash afterwards, one group rinsed lightly, and a third group washed their hands thoroughly with soap and water. Mrs. Bradley directed a class discussion about the experience, concentrating on what students can do for better health behaviors. By doing this lesson, she best addressed which of the following TEKS:

   A. Explain the importance of health information.
   B. Name the five senses.
   C. Name major body parts and their functions.
   D. Explain practices used to control the spread of germs.

   D Option A involves higher level application skills then required in this lesson. Option B is also incorrect, even though some may think that touch was a part of the dipping experiment. However, touch represents only one of the five senses and was not the emphasis of this lesson. Because the skin is a part of the integumentary system, some may believe C is a correct response; however, it is only one body part and the lesson did not emphasize functions of the skin. Only answer D—explain practices used to control the spread of germs—is a viable answer. Mrs. Bradley accomplished this standard through the class discussion related to thorough hand washing following the experiment.

3. A 3rd-grade teacher asks her students to write descriptively about nutrition, using all five senses, in response to individual apple slices placed in front of them. TEKS from which subject areas are met with this assignment:

   A. health education
   B. English language arts and reading
   C. art
   D. Both A and B

   D Health easily integrates with a number of other subjects. In this case, the TEKS for 3rd-grade English language arts and reading includes the standard to "write to record ideas and reflections." Health education for 3rd grade includes the following: "identify types of nutrients" and "describe food combination in a balanced diet." Thus, TEKS from these two subjects can be met with the assignment, making D the best answer. C is not correct, because this particular question calls for a literary response rather than art elements such as color, texture, and form.

4. Mr. Doyle has arranged his 2nd-graders so they are sitting in a circle. In the middle of the circle, he has placed a number of food cards (with names or pictures of familiar foods) face down. Each card has a paper clip on it. Mr. Doyle explains to the students that this is the fish pond and the food cards are the fish. Using a yardstick with a string and magnet, each student gets a turn to "fish." The student will then reel in the food card and decide where his/her catch belongs on the food guide pyramid. In order to learn about the recommended servings, what does Mr. Doyle need to do when preparing the food cards?

    A. Prepare almost equal amounts of fruits and vegetables.

    B. Prepare more protein (meat/beans/fish) cards than grains.

    C. Prepare almost equal amounts of fats/oils as dairy.

    D. all of the above

A Almost equal servings of fruits and vegetables are recommended on the food group pyramid (2–4 fruits/3–5 vegetables), and on the new MyPyramid for children (1.5–2 cups of each). B is incorrect, because nutritionists recommended 5–11 servings of grains, preferably whole-grain variety, and about half that many servings of protein. C is also incorrect, because fats and oils should be used sparingly; dairy recommendations include 2–3 servings for growing children. Because B and C are incorrect, the final option, D, is also incorrect.

5. Miss Hightower, is a 1st-grade teacher who, unfortunately, suffers from seasonal allergies. One day she comes to school with irritated eyes, a runny nose, and a tendency to sneeze. She decides to use the time as a teachable moment for a health lesson. She tells her students her body has an unusually high sensitivity to certain substances, such as pollens that infiltrate their community during a specific time of year. The result is red eyes, sniffles, and sneezes, but her illness cannot be spread to others. Her impromptu lesson best meets which of the following 1st-grade health TEKS?

    A. Explain common practices that control the way germs are spread.

    B. Identify common illnesses and their symptoms.

    C. Identify and demonstrate use of the five senses.

    D. Identify people who can provide helpful health information such as parents, teachers, nurses, and physicians.

B As stated in the problem, Miss Hightower used the situation to identify her allergy problem and its symptoms, and to explain the relationship of her current health status as a non-contagious illness. Thus, B is a correct answer. A is not correct, because this particular type of illness (allergies) is non-communicable. Although senses may be affected by allergies, Miss Hightower did not elaborate on this, so C is not an appropriate answer. D is likewise not correct. Through this mini-lesson, Miss Hightower did not identify herself as a prime source of information about allergies, nor did she disseminate information about the role of medical assistance with her allergic problem. This may be covered at another time, but the scenario does not reflect D as a suitable answer.

Competency 027 (Physical Education)

The teacher uses knowledge of the concepts, principles, skills, and practices of physical education to plan and implement effective and engaging physical education activities for young children.

Review

Plan and implement appropriate physical education activities

The beginning teacher applies knowledge of physical education content and curriculum, including the Texas Essential Knowledge and Skills (TEKS), and of children in early childhood through 4th grade to plan and implement effective, developmentally appropriate physical education activities.

The curricular focus in physical education from early childhood through 4th grade follows a progressive and sequential framework. The instructional content for early childhood through 2nd grade emphasizes the development of fundamental motor skills, movement concepts, and varied movement experiences as a foundation for individual enjoyment. The curricular activities for 3rd and 4th grades center around producing mature movement patterns within fundamental motor skills, developing higher levels of health-related fitness, playing lead-up games, and understanding the beneficial influences of pursuing physical activity throughout life.

Apply key principles and concepts in physical education

The beginning teacher applies key principles and concepts in physical education (for example cardiovascular endurance, muscular strength, flexibility, weight control, conditioning, safety, stress management, nutrition) and their significance for physical activity, health, and fitness.

Movement is a way of life for young children. Active interaction for themselves, with friends, and within the environment encourages learning. Promoting **health-related fitness** in children is paramount for the development of better health now and in the future. Health-related fitness components include cardiovascular endurance, flexibility, muscular strength/endurance, and body composition. Developing health-related fitness enhances physiological efficiency in every system within the body (cardiopulmonary, immunology, endocrine, pulmonary, vascular), enhances the quality of life at every stage, and can have a targeted impact on preventing or decreasing childhood obesity.

- **Cardiovascular endurance** promotes the efficient exchange of oxygen and carbon dioxide at lung and tissue levels. A healthy heart is capable of providing sufficient blood supply to tissues and lungs for gas exchange to take place. Teachers should lead activities that incorporate vigorous movement and rapid breathing for a minimum of 20 to 30 sustained minutes each day to improve cardiovascular endurance, conditioning, and assist with weight management efforts.

- **Flexibility** enables children to have full range of motion and ease of movement at specific joints. Young children demonstrate better posture when joint flexibility is sufficient. Teachers should lead activities four to five times per week that require all joints to move through the entire range of motion.

- **Body composition** is related to the amount of lean body tissue a child has in comparison to the amount of adipose (fat) tissue. Too little or too much adipose tissue is unhealthy; however, young children need some good fats in their diets to provide for the body's physiological growth needs. Teachers may aide older children's understanding of the balance between caloric intake and expenditure by journaling (tracking) food intake and caloric consumption.

- **Muscular strength and endurance** describes the ability of a muscle to contract with force and continue to contract over a period of time. Muscular strength and endurance are very important to the maintenance of excellent posture, development of body control, and production of efficient movement. At the younger ages, traditional strength activities are not appropriate; therefore, natural strength activities are encouraged. Natural strength activities include games or physical tasks where the child's own body weight is entirely or partially held or lifted. Stunts and tumbling activities are excellent opportunities for children to individually develop strength (cartwheels, mule kick, handstand, crab walk).

Movement offers a natural and effective tool for managing stress at every age. Providing children with beneficial stress management choices encourage the development of healthy adult habits. Establishing movement as a healthy response to managing stress provides young children with an early tool to lessen the harmful affects of stress.

Help students understand the benefits of an active lifestyle

The beginning teacher knows and helps children understand the benefits of an active lifestyle.

Producing physically educated individuals should be a mission for every teacher and community. Teachers must implement a well rounded curriculum that develops nationally recognized characteristics demonstrated by physically educated individuals. A **physically educated person** is one who has the skills necessary to participate in a variety of physical activities, demonstrates a personally active lifestyle sufficient to produce a healthy level of fitness, demonstrates respect for self and others, and values physical activity as a means of self-expression, enjoyment, and health.

Use knowledge of movement principles to help students develop motor skills

The beginning teacher applies knowledge of movement principles and concepts to develop children's motor skills.

Understanding and applying movement principles, such as cephalocaudal and proximodistal, enable the beginning teacher to structure motor skills practice in an appropriate and natural sequence.

- **Cephalocaudal** motor development identifies that young children gain voluntary control of the area of their bodies closest to the head first before the lower portion of the body.

- **Proximodistal** motor development identifies that young children acquire motor skills using large muscle (**gross motor**—more proximal) movements before applying specialized movements produced from the use of small muscles (**fine motor**—more distal).

Teachers develop the fundamental movement (motor) skills in young children, because these fundamental movements are the foundation for all other specialized motor skills. **Specialized motor skills** are made up of fluid combinations of fundamental motor skills and enable children to meet the movement demands of lead-up and traditional game play. Teachers working with young children should explore the vast array of different ways to produce a single skill. Using movement concepts and guided instruction strategies, teachers help young children understand the variety of movements the body can produce. Using more direct teaching methods to teach older students how specialized skills (sport skills) are produced is appropriate when technique and mastery are important outcomes.

Movement concepts are cognitive understandings related to movement which describe the variety of ways to produce a skill and or interact with the environment, objects, or others. The three primary categories of movement concepts are effort, space, and relationship.

- **Effort** involves movements that incorporate time, flow, and force.
- **Space** involves body movement at different levels, directions, and ranges of movements.
- **Relationship** develops conceptual awareness of moving while interacting with objects and or people.

Activities that promote an understanding of how the body moves develop the **effort** movement concept. Moving slowly or quickly, with tight or loose arms, and with strong or light steps are all examples of modifying movement using the effort concept.

Activities that promote the understanding of where the body moves develop the **space movement** concept. Moving at high or low levels, forward or backward, and with narrow or wide movement demonstrates the space concept.

Activities that promote an understanding of moving while interacting with others and objects develop the **relationship** movement concept. Moving in-between or around a cone and with or without a partner demonstrates the relationship concept.

Select and use appropriate learning experience to enhance fundamental motor skills

The beginning teacher selects and uses developmentally appropriate learning experiences that enhance children's loco-motor, non-locomotor, body-control, manipulative, and rhythmic skills.

Fundamental motor skills are the foundation of all movement. Therefore, the importance of developing efficient movers in fundamental movement skills is imperative for proficient future movers. Fundamental movement skills are comprised of locomotor, non-locomotor, and manipulative skills. The emphasis on developing locomotor and non-locomotor skills is heaviest in the EC and 1st-grade curricula.

- **Locomotor** skills serve the primary goal of moving the body from one location to another. Locomotor skills include walking, running, leaping, jumping, hopping, galloping, sliding, and skipping.

- **Non-locomotor** skills develop aspects of body control and balance with limited emphasis on movement. Non-locomotor skills include body control, balance, and stability skills. **Body control skills** incorporate maintaining body control while moving, starting, stopping, and or dodging. **Balance skills** place emphasis on maintaining balance while moving or standing stationary, such as working on a balance beam or doing a cartwheel. **Stability skills** integrate body control and balance skills to produce movements such as a headstand, handstand, or tripod.

- **Manipulative** skills are motor skills that are used to control an object. Manipulative skills include the elemental movements of kicking, trapping, throwing, striking, volleying, catching, bouncing, and ball rolling.

These fundamental motor skills form the foundation of all children's games. Young children respond to rhythmic activities and music. Every motor skill has an underlying rhythm (timing component). The rhythm of a skill is based in the unique sequential pattern and movement timing required to produce a particular skill. Using rhythmic activities to teach fundamental motor skills is a multi-sensory approach to aid learning.

Modify instruction based on individual differences

The beginning teacher modifies instruction based on individual differences in growth and development. The beginning teacher must know and be able to identify the various growth and developmental stages of young children. Movement capabilities are driven by growth and developmental readiness, but are also affected by opportunity to practice and exposure to all the fundamental skills.

Readiness describes a state of being when it is easiest for an individual to learn a task (concept). Readiness is unique for each individual child. Successful teachers understand the common cognitive, social, emotional, and physiological growth and development expectations and can plan activities that promote successful participation regardless of readiness levels of the students within early childhood through 4th-grade ages.

Enhance students' movement patterns

The beginning teacher evaluates movement patterns to help children improve performance of motor skills and to integrate and refine motor and rhythmic skills.

Teachers should know how to select, develop, and use appropriate assessment strategies and instruments to identify whether learning outcomes are being met and for other diagnostic purposes. The use of informal and formal assessment is appropriate at the early childhood through 4th-grade ages. Assessing student performance permits evaluation of individual student competencies and/or deficiencies and instructional effectiveness.

- **Informal assessment** tools (observation checklists, rubrics, portfolios) enable teachers to document student performance and progress. Within the early childhood to 4th-grade curricula, assessments of fundamental motor skills, specialized motor skills, basic game play, and sport-specific skills are often completed using qualitative assessment tools, such as observation checklists and performance rubrics. **Checklists** are used to determine whether the elemental components of a skill or activity are demonstrated. **Performance rubrics** allow the teacher to specify the degree to which elemental components are demonstrated.

- The curricular activities for 3rd and 4th grades center on lead-up games that require a balance between informal and formal assessment. **Formal assessments** (paper-pencil exams, standardized physical fitness tests) are periodically used to measure mastery of information, skill execution, and/or physical fitness levels.

Promote rules, etiquette, and fair play

The beginning teacher selects and uses instructional strategies to promote children's knowledge and application of rules, procedures, etiquette, and fair play in developmentally appropriate games and activities.

Teachers should maximize exposure to a wide variety of lifetime physical activities and sport opportunities to provide children with a knowledge base and skill base foundation for lifelong movement.

Lifelong activities describe activities that are carried over or continued throughout the life span. These activities are typically individual or dual activities and include endeavors, such as archery, camping, dancing, hiking, rock climbing, martial arts, horseshoes, cycling, and water activities. A sports curriculum should include individual sports, dual sports, and team sports:

- The focus for **individual sports** should be on health and social benefits, as well as personal satisfaction gained from participation. Individual sports may be completed without another player required. Examples of individual sports include jogging, aquatics, archery, golf, bowling, gymnastics, orienteering, weight resistance, and rope jumping.

- **Dual sports** are performed with two to four players and are also considered lifetime sports. These sports include tennis, badminton, pickelball, bocce, croquet, Frisbee, fencing, and racquetball.

- **Team sports** provide social experiences for children that require cooperative interaction as a team member (leadership and followship skills). Team sports include activities such as volleyball, basketball, flag football, field hockey, speedball, soccer, and softball.

Physical activities and games are an excellent venue to discuss elements of fair play, organized structure, individual responsibility, and group dynamics. Young children learn the structural procedures of taking turns, fair play, and simple rules though game play. Older children are able to grasp more abstract elements of game play, such as situation-based strategies and the role an individual serves while being part of a team (position play).

Promote positive interaction and active engagement

The beginning teacher designs, manages, and adapts physical education activities to promote positive interaction and active engagement by all children.

Managing children in a physically oriented environment poses different challenges for the classroom teacher. Teachers must plan for all students to be active, regardless of a child's ability (disability). Maximizing participation encourages learning throughout the lesson. Teachers who plan for maximum participation do so by following two key strategies: accommodate diverse skill levels and organize activities to reduce wait time. Maintaining engaged student participation promotes skill development and limits time for off-task behavior. Altering game rules and using multilevel stations are ways to challenge several skill levels at a single learning center; they are examples of adapting to meet the performance capability of children.

Sample Questions

1. Which of the following skills are examples found within the skill category that is responsible for getting you from one place to another while primarily using large muscles to accomplish the movement?

    A.   walk and run
    B.   hop and leap
    C.   throw and bat
    D.   A and B

    D Locomotor skills move you from one place to another, and walking and runing are locomotor skills; however, so are hopping and leaping, found in answer B. Neither throwing nor batting is considered a locomotor skill—they are manipulative skills—so D is correct: Both walk/run and hop/leap contain locomotor skills.

2. Nine-year-old Paschal is having difficulty hitting a pitched ball with a bat. Which of the following activities is likely to be most effective for helping him learn how to hit a ball successfully?

    A.   The teacher should have him work cooperatively with another learner who has similar difficulties.
    B.   The teacher should have him practice striking small whiffle balls on the ground with a short-handled hockey stick.
    C.   The teacher should have him participate in games that require advanced eye-hand coordination skills.
    D.   The teacher should have the pitcher use a larger ball and slow down the pitch.

    D Partnering students with similar difficulties without providing better modeling will reinforce poor skill techniques. B is incorrect: He would be practicing different skill techniques (golf) than the ones required to hit an object in a horizontal plane. C is incorrect: If he is having perceptual-motor difficulties of eye-hand coordination, participating in harder games will only leave him more frustrated. D is correct: Changing the ball to a larger size and reducing the speed of the ball makes it easier to hit.

3. Kickball is the unit you are teaching, and you notice many of your 2nd- and 3rd-grade students need help developing the skill of kicking a moving ball. You change the current lesson to include the following instructional practice for those students struggling with kicking the ball. First, from a stationary position, the students kick a stationary ball. Second, from a stationary position, the students kick a stationary ball to different areas on the field. Third, from a stationary position, the students kick a ball rolled at the same speed, height, and spot each time. Fourth, the students kick a rolled ball as they run toward the ball. Why would a teacher design the lesson this way?

    I.   You want to order the levels in the kicking task from the simplest practice level to more complex practice levels.
    II.   This lesson is designed to develop all possible ways to kick that could be used in game play.
    III. You want to teach students how to analyze their own errors in kicking performance.
    IV.   You want to provide students with more opportunities to progressively practice the basic parts of kicking with success, and then increase the difficulty of the kicking task slowly.

    A.   I and IV
    B.   I and II
    C.   II and III
    D.   III and IV

    A Both I and IV address the practice teachers use to organize lessons and present learning experiences in a sequential and progressive manner. During this lesson adaptation, the students are working on the mechanical and timing components of kicking a moving ball and not on all the different ways to kick the ball. B is incorrect: Option I is correct; however, option II is not correct, because the adaptation concentrates on how to time the body's movement with the movement of the ball and not on how many different ways the ball may be kicked (long, short, to right or left field). C is incorrect: Option II is not correct, because the adaptation concentrates on how to time the body's movement with the movement of the ball and not on how many different ways the ball may be kicked (long, short, to right or left field). Option III is not correct, because the teacher is not asking the student to identify errors in movement. Skill analysis develops much later and follows understanding of how a skill is produced. D is incorrect: Option III is not correct, because the teacher is not asking the student to identify errors in movement. Skill analysis develops much later and follows understanding of how a skill is produced. Option IV is correct, because when a teacher simplifies timing or movement elements, such as ball movement, the task is easier to process and produce. Teachers modifying activities with small incremental changes in task difficulty, allows the child's brain and body to coordinate more efficiently.

4. Miss Talbot wants to assess her health-related fitness unit this year. She completed baseline fitness information at the beginning of the semester and now again at the end. The following shows one female student's beginning and ending semester performances on the health-related fitness tests.

		Beginning Performance	*Ending Performance*
Station #1:	Flexibility: Sit and Reach	19.5 inches	16.75 inches
Station #2:	Crunch (in 1 minute)	55 crunches	65 crunches
Station #3:	Body Composition	15%	12%
Station #4:	1.5 Mile Run/Walk	18:55 minutes	15:03 minutes

Which of the following conclusions may be true?

A. Student's performance improved within each testing component; therefore, no curricular adjustments need to be made within the unit content.

B. Student's performance related to flexibility and muscular endurance improved; therefore, improvement in two of four components is sufficient and no curricular adjustments need to be made within the unit content.

C. The health-related fitness components measuring body composition and cardiovascular endurance are closely related and student's performance improvements in these areas should be expected.

D. Student's performance related to body composition, muscular endurance, and cardiovascular endurance improved, but flexibility performance declined.

D Flexibility did not show improvement. Activities within this unit need to be altered to emphasize joint range of motion. Muscular endurance did improve, because the student was able to do more crunches in one minute than previously; however, flexibility performance was worse. Activities within this unit need to be altered to emphasize joint range of motion. Although body composition and cardiovascular endurance components are strongly tied to each other, one component is not a predictor of the other. The question asked for comparison of all beginning and ending factors and not just body composition and cardiovascular endurance. The decrease in flexibility was not addressed, nor was there a mention of overall unit activity impact on the other health-related fitness performances. D is correct: Unit content was successful in improving three of the four health-related fitness components (cardiovascular endurance, muscle endurance, and body composition); however, the unit activities need to be adjusted to address deficiencies in flexibility performance.

PART II

TExES GENERALIST EC–4 SAMPLE TESTS

Answer Sheet for Practice Test I

1 Ⓐ Ⓑ Ⓒ Ⓓ	51 Ⓐ Ⓑ Ⓒ Ⓓ
2 Ⓐ Ⓑ Ⓒ Ⓓ	52 Ⓐ Ⓑ Ⓒ Ⓓ
3 Ⓐ Ⓑ Ⓒ Ⓓ	53 Ⓐ Ⓑ Ⓒ Ⓓ
4 Ⓐ Ⓑ Ⓒ Ⓓ	54 Ⓐ Ⓑ Ⓒ Ⓓ
5 Ⓐ Ⓑ Ⓒ Ⓓ	55 Ⓐ Ⓑ Ⓒ Ⓓ
6 Ⓐ Ⓑ Ⓒ Ⓓ	56 Ⓐ Ⓑ Ⓒ Ⓓ
7 Ⓐ Ⓑ Ⓒ Ⓓ	57 Ⓐ Ⓑ Ⓒ Ⓓ
8 Ⓐ Ⓑ Ⓒ Ⓓ	58 Ⓐ Ⓑ Ⓒ Ⓓ
9 Ⓐ Ⓑ Ⓒ Ⓓ	59 Ⓐ Ⓑ Ⓒ Ⓓ
10 Ⓐ Ⓑ Ⓒ Ⓓ	60 Ⓐ Ⓑ Ⓒ Ⓓ

11 Ⓐ Ⓑ Ⓒ Ⓓ	61 Ⓐ Ⓑ Ⓒ Ⓓ
12 Ⓐ Ⓑ Ⓒ Ⓓ	62 Ⓐ Ⓑ Ⓒ Ⓓ
13 Ⓐ Ⓑ Ⓒ Ⓓ	63 Ⓐ Ⓑ Ⓒ Ⓓ
14 Ⓐ Ⓑ Ⓒ Ⓓ	64 Ⓐ Ⓑ Ⓒ Ⓓ
15 Ⓐ Ⓑ Ⓒ Ⓓ	65 Ⓐ Ⓑ Ⓒ Ⓓ
16 Ⓐ Ⓑ Ⓒ Ⓓ	66 Ⓐ Ⓑ Ⓒ Ⓓ
17 Ⓐ Ⓑ Ⓒ Ⓓ	67 Ⓐ Ⓑ Ⓒ Ⓓ
18 Ⓐ Ⓑ Ⓒ Ⓓ	68 Ⓐ Ⓑ Ⓒ Ⓓ
19 Ⓐ Ⓑ Ⓒ Ⓓ	69 Ⓐ Ⓑ Ⓒ Ⓓ
20 Ⓐ Ⓑ Ⓒ Ⓓ	70 Ⓐ Ⓑ Ⓒ Ⓓ

21 Ⓐ Ⓑ Ⓒ Ⓓ	71 Ⓐ Ⓑ Ⓒ Ⓓ
22 Ⓐ Ⓑ Ⓒ Ⓓ	72 Ⓐ Ⓑ Ⓒ Ⓓ
23 Ⓐ Ⓑ Ⓒ Ⓓ	73 Ⓐ Ⓑ Ⓒ Ⓓ
24 Ⓐ Ⓑ Ⓒ Ⓓ	74 Ⓐ Ⓑ Ⓒ Ⓓ
25 Ⓐ Ⓑ Ⓒ Ⓓ	75 Ⓐ Ⓑ Ⓒ Ⓓ
26 Ⓐ Ⓑ Ⓒ Ⓓ	76 Ⓐ Ⓑ Ⓒ Ⓓ
27 Ⓐ Ⓑ Ⓒ Ⓓ	77 Ⓐ Ⓑ Ⓒ Ⓓ
28 Ⓐ Ⓑ Ⓒ Ⓓ	78 Ⓐ Ⓑ Ⓒ Ⓓ
29 Ⓐ Ⓑ Ⓒ Ⓓ	79 Ⓐ Ⓑ Ⓒ Ⓓ
30 Ⓐ Ⓑ Ⓒ Ⓓ	80 Ⓐ Ⓑ Ⓒ Ⓓ

31 Ⓐ Ⓑ Ⓒ Ⓓ	81 Ⓐ Ⓑ Ⓒ Ⓓ
32 Ⓐ Ⓑ Ⓒ Ⓓ	82 Ⓐ Ⓑ Ⓒ Ⓓ
33 Ⓐ Ⓑ Ⓒ Ⓓ	83 Ⓐ Ⓑ Ⓒ Ⓓ
34 Ⓐ Ⓑ Ⓒ Ⓓ	84 Ⓐ Ⓑ Ⓒ Ⓓ
35 Ⓐ Ⓑ Ⓒ Ⓓ	85 Ⓐ Ⓑ Ⓒ Ⓓ
36 Ⓐ Ⓑ Ⓒ Ⓓ	86 Ⓐ Ⓑ Ⓒ Ⓓ
37 Ⓐ Ⓑ Ⓒ Ⓓ	87 Ⓐ Ⓑ Ⓒ Ⓓ
38 Ⓐ Ⓑ Ⓒ Ⓓ	88 Ⓐ Ⓑ Ⓒ Ⓓ
39 Ⓐ Ⓑ Ⓒ Ⓓ	89 Ⓐ Ⓑ Ⓒ Ⓓ
40 Ⓐ Ⓑ Ⓒ Ⓓ	90 Ⓐ Ⓑ Ⓒ Ⓓ

41 Ⓐ Ⓑ Ⓒ Ⓓ	91 Ⓐ Ⓑ Ⓒ Ⓓ
42 Ⓐ Ⓑ Ⓒ Ⓓ	92 Ⓐ Ⓑ Ⓒ Ⓓ
43 Ⓐ Ⓑ Ⓒ Ⓓ	93 Ⓐ Ⓑ Ⓒ Ⓓ
44 Ⓐ Ⓑ Ⓒ Ⓓ	94 Ⓐ Ⓑ Ⓒ Ⓓ
45 Ⓐ Ⓑ Ⓒ Ⓓ	95 Ⓐ Ⓑ Ⓒ Ⓓ
46 Ⓐ Ⓑ Ⓒ Ⓓ	96 Ⓐ Ⓑ Ⓒ Ⓓ
47 Ⓐ Ⓑ Ⓒ Ⓓ	97 Ⓐ Ⓑ Ⓒ Ⓓ
48 Ⓐ Ⓑ Ⓒ Ⓓ	98 Ⓐ Ⓑ Ⓒ Ⓓ
49 Ⓐ Ⓑ Ⓒ Ⓓ	99 Ⓐ Ⓑ Ⓒ Ⓓ
50 Ⓐ Ⓑ Ⓒ Ⓓ	100 Ⓐ Ⓑ Ⓒ Ⓓ

Time: 5 hours

100 questions

Directions: The following test consists of questions from each of the five domains that will be on the actual examination. Select the choice that best answers the question. At the end of the test are complete answers and explanations. To help you identify your strengths and weaknesses on this test, we've included the subject area at the end of each answer.

1. How many phonemes does the word "six" contain?

   A. one
   B. two
   C. three
   D. four

2. Which of the following most directly supports receptive language?

   A. encouraging the free expression of ideas
   B. encouraging children to ask questions politely
   C. teaching children active listening strategies
   D. teaching children how to formulate questions

3. Mr. Michaels leads his kindergarten class in a game in which he says words such as "running," "catching," "sleeper," and "helper," and students repeat each word without the "-ing" or "-er" ending. What does Mr. Michaels want to call his students' attention to?

   A. phonemes
   B. morphemes
   C. syntax
   D. semantics

4. When would it benefit early language development for a teacher to think out loud?

   A. when the teacher ties her own shoes
   B. when the teacher selects a book to read to the class
   C. when the teacher decides how to distribute construction paper to the class
   D. all of the above

5. A preschool teacher writes a letter to parents explaining that the class is working on phonemic awareness. Which of the following should the teacher do to encourage parents to help?

   A. Ask parents to continue reading to their children.
   B. Identify some word games, such as wordplay and rhymes, that parents can play with their children.
   C. Encourage parents to prepare flash cards that can be used to practice letter-sound correspondences.
   D. Describe some phonemic awareness exercises that parents can use to help their children learn.

6. If one inch is approximately 2.54 cm, one meter is approximately how many inches?

   A. 0.0254
   B. 40
   C. 72
   D. 254

7. A cake recipe calls for 2½ cups of flour. James is going to triple the recipe. How many cups of flour will he use?

   A. $5\frac{1}{2}$
   B. $6\frac{1}{2}$
   C. $7\frac{1}{2}$
   D. 9

GO ON TO THE NEXT PAGE

8. Which of the following is *not* equivalent to 40(32 + 68)?

    A. $40 \times 32 + 68$

    B. (32 + 68)40

    C. 40(68 + 32)

    D. $40 \times 32 + 40 \times 68$

9. Which of the following is one of the major goals of social studies instruction at the elementary level?

    A. to teach problem-solving skills that can be applied to real-life social situations

    B. to convey basic knowledge about the history of our nation

    C. to promote a sense of tolerance and appreciation for differing points of view

    D. all of the above

10. Which of the following is the most effective way of introducing kindergarten students to differences in the natural and artificial features that cover the earth's surface?

    A. The teacher shows children pictures of some of the features on the earth's surface, and asks the children which ones they recognize.

    B. The teacher defines the terms "natural" and "artificial," and then asks children to think of examples of each type of object.

    C. The teacher leads children through the playground while encouraging them to explore and discuss some of the differences between various materials such as grass, sand, and asphalt.

    D. The teacher leads children through the classroom and playground while pointing to objects and naming them as "natural" or "artificial," and then encourages children to guess what those two words mean.

11. Inquiry teaching most directly promotes which of the following?

    A. appreciation of abstract ideas

    B. understanding of the scientific method

    C. the ability to consider multiple perspectives on an issue

    D. acquisition of facts and concepts through rote learning

12. As a beginning 1st-grade science teacher, Mrs. Fillmore understands that she will be responsible for developing lessons and activities based on a grade-appropriate science curriculum. As she presents concepts and introduces the students to concepts embedded within a lesson, she will want to focus on which of the following activities?

    A. watching videos

    B. reading books

    C. conducting field trips

    D. constructing models

13. Mrs. Chang believes that the environment can provide many examples of objects that can be used to organize ideas. Mrs. Chang decides to take her 1st graders on an excursion to:

    A. put their hands on a tree and note its texture

    B. relate art to everyday life

    C. see the different shapes of the leaves

    D. both A and C

14. Which of the following persons was an American painter?

    A. Salvador Dali

    B. Grandma Moses

    C. Helen Keller

    D. Pablo Picasso

15. A 4th-grade classroom professional plays two selections of dance music from two different cultures: Navaho and Filipino. Although both selections have a steady beat and a vocal line, the accompanying instruments are not similar. What might the professional want the children to understand?

    A. that both cultures had dance music and that they enjoyed dancing

    B. that both cultures employed singing while dancing

    C. that both cultures' music had different instruments because they liked a particular sound better than another sound

    D. that both cultures had different instruments due to the region of the world in which they lived

16. "Happy Birthday" and "The Star Spangled Banner" are similar because

   A. They have the same steady beat.
   B. They have the same words.
   C. They have the same rhythm.
   D. They have the same composer.

Questions 17 though 22 are based on the following information.

Mrs. Lacewell, a 4th-grade teacher, wanted to introduce the students to a lesson built around the motion of a pendulum. She tied a string to one end of the pencil, held the other end of the string fixed, pulled the pencil back a small angle, and released it. As the pencil went back and forth, Mrs. Lacewell asked the students what they noticed about the time taken to complete a round trip. She explained that this time was known as the period of a pendulum, an important feature of a pendulum, and how grandfather clocks used the period to tell time.

After Mrs. Lacewell introduced the concept of a period of a pendulum, she wanted her class to perform a laboratory investigation to determine the effects of certain variables by asking them the following question: Does the mass of the object or the length of the string affect the period of a pendulum? She then had her class sorted in small groups, in which they constructed their own pendulum and set out to design an experiment to answer this question. Each group was assigned specific roles for the experiment: One student would coordinate the different masses and string lengths of the different pendulums; one student would release the pendulum; one would time the object's motion; and one would collect the data. The data one group obtained from its experiment are given in the two following tables.

Experimental Results from Pendulum Investigation (Variable Held Constant = String Length)		
Object Mass (kg)	**String Length (m)**	**Period of the Pendulum (s)**
1	0.25	0.98
5	0.25	1.02
10	0.25	1.16
15	0.25	1.05
20	0.25	1.00

Experimental Results from Pendulum Investigation (Variable Held Constant = Object Mass)		
Object Mass (kg)	**String Length (m)**	**Period of the Pendulum (s)**
10	0.10	0.63
10	0.25	1.08
10	0.50	1.42
10	0.75	1.74
10	1.00	2.00

GO ON TO THE NEXT PAGE

17. In discussing the demonstration, Mrs. Lacewell asked the class whether the object would move faster at the bottom point if the object were held at a greater height above the ground. It turned out that this was true, which is an example of

    A. conservation of energy

    B. conservation of mass

    C. kinetic energy

    D. potential energy

18. As Mrs. Lacewell set the pendulum in motion, the class was asked for how long the back-and-forth motion would continue. In other words, would the object eventually come to a stop? It turned out that the object did, indeed, eventually come to a stop. The reason the object came to a stop was

    A. shape of object

    B. gravity

    C. object weight

    D. friction

19. In comparing the data in the two tables, the period for the 10 kg object mass and string length of 0.25 m yielded values of 1.16 s and 1.08 s, respectively. The most likely reason for this inconsistency in data values is

    A. defective stopwatch

    B. different students making measurements

    C. student reaction times

    D. pendulum turned out to be slightly slower in the second table

20. In order to minimize any possible inconsistencies in the data, Mrs. Lacewell might suggest which of the following to her students:

    A. Each group performs several measurements and takes the average.

    B. All groups average their results together.

    C. Every group performs the same experiment over the next two days and averages the values.

    D. Each team member makes a measurement of the period, and the team averages the values.

21. For the data in the first table, which are the independent and dependent variables?

    A. Mass is an independent variable; period is a dependent variable.

    B. Length is an independent variable; period is a dependent variable.

    C. Mass is an independent variable; length is a dependent variable.

    D. Length is an independent variable; mass is a dependent variable.

22. From the data displayed in the two tables, students can conclude that which variable(s) affected the period of the pendulum?

    A. object mass

    B. string length

    C. both string length and object mass

    D. neither string length nor object mass

23. Mr. Herdez wants his kindergarten students to realize that their own behaviors result in healthy or unhealthy conditions. This is best done by all of these activities except

    A. naming harmful effects of drugs

    B. identifying safe and unsafe places to play

    C. learning how to dial 911

    D. discussing the basic parts of the body that fight diseases

24. Mr. Metcalf, the physical education teacher, expects his kindergarten students to be proficient in specialized movement forms. An activity that is appropriate for this is which of the following:

    A. Have students demonstrate a clear contrast between moving slow and fast when traveling from point A to point B.

    B. Describe to them the benefits from involvement in daily activities.

    C. Have the students locate the lungs and tell why they are important in exercising.

    D. Get students to follow the rules of each game.

25. There have been many accidents at Benavidez Elementary, and the principal wants the number of accidents reduced. She has solicited the help of the PE teachers, who can help in which of the following ways?

    A. Have students memorize rules of play.
    B. Explain how proper shoes and clothing promote safe play.
    C. Do the exercises with the students.
    D. Get the students to get more hours of sleep.

26. During a presidential election campaign, a 4th-grade teacher helps her students formulate opinions about the major candidates, create a ballot box for the class, vote, and then tabulate the results. Which of the following would be most important to include in this activity?

    A. A competition in which the supporters of each candidate form a group and generate a written statement as to why its candidate is the best. The teacher then compares the two statements and declares one the "winner."
    B. A written assignment in which each student describes the merits of the candidate that he/or she does *not* support.
    C. A structured debate involving one supporter of each candidate, with the teacher acting as moderator and the rest of the class serving as the audience.
    D. A round robin exercise in which each student is asked to explain to the rest of the class why he or she favors a particular candidate.

27. During the Archaic Period, why did the peoples of the Trans Pecos build rock shelters that were partially underground?

    A. The shelters stayed relatively cool in the intense summer heat of the desert.
    B. The shelters served as protection against the flooding that is common in the region.
    C. The shelters provided access to rivers that flowed underground.
    D. The shelters offered protection against a variety of human and animal predators.

28. What was the primary cause of the Mexican-American War?

    A. disagreements about grazing rights
    B. desire for petroleum-rich land
    C. boundary disputes concerning Texas and Mexico
    D. conflicting claims to water rights

29. What is the origin of the word "Texas"?

    A. It comes from a Karankawan word that means "kin" or "family."
    B. It comes from a Caddo word that means "friends" or "allies."
    C. It comes from a Comanche word meaning "wide land."
    D. all of the above are possible origins

30. What is one of the main advantages of using primary sources in teaching history?

    A. Primary sources tend to be more accurate than secondary sources.
    B. Primary sources tend to be highly engaging, given that they represent personal views on historical events and situations.
    C. Primary sources tend to be more comprehensive and complete than secondary sources.
    D. Primary sources tend to present multiple points of view on a particular historical event or situation.

31. Sam earned an 8% raise. He made $32,000 before his raise. What does he make now?

    A. $2,560
    B. $32,008
    C. $34,560
    D. $256,000

32. Sheena bought four apples for $0.75. How much would she spend for a dozen apples?

    A. $2.25
    B. $3.00
    C. $7.52
    D. $9.00

GO ON TO THE NEXT PAGE

33. A teacher has her students to create maps in order to help them appreciate the general topography of the United States. Which of the following maps would be most useful in helping children appreciate differences in the elevations of different regions?

   A. outline map
   B. geographic map
   C. topographic map
   D. relief map

34. A temperate environment, located between a desert and a forest that is dominated by grasslands, is likely to be which of the following biomes?

   A. taiga
   B. savanna
   C. tundra
   D. steppe

Questions 35 through 38 are based on the following information:

In presenting a lesson on plants to her 4th-grade class, Mrs. Luna discussed the major features of plants, the life cycle of plants, the process of photosynthesis, and the required elements for plants to survive. Following this discussion, Mrs. Luna posed the following question to her class: Do plants grow better in sunlight or in artificial light? Working in small groups, her students were given bean seeds, soil, water, and small planter pots. Each group was to plant the same number of seeds in four different planter pots, and then place each pot under different lighting conditions: near a window for sunlight, under a box subjected to artificial white light, under a box subjected to artificial green light, and in an enclosed space in total darkness. All plants were to be watered each day in the same amount at the same time for 5 days. After the plants are watered, a student in each group would measure the length of the bean sprout.

35. In this experiment, the dependent variable is:

   A. amount of soil
   B. amount of water
   C. length of sprout
   D. amount of light exposure

36. Mrs. Luna had one group place their data table (shown below) on the blackboard. Which bean sprout grew the fastest?

   A. sunlight
   B. white light
   C. green light
   D. darkness

Various Sources Of Light Exposure Versus Bean Sprout Length				
Day	Sprout Length (Sunlight) [cm]	Sprout Length (White Light) [cm]	Sprout Length (Green Light) [cm]	Sprout Length (Darkness) [cm]
1	0	0	0	0
2	0.6	0.4	0.3	0.7
3	0.8	0.7	0.6	1.2
4	1.4	0.9	0.8	2.4
5	1.9	1.1	1.0	3.6
6	3.2	3.0	2.7	5.7

37. Which line graph best summarizes the data displayed in the table of the bean sprout grown in total darkness?

A.

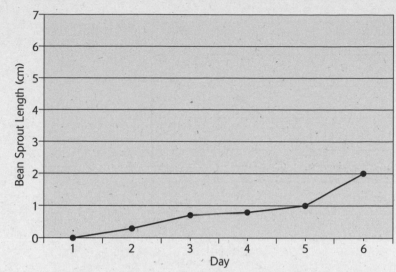

B.

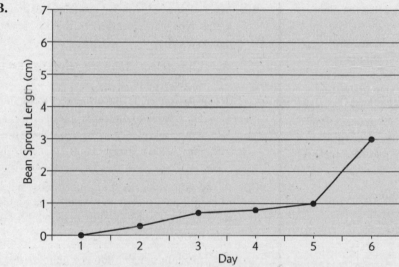

C.

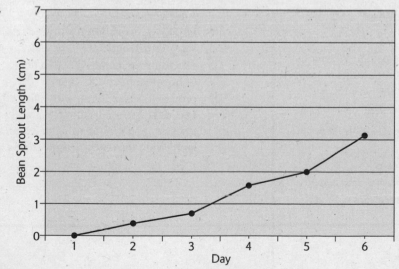

GO ON TO THE NEXT PAGE

D.

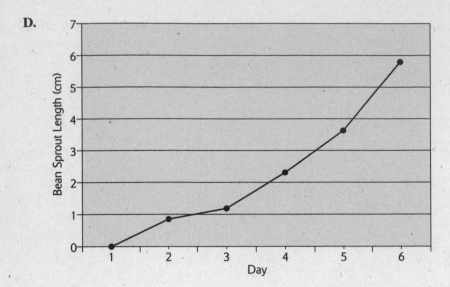

38. The students expressed amazement that the plant placed in total darkness grew faster then those exposed to light. Mrs. Luna asked them if they noticed any differences as they compared the sprout grown in darkness to the other sprouts grown in light. One thing they noticed was that the sprout grown in darkness, although it was longer, was not as green as the other plants. Mrs. Luna was trying to think of an analogy to support the student's observation. The best possible analogy(ies) for this question would be:

   I.   seasonal change of plant colors
   II. the ripening of bananas
  III. the enormous height of redwoods
  A. I only
  B. II only
  C. I and II
  D. I, II, and III

39. Mrs. Perales has the students select an art print to take home. She has a variety of artists represented. One of the things that Mrs. Perales will learn about her students through this activity is:

  A. their ability to share materials with other students
  B. who likes art and who does not
  C. student preferences in personal artwork
  D. that some students will prefer not to participate

40. Mr. Welch wants his 3rd graders to express themselves using a variety of media. He should make sure that:

  A. The students know the terms needed to express themselves.
  B. The school has an art class for his students.
  C. He is hooked up to the Internet.
  D. There are plenty of art supplies in the classroom.

41. A 2nd-grade class is studying sounds. Which of the following activities would best highlight the relation between length and sound for the students?

  A. providing the children with materials to manipulate to discover how length effects sounds
  B. providing the children with materials that show how length effects sound
  C. providing the children with a demonstration of how length effects sound
  D. providing the children with a field experience to a museum of natural science so that they can benefit from an expert showing and telling them how length effects sound

42. A kindergarten class is moving to a selection of western art music. Throughout the selection, the children are walking around the room and either placing their finger over their mouths ("shhh") and squatting or cupping their hands around their mouths ("shout!") and standing as the music plays. What element of music do these motions reinforce?

    A. pitch
    B. dynamics
    C. harmony
    D. instrumentation

43. The 4th-grade students in Mrs. James' class were surprised to learn that the largest organ of the body helps protect them from pathogens such as bacteria and fungi. Taking good care of this organ is their responsibility. This organ is

    A. the liver
    B. the skin
    C. the brain
    D. the small intestine

44. Many 2nd-grade children have poor habits that lead to sedentary lifestyles. This is a concern to the principal, Mr. Poy. He has entrusted the 2nd-grade lead teacher to come up with activities that will improve their health. One activity that they can do to reduce their sedentary lifestyle is to

    A. Demonstrate how to mirror a partner.
    B. Identify foods that enhance a healthy heart.
    C. Use equipment and space safely and properly.
    D. Lift and support their own weight.

45. Many 3rd graders are still showing slow development of their fine motor skills. Mr. Cantu complains that the physical education (P.E.) teachers are not moving fast enough in their development. Mr. Cantu does not understand that

    A. Fine motor development skills are developed after 3rd grade.
    B. Fine motor development skills take practice, attention, and effort to develop.
    C. It is not the responsibility of the P.E. teacher to develop these skills.
    D. Students should not be rushed in developing these skills.

46. What term is used to describe the way sounds can be combined in order to pronounce a word?

    A. segmentation
    B. fluency
    C. blending
    D. phonic conjunction

47. A kindergarten teacher notices that one of her students has difficulty isolating phonemes. When the teacher says the word "bat," for example, the student is unable to reproduce or otherwise identify the first sound of the word. Which of the following is most likely to help this student?

    A. repeated exposure to the word
    B. development of reading skills that would allow the student to visually discriminate key phonemes
    C. listening to the teacher model phoneme identification strategies
    D. practice saying the word at different tempos

48. How many graphemes does the word "bright" contain?

    A. three
    B. four
    C. five
    D. six

49. As a teacher introduces letter-sound correspondences, which of the following is problematic?

    A. In English, certain sounds can be represented by more than one letter.
    B. In English, certain letters represent more than one sound.
    C. At first, students sometimes confuse similar letters and sounds.
    D. all of the above

50. Which of the following is especially problematic for English Language Learners?

    A. English has complex grammatical rules.
    B. English is one of the most phonetically irregular languages.
    C. English has many vocabulary words that do not appear in other languages.
    D. English is unique in the way that its words are pronounced.

GO ON TO THE NEXT PAGE

51. Which of the following reflects an increase in graphophonemic knowledge?

    A.   A child learns how to distinguish between highly similar phonemes.

    B.   A child learns how to write the first letter of her name and pronounce the sound it makes.

    C.   A child learns how to sing the alphabet song.

    D.   A child learns how to write most of the letters of the alphabet correctly.

52. A pre-kindergarten teacher might encourage a parent to engage in which of the following activities?

    A.   Sitting next to the child and asking the child to turn the pages of a storybook while the parent reads it out loud.

    B.   Asking the child to review each of the preschool day's activities.

    C.   Using index cards with letters on them to drill children in letter recognition.

    D.   Teaching their child how to write letters and words.

53. The average of three numbers is 8. Two of the numbers are 6 and 11. What is the third number?

    A.   –1

    B.   7

    C.   9

    D.   31

54. Blaire and Carl, along with Dalys and Halo, chip in to buy Miss Frieze some flowers. Carl agrees to put in twice as much as Halo. Dalys puts in $1 less than Halo. Blaire puts in $4, which is exactly what Carl puts in for the flowers. What is the total amount they put in for the flowers?

    A. $11

    B. $13

    C. $23

    D. $25

55. The 3rd graders make a square garden with a perimeter of 20 feet. The garden's area is how many square feet?

    A.   16

    B.   20

    C.   25

    D.   400

56. Which of the following is most likely to foster print awareness among preschoolers?

    A.   The teacher leads a discussion of the lyrics of a song that the entire class knows.

    B.   The teacher slowly spells new vocabulary words out loud.

    C.   Before reading a big book to children, the teacher identifies the author and points to the title while saying it.

    D.   While reading a story to children, the teacher pauses occasionally to ask for children's reactions to the characters and events in the story.

57. Which of the following props are most appropriate for emergent literacy activities in a pre-kindergarten classroom?

    A.   puppets

    B.   wordless books

    C.   pictures

    D.   all of the above

58. Which of the following words contains a diphthong?

    A.   sand

    B.   boys

    C.   feet

    D.   build

59. Why might a kindergarten teacher articulate the phonemes in a word very slowly?

    A.   The teacher wants to model a blending strategy.

    B.   The teacher wants to make sure that everyone in the class can hear the word.

    C.   The teacher wants to promote auditory discrimination among students in the class.

    D.   The teacher wants to instill alphabetic knowledge among the class.

60. Decodable texts contain a high frequency of which of the following?

    A.   monosyllabic words

    B.   nouns

    C.   phonetically regular words

    D.   sight words

61. A 4th-grade class reads a book about families of 19th-century immigrants from Eastern Europe who quickly adopt the language and customs of their new country. What term best describes the process of change in these families after they immigrate?

- **A.** diffusion
- **B.** acculturation
- **C.** exchange
- **D.** accommodation

62. Which of the following could account for the presence of highly similar hunting and foraging strategies observed in two small tribal societies in southern Africa that live approximately 100 miles away from each other and are unaware of each other's existence?

- **A.** In the past, the two societies had contact with each other, and a process of cultural diffusion took place.
- **B.** The two societies independently developed similar forms of adaptation to relatively similar geographic conditions.
- **C.** In the past, a third society shared their hunting and foraging strategies with these two societies through a process of cultural exchange.
- **D.** all of the above

63. Why was the Bill of Rights created?

- **A.** to define the structure of the federal government
- **B.** to provide for a separation of powers across the different branches of government
- **C.** to guarantee protection of individuals against the power of the government
- **D.** to ensure cooperation between federal and state governments

64. Photosynthesis is the process used by plants to make food in which carbon dioxide and water coupled with sunlight and chlorophyll create glucose and oxygen. The creation of oxygen is particularly important to animals in nature because it serves as a primary source of:

- **A.** shelter
- **B.** food
- **C.** respiration
- **D.** protection

65. Photosynthesis is an example of the conservation of energy in which:

- **A.** Mechanical energy is converted to solar energy.
- **B.** Chemical energy is converted to solar energy.
- **C.** Solar energy is converted to mechanical energy.
- **D.** Solar energy is converted to chemical energy.

66. In an experiment, students investigated whether plants grow better in sunlight or artificial light. A logical extension of this experiment would be to investigate the effect of light exposure on sprout length using

- **A.** different seeds
- **B.** different amounts of soil
- **C.** longer time period
- **D.** different color lights

67. A 3rd-grade class is reading a story. The children are delighted by the characters and the plot and have begun working on a creative dramatic presentation of the story. As a way of extending their experience, the classroom professional borrows some non-tuned percussion instruments from the school's music specialist. Over the next few days the children begin adding instrumental sounds to their story. Toward the end of the class project, every character can be easily identified by the sound of a different instrument. The class presents its adaptation of the story for their parents. As the story is retold, each instrument is played when the corresponding character is speaking. Why did the children choose different instruments for different characters and what element of music did they vary?

- **A.** steady beat
- **B.** timbre
- **C.** harmony
- **D.** form

GO ON TO THE NEXT PAGE

68. Which of the following is most important for a teacher to keep in mind when choosing texts for early readers?

- **A.** The texts chosen should always correct deficiencies in content-area knowledge.
- **B.** The texts chosen should match students' current knowledge of letter-sound relationships as closely as possible.
- **C.** The texts chosen should always match each student's current interests as closely as possible.
- **D.** The texts chosen should be written at a level that is especially difficult for students, in order to challenge them.

69. Which of the following is one of the most important consequences of acquiring a large store of sight words?

- **A.** substantial improvement in phonological awareness
- **B.** a significant increase in oral language skill
- **C.** a shift from learning to read to reading to learn
- **D.** a larger vocabulary

70. As a teacher listens to one of his 3rd graders read a new book out loud, he notices that the student pronounces the words in a slow and halting way. Which of the following is an appropriate response by the teacher?

- **A.** Encourage the student to read an easier book.
- **B.** Ask the student to practice at home in front of a mirror.
- **C.** Provide the student with phonics exercises.
- **D.** Reassure the student that it is natural to struggle with written text.

71. Which of the following reflects sensitivity to prosodic cues?

- **A.** A student uses knowledge of morphology to guide her decoding of unfamiliar words.
- **B.** A student corrects himself when misreading a word because he realizes that his initial reading makes no sense in the present context.
- **C.** A student speaks more loudly when reading sentences ending with exclamation points.
- **D.** A student successfully decodes unfamiliar words largely on the basis of structural information.

72. Nancy gets embarrassed when she reads out loud, because she is one of the least fluent readers in the class. What should Nancy's teacher do?

- **A.** Correct Nancy's mistakes whenever possible.
- **B.** Tell Nancy that it is natural for people to make mistakes when they read.
- **C.** Make sure that Nancy has familiar books when she reads out loud.
- **D.** all of the above

73. What is the perimeter of a rectangular room that is 10 strides by 14 strides?

- **A.** 48 strides
- **B.** 48 square strides
- **C.** 140 strides
- **D.** 140 square strides

74. Butch stands at the cookie counter at Hearts and Tarts. He cannot decide whether to choose a brownie, a chocolate chip cookie, a gingerbread man, or a macaroon. What is the probability that he will *not* choose a gingerbread man?

- **A.** $\frac{1}{4}$
- **B.** $\frac{1}{3}$
- **C.** $\frac{3}{4}$
- **D.** $\frac{3}{1}$

75. Which of the following would be the best preliminary for introducing 4th graders to economic concepts such as circular flow and interdependence?

- **A.** The teacher discusses with students where their families go shopping.
- **B.** The teacher defines each concept and provides concrete examples.
- **C.** The teacher asks students what they think each concept means.
- **D.** The teacher draws a diagram of each concept and then defines it.

76. Currently, what is the largest export from Texas?

- **A.** cotton
- **B.** petroleum
- **C.** electronic products
- **D.** cattle

For questions 77 through 79, refer to the following scenario:

Students are asked to read the following passage silently: *One night, Sally was sitting in her room. Sally heard a noise behind her. The noise scared her. Sally turned around and saw a tiny mouse. Sally smiled.*

77. After reading the passage, students are asked questions such as why Sally was scared, what made the noise, and why Sally smiled. What is the highest level of comprehension tapped into by these questions?

    A. literal comprehension
    B. inferential comprehension
    C. analytical comprehension
    D. evaluative comprehension

78. After reading the passage, students are asked questions such as where Sally was sitting when she heard a noise, and what she saw when she turned around. What is the highest level of comprehension tapped into by these questions?

    A. literal comprehension
    B. inferential comprehension
    C. analytical comprehension
    D. evaluative comprehension

79. After reading the passage, the teacher asks students what they think the writer should describe next. What is the highest level of comprehension tapped into by this question?

    A. literal comprehension
    B. inferential comprehension
    C. analytical comprehension
    D. evaluative comprehension

80. Which of the following is a useful strategy for a student to use if she already knows a little bit about whales and is planning to do more research for a report?

    A. Write and revise a draft of the report.
    B. Brainstorm, and then examine pertinent reference materials.
    C. Use the K-W-L method while examining pertinent reference materials.
    D. Ask classmates for their thoughts on how to proceed.

81. Which of the following contributes most directly to content literacy?

    A. sensitivity to textual cues as a source of meaning in written passages
    B. knowing what text organizers are and how they can be used
    C. understanding basic word-identification strategies
    D. being able to read expressively

82. A teacher is planning to introduce bar graphs to her students. Which of the following is the best way for the teacher to begin conveying the idea that each bar represents a different quantity?

    A. The teacher labels the two axes and gives examples.
    B. The teacher hands out worksheets depicting a variety of bar graphs, and then leads a class discussion of similarities and differences among the graphs.
    C. The teacher asks each student how many inhabitants (including people and pets) live with the student, and then works with the class to construct a bar graph on the board.
    D. The teacher familiarizes students with line graphs before moving on to bar graphs.

83. Jana, a 4th grader, seems to be interested in and knowledgeable about class material during group discussions, but she shows poor comprehension on tests. Which of the following is most likely to be the source of her difficulty?

    A. the quality of her class notes
    B. low intelligence
    C. oral language limitations
    D. lack of motivation

84. What is the sum of the digit in the ten's place and the digit in the hundred's place in 6,543,201?

    A. 0
    B. 2
    C. 3
    D. 20

GO ON TO THE NEXT PAGE

85. What is the remainder when the digit in the million's place of 9,452,106 is divided by the digit in its thousand's place?

    A. 0
    B. 1
    C. 3
    D. 4

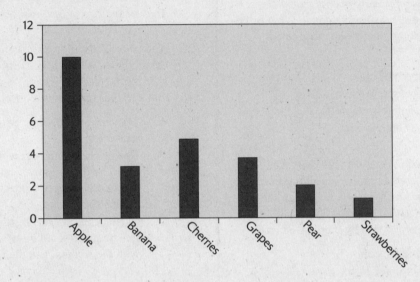

86. This graph shows the consumption of fruit by Mr. Tooler's class. The vertical axis represents the number of students who enjoyed each type of fruit. What fruit is the mode?

    A. apple
    B. banana
    C. grapes
    D. strawberries

Questions 87 through 90 are based on the following:

Ms. Farber, a 2nd-grade teacher, has spent one week teaching a unit on rocks and minerals, and she would now like to supplement the lessons with a laboratory investigation on the characteristics of rocks. She separated her class of 20 students into small groups of four, and they went on a nature field trip around the school in a scavenger hunt for rocks. They were told to collect six different rocks. They then returned to the classroom to conduct an investigation of their rocks, looking for differences in their size, shape, color, and mass.

87. As the students prepare to make observations of their rocks, the first thing that they should be asked to do would be to:

    A. Wash the rocks off with water.
    B. Look at each rock closely.
    C. Make sure each group has a variety of rocks.
    D. Check with other groups to see what types of rocks they found.

88. An important safety consideration for Ms. Farber to emphasize before the nature field trip is to

    A. inspect the rocks before the students handle them
    B. ask whether they all have eye goggles on before they begin their field trip
    C. ensure that each student has a writing utensil and a pad of paper to write down observations
    D. limit the amount of time outside so that the students can complete their experiment

Ms. Farber compiled the data from each of the groups and recorded them into a table that she placed on an overhead.

Group	Number of Small-Sized Rocks	Number of Medium-Sized Rocks	Number of Large-Sized Rocks
1	5	1	0
2	4	1	1
3	3	2	1
4	4	2	0
5	4	2	0

89. Ms. Farber, trying to incorporate concepts learned in a recent mathematics lesson, asked the students what the percentage of small-sized rocks was. The answer, found on the table, is:

   A.   100%
   B.   67%
   C.   33%
   D.   0%

90. Ms. Farber wanted her students to prepare a pie chart of the information reported in the table. The pie chart which correctly represents the data in the table is given by:

   A.

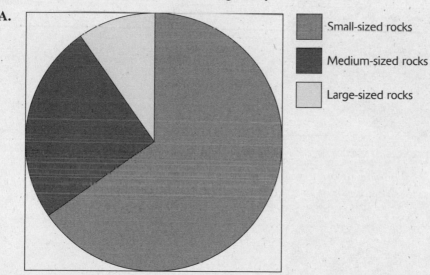

Small-sized rocks

Medium-sized rocks

Large-sized rocks

GO ON TO THE NEXT PAGE

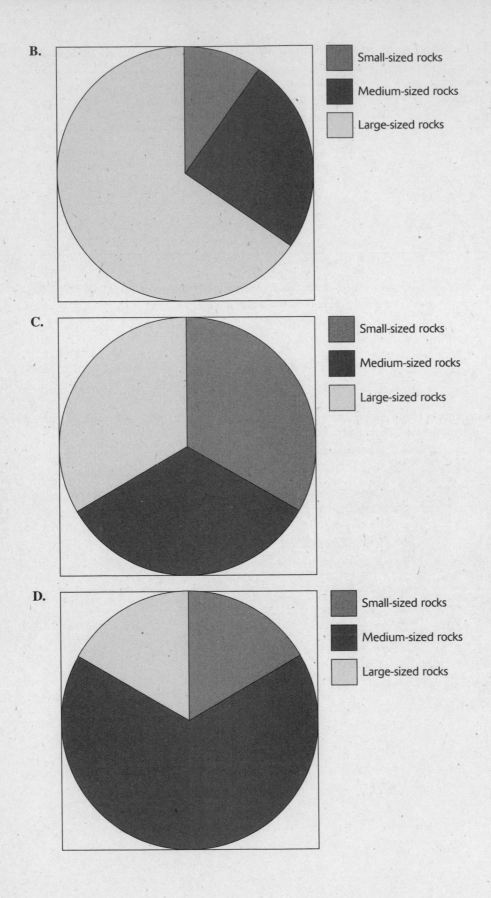

91. When teaching students what bibliographies are, which of the following is the prerequisite of most immediate importance?

   A. an appreciation for the limitations of narrative as a source of information

   B. interest in independent research

   C. an understanding of other text organizers such as chapter titles, headings, and summaries

   D. the concept of authorship

92. Knowledge of spelling reflects what dimension of language?

   A. alphabetic

   B. pragmatics

   C. prosody

   D. orthography

93. Which of the following activities for 1st graders is most likely to promote a range of literacy skills, including phonemic awareness, reading, and writing?

   A. Children choose small magnetic letters out of a bowl to spell familiar words.

   B. Children are asked to draw a picture and discuss it with the class.

   C. Children are invited to bring objects from home for show-and-tell.

   D. Children play a game in which the object is to take turns thinking of things that begin with a particular letter.

94. The parents of a kindergartener tell the teacher that they have noticed their son trying to write words, although what the boy writes is mostly incomprehensible. What should the teacher advise the parents to do?

   A. Buy the child a journal and encourage him to write a little bit each day.

   B. Ask the child about what he writes, and be appreciative of his response.

   C. Discourage the child from writing until he is more familiar with letter-sound correspondences.

   D. Work with the child on correct formation of letters and words.

95. Mike, a 3rd grader, writes the following poem about a walk in the forest.

> I wandered past the purpel trees.
> I felt a cool and pleasant breez.
> I saw abov the twinkling stars.
> I heard the whiz of distant cars.

Which approach to assessment would yield the most useful information about Mike's writing?

   A. holistic scoring

   B. primary trait scoring

   C. analytic scoring

   D. error analysis

96. Which of the following names this figure?

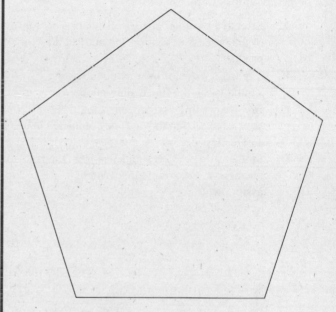

   A. decagon

   B. hexagon

   C. octagon

   D. pentagon

97. If a cube's edge measures five decimeters, what is the surface area of the entire cube?

   A. 25 cubic decimeters

   B. 50 decimeters

   C. 125 cubic decimeters

   D. 150 square decimeters

GO ON TO THE NEXT PAGE

98. A 3rd-grade class is reading a book about a little girl who grows up in Vietnam. What can the teacher do to help students be actively engaged in the book?

   A. Ask students to keep a journal in which they describe their own lives.

   B. Teach children facts about Vietnam and the Vietnamese people.

   C. Have students keep response journals as they read.

   D. Have students keep a learning log that focuses on what they are learning about life in Vietnam.

99. Which of the following is one of the key assumptions of process writing?

   A. Effective writing depends on an appreciation of the process of writing and not just the product.

   B. The main focus of instruction in writing should be on the finished product.

   C. In-class writing assignments should be structured so that they can be completed in a single class period.

   D. Students do not need guidance from their teachers when completing written assignments.

100. Aya is an English Language Learner whose 1st-grade teacher sometimes allows her to complete writing assignments in her home language. Why does Aya's teacher allow her to do that?

   A. to help Aya understand the correspondences between her home language and English

   B. to make sure that Aya doesn't fall too far behind her peers

   C. to make it easier to compare Aya's work to that of her classmates when assigning grades

   D. to help ensure that Aya continues to be interested and engaged in the process of writing

Answer Key for Practice Test I

1. D	**26.** B	**51.** B	**76.** C
2. C	**27.** A	**52.** A	**77.** B
3. B	**28.** C	**53.** B	**78.** A
4. D	**29.** B	**54.** A	**79.** D
5. B	**30.** B	**55.** C	**80.** C
6. B	**31.** C	**56.** A	**81.** B
7. C	**32.** A	**57.** D	**82.** C
8. A	**33.** D	**58.** B	**83.** A
9. D	**34.** D	**59.** A	**84.** B
10. C	**35.** C	**60.** D	**85.** B
11. B	**36.** D	**61.** B	**86.** A
12. D	**37.** D	**62.** D	**87.** A
13. D	**38.** C	**63.** C	**88.** A
14. B	**39.** C	**64.** C	**89.** B
15. D	**40.** D	**65.** D	**90.** A
16. C	**41.** A	**66.** A	**91.** D
17. A	**42.** B	**67.** B	**92.** D
18. D	**43.** B	**68.** B	**93.** A
19. C	**44.** D	**69.** C	**94.** B
20. A	**45.** B	**70.** A	**95.** D
21. A	**46.** C	**71.** C	**96.** D
22. B	**47.** C	**72.** C	**97.** D
23. D	**48.** B	**73.** A	**98.** C
24. A	**49.** D	**74.** C	**99.** A
25. B	**50.** B	**75.** A	**100.** D

1. **D.** A phoneme is the smallest unit of sound. The word "six" consists of four phonemes: /s/ /i/ /k/ /s/. Hence, D is the correct answer. **(Competency 001, Oral Language)**

2. **C.** Receptive language is based on the ability to understand what is being said. C is the correct answer, because it is the only option that pertains to comprehension rather than production. **(Competency 001, Oral Language)**

3. **B.** Morphemes are the smallest meaningful components of words, so B is the correct answer. **(Competency 001, Oral Language)**

4. **D.** Whenever possible, early childhood teachers should use verbal descriptions to accompany their actions. Hence, D is the correct answer. **(Competency 001, Oral Language)**

5. **B.** Children benefit most from phonemic awareness exercises that parents incorporate into games and other fun activities, rather than the drills described in options C and D. Although reading to children is beneficial for all aspects of language development, option A is not the best answer, because option B describes fun games that focus more specifically on phonemic awareness. **(Competency 002, Phonological and Phonemic Awareness)**

6. **B.** One meter is equal to 100 cm. So, the proportion $\frac{1 \text{ inch}}{2.54 \text{ cm}} = \frac{x}{100 \text{ cm}}$ will provide this solution:

$$\frac{1 \text{ inch}}{2.54 \text{ cm}} = \frac{x}{100 \text{ cm}}$$
$$2.54x = 100$$
$$\frac{2.54x}{2.54} = \frac{100}{2.54}$$

Wait! The question asks only for an approximate answer. So $x = \frac{100}{2.5} = \frac{100(10)}{2.5(10)} = \frac{1,000}{25} \approx 40$. The correct answer is B. **(Competency 014, Geometry, Measurement, Probability, and Statistics)**

7. **C.** James needs three times as much flour as is called for in the recipe. James calculates $3 \times 2\frac{1}{2} = \frac{3}{1} \times \frac{5}{2} = \frac{15}{2} = 7\frac{1}{2}$. The correct answer is C. **(Competency 015, Mathematical Process)**

8. **A.** Choice A is false, and that's the answer, because the exercise asks for the choice that is *not* equivalent. By the way, choice B is equivalent, because it applies the commutative property of multiplication. Choice C is equivalent, because it applies the commutative property of addition. Choice D is equivalent, because it applies the distributive property. **(Competency 013, Number Concepts, Patterns, and Algebra)**

9. **D.** All of the options describe important goals of elementary-level social studies instruction. **(Competency 016, Social Science Instruction)**

10. **C.** It is the only option in which the children obtain the hands-on experience that is critical at their age to the appreciation of key conceptual distinctions. **(Competency 016, Social Science Instruction)**

11. **B.** Inquiry teaching occurs when teachers ask and then help students answer questions by proposing hypotheses, gathering and evaluating data, and generating conclusions. Because inquiry teaching promotes an understanding of the scientific method, B is the correct answer. **(Competency 016, Social Science Instruction)**

12. **D.** As Mrs. Fillmore prepares activities for a science lesson, she needs to integrate activities based upon the higher levels of cognitive learning according to Bloom's Taxonomy. Although all of these activities do play an important role in the presentation of a lesson, it can be seen that by mere inspection of the activities, D is much more of a learner-centered activity where the student takes charge of his/her learning. **(Competency 020, Science Instruction)**

13. **D.** Both A and C are related activities where students can experience the environment and find art in nature. **(Competency 024, Visual Arts)**

14. B. Salvador Dali was a Spanish surrealist painter. Pablo Picasso was also a Spanish painter and sculptor. Helen Keller was an American writer. Anna Mary "Grandma" Moses was an American artist. **(Competency 024, Visual Arts)**

15. D. The question revolves around culture and music. It asks the reader, "How does culture influence music?" In this question, two different cultures are cited: Navaho and Filipino. When cultures are specified, you should envision a globe and locate each culture. For this question, one culture is located in North America and the other is located in Southeast Asia. Having identified where each culture is located, the reader is asked a question regarding 1) steady beat, 2) vocal singing, and 3) differences in instrumentation. D is the correct answer choice. Notice that this choice uses the word "different," as does answer C. The question stem mentions differences as well (that is, accompanying instruments are not similar). Answer C is not the best answer, because you may assume that a culture will make and use instruments that produce sounds they like to hear. Answer D is the best choice, because it brings together the idea that the two cultures are "worlds apart" and that indigenous peoples would rely on readily available resources to make instruments. (One culture lives in a tropical region of the world and the other lives in a more arid and temperate part of North America.) Based on our knowledge of geography and science, these two cultures would not have similar instruments. **(Competency 025, Music)**

16. C. This question addresses knowledge of the elements of music. Note that three of the answer choices are related to steady beat or rhythm. Remember that clapping the individual syllables of words creates rhythms. Realizing that three answers are similar, you can eliminate answer D. Even though you may not really know who wrote "Happy Birthday" or "The Star Spangled Banner," you may have a suspicion that they were not written by the same person. One song is a "campy" type of tune that is usually sung without accompaniment at birthdays. The other song is usually heard with some type of accompaniment (for example, band, orchestra) and is sung at special events (for example, ballgames, patriotic ceremonies). A more obvious distracter is answer choice B. The two songs do not have the same words. This leaves choice A or choice C. Relying on our understanding of the elements of music we can eliminate answer choice A. Steady beat relates to the tempo of the song. All songs will have a steady beat. That steady beat could indicate a quick tempo (for example, allegro) or a slow tempo (for example, andante). Answer choice C is the only logical choice for one important reason. If you clap the words and syllables as you sing or chant the words of the two songs, you will note that you are clapping the same rhythm, even though the melodies are completely different. If you clap the words to "Baa, Baa Black Sheep," the "ABC Song," and "Twinkle, Twinkle," you will note that each song has the same rhythm. **(Competency 025, Music)**

17. A. In asking the class about the differences in the pendulum before it was released and after it was set in motion, Mrs. Lacewell describes the conservation of energy. Prior to release, the object has potential energy which converts to kinetic energy as it gains speed at the bottom of the cycle. Conservation of mass is not a viable option, because the object remains the same and does not change with position in the pendulum cycle. The pendulum does have both kinetic energy and potential energy, but the question was referring to the transfer or conversion between the two, or the conservation of energy. The correct answer is represented by option A. **(Competency 021, Physical Science)**

18. D. In order for the pendulum to come to a stop, there must be some force acting in a direction opposite to the motion of the object, which in turn poses a resistance and slows the object down. Although gravity seems the most likely solution, gravity acts in a constant manner downward. This means that although gravity acts to slow down the object on the opposite side of release, it also speeds up at the same rate. Because it is acting in a constant manner, gravity does not act to slow it down. Object weight is closely related to gravity and the same explanation applies. The shape of the object does not factor in the slowing down of a pendulum and can be easily demonstrated using objects of different shapes. The correct answer is D. Friction occurs as the string rubs against the pivot of the pendulum. Friction always opposes motion and thus causes the pendulum to slow down and eventually come to a stop. **(Competency 021, Physical Science)**

19. C. In this case, each student in a workgroup assumed the same responsibility in their experiment so it could not have been option B. A defective stopwatch would not yield values so close together, and option D only reiterates the problem and does not propose a reason for the observation. The correct answer is option C. The time measurement depends on the student's reaction time and varies for each measurement. **(Competency 021, Physical Science)**

20. A. In laboratory experiments, the best way to minimize possible inconsistencies and reduce bias is to have the same group perform several trials of an experiment and average the values together to get a more accurate value of the measurement. The suggestions represented by the other options are scientifically invalid and would have no significance in the accuracy and meaning of the data. The correct answer is option A. **(Competency 021, Physical Science)**

21. A. In the first table, object mass is independent (free to take on any value by the experiment), so it's called the independent variable. The period of the pendulum, another variable, depends on what the mass is and, thus, is a dependent variable. **(Competency 021, Physical Science)**

22. B. Analyzing the data in both tables, the students can see that the period changes its values only when the string length changes. As the object mass changes (the first table), the period values remain the same, at least within the error of the operator using the stopwatch. **(Competency 021, Physical Science)**

23. D. A, B, and C are all activities that help children learn to be safe. Discussing the parts that fight diseases is not a behavior that leads to healthy or unhealthy conditions. **(Competency 026, Health)**

24. A. This is the only response that mentions movement. Knowing the benefits of daily activities, where the lungs are located, and following game rules do not make the students proficient in movement forms. **(Competency 027, Physical Education)**

25. B. Many students are not properly dressed for physical activities. The clothing they wear can get in the way and cause an accident. Memorizing rules does not guarantee safety. Not having the proper attire, even when the student has had enough sleep or if the teacher is doing the activity alongside the student, can be the cause of a serious accident. **(Competency 027, Physical Education)**

26. B. One goal of social studies instruction is to help students appreciate and respect opposing points of view. Because the students are already formulating and expressing their own opinions, an exercise in which they describe the merits of the candidate they do not support would be useful and, thus, B is the correct answer. **(Competency 016, Social Science Instruction)**

27. A. Options B, C, and D are unlikely, given what we know about the rock shelters. A is the correct answer. **(Competency 017, History)**

28. C. The Mexican-American war was fought over boundary disputes. **(Competency 017, History)**

29. B. "Texas" stems from the Caddo word for "friends" or "allies." **(Competency 017, History)**

30. B. Options A, C, and D are sometimes incorrect in practice. B is the correct answer, because the personal views expressed in primary sources are often engaging. **(Competency 017, History)**

31. C. Sam's raise is 8% of $32,000 or $0.08 \times \$32,000 = \$2,560$. Another way to calculate this answer is to use the proportion:

$$\frac{\text{percent}}{100} = \frac{\text{part}}{\text{whole}}$$

$$\frac{8}{100} = \frac{\text{raise}}{\$32,000}$$

$$100\,(\text{raise}) = 8\,(\$32,000)$$

$$100\,(\text{raise}) = \$256,000$$

$$\frac{100\,(\text{raise})}{100} = \frac{\$256,000}{100}$$

$$\text{raise} = \$2,560$$

However, the exercise is to find Sam's new salary: $32,000 + $2,560 = $34,560. **(Competency 015, Mathematical Process)**

32. **A.** Sheena wants to buy one dozen (twelve) apples. That is three times the number that she can buy for $0.75. So, she should multiply $0.75 by three. The result is $2.25. Another approach is to make a proportion.

$$\frac{4 \text{ apples}}{\$0.75} = \frac{12 \text{ apples}}{p}$$

$$4p = 12\,(\$0.75)$$

$$\frac{4p}{4} = \frac{12\,(\$0.75)}{4}$$

$$p = \frac{12\,(\$0.75)}{4} = 3\,(\$0.75) = \$2.25$$

The correct answer is A. **(Competency 015, Mathematical Process)**

33. **D.** Because a relief map would include concrete representations of different elevations, D is the correct answer. **(Competency 018, Geography and Culture)**

34. **D.** A steppe best fits this description and, thus, D is the correct answer. **(Competency 018, Geography and Culture)**

35. **C.** In an experiment, the independent variable is the variable allowed to move or change, and the dependent variable is measured as a result of the independent variable. All other possible variables in an experiment are, or should be, controlled (held constant) so that any trend observed by the dependent variable can be attributed only to the independent variable and nothing else. In this experiment, the independent variable is the type of light exposure and the dependent variable is the length of the bean sprout. All other variables, including the type of seeds, amount of soil, amount of water, and time and frequency of feeding, should be held constant. **(Competency 022, Life Science)**

36. **D.** This problem can be answered by referring to the data table and looking at the rate of sprout growth or difference between the sprout growth over the duration of the experiment. Over the six-day period measured for each of the four seed sprouts, the sprout in darkness grew the fastest. Thus, option D is the correct response. **(Competency 022, Life Science)**

37. **D.** By coordinating the data points in the table and comparing them with the corresponding data points in the graphs, you can see that the graph in option D is the one that most closely represents the data of the sprouts placed in darkness. **(Competency 022, Life Science)**

38. **C.** Chlorophyll, which requires sunlight, is responsible for the green color of plants. Because the problem had to do with observations regarding the color pf plants, the two options that are appropriate in this discussion are I and II. The seasonal change of plant colors as well as the ripening of bananas have to do with the lack of or breakdown of chlorophyll in the plant. The height of redwoods is not directly related to the function of chlorophyll. Option C is the correct choice. **(Competency 022, Life Science)**

39. **C.** This is an informal way to assess students' preferences as they select the print they want to take home. Students are not sharing materials; the teacher is sharing the prints with the students. The students are not given a choice whether to take or not take a print. They are asked to select a print. **(Competency 024, Visual Arts)**

40. **D.** Without a variety of art supplies, students are limited in how they will express themselves. Students do not need to have an art class, be hooked up to the Internet, or know artistic terms to express themselves artistically using a variety of media. **(Competency 024, Visual Arts)**

41. **A.** Most of the questions on the exam will refer to a specific age or grade level. This is important in determining the answer that is developmentally appropriate for the age or grade. In this question, you are asked to select a developmentally appropriate answer for a science lesson involving sounds. 2nd grade is considered to be at the upper end of early childhood. Because this is early childhood, you want to identify both "best practice" and "inappropriate practice." Begin by looking for choices that focus on children listening to an adult or children that are passively engaged in an activity. Choice C indicates that the children will see a demonstration. Although the demonstration may be engaging, it still requires children to sit and watch. Choice D is similar to C in that the children are watching a show-and-tell demonstration. The change of venue may increase their learning but they are still sitting and watching. Choices A and B mention the inclusion of materials, possible things that could be manipulated—a hands-on experience. Looking closely at choice B, you can see that the materials are there to show how length effects sound. Choice A is similar to B, except that the children are expected to manipulate the

materials. In a child-centered curriculum, children should have hands-on experiences. This is the best answer. **(Competency 025, Music)**

42. B. This question assesses your knowledge of how music can be altered. As you recall, a song can be sung or played in many different ways. It can be performed fast, slow, loud, soft, and with different vocal timbres. This question also includes a specific grade level. Reading the question carefully, you will note that the specific age mentioned in the question stem does not relate to the answer choices. The important information in the stem is that the children are walking about the room moving their hands as the music plays. Using a "shhh" finger and cupped hands around the mouth leads the reader to the assumption that the movements must have something to do with soft ("shhh") and loud (cupped hands). Relying on your knowledge of musical terms, dynamics is the most logical choice. Without the ability to hear the selection, the other choices cannot be easily justified. Given the information presented in the question stem, the best answer is B. **(Competency 025, Music)**

43. B. Although the other organs can play a role in fighting pathogens, they are not as large as the skin. This organ is accessible to the students, and they can learn ways to care for it in a personal manner. **(Competency 026, Health)**

44. D. For this to happen, the students have to engage in many different types of physical activities. Mirroring a partner is just one activity, and it could be done in a sedentary position. Identifying foods does not require physical activity, neither does using space and equipment safely. **(Competency 027, Physical Education)**

45. B. This question addresses Competency 027: The teacher uses knowledge of the concepts, principles, skill, and practices of physical education to plan and implement effective and engaging physical education activities for young children. **(Competency 027, Physical Education)**

46. C. Blending is the term used to describe the way sounds are combined in pronunciation and, thus, C is the correct answer. **(Competency 002, Phonological and Phonemic Awareness)**

47. C. Difficulty isolating phonemes is not readily overcome by repeated exposure or mere practice at repeating words, nor does it call for a strategy based on visual discrimination or other written language skills. C is the correct answer, because phoneme identification strategies can help young children isolate phonemes. **(Competency 002, Phonological and Phonemic Awareness)**

48. B. A grapheme is the letter or letters that represent a phoneme. B is the correct answer, because the word "bright" contains four graphemes, one corresponding to each of the following sounds: /b/ /r/ /i/ /t/. **(Competency 003, Alphabetic Principle)**

49. D. All of the options describe obstacles that teachers must contend with when introducing letter-sound correspondences. Hence, D is the correct answer. **(Competency 003, Alphabetic Principle)**

50. B. Although options A, B, and D are correct, they describe challenges that any child would face when learning a new language. B is the correct answer, because English contains a relatively high incidence of phonetic irregularities. **(Competency 003, Alphabetic Principle)**

51. B. Graphophonemic knowledge is knowledge about letter-sound correspondences. B is the correct answer, because it is the only option that describes learning about such correspondences. **(Competency 003, Alphabetic Principle)**

52. A. Emergent literacy is most effectively promoted in the context of natural, meaningful, "fun" activities. Option A is, therefore, the correct answer. **(Competency 004, Literacy Development)**

53. B. The average is found by adding the values, then dividing by the number of values.

$$\frac{6 + 11 + ?}{3} = 8$$

$$\frac{17 + ?}{3} = 8$$

Multiplying both sides by 3, we cancel the division by 3 on the left and multiply 8 by 3.

$$17 + ? = 24$$

$$? = 7$$

The correct answer is B. **(Competency 014, Geometry, Measurement, Probability, and Statistics)**

54. A. Set up a chart to organize the given information, and fill in the amount that Blaire puts in, because that amount is given.

Child	Money Put In for the Flowers
Blaire	$4
Carl	
Dalys	
Halo	

Because Carl agrees to put in exactly as much as Blaire puts in, fill in his amount.

Child	Money Put In for the Flowers
Blaire	$4
Carl	$4
Dalys	
Halo	

The exercise claims that Carl agrees to put in twice as much as Halo. In other words, Halo puts in one-half the amount that Carl put in for the flowers. One-half of $4, $\frac{1}{2} \times \frac{4}{1} = \frac{1}{1} \times \frac{2}{1} = 2$, is $2.

Child	Money Put In for the Flowers
Blaire	$4
Carl	$4
Dalys	
Halo	$2

Finally, Dalys puts in $1 less than Halo.

Child	Money Put in for the Flowers
Blaire	$4
Carl	$4
Dalys	$1
Halo	$2

The total amount they put in for the flowers is $4 + $4 + $1 + $2 = $11. The correct answer is A. (**Competency 013, Number Concepts, Patterns, and Algebra**)

55. C. A square has four equal sides. Therefore, each side is 5 feet, $\frac{20 \text{ feet}}{4}$. The area of a square is calculated by multiplying the length of the base of the square, 5 feet, by its height, 5 feet. Hence, 5 feet × 5 feet = 25 square feet. The correct answer is C. (**Competency 014, Geometry, Measurement, Probability, and Statistics**)

56. A. All four options describe activities that may contribute to emergent literacy. However, A is the correct answer, because it is the only option of specific relevance to print awareness. (**Competency 004, Literacy Development**)

57. D. All of the props mentioned can contribute to the development of emergent literacy, and thus D is the correct answer. **(Competency 004, Literacy Development)**

58. B. A diphthong is a pair of adjacent vowels in a word that are both audible. B is the correct answer, because the word "boys" contains the diphthong "oy." **(Competency 005, Word Analysis and Decoding)**

59. A. Although options B, C, and D represent useful goals, the slow articulation of phonemes in a word allows teachers to model strategies for blending sounds and, hence, A is the correct answer. **(Competency 005, Word Analysis and Decoding)**

60. D. Decodable texts contain a high frequency of words that children can recognize by sight and, thus, D is the correct answer. **(Competency 005, Word Analysis and Decoding)**

61. B. Acculturation occurs when an individual or group adopts much or all of another society's culture and, thus, B is the correct answer. **(Competency 018, Geography and Culture)**

62. D. All of the options describe plausible ways that two geographically remote societies could share similar cultural practices. **(Competency 018, Geography and Culture)**

63. C. The first ten amendments to the Constitution, the Bill of Rights, were created to protect citizens against the powers of government outlined in the Constitution. **(Competency 019, Government, Citizenship, and Economics)**

64. C. The general reaction of photosynthesis involves carbon dioxide and water combining with sunlight to yield glucose and oxygen. The glucose is a source of food for the plant itself but, for the animals in nature, the oxygen generated from photosynthesis becomes a source of respiration. **(Competency 022, Life Science)**

65. D. Photosynthesis is the process by which plants use sunlight to produce food on their own. With regard to energy, the energy provided by the sun needed to drive photosynthesis is solar energy, so you can exclude options A and B. Photosynthesis is the process by which plants produce food where food is chemical energy. So photosynthesis converts solar energy to chemical energy, given the response in option D. **(Competency 022, Life Science)**

66. A. Although either of these scenarios could pose as a viable extension to this investigation, the most logical extension would be to investigate different seeds. The purpose of this experiment was to investigate the effects of light exposure on plant growth. Options B, C, and D are well represented in the experiment and, if changed or varied, would probably effect the overall results minimally, if at all. The most logical extension to this experiment would be different seeds, given by option A. **(Competency 022, Life Science)**

67. B. With this question, you were to use your knowledge of the elements of music to select the best answer. There was a specific grade level mentioned, but that information was not relevant for arriving at the best answer. The question asked whether you knew that the musical term for different musical sounds is timbre. Each musical instrument has a distinct sound, called timbre. Looking at the other answer choices, you could eliminate harmony, because non-tuned percussion instruments do not produce pitches, hence the term non-tuned. The question stem did not mention music, it only mentioned instrumental sounds. Therefore, you could eliminate "steady beat," because you have to have music in order to have a steady beat, and eliminate "form," because this relates to a larger piece of music—not just sounds. The best answer for this question is timbre. **(Competency 025, Music)**

68. B. Early readers should not use texts that are "especially" difficult for them. Although the texts they use may provide content knowledge and may be chosen to match their current interests, these conditions should be met sometimes rather than always. B is the correct answer, because it is important that texts correspond to the students' current level. **(Competency 005, Word Analysis and Decoding)**

69. C. "Reading to learn" occurs when children have acquired enough sight words that they do not need to make frequent pauses for decoding. Instead, they can attend more closely to the meaning of what they are reading. Hence, C is the correct answer. **(Competency 006, Reading Fluency)**

70. A. A is the correct answer, because the other options would not help the student. **(Competency 006, Reading Fluency)**

71. C. The knowledge that students in options A, B, and D make use of does not fall under the heading of prosody. Exclamation points are among the many prosodic cues to the loudness, pitch, tempo, and rhythm that should be used when reading a passage. **(Competency 006, Reading Fluency)**

72. C. Nancy's embarrassment indicates that she is already quite aware of her mistakes, so calling attention to them will not be as productive as giving her materials that are more closely matched to her level. C is, therefore, the correct answer. (**Competency 006, Reading Fluency**)

73. A. The room looks like this.

10 strides

The perimeter of the room is the total length to walk around the room. That would be 14 strides + 10 strides + 14 strides + 10 strides = 48 strides. The correct answer is A. (**Competency 014, Geometry, Measurement, Probability, and Statistics**)

74. C. Butch has four sweets from which to choose. Three of them are *not* a gingerbread man. The probability is $\frac{\text{number of times the successful event occurs}}{\text{number of attempts that were made}} = \frac{3}{4}$. The correct answer is C. (**Competency 014, Geometry, Measurement, Probability, and Statistics**)

75. A. A is the correct answer, because a discussion about shopping would allow the abstract concepts of circular flow and interdependence to take on personal meaning for students. (**Competency 019, Government, Citizenship, and Economics**)

76. C. Electronic products are currently the largest Texas export, so C is the correct answer. (**Competency 019, Government, Citizenship, and Economics**)

77. B. "Why" questions such as these require inferences to be made and, thus, B is the correct answer. (**Competency 007, Reading Comprehension**)

78. A. A is the correct answer, because these questions are directly answered in the content of the passage. (**Competency 007, Reading Comprehension**)

79. D. Formulating opinions about what the writer should describe next requires the aesthetic judgment associated with evaluative comprehension, so D is the correct answer. (**Competency 007, Reading Comprehension**)

80. C. Although the other options are not necessarily counterproductive, A is the correct answer, because the child already knows something about whales. Through the K-W-L method, the child would identify what she already knows, as well as what she wants to know and, later, what she learns following additional research. (**Competency 007, Reading Comprehension**)

81. B. Although all of the options reflect contributions to content literacy, B is the correct answer, because the use of text organizers would make the most direct contribution. (**Competency 008, Research and Comprehension Skills in the Content Areas**)

82. C. C is the correct answer, because it is the only option in which bar graphs are used to convey meaningful, personally relevant information. (**Competency 008, Research and Comprehension Skills in the Content Areas**)

83. **A.** Options B, C, and D are incorrect in light of the student's performance during class discussion. Although there are many possible explanations for poor test performance in a situation like this, given the available options, the quality of the student's notes is the most likely culprit, so A is the correct answer. **(Competency 008, Research and Comprehension Skills in the Content Areas)**

84. **B.** The digit in the ten's place is 0, while the digit in the hundred's place is 2. The sum is $0 + 2 = 2$. The correct answer is B. **(Competency 013, Number Concepts, Patterns, and Algebra)**

85. **B.** The digit in the million's place is 9, while the digit in the thousand's place is 2. The division is:

$$
\begin{array}{r}
4\text{r}1 \\
2\overline{)\;9\;} \\
-8 \\
\hline
1
\end{array}
$$

The quotient is 4; the remainder is 1. The correct answer is B. **(Competency 013, Number Concepts, Patterns, and Algebra)**

86. **A.** The mode is the most frequently occurring value. Apple is the most frequently occurring value, as is evidenced on the graph. The "Apple" bar appears to reach 10, which is higher than any other bar. **(Competency 014, Geometry, Measurement, Probability, and Statistics)**

87. **A.** Because the rocks used in the investigation were acquired during a nature field trip, it was very possible that each rock could have dirt, mud, or another type of debris on them. Because the presence of dirt or mud could impact the rock's size, shape, color, and mass, it is important that each group wash the rocks thoroughly with water to ensure they are all clean and that all observations noted for each rock are as accurate as possible. **(Competency 023, Earth and Space Science)**

88. **A.** As the class embarks on their nature field trip, the students will be looking for rocks. However, there are also objects which may look like rocks or, at the very least, garner the curiosity of the students, prompting them to pick them up and look at them. These objects could pose safety hazards. Glass from a broken bottle is such an example. Thus, it is important for Ms. Farber to inspect each rock that a group collects to make sure it is a rock and nothing that may be dangerous. **(Competency 023, Earth and Space Science)**

89. **B.** In order to calculate the percentage of the small-sized rocks, one must sum up the total number of small-sized rocks and divide that number by the total number of all rocks. The total number of small-sized rocks is 20 and the total number of all rocks is 30. Thus the percentage of small-sized rocks can be calculated by:

% small-sized rocks = (total number of small-sized rocks)/(total number of all rocks) $\times$ 100% =

$20 \div 30 \times 100\% = 66.66$, which is approximately equal to 67%

Any of the other options can be eliminated by simple inspection. The student should know that it cannot be 100%, because there were medium-sized and large-sized rocks collected by some of the groups and it cannot be 0%, because small-sized rocks were recorded. Because the majority of rocks is small-sized, 33% cannot be correct either. Thus, option B is the only correct response. **(Competency 023, Earth and Space Science)**

90. **A.** The pie chart is the best graph for looking at pieces of a whole. The pieces in this case are the number of small-sized, medium-sized, and large-sized rocks, and the whole is the total number of rocks combined from each group (which is equal to 30, because the 5 groups were asked to locate 6 rocks). The clear majority (67%) of rocks found by each of the groups were small-sized so the pie chart which represents the data will have a piece of the pie that is larger than the other two. This can only be represented by option A. **(Competency 023, Earth and Space Science)**

91. **D.** All of the options represent important knowledge, but the prerequisite of most direct and immediate relevance to the understanding of what bibliographies are is the concept of authorship, including the idea that bibliographies consist of written works created by different authors. D is, therefore, the correct answer. **(Competency 008, Research and Comprehension Skills in the Content Areas)**

92. **D.** Orthography refers to the nature and use of written symbols in a language, including conventions of spelling. **(Competency 009, Writing Conventions)**

93. A. In contrast to the other options, the task described in option A would promote a variety of literacy skills ranging from letter identification to spelling, reading, and writing. **(Competency 009, Writing Conventions)**

94. B. The child should not be discouraged from writing, nor does the child need encouragement to write each day or to practice on correct formation of letters and words. The teacher should advise the parents to show interest in whatever the child chooses to write and to be appreciative of the child's descriptions of both the process and the product of any writing. **(Competency 009, Writing Conventions)**

95. D. The student is clearly a talented and expressive writer, but he is having some difficulty with the orthography of the silent "e." Error analysis would reveal this very specific problem and, thus, D is the correct answer. **(Competency 010, Development of Written Communication)**

96. D. The figure has five sides—a pentagon. By the way, a decagon has ten sides, a hexagon has six sides, and an octagon has eight sides. The correct answer is D. **(Competency 014, Geometry, Measurement, Probability, and Statistics)**

97. D. A cube has equal length, width, and height. The surface area of a cube is found by determining the area of one face, and then multiplying by six, because the cube has six congruent faces. Each face is a square, with dimensions 5 dm by 5 dm. The area of a square is calculated by multiplying the base times the height. In this case, both of those dimensions measure 5 dm. Hence, the area of one face is 25 square decimeters. Multiplying 25 square decimeters by 6 results in 150 square decimeters. The correct answer is D. **(Competency 014, Geometry, Measurement, Probability, and Statistics)**

98. C. Options A and D may be useful activities, but they would draw students' attention away from the book. Option B would not be especially engaging. Option C is the correct answer, because it would give students the opportunity to express their responses to the story. **(Competency 010, Development of Written Communication)**

99. A. Process writing is typically carried out over a period of days, with guidance from the teacher, and with emphasis on the writing process rather than the final product. A is the correct answer. **(Competency 010, Development of Written Communication)**

100. D. Although options A, B, and C reflect worthwhile goals, student interest and engagement in writing is critical to early literacy development. D is, therefore, the correct answer. **(Competency 010, Development of Written Communication)**

Answer Sheet for Practice Test II

1 Ⓐ Ⓑ Ⓒ Ⓓ	51 Ⓐ Ⓑ Ⓒ Ⓓ
2 Ⓐ Ⓑ Ⓒ Ⓓ	52 Ⓐ Ⓑ Ⓒ Ⓓ
3 Ⓐ Ⓑ Ⓒ Ⓓ	53 Ⓐ Ⓑ Ⓒ Ⓓ
4 Ⓐ Ⓑ Ⓒ Ⓓ	54 Ⓐ Ⓑ Ⓒ Ⓓ
5 Ⓐ Ⓑ Ⓒ Ⓓ	55 Ⓐ Ⓑ Ⓒ Ⓓ
6 Ⓐ Ⓑ Ⓒ Ⓓ	56 Ⓐ Ⓑ Ⓒ Ⓓ
7 Ⓐ Ⓑ Ⓒ Ⓓ	57 Ⓐ Ⓑ Ⓒ Ⓓ
8 Ⓐ Ⓑ Ⓒ Ⓓ	58 Ⓐ Ⓑ Ⓒ Ⓓ
9 Ⓐ Ⓑ Ⓒ Ⓓ	59 Ⓐ Ⓑ Ⓒ Ⓓ
10 Ⓐ Ⓑ Ⓒ Ⓓ	60 Ⓐ Ⓑ Ⓒ Ⓓ
11 Ⓐ Ⓑ Ⓒ Ⓓ	61 Ⓐ Ⓑ Ⓒ Ⓓ
12 Ⓐ Ⓑ Ⓒ Ⓓ	62 Ⓐ Ⓑ Ⓒ Ⓓ
13 Ⓐ Ⓑ Ⓒ Ⓓ	63 Ⓐ Ⓑ Ⓒ Ⓓ
14 Ⓐ Ⓑ Ⓒ Ⓓ	64 Ⓐ Ⓑ Ⓒ Ⓓ
15 Ⓐ Ⓑ Ⓒ Ⓓ	65 Ⓐ Ⓑ Ⓒ Ⓓ
16 Ⓐ Ⓑ Ⓒ Ⓓ	66 Ⓐ Ⓑ Ⓒ Ⓓ
17 Ⓐ Ⓑ Ⓒ Ⓓ	67 Ⓐ Ⓑ Ⓒ Ⓓ
18 Ⓐ Ⓑ Ⓒ Ⓓ	68 Ⓐ Ⓑ Ⓒ Ⓓ
19 Ⓐ Ⓑ Ⓒ Ⓓ	69 Ⓐ Ⓑ Ⓒ Ⓓ
20 Ⓐ Ⓑ Ⓒ Ⓓ	70 Ⓐ Ⓑ Ⓒ Ⓓ
21 Ⓐ Ⓑ Ⓒ Ⓓ	71 Ⓐ Ⓑ Ⓒ Ⓓ
22 Ⓐ Ⓑ Ⓒ Ⓓ	72 Ⓐ Ⓑ Ⓒ Ⓓ
23 Ⓐ Ⓑ Ⓒ Ⓓ	73 Ⓐ Ⓑ Ⓒ Ⓓ
24 Ⓐ Ⓑ Ⓒ Ⓓ	74 Ⓐ Ⓑ Ⓒ Ⓓ
25 Ⓐ Ⓑ Ⓒ Ⓓ	75 Ⓐ Ⓑ Ⓒ Ⓓ
26 Ⓐ Ⓑ Ⓒ Ⓓ	76 Ⓐ Ⓑ Ⓒ Ⓓ
27 Ⓐ Ⓑ Ⓒ Ⓓ	77 Ⓐ Ⓑ Ⓒ Ⓓ
28 Ⓐ Ⓑ Ⓒ Ⓓ	78 Ⓐ Ⓑ Ⓒ Ⓓ
29 Ⓐ Ⓑ Ⓒ Ⓓ	79 Ⓐ Ⓑ Ⓒ Ⓓ
30 Ⓐ Ⓑ Ⓒ Ⓓ	80 Ⓐ Ⓑ Ⓒ Ⓓ
31 Ⓐ Ⓑ Ⓒ Ⓓ	81 Ⓐ Ⓑ Ⓒ Ⓓ
32 Ⓐ Ⓑ Ⓒ Ⓓ	82 Ⓐ Ⓑ Ⓒ Ⓓ
33 Ⓐ Ⓑ Ⓒ Ⓓ	83 Ⓐ Ⓑ Ⓒ Ⓓ
34 Ⓐ Ⓑ Ⓒ Ⓓ	84 Ⓐ Ⓑ Ⓒ Ⓓ
35 Ⓐ Ⓑ Ⓒ Ⓓ	85 Ⓐ Ⓑ Ⓒ Ⓓ
36 Ⓐ Ⓑ Ⓒ Ⓓ	86 Ⓐ Ⓑ Ⓒ Ⓓ
37 Ⓐ Ⓑ Ⓒ Ⓓ	87 Ⓐ Ⓑ Ⓒ Ⓓ
38 Ⓐ Ⓑ Ⓒ Ⓓ	88 Ⓐ Ⓑ Ⓒ Ⓓ
39 Ⓐ Ⓑ Ⓒ Ⓓ	89 Ⓐ Ⓑ Ⓒ Ⓓ
40 Ⓐ Ⓑ Ⓒ Ⓓ	90 Ⓐ Ⓑ Ⓒ Ⓓ
41 Ⓐ Ⓑ Ⓒ Ⓓ	91 Ⓐ Ⓑ Ⓒ Ⓓ
42 Ⓐ Ⓑ Ⓒ Ⓓ	92 Ⓐ Ⓑ Ⓒ Ⓓ
43 Ⓐ Ⓑ Ⓒ Ⓓ	93 Ⓐ Ⓑ Ⓒ Ⓓ
44 Ⓐ Ⓑ Ⓒ Ⓓ	94 Ⓐ Ⓑ Ⓒ Ⓓ
45 Ⓐ Ⓑ Ⓒ Ⓓ	95 Ⓐ Ⓑ Ⓒ Ⓓ
46 Ⓐ Ⓑ Ⓒ Ⓓ	96 Ⓐ Ⓑ Ⓒ Ⓓ
47 Ⓐ Ⓑ Ⓒ Ⓓ	97 Ⓐ Ⓑ Ⓒ Ⓓ
48 Ⓐ Ⓑ Ⓒ Ⓓ	98 Ⓐ Ⓑ Ⓒ Ⓓ
49 Ⓐ Ⓑ Ⓒ Ⓓ	99 Ⓐ Ⓑ Ⓒ Ⓓ
50 Ⓐ Ⓑ Ⓒ Ⓓ	100 Ⓐ Ⓑ Ⓒ Ⓓ

Practice Test II

Time: 5 hours

100 questions

Directions: The following test consists of questions from each of the five domains that will be on the actual examination. Select the choice that best answers the question. At the end of the test are complete answers and explanations. To help you identify your strengths and weaknesses on this test, we've included the subject area at the end of each answer.

---

1. What skill is promoted by an activity in which a preschool class says each student's name out loud while stomping their feet one time for each syllable?

    A. alliteration
    B. phonological awareness
    C. blending
    D. structural analysis

2. Juan is a new student in Mrs. Arlen's 1st-grade class. Mrs. Arlen knows that Juan is an English Language Learner whose command of English is very limited. What should Mrs. Arlen do to promote Juan's oral language development?

    A. Encourage Juan to express himself in either his home language or English, through writing, drawing pictures, and any other method.
    B. Encourage Juan to participate in show and tell and other oral language activities, but tell Juan what to say in advance.
    C. Treat Juan no differently from the rest of the class.
    D. all of the above

3. Every morning, a kindergarten teacher enlists a different helper from her class. Helpers assist the teacher in giving instructions to the other students about class activities. How is being a helper most likely to benefit children?

    A. It reinforces children for using complex syntactic structures.
    B. It strengthens children's vocabulary.
    C. It encourages children to use their home language, thereby enhancing oral language development.
    D. It helps children learn how to adapt spoken language for different purposes and occasions.

4. Which of the following kindergarten activities is designed to promote segmentation?

    A. The entire class is involved in choral reading of a familiar story.
    B. Children are taught each others' names.
    C. Children are taught how to use Elkonin boxes for familiar words.
    D. none of the above

5. A pre-kindergarten teacher is discussing her students' names. It is Mike's turn, and the teacher is encouraging the entire class to say "Mmmm" together before pausing and saying "ike." What does this activity contribute to?

    A. metalinguistic knowledge
    B. the ability to recognize digraphs
    C. oral language comprehension
    D. the ability to distinguish between onsets and rimes

GO ON TO THE NEXT PAGE

6. The products of the two numbers on each diagonal are all equal. Which of the following is true?

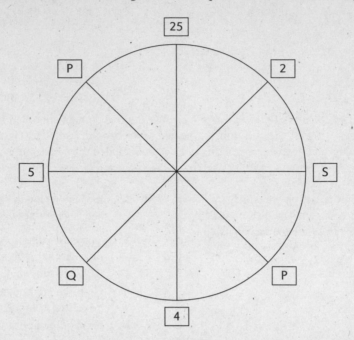

A. P = 10
B. P = 50
C. Q = 5
D. S = 10

7. Mr. Grant establishes this rule: $a \, \Omega \, b = a \times b + a - b$ for students to use to practice addition, subtraction, multiplication, and working with expressions. Which of the following equals 7?

A. $1 \, \Omega \, 4$
B. $3 \, \Omega \, 5$
C. $4 \, \Omega \, 1$
D. $4 \, \Omega \, 2$

8. Mrs. Parkes is showing her class equivalencies on two thermometers. She has each child fill in a chart organized as follows. What is the most reasonable temperature, in degrees Celsius, to go in the empty box.

Fahrenheit	*Celsius*
25	−4
50	
80	27
100	38

A. −10
B. 10
C. 25
D. 30

9. Which of the following best characterizes the structure of EC-4 social studies in the TEKS?

   A. vertical alignment, in the sense that as students get older, the social studies content they are taught becomes increasingly narrow, so that by 4th grade, the focus is on the student's school and local community

   B. vertical alignment, in the sense that as students get older, the social studies content they are taught becomes increasingly broad, so that by 4th grade, the focus is on Texas in the western hemisphere

   C. vertical alignment, in the sense that as students get older, the social studies content they are taught becomes interdisciplinary

   D. no vertical alignment, but simply horizontal alignment across disciplines

10. A teacher has just defined the term "citizenship" for his 2nd-grade class, and he is now helping the students generate examples. Why would the teacher encourage students to talk about their own classroom behavior as examples?

    A. because the fundamental goal of social studies instruction is good citizenship in the classroom

    B. because citizenship is defined primarily in terms of interactions with one's immediately present peer group

    C. because citizenship is an abstract concept, and children will be able to grasp it more readily by means of personal, concrete examples

    D. all of the above

11. Which of the following might be an effective way of helping elementary students understand how climate and other aspects of physical geography influence cultural practices?

    A. A collaborative activity in which the entire class, working together, creates a fictionalized account of how the Caddo came to Texas and adapted to new geographic conditions.

    B. A collaborative activity in which the entire class, working together, creates a chart listing some of the different Native American tribes in Texas during the Archaic Period. The chart contains information on the geographic region each tribe occupied, as well as each tribe's approach to obtaining food, making clothing, and constructing shelters.

    C. A collaborative role-play activity, in which the class is divided into four groups, each representing a Native American tribe that occupied a different geographic region in Texas during the Archaic period. During the role-play, children in each group are instructed to find ways of interacting positively with the other groups, through communication, trade, and other peaceful interactions.

    D. A collaborative role-play activity, in which the class is divided into four groups, each representing a Native American tribe that occupied a different geographic region in Texas during the Archaic Period. During the role-play, children in each group imagine that their tribe has just migrated to their particular region, and that they are now figuring out how to survive in their new environment. Later, the solutions generated by each group are shared and discussed with the entire class.

GO ON TO THE NEXT PAGE

12. In a 3rd-grade class, Mr. Hanson was interested in engaging his students in an experiment on density and what makes objects sink or float. He first assembled his class into small groups and then gave each group 3 unlabeled beakers (one filled with water, one filled with alcohol, and one filled with glycerol). He then distributed the following objects to each group (paper clip, thumb tack, crumpled sticky note, penny, and a marble. Each group was instructed to place each object in all three beakers and note whether they sank or floated. From a safety concern, which of the following should Mr. Hanson emphasize first before the experiment begins?

   I.   Grab the fire extinguisher if a fire breaks out.

   II.   Do not taste any of the liquids in the beakers.

   III.   Do not place any of the objects in your mouth.

   IV.   Make sure your eye goggles are being worn.

   A. I only

   B. I and II

   C. II, III, and IV

   D. I and IV

13. Which of the following is *not* an element of art?

   A. color

   B. texture

   C. form

   D. balance

14. David is a 4th-grade student. His parents took him to visit Teotihuacán, outside of Mexico City. He told his art teacher that his parents, while visiting the pyramids, bought some obsidian sculptures representing the sun and moon gods. His art teacher asked him to bring the sculptures to class so that the other students could see them. David agreed to do it if his parents gave him permission. David's teacher should use this opportunity to:

   A. Show how fortunate David is to have visited Teotihuacán.

   B. Have his students design their own sculptures.

   C. Expose students to cultural art from Central America.

   D. Relate art to everyday life.

15. In the following example, what element of music is represented by the higher and lower notation?

   A. harmony

   B. steady beat

   C. pitch

   D. text

16. A 4th-grade teaching professional interested in developing her students' critical-thinking skills presents to her class several listening examples of indigenous folk music from Latin America. In small groups, the children discuss each listening selection and take notes about each other's comments. The teacher then asks students to select several resource textbooks from the classroom library and begin creating a class report on the music to which they were listening. At the conclusion of the activity, the teacher has each group share its information with the rest of the class. As the students share, the teacher occasionally interjects questions. Which of the following questions would *not* show that the children were thinking critically about the listening assignment?

   A. asking her students where this music was written and to locate that country on a map of Latin America

   B. asking her students to compare and contrast each selection's melody, harmony, instrumentation, and rhythms

   C. asking her students to hypothesize why the selections sound the same

   D. asking her students to explain why they did or did not like the music based on the elements of music

17. Students in Mr. Frank's 2nd-grade class are showing poor judgment in their choice of snacks during the afternoon break. In addition, many parents are sending snacks that are high in sugar. Mr. Frank wants to teach his students how to select snacks that are low in sugar. Which of the following activities is best for this purpose?

A. weighing the snacks and selecting the lightest ones

B. selecting the snacks that have the most fruit

C. learning to read the grams of sugar listed on the nutrition label

D. bringing to class only snacks that are low in sugar.

18. Responding to winning and losing with dignity and understanding contributes to:

A. positive social development and fair play

B. physical activity and healthy living

C. learning concepts and principles of movement

D. increased participation in group sports

19. Two students from the Life Skills Unit have in their IEPs inclusion in regular physical education (P.E.). Mr. Simmerman is one of the P.E. teachers in their school. What Mr. Simmerman needs to do is:

A. Separate these students and give them a safer place to play.

B. Require that an aid be with them at all times.

C. Adapt the activities so that they can participate as much as possible.

D. Not make a distinction and treat them as regular P.E. students.

20. A pre-kindergarten teacher plays a game with students that calls their attention to alliteration. What aspect of literacy is this game most likely to benefit?

A. phonemic awareness

B. semantic development

C. auditory discrimination

D. all of the above

21. Which of the following is likely to foster the development of phonological awareness?

A. language games

B. informal conversations

C. direct instruction

D. all of the above

22. Which of the following would be expected from young children as they acquire alphabetic knowledge?

A. quick mastery of graphophonemic associations

B. difficulty learning letter names by means of "The Alphabet Song"

C. relatively effortless decoding

D. confusion between similar letters such as "b" and "d"

23. Which of the following is most important to the development of reading among children entering the 1st grade?

A. the ability to say the alphabet in correct order

B. the ability to speak with good grammar

C. the ability to recognize letters

D. the ability to enunciate clearly

24. Which of the following instructional approaches should be most effective at helping kindergarten children acquire alphabetic knowledge?

A. a multisensory approach, including activities such as read alouds, letter-identification games, air-writing, and the creation of art projects that focus on letter shapes

B. a skill-and-drill approach in which the goal is quick and accurate identification of individual letters, in isolation at first, and then in the context of meaningful words

C. a collaborative approach, in which each child is given responsibility for learning a particular letter, and then teaching the letter to the rest of the class

D. a direct instruction approach, in which the teacher introduces each letter to students, and the students engage in active listening

25. Mary, a student, points to a picture on the wall and asks what it is. The teacher asks the class whether anyone knows. "Octopus," respond several children. "That's right," says the teacher, "Octopus. Oc . . . to . . . pus." As the teacher says the word the second time, she moves her finger across the word printed beneath the picture. Which of the following skills is the teacher contributing to?

A. syntactic awareness

B. semantic awareness

C. phonemic awareness

D. print awareness

GO ON TO THE NEXT PAGE

26. Penelope drives to her beach house in three and one-quarter hours. If she drives twice as fast on her way back home, what is her estimated return trip travel time?

    A.   one and five-eighths hours

    B.   one and three-quarter hours

    C.   six and one-quarter hours

    D.   six and one-half hours

27. Kent and Lily are learning to add multi-digit numbers. Mrs. Drain wants them to "see" what they are adding. Which of the following manipulatives should she give the children to use?

    A.   Dienes blocks

    B.   Cuisenaire rods

    C.   geoboards

    D.   tangrams

28. Why are thematic units especially important to social studies instruction?

    A.   Because social studies instruction is fundamentally interdisciplinary.

    B.   Because children find thematic units interesting.

    C.   Because thematic units permit language arts instruction along with the teaching of content.

    D.   Because thematic units provide a structured curriculum that is convenient for teachers to use.

29. Why did Spanish explorers come to Texas in the 16th and 17th centuries?

    A.   to find suitable locations for the establishment of colonies

    B.   to find gold and other material resources

    C.   to find straits and establish trade routes

    D.   all of the above

30. Why is Stephen F. Austin referred to as the "father of Texas"?

    A.   Because he was the first Anglo to become a father in Texas.

    B.   Because he established the first Anglo colony in Texas.

    C.   Because he was the first governor of the Republic of Texas.

    D.   Because he was the principal author of the Texas Constitution that is still in force today.

31. The "six flags over Texas" do not include the flag of which of the following countries?

    A.   England

    B.   France

    C.   Mexico

    D.   United States

Questions 32 through 37 are based on the following information:

    Mr. Browning introduced motion and forces to his 3rd-grade class by having them conduct an experiment to measure the distance that a toy race car would attain as a result of force. The experiment was conducted in two parts.

    Part I: In the first part of the experiment, one student in a group of four applied a force to the same race car on the same flat surface while the other students in the group measured the distance and recorded the data. The following results are displayed in a table:

Distance Reached by a Race Car on a Flat Surface	
Trial	**Distance (m)**
1	1.34
2	1.38
3	1.42
4	1.40
5	1.39
6	1.34

Part II: In the second part of the experiment, the student lab groups took a 1-meter wooden plank and created a ramp using textbooks to elevate one end of the ramp. A student would release the car from the top of the ramp, let it roll down the ramp and measure how far from the ramp the car would end up. The data that the group obtained is summarized in the following table:

Distance Reached by a Race Car on a Wooden Ramp	
Number of Books	**Distance (m)**
2	1.56
4	1.84
6	2.42
8	2.60
10	2.98
12	3.34

32. In introducing the experiment to the students, Mr. Browning demonstrated the distance covered due to a force by throwing a book along the floor. He pointed out that the book covered a certain distance before coming to a stop. Mr. Browning asked the students for a reason why the book came to a stop. The correct explanation as to why the book eventually stops would be

    A. type of book
    B. weight of the book
    C. gravity
    D. surface friction

33. After reviewing the results from their experiment, the students were asked why the distance changed between trials. A possible reason would be

    A. air resistance
    B. surface friction
    C. initial force imparted to the car
    D. change in mass of the car

34. As an extension to the first experiment, Mr. Browning had the student push the car on the surface at varying levels, first imparting to it a small push, and then a progressively harder push followed by a forceful push. The students noticed that the distance that the car traveled was directly impacted by the amount of force or push imparted to the car. This illustrated which physical science principle?

    A. Newton's First Law
    B. Newton's Second Law
    C. Newton's Third Law
    D. Newton's Fourth Law

35. In drawing comparisons between the two experiments, Mr. Browning asked his students to describe the motion of the car and identify the force behind the motion. The students readily responded that it was their initial force or push that caused the car to move in the second experiment. Following in this line of questioning, Mr. Browning then asked the students to identify the force that caused the race car to move. The correct response would be

    A. friction
    B. gravity
    C. torque
    D. car mass

GO ON TO THE NEXT PAGE

36. As the car was placed at the top of the ramp, Mr. Browning extended his discussion of motion and forces to include energy. The energy that the toy car had at the top of the ramp was

 A. heat energy
 B. rotational energy
 C. potential energy
 D. kinetic energy

37. When the car was released from the top of the ramp, the potential energy that the car had at the top of the ramp was converted to kinetic energy as the car reached the bottom of the ramp. This is an example of the conservation of energy. However, when the students performed the experiments, the students found that the kinetic energy at the bottom of the ramp was slightly less than the potential energy of the car at the top. The students could probably conclude that:

 A. Conservation of energy was violated because the total energy before the car was released must equal the total energy of the car after it was released.
 B. Conservation of energy was not violated because some of the potential energy lost by the car was transferred to heat energy while the rest was transferred to kinetic energy.
 C. Conservation of energy was violated because there was no kinetic energy at the top of the ramp and no potential energy at the bottom of the ramp.
 D. Conservation of energy was not violated because all of the potential energy lost by the car was transferred to elastic potential energy.

38. Mrs. Haines, the art teacher, asked her students to bring an empty box of cereal to class. She can use these boxes to:

 A. show how the elements of art are used
 B. show the nutritious value of their content
 C. show how the environment is reflected in their design
 D. show how students can communicate with the cereal companies

39. A student reads the passage, "The pirate climbed up the hull" as "The pirate climbed up the hall." Immediately, the student pauses and corrects himself. What prompted the student's self-correction?

 A. word-attack skills
 B. syntactic cues
 C. semantic context
 D. structural cues

40. A student who has difficulty reading words like "cherry," "edge," and "calm" is probably struggling with which of the following?

 A. diphthongs
 B. digraphs
 C. consonant blend
 D. single consonants

41. Which of the following activities is likely to have the most positive impact on reading fluency among 1st graders?

 A. inviting students to read challenging books instead of returning to familiar ones
 B. guiding students through extensive phonic analysis exercises that focus on isolated letter groups and words
 C. encouraging students to read new texts independently, without modeling by the teacher
 D. encouraging students to engage in repeated reading

42. Which of the following can be expected among children in the initial reading (that is, decoding) stage?

 A. poor comprehension
 B. inability to sound out words
 C. no knowledge of sight words
 D. all of the above

43. What stage is reflected by the child who can read his own name as well as several brand names?

 A. fluency stage
 B. pre-reading stage
 C. reading to learn stage
 D. initial reading stage

44. Which is the most appropriate way for 2nd-grade children to respond to changes in tempo in a listening selection?

    A. Provide each child a sheet of paper with a picture of the musical characters. As the music plays, the children move their fingers across the page.

    B. Have the children walk about the room when the music is slow, and then increase the speed of their movements when the music is very fast.

    C. Create a movement pattern that requires the children to clap their hands to the slow tempo and pat their laps to the fast tempo.

    D. Have the children create a stationary movement pattern for the slow tempo and an entirely different stationary movement pattern for the fast tempo.

45. A 2nd-grade teaching professional is planning a unit on the countries of Latin America. As a culminating activity, she plans to have her students engage in a traditional folk dance from Guatemala. Because her students have limited experience with music, to which of the following should she have her students dance and move?

    A. harmony
    B. words
    C. rhythm
    D. syncopation

46. More children in the upper elementary grades are showing signs of becoming overweight. This is a problem that needs to be addressed in the early grades. One of the things the school can do is to

    A. Teach the students to use time management skills to control when they eat and the number of times they eat.

    B. Weigh the students and give them a goal for proper weight loss.

    C. Send brochures home informing the parents of the dangers of overeating.

    D. Show the students a video of overweight teens and their social problems.

47. Which of the following contains examples of invented spelling?

    A. Mary walked to the store.
    B. Mary walkd to the store.
    C. Meri wokd to th stour.
    D. M w t s.

48. Which of the following is typically *not* learned during the emergent literacy stage?

    A. the concept of authorship
    B. the directionality of print
    C. the idea that print conveys meaning
    D. the use of graphic organizers

49. When very young children are first able to recognize environmental print, what do they still lack?

    A. an appreciation that certain signs and symbols convey meaning

    B. an appreciation that text conveys a different kind of information than logos and other graphic images do

    C. an interest in particular objects and places in their environments

    D. all of the above

50. A teacher who is introducing words to beginning readers should keep in mind which of the following suggestions?

    A. Words should always be introduced in isolation, so that children can make use of decoding strategies one word at a time.

    B. Words such as "bad" and "dab" should be introduced early, so that children can practice visual discrimination between highly similar letters.

    C. Words with consonants such as "t" should be introduced before words with consonants such as "j."

    D. A mix of multisyllabic and monosyllabic words should be introduced from the beginning.

GO ON TO THE NEXT PAGE

51. Yvette, a 2nd grader, is a slow, clear, expressive reader who is having difficulty decoding some of the multisyllabic words in the following passage: *Steve kicked the basketball as hard as he could. The basketball hit the bush where the ducks were standing. The ducks flew off, honking loudly.*

What should Yvette's teacher do to help her?

A. Tell Yvette that she needs to read more carefully.

B. Ask Yvette to read the passage even more slowly.

C. Help Yvette apply structural analysis to the difficult words.

D. Encourage Yvette to make use of contextual information.

52. Zachary Taylor Elementary is having an assembly. Some of the physical education (P.E.) classes had to be combined to accommodate the schedule changes. Ms. De León will have kindergarten and 3rd-grade students coming to her class at the same time. Ms. De León has to

A. Modify her activities to accommodate their differences in growth and development.

B. Match one kindergartener with one 3rd grader as partners in all activities.

C. Combine all of the students and recognize that children of mixed abilities and ages are always at play.

D. Refuse to have the mixed students in the same class.

53. The kindergarten students in Mr. Abrego's third period physical education (P.E.) class frequently quarrel during play and other activities. Mr. Abrego needs to:

A. Refer the instigators to the school counselor.

B. Call the parents and work out a plan of action.

C. Have the classroom teacher stay with them and help with the discipline.

D. Understand that students at this age quarrel frequently, but the quarrels tend to be of short duration.

54. Which of the following would be an important distinction to help 1st graders recognize in the context of learning about history?

A. the distinction between major periods in world history

B. the distinction between induction and deduction

C. the distinction between fact and opinion

D. the distinction between proximal and distal causes

55. Most weather takes place in which of the following layers of the atmosphere?

A. mesosphere

B. troposphere

C. stratosphere

D. thermosphere

56. What is the geographic term for the westernmost area of Texas?

A. Trans-Pecos region

B. High Plains

C. Piney Woods

D. all of the above

57. Tests of reading fluency typically measure which of the following?

A. rate

B. accuracy

C. expression

D. all of the above

58. Mrs. Jones notices that Mark, one of her 2nd-grade students, shows poor comprehension of expository texts but seems to understand narratives just fine. What should Mrs. Jones do?

A. Make sure that Mark always has narratives to read.

B. Talk with Mark before he reads an expository text to find out what his goals are in reading.

C. Encourage Mark to try harder when he reads expository texts and to approach the teacher with questions.

D. Annotate expository texts for Mark before he reads them.

59. Ebony made the following number line. While she made it, she received a telephone call. When she went back to work on it, she had forgotten what she had been doing. She remembered that she had been about to put a number in place of the E. What number should she put where the E is?

-28 -21 -14   0   7   14   E   F   G

A. 15
B. 16
C. 21
D. 35

60. Dolly sees a poncho in Coats and Totes that she just has to have! Her friend asks her how much it costs. If she truthfully tells her friend the cost, rounded to the nearest ten dollars, how much the $346 poncho costs, what does she tell her?

A. $300
B. $340
C. $350
D. $400

61. What is the area, in boxes, of this diagram?

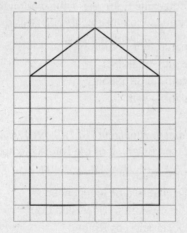

A. 34
B. 42
C. 76
D. 96

62. A kindergarten class is adding different instruments to a familiar chant. They are also playing around with the words and the syllables of the chant, making some syllables longer and some shorter, and adding words with a different number of syllables. As they say the chant, they change the volume of their speaking voices. While they are doing this, the teacher provides the class a constant steady beat to help them stay together more easily. Which of the following is *not* being varied?

A. dynamics
B. tempo
C. timbre
D. rhythm

Questions 63 and 64 are based on the following:

As she was presenting a lesson to her 1st-grade class on earthworms, Ms. Perkins wanted her students to explore the living environment of earthworms. She arranged to take her students on a nature walk in a park adjacent to the school to look for earthworms. Once they found ten earthworms, they returned to class for a discussion.

63. As Ms. Perkins embarked on a nature walk with her students, which would be least helpful in performing the investigation:

A. shovel
B. container
C. gloves
D. stopwatch

64. Ms. Perkins asked her students whether the earthworms would prefer to live under dark conditions or light conditions. The correct response she should expect from her students would be:

A. only dark conditions
B. only light conditions
C. both light and dark conditions
D. either light or dark conditions

Practice Test II

65. Before a 4th-grade class reads a story about a police officer, the teacher asks students what they know about the police, apart from fictionalized accounts in movies and on television. The teacher then leads a discussion of the various roles that police officers play in our society. What is the general purpose of the discussion?

  A. to activate appropriate schemata about the police, so that children's understanding of the story can be connected with their existing knowledge

  B. to foster a positive attitude about police officers, so that students will become interested in the story and read it attentively

  C. to encourage the use of vocabulary that is relevant to law enforcement

  D. to demonstrate the importance of the topic

66. Which of the following is the best approach for a teacher to introduce 2nd graders to the idea that reference materials serve an expository rather than narrative function?

  A. The teacher encourages students to create two graphic organizers, one for a reference book and one for a story. Students are then asked to compare the two in order to see the differences between them.

  B. The teacher discusses the difference between expository and narrative texts. Students are then given study questions to guide their examination of reference materials written at their level.

  C. Students are asked to find key information from reference materials.

  D. Students are encouraged to compare narrative and expository texts on their own, and to identify some of the differences between them.

67. Before reading a story about a lion and an ant, a kindergarten teacher says to her class, "As I read this story, I want you to think about what the lion does for the ant, and how the ant helps the lion." How is the teacher's comment likely to help the students?

  A. by identifying the underlying story grammar

  B. by distinguishing between the motives of the main characters

  C. by providing children with a purpose for listening

  D. by summarizing the plot of the story

68. The SQ3R method would be the best tool for 4th graders to use for which of the following projects?

  A. a poem focusing on the United States in the mid-19th century

  B. a response journal focusing on classroom discussion of the American civil war

  C. a simulated journal in which students take the perspective of civil war soldiers and nurses

  D. a biography of Abraham Lincoln in which students use a variety of reference materials

69. Which of the following would be the most effective use of a graphic organizer?

  A. Students illustrate the beginning, middle, and end of a story.

  B. Students create an alphabetized list of class members.

  C. Students depict the main characters in a story and the relationships between them.

  D. Students look at pictures of trees and classify each one as "evergreen" or "deciduous."

70. A teacher leads a discussion of the foods each of his students likes, while using a map to illustrate where each food came from. What concept might the teacher intend to illustrate through this exercise?

  A. nature-nurture interaction

  B. continental drift

  C. cultural diffusion

  D. nationalism

71. The fundamental rights of U.S. citizens are guaranteed in which of the following documents?

  A. Constitution

  B. Declaration of Independence

  C. Articles of the Confederation

  D. Declaration of Rights

72. The surface area of a cylindrical soup can is comprised of which of the following?

  A. a rectangle and a circle

  B. two little circles and a big circle

  C. two circles and a rectangle

  D. one rectangle

73. How many decimeters are in a hectometer?

A. $\frac{1}{1,000}$

B. 10

C. 100

D. 1,000

74. Mr. Ramjey has twenty-four students in his class. Three-fourths of them are girls. What is the probability that Mr. Ramjey will pick a boy, if he randomly chooses a student from his class to run an errand for him?

A. $\frac{1}{24}$

B. $\frac{1}{4}$

C. $\frac{1}{3}$

D. 6

75. Which of the following is a benefit of electronic texts?

A. Readers generally enjoy electronic texts more than printed ones.

B. Readers have an enhanced ability to search for information in electronic texts.

C. Electronic texts are easier to read than printed ones.

D. The flow of information in an electronic text is much more easily controlled.

76. A kindergarten teacher helps each of her students create a project in which they describe their families. Some students turn in pictures with labels for key objects and people. Some students turn in pictures that contain no text. Two students turn in simple narrative descriptions. By accepting each of these projects and praising them in front of the class, what is the teacher attempting to do?

A. Encourage students to express themselves.

B. Help students understand that pictures and text are interchangeable.

C. Motivate students to do their best written work.

D. Model appropriate strategies for giving constructive criticism.

77. What stage of writing is exemplified by the child who writes, "I hav a pupy named Bill. He is very littel and he licks my face a lot. He is a goldun rutreevur."

A. prephonemic

B. phonemic

C. transitional

D. conventional

78. Which of the following can be expected in the handwriting of 1st graders?

A. inconsistencies in the size of letters

B. upper- and lower-case letters of the same size

C. insufficient spacing between words

D. all of the above

79. Which of the following is most indicative of a problem that a kindergarten teacher needs to address?

A. A student complains of discomfort during handwriting.

B. A student sometimes writes mock letters instead of real ones.

C. A student sometimes reverses letters during writing.

D. A student sometimes writes words that are inconsistent in size.

GO ON TO THE NEXT PAGE

Questions 80 though 85 are based on the following:

In an effort to introduce his students to the environment, Mr. Ramirez had originally planned to take his 4th-grade class on a nature field trip around the schoolyard but was disappointed when it began to rain in the morning and then stopped about 30 minutes later. During this time, Mr. Ramirez had his class line up at the windows and asked them questions about what they observed. One student (Student 1) noted that the level of water in a small puddle had become smaller during the day until it eventually dried up. Another student (Student 2) noted that an empty soda bottle outside had some water in it and he wondered how much water was in it. Yet another student (Student 3) noted that a large area of field that had more water on it than the surrounding area was greener. Mr. Ramirez then proceeded to engage his class in a discussion based on the observations of these students.

80. Mr. Ramirez asked Student 1 for a possible explanation as to why the level of water in the small puddle became smaller during the day. The most logical explanation would be:

   A. transpiration
   B. condensation
   C. precipitation
   D. evaporation

81. An explanation of Student 1's observation provides an excellent opportunity for which concept to be introduced by Mr. Ramirez to his students?

   A. water cycle
   B. earth cycle
   C. sun cycle
   D. rock cycle

82. Mr. Ramirez encouraged Student 2 to retrieve the empty soda bottle outside and measure the amount of water in the soda bottle. He then asked the student what information could be revealed by the water in the bottle. The most appropriate answer would be:

   A. time duration of rainfall
   B. type of rainfall
   C. amount of rainfall
   D. temperature at rainfall

83. Addressing the class, Mr. Ramirez asked what type of weather instrument that empty soda bottle represented. The best answer to this question would be:

   A. barometer
   B. rain gauge
   C. weather thermometer
   D. altimeter

84. Student 3 notes that areas that have more water tend to be greener. Mr. Ramirez takes this opportunity to explain this student's observation by introducing the students to which process?

   A. precipitation
   B. condensation
   C. transpiration
   D. evaporation

85. After discussing the observations with his students, Mr. Ramirez then instructs his students to find the amount of rainfall that has fallen in the city over the past month. Once the students acquire the data, which graph type(s) would be the best way to display this information?

   I. bar graph
   II. line graph
   III. pie chart

   A. I only
   B. I and II
   C. I and III
   D. I, II, and III

86. Which of the following is most appropriate during the prewriting stage of the writing process?

   A. freewriting
   B. revising
   C. editing
   D. annotation

87. A 2nd-grade teacher asks his class to write their parents a description of their field trip that morning. Which of the following is the most appropriate comment to add to the instructions?

A. Be sure to do your best work, so that whoever reads it can be proud of you.

B. Jot down some thoughts in the margin of your paper. Then write a five paragraph description of what you found most interesting about the trip. Be sure to provide an introduction and a conclusion.

C. Be sure to keep in mind what you want to say. Have your theme in mind and develop it as you write.

D. Write down what you found most interesting about the trip. Don't worry about your spelling or your handwriting yet. Just write down some things you found really interesting. Later, you'll have a chance to go back and make corrections.

88. Amie bought two notebooks for $1.25 each and one pencil for $0.92. Barton bought three pens for $0.85 each and one ruler for $0.86. Who spent more money and how much more?

A. Barton: $0.01

B. Amie: $1.00

C. Amie: $3.42

D. Amie: $0.01

Questions 89 and 90 are based on the following:

Ms. Carleigh determined that a group of children with whom she worked had weights that approximated a normal distribution. The weights of the eight children had a mean of 550 kilograms. The standard deviation was calculated to be 150 kilograms.

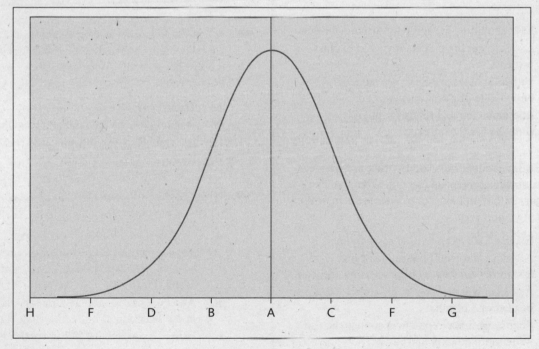

89. What value should be in position D, if each letter is one standard deviation from the next?

A. 0

B. 400

C. 250

D. 850

GO ON TO THE NEXT PAGE

90. What is the difference between the C and D values?

    A. 250

    B. 450

    C. 700

    D. 950

91. What manipulatives should Mr. Clymer use to best help Jaime correct his misunderstanding of place value? (Jaime presented the following exercise to Mr. Clymer.)

$$\begin{array}{r} 52 \\ +37 \\ \hline 17 \end{array}$$

    A. calculator

    B. fraction bars

    C. stopwatch

    D. Dienes blocks

92. Mr. Reynolds has asked his students to bring a white T-shirt to art class. In class, they will be asked to express themselves artistically by using the T-shirt as a canvas. The students are free to use any medium in class. When this project is finished, they will wear their creations and visit several classes to show their work. Mr. Reynolds can use the T-shirts as

    A. a way to boost the students' artistic abilities

    B. a way to get the parents involved in class projects

    C. authentic assessments of the students' knowledge of the elements of art

    D. sale items to raise funds for buying art supplies for the art class

93. Lisa, a 3rd grader, finds handwriting to be a slow and somewhat laborious process. What can the teacher do to help Lisa express her ideas in written form?

    A. Excuse Lisa from written assignments.

    B. Allow Lisa to complete some of her assignments using word processing software.

    C. Ask Lisa whether she would rather use a pen instead of a pencil.

    D. Encourage Lisa to practice, so that she can write more quickly and easily.

94. A 3rd-grade student expresses interest in reading a relatively advanced book on motorcycles. The teacher asks the student to read a passage from the book to her. The teacher finds that the student reads less than half of the words correctly, and has limited comprehension of what was read. What should the teacher do?

    A. Create a list consisting of the words the student cannot read correctly, and then work with the student on making those into sight words.

    B. Tell the student to keep reading, because it will be easier in time.

    C. Help the student select a less advanced book.

    D. Spend five minutes per day helping the student with a chosen passage.

95. A 2nd-grade teacher notices that one of her students is reading well on the whole but still struggles with words such as "though" and "which." Instructional emphasis on what types of words would benefit this student the most?

    A. high-frequency words with irregular spellings

    B. complex morphemes

    C. low-frequency, morphemically simple words

    D. phonetically regular words

96. A 2nd-grade teacher is worried that her book basket contains books that are too difficult for most of her students. What assessment should the teacher use?

    A. Texas Primary Reading Inventory (TPRI)

    B. Peabody Picture Vocabulary Test (PPVT)

    C. Informal Reading Inventory (IRI)

    D. Reading Miscue Inventory (RMI)

97. Which of the following is the most accurate statement about assessment?

    A. Teachers need to assess the literacy development of each student on a regular basis by means of both informal and formal evaluations.

    B. Assessment should play a minor role, at most, in the selection of books for student use.

    C. Formal assessments of literacy development are a more important source of information for teachers than informal assessments.

    D. Assessment of literacy development is not needed if a teacher is attentive to the progress of each student in the class.

98. Which of the following is a disadvantage of describing the quality of life in a particular country in terms of its Gross National Product (GNP)?

   A. Other factors, such as unemployment rates, literacy, and life span, are central to considerations of quality of life.

   B. The Gross National Product does not provide an overall sense of the financial health of a country.

   C. "Quality of life" is a highly subjective concept and, thus, it is not analyzed by social scientists.

   D. The Gross Domestic Product (GDP) provides a much more accurate portrayal of the financial condition of a country.

99. A teacher asks each student in his class to name the type(s) of pet(s) he or she owns. As each student responds, the teacher writes the types of animals on the board and makes a note of how many times each animal is named. Which number should the teacher calculate in order to answer the question, "What kind of pet is most common"?

   A. mean
   B. median
   C. mode
   D. range

100. From earliest to most recent, which of the following is the correct sequence of industries that dominated the Texas economy over the past two centuries?

   A. cattle ranching, cotton, petroleum, electronics
   B. cotton, cattle ranching, petroleum, electronics
   C. cotton, petroleum, cattle ranching, electronics
   D. cattle ranching, petroleum, cotton, electronics

Answer Key for Practice Test II

1. B	26. A	51. C	76. A
2. A	27. A	52. A	77. C
3. D	28. A	53. D	78. D
4. C	29. D	54. C	79. A
5. D	30. C	55. B	80. D
6. A	31. A	56. A	81. A
7. C	32. D	57. D	82. C
8. B	33. C	58. B	83. B
9. B	34. B	59. C	84. C
10. C	35. B	60. C	85. B
11. D	36. C	61. C	86. A
12. C	37. B	62. B	87. D
13. D	38. A	63. D	88. D
14. C	39. C	64. A	89. C
15. C	40. B	65. A	90. B
16. A	41. D	66. A	91. D
17. C	42. A	67. C	92. C
18. A	43. B	68. D	93. B
19. C	44. D	69. C	94. C
20. A	45. C	70. C	95. A
21. D	46. A	71. A	96. C
22. D	47. C	72. C	97. A
23. C	48. D	73. D	98. A
24. A	49. B	74. B	99. C
25. D	50. C	75. B	100. B

Practice Test II—Answer Explanations

1. **B.** Phonological awareness includes the ability to hear the individual syllables of spoken words. (**Competency 001, Oral Language**)

2. **A.** It is important for English Language Learners to have opportunities to express themselves while they are in the process of catching up to their classmates in English. So A is the correct answer. (**Competency 001, Oral Language**)

3. **D.** Although options A, B, and C all reflect benefits that children may experience by giving instructions, D is the best answer, because it describes the benefit that is most specific to the practice of conveying instructions. (**Competency 001, Oral Language**)

4. **C.** Elkonin boxes are specifically designed to promote segmentation skills, so C is the correct answer. (**Competency 002, Phonological and Phonemic Awareness**)

5. **D.** The teacher is dividing Mike's name into the onset sound and accompanying rime. D is, therefore, the correct answer. (**Competency 002, Phonological and Phonemic Awareness**)

6. **A.** One of the diagonals has 25 and 4. The product of 25 and 4 is 100. Every diagonal, then, must have a product of 100. P is on both ends of one of the diagonals. Choice A claims that P = 10. That works: $10 \times 10 = 100$. Choice B, P = 50, would result in 2,500. That is incorrect. Choice C, Q = 5, multiplied by 2, on the other end of the diagonal, would give 10. That does not work! Choice D, S = 10, multiplied by 5, results in 50: No good! The correct answer is A. (**Competency 013, Number Concepts, Patterns, and Algebra**)

7. **C.** The rule requires multiplying the two values together, adding the first value to that product, then subtracting the second value from that sum. Choice A results in $1 \times 4 + 1 - 4 = 4 + 1 - 4 = 5 - 4 = 1$. That is not 7, which is the desired answer. Choice B results in $3 \times 5 + 3 - 5 = 15 + 3 - 5 = 18 - 5 = 13$. Wrong again! The result from choice C is $4 \times 1 + 4 - 1 = 4 + 4 - 1 = 8 - 1 = 7$. Yes! That is the winner! Choice D results in $4 \times 2 + 4 - 2 = 8 + 4 - 2 = 12 - 2 = 10$. That clearly is wrong. The correct answer is C. (**Competency 013, Number Concepts, Patterns, and Algebra**)

8. **B.** The values in the first column get progressively larger from top to bottom. Likewise, the second column will have to get larger from top to bottom. Oops! Two answers are between –4 and 27: 10 and 25. However, 50 is about halfway between 25 and 80. So, the number in the empty box in the second column should be about halfway between –4 and 27. Choice C, 25, is too close to 27. The correct answer is B. (**Competency 015, Mathematical Process**)

9. **B.** EC–4 social studies in the TEKS is vertically aligned, and B is the only option in which the vertical alignment is correctly summarized. (**Competency 016, Social Science Instruction**)

10. **C.** One goal of social studies instruction is good classroom citizenship, and this goal can be defined in terms of interactions with peers. But there is much more to citizenship, and because it is an abstract concept, students need personal, concrete examples in order to help them understand what it is. (**Competency 016, Social Science Instruction**)

11. **D.** Although all of the options would be potentially beneficial, the influence of climate on culture may be conveyed most directly, and in the most personally engaging way, through the collaborative role-play activity described in option D. (**Competency 016, Social Science Instruction**)

12. **C.** It is important to emphasize lab safety in any laboratory investigation, and all four directives are important. However, in this experiment, because fire will not be incorporated into the project, emphasizing the fire extinguisher is not as important as the other directives represented by option C. The responses provided by II, III, and IV all are important in guaranteeing the safety of students performing this investigation. (**Competency 016, Social Science Instruction**)

13. **D.** Balance is a principle of art, not an element of art. (**Competency 024, Visual Arts**)

14. C. The teacher can use this opportunity to show examples of art work found outside of the United States. Designing their own sculptures can be an extended activity, through which students can express their own artistic skill. Speaking about how fortunate a person is would not be an art objective. Although religion can be a part of everyday life, religion is only one aspect of culture. Cultural art encompasses much more than religion. **(Competency 024, Visual Arts)**

15. C. This question assesses your knowledge of written notation. You can easily eliminate answer choice D; there is no text in the music example. You can also eliminate answer choice A, because only one is presented at a time in the example. For the answer to be choice A, you would need at least two notes stacked upon one another. Of the remaining two choices, C is the best choice, because the stem specifically asks about "higher and lower notation." Recall that the "round circles" in the example are the note heads that are placed on specific lines and/or spaces to represent pitch—high or low. Choice B relates to the rhythms of the example, which are represented by the "sticks" attached to the "round circles." **(Competency 025, Music)**

16. A. Critical, higher-order thinking is assessed in all domains throughout the exam. Although the question is couched in a music domain, the thrust of the question is to assess your ability to recognize developmentally appropriate questioning strategies. What makes this question difficult is that it asks for the negative response mode (that is, would not). Recognizing that the question relates to critical thinking and not music, per se, you should look for words that correspond to higher order thinking skills. Choices B, C, and D ask children to compare and contrast, hypothesize, and defend (explain) a musical preference. All of these are higher-order thinking questions. Answer choice A asks "where" the music was written and to "locate" that country on a map. Both of these tasks rely on lower-level thinking skills. **(Competency 025, Music)**

17. C. Although D could be a correct answer, answer C is better, because students can then take this skill outside the classroom and together with their parents select those snacks that are low in sugar. **(Competency 026, Health)**

18. A. The stem refers to an affective behavior important in social development. The only response that targets an affective response is answer A. **(Competency 027, Physical Education)**

19. C. The other options do not assure participation in a least restrictive environment which is a major component of inclusion. **(Competency 027, Physical Education)**

20. A. Alliteration is the repetition of sounds in stressed syllables or at the beginnings of words. A game that calls attention to alliteration would not necessarily contribute to semantic development or auditory discrimination and, thus, A is the correct answer. **(Competency 002, Phonological and Phonemic Awareness)**

21. D. All of the options can promote phonological awareness and, thus, D is the correct answer. **(Competency 002, Phonological and Phonemic Awareness)**

22. D. Children learn letter names through "The Alphabet Song" fairly easily, but graphophonemic associations and decoding skills are not quick and easy developments. Moreover, as children acquire alphabetic knowledge, confusion between similar letters is common. Thus, D is the correct answer. **(Competency 003, Alphabetic Principle)**

23. C. Among the available options, letter recognition is by far the most important prerequisite to the development of reading and, thus, C is the correct answer. **(Competency 003, Alphabetic Principle)**

24. A. Skill-and-drill techniques, direct instruction, and peer collaboration are not the most effective methods for early literacy instruction. A is the correct answer, because the multisensory approach it describes is meaningful, engaging, and varied. **(Competency 003, Alphabetic Principle)**

25. D. By moving her finger across the word, the teacher is calling children's attention to the fact that the printed word conveys the name of the picture. Hence, D is the correct answer. **(Competency 004, Literacy Development)**

26. A. If Penelope drives twice as fast, it will take her one-half the time. One-half of $3\frac{1}{4}$, or $\frac{1}{2} \times 3\frac{1}{4}$, is $\frac{1}{2} \times 3\frac{1}{4} = \frac{1}{2} \times \frac{13}{4} = \frac{13}{8} = 1\frac{5}{8}$. The correct answer is A. **(Competency 015, Mathematical Process)**

27. A. Mrs. Drain needs to use manipulatives that will show the children place value. Dienes blocks are base-10 blocks. Perfect! The correct answer is A. **(Competency 012, Mathematics Instruction)**

28. A. The fundamentally interdisciplinary nature of social studies instruction is ideally suited to thematic units. **(Competency 016, Social Science Instruction)**

29. D. All of the options describe reasons for the Spanish exploration of Texas in the 16th and 17th centuries. **(Competency 017, History)**

30. C. Stephen F. Austin was the first governor of Texas and, thus, C is the correct answer. **(Competency 017, History)**

31. A. England is the only country among those mentioned that has not governed some part of modern-day Texas. **(Competency 017, History)**

32. D. Surface friction occurs when an object is moving along a surface, such as the book moving along the floor. So D is the correct response. "Type of book" is not a force, and the options described in options B and C are essentially the same quantity. **(Competency 021, Physical Science)**

33. C. The teacher needs to encourage the student to analyze the data and compare the results with information regarding the procedure of the experiment. Air resistance, surface friction, and change in the mass of the car were all controlled variables, because the same car was pushed by the same student over the same surface. The only variable that changed for any given trial was the amount of force or push imparted to the car for each trial. There was nothing implemented into the procedure of the experiment to control for it. **(Competency 021, Physical Science)**

34. B. The results from this extension to the experiment illustrates Newton's Second Law or the fact that force is proportional to the mass of the object multiplied by the acceleration of the object as a result of the force. **(Competency 021, Physical Science)**

35. B. Because the car is suspended above the ground, regardless of whether it is held or placed on a ramp, gravity is acting on the object, pulling it straight down or, in this case, pulling it down along the slanted ramp. Thus, by releasing the car at the top of the ramp, gravity acts to pull it down along the ramp, starting the motion of its wheels. Friction is the force that occurs between two surfaces in motion, while torque is the rotational equivalent of force. Car mass, of course, is not a force and, thus, is not a viable option. **(Competency 021, Physical Science)**

36. C. The toy car held motionless at the top of the ramp has energy stored due to its location. This is the definition of potential energy. Rotational and kinetic energy imply that the car is moving. Heat energy, which usually occurs as a direct result of motion, cannot be considered as a possible option, because the car is held still. **(Competency 021, Physical Science)**

37. B. Conservation of energy—the fact that energy can neither be created nor destroyed, only transferred—must always hold true. It *cannot* be violated under any circumstances. Thus A and C can immediately be eliminated. The toy car held motionless at the top of the ramp has energy stored due to its location. This is the definition of potential energy. Rotational and kinetic energy imply that the car is moving and heat energy, which usually occurs as a direct result of motion, cannot be considered as a possible option, because the car is held still. Choice D is not correct, because although conservation of energy is not violated, there are no springs involved in the system and, thus, no elastic potential energy. **(Competency 021, Physical Science)**

38. A. There is so much artwork that goes into the design of a cereal box. They are designed to appeal to the eye. Although other content areas can be included in art activities (for example, writing and health), a primary reason for looking at cereal boxes in an art class is to observe how the elements of art are evident on the boxes' artwork. **(Competency 024, Visual Arts)**

39. C. The student most probably noticed that his first reading didn't make sense, given that a pirate would not climb up a "hall." C is therefore the correct answer. **(Competency 005, Word Analysis and Decoding)**

40. B. B is the correct answer, because a digraph is a pair of adjacent vowels or consonants that are heard as a single sound, such as the "ch" in "cherry." **(Competency 005, Word Analysis and Decoding)**

41. D. Options A, B, and C are not optimal. D is the correct answer, in part because it is the only option that would specifically benefit fluency. **(Competency 006, Reading Fluency)**

42. A. During the initial reading stage, children are focused heavily on decoding and, as a result, comprehension may be poor. Hence, A is the correct answer. **(Competency 006, Reading Fluency)**

43. B. During the pre-reading stage, the ability to read is limited to a few sight words, such as the child's own name. Hence, B is the correct answer. **(Competency 006, Reading Fluency)**

44. **D.** The best choice for this question is grounded on the fact that it is child-centered. A is inappropriate, because it requires minimal movement from the children. In a developmentally appropriate early childhood curriculum, you want to include many gross motor movement activities, especially in music. B may be plausible in that it does engage children in gross motor movement. However, note that it does not include any provision for "out of control children." If there is no upper limit on how fast children can walk, it will turn into a "dead run," which may be unsafe. C and D are valid. There are safety guidelines that help children manage their physical movements. Of the two, D is the best, because it encourages child-centered learning. **(Competency 025, Music)**

45. **C.** This question assesses your knowledge of musical elements, namely steady beat and rhythm. When you dance to music, you most likely move to either the steady beat or to a prominent rhythm heard in the music. In a folk dance tradition, you will most likely never move to harmony or to the words (often, folk dances are instrumental pieces that have no words). Syncopation relates to rhythm, and is a specific type of rhythm, but is too restrictive to be used to generalize across multiple examples of Guatemalan folk music. Note that there is no musical example to be heard. Therefore, you need to select the broadest possible word to account for many examples of music. Answer choice C, rhythm, is a broad enough term to be used with this question. If "steady beat" were a choice, it would be a better answer than rhythm. Steady beat is found in all music and is the thing to which we most often dance. **(Competency 025, Music)**

46. **A.** Students need to learn to use time-management skills when making health-promoting decisions. Option C is important; however, students have to learn decision-making skills and take control of their own decision-making process. **(Competency 026, Health)**

47. **C.** Option A depicts correct spelling. Option B depicts correct spelling with a single error. In option D, the child is simply using one letter to stand for each word. C is the correct answer, because the child is using his or her own creative method of representing sounds with letters. **(Competency 004, Literacy Development)**

48. **D.** Unlike the competencies described in options A, B, and C, the use of graphic organizers is typically not learned until after the emergent literacy stage and, thus, D is the correct answer. **(Competency 004, Literacy Development)**

49. **B.** Because children typically recognize environmental print before they can read, they may associate meanings with entire words as well as logos and other images and, thus, B is the correct answer. **(Competency 004, Literacy Development)**

50. **C.** Options A, B, and D are not optimal approaches according to current thinking about literacy instruction. C is the correct answer, because high-frequency consonants should be introduced before low-frequency ones. **(Competency 005, Word Analysis and Decoding)**

51. **C.** A is incorrect, because the student's expressiveness indicates that she is reading carefully. B is incorrect, because simply asking the student to read more slowly will not help. Although contextual information is often useful, D is incorrect, because in this particular passage, context is not consistently informative (basketballs are rarely kicked, and ducks are not commonly described in early readers as "standing"). C is the correct answer, because each of the multisyllabic words in the passage can be divided into meaningful components using structural analysis. **(Competency 005, Word Analysis and Decoding)**

52. **A.** Kindergarten and 3rd-grade children are very different developmentally. The activities planned have to be modified in order to be age appropriate. B and C, if applied, can cause serious physical problems. D is not an option for this teacher. **(Competency 027, Physical Education)**

53. **D.** There is no need for this teacher to do what is mentioned in the other options. If this teacher understands the social development of kindergarten students, he will realize that these students quarrel frequently and that their quarrels are short lived. **(Competency 027, Physical Education)**

54. **C.** Options A, B, and D represent important distinctions, but they may be somewhat advanced for 1st graders. One of the most basic concepts that students must grasp as they begin to learn about history is the distinction between fact and opinion and, thus, C is the correct answer. **(Competency 017, History)**

55. **B.** Most weather takes place in the troposphere. **(Competency 018, Geography and Culture)**

56. **A.** The Trans-Pecos region is the westernmost area of Texas. **(Competency 018, Geography and Culture)**

57. D. D is the correct answer, because tests of reading fluency measure each of the variables mentioned. **(Competency 006, Reading Fluency)**

58. B. It would be unrealistic to annotate every text for a student, to allow the student to read narratives exclusively, or to assume that telling the student to try harder would benefit the student's comprehension. Comprehension of an expository text may be increased if the student understands the purpose for reading the text and, thus, B is the correct answer. **(Competency 007, Reading Comprehension)**

59. C. Moving from left to right, each value is seven more than the previous value. Keep going: 14 + 7 = 21. That is it! The correct answer is C. **(Competency 013, Number Concepts, Patterns, and Algebra)**

60. C. The poncho cost $346. Rounding $46 to the nearest ten dollars is $50. In other words, 46 is closer to 50 than it is to 40. Therefore, rounding $346 to the nearest ten dollars is $350. The correct answer is C. **(Competency 013, Number Concepts, Patterns, and Algebra)**

61. C. The bottom measures 8 boxes by 8 boxes. Adjacent sides are perpendicular (that is, they form right angles). This figure is a square. A square's area is calculated by multiplying the base times the height. In this case, both dimensions measure 8 boxes. Hence, the area of this square is 64 square boxes.

A triangle is on top of the square. The triangle on the top of the square takes up one-half of the area inside the rectangle on the top, as can be seen in the following diagram.

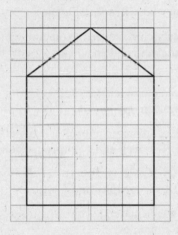

The top rectangle has dimensions 8 boxes by 3 boxes. The area of the rectangle is 24 square boxes. However, the triangle's area is one-half of that. (If that is not clear to you, imagine a line splitting the rectangle right down the middle, as shown in the following diagram.)

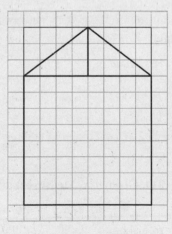

The triangle's area is one-half of 24 square boxes. That area is 12 square boxes. The original diagram is made of the square and the triangle. That total area is 64 square boxes plus 12 square boxes, for a total of 64 + 12 square boxes, which equals 76 square boxes. The correct answer is C. **(Competency 014, Geometry, Measurement, Probability, and Statistics)**

62. B. In the question stem, note that the class is using different instruments (that is, altering timbre), playing around with words and syllables making some longer and shorter (that is, altering rhythm), and changing the volume of their speaking voices (that is, altering dynamics). You will also note that the teacher provides a steady beat. The steady beat ensures a steady tempo, one that does not speed up or slow down. **(Competency 025, Music)**

63. D. The classroom investigation involves looking for earthworms in a field. Because earthworms live in damp, dark places in the soil, the students will need to have a shovel or some type of digging implement, a container to put the worms in and gloves to protect their hands. A stopwatch is used in investigations involving motion or to make measurements of time. Because time is not an important variable in the experimental investigation, a stopwatch would be least helpful to Ms. Perkins and her class. **(Competency 022, Life Science)**

64. A. The teacher should call upon the past experience of the field trip as she discusses this question with her students. As they were on their nature walk looking for worms, they should have noticed that no earthworms were on the surface and that they had to dig to find the earthworms. By virtue of that experience alone, the students should be able to deduce that earthworms survive only in dark conditions. **(Competency 022, Life Science)**

65. A. Although Options B, C, and D represent important instructional goals, A is the correct answer, because the general purpose of the discussion is to activate schemata about the police, so that the new story can be linked to children's existing knowledge. **(Competency 006, Reading Fluency)**

66. A. A is the best answer, because the other options would either confuse children or not incorporate enough guidance from the teacher. **(Competency 006, Reading Fluency)**

67. C. Options A, B, and D do not accurately characterize the function of the teacher's comment. C is the correct answer, because the teacher's comment gives children an idea of what to listen for. **(Competency 006, Reading Fluency)**

68. D. The SQ3R method is most appropriate for reading expository texts, and thus D is the correct answer. **(Competency 008, Research and Comprehension Skills in the Content Areas)**

69. C. Because a graphic organizer is a visual representation of a text and the relationships among its elements, C is the correct answer. **(Competency 008, Research and Comprehension Skills in the Content Areas)**

70. C. Cultural diffusion is the transmission of objects, ideas, and behaviors from one society to another, and thus C is the correct answer. **(Competency 018, Geography and Culture)**

71. A. The Constitution guarantees the fundamental rights of U.S. citizens, so A is the correct answer. **(Competency 019, Government, Citizenship, and Economics)**

72. C. A cylindrical soup can has a top that is a circle, a bottom that is also a circle, and a label around the can. That label is actually a rectangle. (See for yourself by taking a label off a cylindrical soup can.) **(Competency 012, Mathematics Instruction)**

73. D. A decimeter is $\frac{1}{10}$ of a meter. A hectometer is 100 meters. However, rather than thinking this through using this information, here's an easier method.

Kyle hurriedly drew mandolins during class Monday.

_____ dm = 1 hm

1 hm = _____ dm

Moving from *hurriedly* to *during* requires movement to the right three places.

1 hm = 1,000 dm

The correct answer is D. **(Competency 014, Geometry, Measurement, Probability, and Statistics)**

74. B. Three-fourths of 24 is 18: $\frac{3}{4} \times \frac{24}{1} = \frac{3}{1} \times \frac{6}{1} = \frac{18}{1} = 18$. So, 18 girls are in Mr. Ramjey's class. That means that the rest of the class is boys: 6 of the 24. Probability is $\frac{\text{number of times the successful event occurs}}{\text{number of attempts that were made}} = \frac{6}{24} = \frac{1}{4}$.

The correct answer is B. **(Competency 014, Geometry, Measurement, Probability, and Statistics)**

75. B. Options A, C, and D may be true in some instances, but they are not generally true. B is the correct answer, because electronic texts generally include powerful search capacities. (**Competency 008, Research and Comprehension Skills in the Content Areas**)

76. A. The teacher's actions do not place special emphasis on picture-text correspondences, nor is her praise likely to contain constructive criticism or to motivate the creation of students' best written work. A is the correct answer, because the teacher's actions are likely to encourage self-expression in her students. (**Competency 009, Writing Conventions**)

77. C. The child is clearly beyond the prephonemic stage, but has not yet achieved conventional spelling. C is the correct answer, because like other children at the transitional stage, this child appreciates that every syllable should contain a vowel, and the child makes use of patterns (such as the "ee" for the long /i/ sound) that appear in other words. (**Competency 009, Writing Conventions**)

78. D. All of the options describe characteristics that can be found in early handwriting. (**Competency 009, Writing Conventions**)

79. A. Options B, C, and D are normally observed among kindergarteners. Discomfort during handwriting is indicative of a problem that the teacher should immediately address. Hence, A is the correct answer. (**Competency 009, Writing Conventions**)

80. D. Any question pertaining to the water that accumulates after a rain has to do, in general, with the water cycle or how water interacts with the environment. There are four major steps involved in the water cycle, as shown in the following figure, with each step represented as a possible option. The step that best characterizes the reason why the water level in the puddle decreases is evaporation, given by choice D. (**Competency 023, Earth and Space Science**)

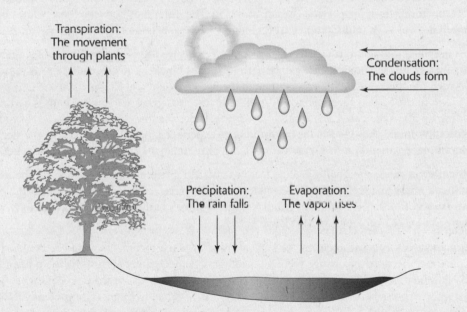

81. A. Water that accumulates from precipitation is a major step in the water cycle. The water cycle consists of four major steps: condensation, precipitation, evaporation, and transpiration. Thus, option A is the correct response. (**Competency 023, Earth and Space Science**)

82. C. The empty soda bottle that was left outside during the rainfall and collected water from the precipitation is a makeshift rain gauge. A rain gauge measures the amount of precipitation or rainfall during a storm. (**Competency 023, Earth and Space Science**)

83. B. A weather instrument that measures the amount of precipitation from a storm is a rain gauge. A barometer measures atmospheric pressure, a thermometer measures outside temperature, and an altimeter measures height. (**Competency 023, Earth and Space Science**)

84. C. There is a common link between the observations of Students 1 and 3 in that they both pertain to the water cycle. In this problem, the link between water and the green color of the grass can be explained by incorporating the process of transpiration into the discussion. Transpiration is the movement of water through plants. **(Competency 023, Earth and Space Science)**

85. B. Given the type of information, an amount of rainfall over the past 30 days, the best ways to display this information would be as a bar graph or a line graph. A line graph and a bar graph are appropriate when one variable (amount of rainfall) is continuously measured over another variable (time or date). A pie chart is used when making measurements which are part of a whole. This would not be a good type of graph for this data and, thus, any option with III (bar graph) can be immediately eliminated. **(Competency 023, Earth and Space Science)**

86. A. One of the main activities during prewriting is the generation of ideas through methods such as freewriting and, thus, A is the correct answer. **(Competency 010, Development of Written Communication)**

87. D. Options A, B, and C seem inordinately pressuring. D is the correct answer, because it would facilitate the expression of ideas through writing that could be polished later. **(Competency 010, Development of Written Communication)**

88. D. Amie spent $(2 \times \$1.25) + \$0.92 = \$2.50 + \$0.92 = \$3.42$. Barton spent $(3 \times \$0.85) + \$0.86 = \$2.55 + \$0.86 = \$3.41$. Amie spent more than Barton. She spent $\$3.42 – \$3.41 = \$0.01$ more. Be sure to answer the question(s) being asked. The correct answer is D. **(Competency 013, Number Concepts, Patterns, and Algebra)**

89. C. The mean, 550, is at A. D is two standard deviations below A. Each standard deviation is 150 kilograms, so two standard deviations total 300 kilograms. D's position is $550 – 300 = 250$. The correct answer is C. **(Competency 014, Geometry, Measurement, Probability, and Statistics)**

90. B. Position C is located one standard deviation, 150, above the 550 mean: 550 kilograms + 150 kilograms = 700 kilograms. D's position (from the previous exercise) is 250. The difference between these values is $700 – 250 = 450$. The correct answer is B. **(Competency 014, Geometry, Measurement, Probability, and Statistics)**

91. D. Jaime just added all of the digits together: $5 + 2 + 3 + 7 = 17$. He needs work with place value. Mr. Clymer should show him a representation of each number, using Dienes blocks. The 10-cm long rods represent the ten's place digit in each number: five in the 52 and three in the 37. The 1 cm^3 cubes represent the unit's place digit in each number: two in the 52 and seven in the 37. Adding up the rods gives $5 + 3 = 8$. There is a total of eight of the rods. Adding up all of the cubes, the result is $2 + 7 = 9$. There is a total of nine cubes. Eight rods and nine cubes represents 89. Jaime should have the opportunity to experience these Dienes blocks in order to improve his understanding of place value. The correct answer is D. **(Competency 012, Mathematics Instruction)**

92. C. The design they make on the T-shirt and the media selected for expressing the design can be used to assess the student's choice of color, shape, form, and their use of lines and space. The only involvement the parents will have is supplying the T-shirts. The students could sell the T-shirts, but the purpose of this activity was to express themselves artistically. **(Competency 024, Visual Arts)**

93. B. Option A is incorrect, because excusing the student from written assignments would be counterproductive. Option C is incorrect, because the change probably would not help. Option D is also likely to be ineffective if the teacher's only comment is to "practice more." B is the correct answer, because word processing software would allow the student to express herself without having to struggle with handwriting. **(Competency 010, Development of Written Communication)**

94. C. The book falls within the student's frustration reading level and, thus, C is the correct answer. **(Competency 011, Assessment of Developing Literacy)**

95. A. "Though" and "which" are irregularly spelled, high-frequency words and, thus, A is the correct answer. **(Competency 011, Assessment of Developing Literacy)**

96. C. An Informal Reading Inventory (IRI) is used to assess general reading level and, thus, C is the correct answer. **(Competency 011, Assessment of Developing Literacy)**

97. A. Options B, C, and D are each incorrect to some extent. A is the correct answer, because teachers should keep track of the literacy development of each student through both formal and informal assessments. **(Competency 011, Assessment of Developing Literacy)**

98. A. There are many factors that contribute to quality of life other than economic indicators such as the GNP. **(Competency 019, Government, Citizenship, and Economics)**

99. C. The mode is the measure of central tendency that describes the most frequent observation in a set. **(Competency 014, Geometry, Measurement, Probability, and Statistics)**

100. B. Option B is the only option in which the chronological order is accurate. **(Competency 019, Government, Citizenship, and Economics)**